Urinary incontinence

the management of urinary incontinence in women

National Collaborating Centre for Women's and Children's Health

Commissioned by the National Institute for Health and Clinical Excellence

October 2006

RCOG Press

Published by the **RCOG Press** at the Royal College of Obstetricians and Gynaecologists, 27 Sussex Place, Regent's Park, London NW1 4RG

www.rcog.org.uk

Registered charity no. 213280

First published 2006

© 2006 National Collaborating Centre for Women's and Children's Health

ISBN 1-904752-32-2

RCOG Editor: Andrew Welsh
Original design by FiSH Books, London
Typesetting by techbooks, Delhi
Index by Cath Topliff

Printed by Henry Ling Ltd, The Dorchester Press, Dorchester DT1 1HD

Contents

Guideline Development Group membership and acknowledgements

Guideline Development Group

GDG members

Elisabeth Adams	Subspecialist in Urogynaecology
Alison Bardsley	Continence Adviser/Service Manager
Linda Crumlin	Patient/Carer Representative
Ian Currie	Consultant Gynaecologist (with an interest in urogynaecology)
Lynda Evans	Patient/Carer Representative
Jeanette Haslam	Women's Health Physiotherapist
Paul Hilton	Consultant Gynaecologist and Urogynaecologist (GDG Leader)
Margaret Jones	General Practitioner
Malcolm Lucas	Consultant Urological Surgeon
Julian Spinks	General Practitioner
Joanne Townsend	Urogynaecology Nurse Specialist
Adrian Wagg	Consultant Geriatrician

National Collaborating Centre for Women's and Children's Health (NCC-WCH) staff

Martin Dougherty	Executive Director
Beti Wyn Evans	Research Fellow
Paul Jacklin	Senior Health Economist
Irene Kwan	Research Fellow
Debbie Pledge	Information Specialist
Samantha Vahidi	Work Programme Co-ordinator

Acknowledgements

Additional support was received from Francoise Cluzeau, Wendy Riches, Rona McCandlish, Moira Mugglestone and colleagues at the NCC-WCH. We also thank the Patient and Public Involvement Programme (PPIP) of the National Institute for Health and Clinical Excellence (NICE) whose glossary was adapted for use in this guideline.

Stakeholder organisations

3M Health Care Limited
Addenbrookes NHS Trust
Airedale General Hospital – Acute Trust
Albyn Medical Ltd
Allergan Ltd
Amdipharm plc
American Medical Systems UK
Anglesey Local Health Board

Association for Continence Advice
Association for Improvements in Maternity Services (AIMS)
Association of British Healthcare Industries
Association of British Neurologists
Association of the British Pharmaceutical Industry (ABPI)
Astellas Pharma Ltd
Astra Tech Ltd
Bard Ltd
Barnet Primary Care Trust
Barnsley Primary Care Trust
BES Rehab Ltd
Boehringer Ingelheim Ltd
Boston Scientific Ltd
Bradford Teaching Hospitals NHS FoundationTrust
Britannia Pharmaceuticals Ltd
British Association for Behavioural and Cognitive Psychotherapies (BABCP)
British Association for Counselling and Psychotherapy (BACP)
British Association of Paediatric Surgeons
British Association of Urological Surgeons (BAUS)
British Dietetic Association
British Geriatrics Society
British Healthcare Trades Association
British Menopause Society
British National Formulary (BNF)
British Psychological Society
British Society of Urogynaecologists
Cancer Services Collaborative 'Improvement Partnership' (CSCIP)
CASPE
Central Liverpool Primary Care Trust
Chartered Society of Physiotherapy
CIS'ters
City Hospitals Sunderland NHS Trust
Clinimed Ltd
Colchester Primary Care Trust
College of Occupational Therapists
Coloplast Ltd
Commission for Social Care Inspection
Connecting for Health
Continence Foundation
Conwy & Denbighshire NHS Trust
Co-operative Pharmacy Association
Croydon Primary Care Trust
David Lewis Centre
Department of Health
Department of Health Sciences, University of Leicester
Diagnostic Ultrasound (UK) Ltd
Dudley Group of Hospitals NHS Trust
Eli Lilly and Company Ltd
English Community Care Association
Faculty of Public Health
Ferring Pharmaceuticals Ltd
Fibroid Network Charity
Galen Ltd
Gloucestershire Hospitals NHS Trust
Good Hope Hospitals NHS Trust
Guy's & St Thomas' NHS Foundation Trust
Hampshire Partnership NHS Trust

Health Protection Agency
Healthcare Commission
Heart of England NHS Foundation Trust
Help the Hospices
Herefordshire Primary Care Trust
Hertfordshire Partnership NHS Trust
Hollister Ltd
Hospital Infection Society
Incontact (Action on Incontinence)
Janssen-Cilag Ltd
Johnson & Johnson Medical
King George's Hospital NHS Trust
Kingston Primary Care Trust
Knowsley Primary Care Trust
Leeds Teaching Hospitals NHS Trust
Liverpool Women's Hospital NHS Trust
Long-term Medical Conditions Alliance
Luton and Dunstable Hospital NHS Foundation Trust
Maternity Health Links
Medicines and Healthcare products Regulatory Agency (MHRA)
Medtronic Europe Sarl
Medtronic Ltd
Mid Staffordshire General Hospitals NHS Trust
Multiple Sclerosis Society
National Childbirth Trust
National Council for Disabled People, Black, Minority and Ethnic Community (Equalities)
National Patient Safety Agency
National Public Health Service – Wales
Newcastle Primary Care Trust
Newcastle Upon Tyne Hospitals NHS Trust
Newham Primary Care Trust
NHS Direct
NHS Health and Social Care Information Centre
NHS Quality Improvement Scotland
Norgine Ltd
North Essex Mental Health Partnership NHS Trust
North Tees and Hartlepool NHS Trust
North Tyneside Primary Care Trust
North West London Hospitals NHS Trust
Northumberland Care Trust
Nottingham City Hospital
Nottingham City Primary Care Trust
Novartis Pharmaceuticals UK Ltd
Novo Nordisk
Oxfordshire Mental Healthcare NHS Trust
Parkinson's Disease Society
Patient and Public Involvement Programme for NICE
Pembrokeshire and Derwen NHS Trust
PERIGON (formerly The NHS Modernisation Agency)
Peterborough and Stamford Hospitals NHS Foundation Trust
Pfizer Ltd
Princess Alexandra Hospital NHS Trust
PromoCon (Disabled Living)
Q-Med (UK) Ltd
Queen Victoria Hospital NHS Foundation Trust
RCM Consultant Midwives Forum
Regional Public Health Group – London

Robert Jones & Agnes Hunt Orthopaedic and District Hospital NHS Trust
Rotherham General Hospitals NHS Trust
Rotherham Primary Care Trust
Royal College of General Practitioners
Royal College of General Practitioners Wales
Royal College of Midwives
Royal College of Nursing
Royal College of Obstetricians and Gynaecologists
Royal College of Physicians of Edinburgh
Royal College of Physicians of London
Royal College of Psychiatrists
Royal National Orthopaedic Hospital NHS Trust
Royal Society of Medicine
Royal West Sussex Trust
Schwarz Pharma
Scottish Intercollegiate Guidelines Network (SIGN)
Sheffield Children's Hospital NHS Trust
Sheffield South West Primary Care Trust
Sheffield Teaching Hospitals NHS Trust
Society and College of Radiographers
South Birmingham Primary Care Trust
South East Sheffield Primary Care Trust
South Essex Partnership NHS Trust
South West Kent Primary Care Trust
Spinal Injuries Association
Staffordshire Moorlans Primary Care Trust
Stockport Primary Care Trust
Stroke Association
Survivors Trust
Tameside and Glossop Acute Services NHS Trust
Tissue Viability Nurses Association
Tissue Viability Society (UK)
Trafford Primary Care Trusts
UCB Pharma Ltd
UK Specialised Services Public Health Network
University College London Hospitals NHS Trust
University Hospital Birmingham NHS Trust
Vale of Aylesbury Primary Care Trust
Welsh Assembly Government
West of Cornwall Primary Care Trust
West Sussex Health and Social Care NHS Trust
Whipps Cross University Hospital NHS Trust
Wirral Hospital NHS Trust
Women's Health Concern

Peer reviewers

Paul Abrams, Linda Cardozo, June Cody, Carol Coupland

Abbreviations

ADL	activities of daily living
AE	adverse effects
AFR	acceleration of flow rate
ALPP	abdominal leak point pressure
AM	ambulatory monitoring
AUS	artificial urinary sphincter
BAUS–SFRU	British Association of Urological Surgeons Section of Female and Reconstructive Urology
b.d.	to be taken twice a day (*bis die*)
BFLUTS	Bristol Female Urinary Tract Symptoms (questionnaire)
BMI	body mass index
BNF	British National Formulary
BOA	basic office assessment
BSUG	British Society of Urogynaecology
CEE	conjugated equine oestrogens
CI	confidence interval
CISC	clean intermittent self-catheterisation
CNS	central nervous system
CT	computed tomography
DB	double-blind
DO	detrusor overactivity
DS	diagnostic study
EL	evidence level (level of evidence)
EMG	electromyography
ER	extended release
ES	electrical stimulation
FB	Fluid-Bridge
GA	general anaesthesia
GDG	Guideline Development Group
GP	general practitioner
GPP	good practice point
HRT	hormone replacement therapy
HTA	health technology assessment
ICER	incremental cost effectiveness ratio
ICI	International Consultation on Incontinence
ICIQ	International Consultation on Incontinence questionnaire
ICS	International Continence Society
IIQ	incontinence impact questionnaire
IP	Interventional Procedures (*see* IPAC)
IPAC	Interventional Procedures Advisory Committee (of NICE)
I-QOL	incontinence quality of life (questionnaire)
IQR	interquartile range
IR	Immediate release
ISC	intermittent self-catheterisation
ISD	intrinsic sphincter deficiency
ISI	incontinence severity index
ITT	intention-to-treat analysis
IVS	intravaginal slingplasty
KHQ	King's Health Questionnaire
LA	local anaesthesia
LOCF	last observation carried forward

LPP	leak point pressure
LUTS	lower urinary tract symptoms
MC	multichannel (cystometry)
MHRA	Medicines and Healthcare products Regulatory Agency
MMK	Marshall–Marchetti–Krantz
MMSE	Mini Mental State Examination
MPA	medroxyprogesterone acetate
MRI	magnetic resonance imaging
MUCP	maximum urethral closure pressure
MUI	mixed urinary incontinence
n	number of patients
NA	not applicable
NCC-WCH	National Collaborating Centre for Women's and Children's Health
NHS	National Health Service
NICE	National Institute for Health and Clinical Excellence
NPV	negative predictive value
NS	not statistically significant
OAB	overactive bladder
OAB-q	overactive bladder questionnaire
o.d.	to be taken once daily
OR	odds ratio
PCT	primary care trust
PFMT	pelvic floor muscle training
PFM	pelvic floor muscle
PGI-I	patients global impression of improvement
PNE	percutaneous nerve evaluation
POP	pelvic organ prolapse
POP-Q	pelvic organ prolapse quantification system
PPIP	Patient and Public Involvement Programme
PPV	positive predictive value
PTFE	polytetrafluoroethylene
PTNS	posterior tibial nerve stimulation
PTR	pressure transmission ratio
PVR	post void residual
pt(s)	patient(s)
QALY	quality-adjusted life year
q.d.s.	to be taken four times a day (*quarter die sumendus*)
QOL	quality of life
r	correlation coefficient
RCT	randomised controlled trial
RR	relative risk
SA	spinal anaesthesia
SB	single-blind
SD	standard deviation
SE	standard error
SF-36	Short form 36
SIGN	Scottish Intercollegiate Guidelines Network
SII	symptom impact index
SNS	sacral nerve stimulation
SPARC	suprapubic arc sling
SSI	symptom severity index
SUI	stress urinary incontinence
SUIQQ	stress and urge incontinence quality of life questionnaire
t.d.s.	to be taken three times a day (*ter die sumendus*)
TENS	transcutaneous electrical nerve stimulation
TOT	transobturator tape

TVT	tension-free vaginal tape
UCP	urethral closure pressure
UD	urodynamics
UDI	urogenital distress inventory (questionnaire)
UI	urinary incontinence
UISS	urinary incontinence severity score
UPP	urethral pressure profile or profilometry
USI	urodynamic stress urinary incontinence
UTI	urinary tract infection
UUI	urge urinary incontinence
VAS	visual analogue scale
VCU	videocystourethrography
VLPP	Valsalva leak point pressure
WVC	weighted vaginal cone

Glossary of terms

Acute trust

A trust is an NHS organisation responsible for providing a group of healthcare services. An acute trust provides hospital services (but not mental health hospital services which are provided by a mental health trust).

Afferent nerve

Nerve carrying sensory nerve impulses from a peripheral receptor towards the central nervous system.

Anterior colporrhaphy

Vaginal operation for the treatment of cystocele (anterior vaginal wall prolapse). Involves plication of the fascia between vaginal and bladder walls. With the addition of plication of the fascia beneath the urethra, it has commonly been used for treatment of stress incontinence. Can be used as an additional procedure for prolapse repair along with a continence procedure.

Antimuscarinic drugs

Class of pharmacological agents acting on neuromuscular junctions in the autonomic nervous system, used for overactive bladder syndrome.

Applicability

The extent to which the results of a study or review can be applied to the target population for a clinical guideline.

Appraisal of evidence

Formal assessment of the quality of research evidence and its relevance to the clinical question or guideline under consideration, according to predetermined criteria.

Best available evidence

The strongest research evidence available to support a particular guideline recommendation.

Bias

Influences on a study that can lead to invalid conclusions about a treatment or intervention. Bias in research can make a treatment look better or worse than it really is. Bias can even make it look as if the treatment works when it actually does not. Bias can occur by chance or as a result of **systematic errors** in the design and execution of a study. Bias can occur at various stages in the research process, e.g. in the collection, analysis, interpretation, publication or review of research data. For examples, see **selection bias, performance bias, information bias, confounder or confounding factor, publication bias**.

Bimanual examination

Vaginal examination carried out using the examiner's fingers of one hand in the vagina and of the other hand on the abdomen. Allows the description of observed and palpable anatomical abnormalities and the assessment of pelvic floor muscle function.

Biofeedback

The technique by which information about a normally unconscious physiological process is presented to the patient and/or the therapist as a visual, auditory or tactile signal.

Bladder diary

A diary that records voiding times and voided volumes, leakage episodes, pad usage and other information such as fluid intake, degree of urgency, and degree of incontinence. See also **frequency–volume chart**.

Bladder pain

Pain felt suprapubically or retropubically, and usually increases with bladder filling, and may persist after voiding.

Bladder training	Bladder training (also described as bladder retraining, bladder drill, bladder re-education, bladder discipline) actively involves the individual in attempting to increase the interval between the desire to void and the actual void.
Blinding or masking	The practice of keeping the investigators or subjects of a study ignorant of the group to which a subject has been assigned. For example, a clinical trial in which the participating patients or their doctors are unaware of whether they (the patients) are taking the experimental drug or a placebo (dummy treatment). The purpose of 'blinding' or 'masking' is to protect against **bias**. See also **double-blind (DB) study**, **single-blind study**.
Body mass index (BMI)	A person's weight in kilograms divided by the square of their height in metres. Overweight is defined as a BMI of 25 or more, and obese as 30 or more.
Case–control study	A study that starts with the identification of a group of individuals sharing the same characteristics (e.g. people with a particular disease) and a suitable comparison (control) group (e.g. people without the disease). All subjects are then assessed with respect to things that happened to them in the past, e.g. things that might be related to getting the disease under investigation. Such studies are also called **retrospective** as they look back in time from the outcome to the possible causes.
Case report (or case study)	Detailed report on one patient (or case), usually covering the course of that person's disease and their response to treatment.
Case series	Description of several cases of a given disease, usually covering the course of the disease and the response to treatment. There is no comparison (**control**) group of patients.
Causal relationship	Describes the relationship between two **variables** whenever it can be established that one causes the other. For example there is a causal relationship between a treatment and a disease if it can be shown that the treatment changes the course or outcome of the disease. Usually **randomised controlled trials** are needed to ascertain causality. Proving cause and effect is much more difficult than just showing an association between two variables. For example, if it happened that everyone who had eaten a particular food became sick, and everyone who avoided that food remained well, then the food would clearly be associated with the sickness. However, even if leftovers were found to be contaminated, it could not be proved that the food caused the sickness – unless all other possible causes (e.g. environmental factors) had been ruled out.
Clinical audit	A **systematic** process for setting and monitoring standards of clinical care. Whereas 'guidelines' define what the best clinical practice should be, 'audit' investigates whether best practice is being carried out. Clinical audit can be described as a cycle or spiral. Within the cycle there are stages that follow a systematic process of establishing best practice, measuring care against specific criteria, taking action to improve care, and monitoring to sustain improvement. The spiral suggests that as the process continues, each cycle aspires to a higher level of quality.
Clinical effectiveness	The extent to which a specific treatment or intervention, when used under *usual or everyday conditions*, has a beneficial effect on the course or outcome of disease compared with no treatment or other routine care. (Clinical trials that assess effectiveness are sometimes called management trials.) Clinical 'effectiveness' is not the same as **efficacy**.

Clinical governance	A framework through which NHS organisations are accountable for both continuously improving the quality of their services and safeguarding high standards of care by creating an environment in which excellence in clinical care will flourish.
Clinical impact	The effect that a guideline recommendation is likely to have on the treatment, or treatment outcomes, of the target population.
Clinical importance	The importance of a particular guideline recommendation to the clinical management of the target population.
Clinical question	This term is sometimes used in guideline development work to refer to the questions about treatment and care that are formulated in order to guide the search for research evidence. When a clinical question is formulated in a precise way, it is called a **focused question**.
Clinical trial	A research study conducted with patients which tests out a drug or other intervention to assess its effectiveness and safety. Each trial is designed to answer scientific questions and to find better ways to treat individuals with a specific disease. This general term encompasses **controlled clinical trials** and **randomised controlled trials**.
Clinician	A healthcare professional providing patient care, e.g. doctor, nurse, physiotherapist.
Cluster	A group of patients, rather than an individual, used as the basic unit for investigation. See also **cluster design** and **cluster randomisation**.
Cluster design	Cluster designs are those where research subjects are not sampled or selected independently, but in a group. For example a clinical trial where patients in a general practice are allocated to the same intervention; the general practice forming a cluster. See also **cluster** and **cluster randomisation**.
Cluster randomisation	A study in which groups of individuals (e.g. patients in a GP surgery or on a hospital ward) are randomly allocated to treatment groups. Take, for example, a smoking cessation study of two different interventions – leaflets and teaching sessions. Each GP surgery within the study would be randomly allocated to administer one of the two interventions. See also **cluster** and **cluster design**.
Cochrane Collaboration	An international organisation in which people find, appraise and review specific types of studies called **randomised controlled trials**. The Cochrane Database of Systematic Reviews contains regularly updated reviews on a variety of health issues and is available electronically as part of the **Cochrane Library**.
Cochrane Library	The Cochrane Library consists of a regularly updated collection of evidence-based medicine databases including the Cochrane Database of Systematic Reviews (reviews of **randomised controlled trials** prepared by the **Cochrane Collaboration**). The Cochrane Library is available on CD-ROM and the internet.
Cohort	A group of people sharing some common characteristic (e.g. patients with the same disease), followed up in a research study for a specified period of time.
Cohort study	An observational study that takes a group (cohort) of patients and follows their progress over time in order to measure outcomes such as disease or mortality rates and make comparisons according to the treatments or interventions that patients received. Thus, within the study group, subgroups of patients are identified (from information collected about patients) and these groups are compared with respect to outcome,

e.g. comparing mortality between one group that received a specific treatment and one group that did not (or between two groups that received different levels of treatment). Cohorts can be assembled in the present and followed into the future (a 'concurrent' or **'prospective'** cohort study) or identified from past records and followed forward from that time up to the present (a 'historical' or **'retrospective'** cohort study). Because patients are not randomly allocated to subgroups, these subgroups may be quite different in their characteristics and some adjustment must be made when analysing the results to ensure that the comparison between groups is as fair as possible.

Co-morbidity	Co-existence of a disease or diseases in the people being studied in addition to the health problem that is the subject of the study.
Confidence interval (CI)	A way of expressing certainty about the findings from a study or group of studies, using statistical techniques. A confidence interval describes a range of possible effects (of a treatment or intervention) that are consistent with the results of a study or group of studies. A wide confidence interval indicates a lack of certainty or precision about the true size of the clinical effect and is seen in studies with too few patients. Where confidence intervals are narrow they indicate more precise estimates of effects and a larger sample of patients studied. It is usual to interpret a '95%' confidence interval as the range of effects within which we are 95% confident that the true effect lies.
Confounder or confounding factor	Something that influences a study and can contribute to misleading findings if it is not understood or appropriately dealt with. For example, if a group of people exercising regularly and a group of people who do not exercise have an important age difference then any difference found in outcomes about heart disease could well be due to one group being older than the other rather than due to the exercising. Age is the confounding factor here and the effect of exercising on heart disease cannot be assessed without adjusting for age differences in some way.
Consensus methods	A variety of techniques that aim to reach an agreement on a particular issue. Formal consensus methods include **Delphi** and **nominal group** techniques. In the development of clinical guidelines, consensus methods may be used where there is a lack of strong research evidence on a particular topic.
Consensus statement	A statement of the advised course of action in relation to a particular clinical topic, based on the collective views of a body of experts.
Considered judgement	The application of the collective knowledge of a guideline development group to a body of evidence, to assess its applicability to the target population and the strength of any recommendation that it would support.
Consistency	The extent to which the conclusions of a collection of studies used to support a guideline recommendation are in agreement with each other. See also **homogeneity**.
Conservative management	Treatment or management strategies that do not involve surgery.
Control group	A group of patients recruited into a study that receives no treatment, a treatment of known effect, or a placebo (dummy or sham treatment), in order to provide a comparison for a group receiving an experimental treatment, such as a new drug.
Controlled clinical trial	A study testing a specific drug or other treatment involving two (or more) groups of patients with the same disease. One (the experimental group) receives the treatment that is being tested, and the other

(the comparison or control group) receives an alternative treatment, a placebo (dummy treatment) or no treatment. The two groups are followed up to compare differences in outcomes to see how effective the experimental treatment was. A controlled clinical trial where patients are randomly allocated to treatment and comparison groups is called a **randomised controlled trial**.

Correlation coefficient

A measure of the degree of linear association between two variables. A significant association does not imply causation.

Cost–benefit analysis

A type of **economic evaluation** where both costs and benefits of healthcare treatment are measured in the same monetary units. If benefits exceed costs, the evaluation would recommend providing the treatment.

Cost–consequence analysis

A limited form of economic evaluation that considers costs alongside consequences (or outcomes) without calculating an incremental cost effectiveness ratio.

Cost effectiveness

Value for money. A specific healthcare treatment is said to be 'cost effective' if it gives a greater health gain than could be achieved by using the resources in other ways.

Cost effectiveness analysis

A type of **economic evaluation** comparing the costs and the effects on health of different treatments. Health effects are measured in 'health-related units', for example, the cost of preventing one additional heart attack.

Cost–utility analysis

A special form of **cost effectiveness analysis** where health effects are measured in **quality-adjusted life years**. A treatment is assessed in terms of its ability to both extend life and to improve the quality of life.

Crossover study design

A study comparing two or more interventions in which the participants, upon completion of the course of one treatment, are switched to another. For example, for a comparison of treatments A and B, half the participants are randomly allocated to receive them in the order A, B and half to receive them in the order B, A. A problem with this study design is that the effects of the first treatment may carry over into the period when the second is given. Therefore a crossover study should include an adequate 'wash-out' period, which means allowing sufficient time between stopping one treatment and starting another so that the first treatment has time to wash out of the patient's system.

Cross-sectional study

The observation of a defined set of people at a single point in time or time period – a snapshot. (This type of study contrasts with a **longitudinal study**, which follows a set of people over a period of time.)

Cystocele

Herniation (protrusion) of the bladder through the wall of the vagina.

Cystometric (bladder) capacity

Bladder volume at the end of the filling phase of **cystometry**.

Cystometry

Cystometry is the measurement of intravesical pressure that can be carried out through a single recording channel (simple cystometry) or, more commonly, by multichannel cystometry, which involves the synchronous measurement of both bladder and intra-abdominal pressures by means of catheters inserted into the bladder and the rectum or vagina. The aim is to replicate the patient's symptoms by filling the bladder and observing pressure changes or leakage caused by provocation tests. See also **urodynamics**.

Data set

A list of required information relating to a specific disease.

Decision analysis

Decision analysis is the study of how people make decisions or how they *should* make decisions. There are several methods that decision analysts use to help people to make better decisions, including **decision trees**.

Decision tree	A decision tree is a method for helping people to make better decisions in situations of uncertainty. It illustrates the decision as a succession of possible actions and outcomes. It consists of the probabilities, costs and health consequences associated with each option. The overall effectiveness or overall cost effectiveness of various actions can then be compared.
Declaration of interest	A process by which members of a working group or committee 'declare' any personal or professional involvement with a company (or related to a technology) that might affect their objectivity, e.g. if their position or department is funded by a pharmaceutical company.
Delphi method	A technique used for the purpose of reaching an agreement on a particular issue, without the participants meeting or interacting directly. It involves sending participants a series of postal questionnaires asking them to record their views. After the first questionnaire, participants are asked to give further views in the light of the group feedback. The judgements of the participants are statistically aggregated, sometimes after weighting for expertise. See also **consensus methods**.
De novo	New onset.
Detrusor overactivity (DO)	An **urodynamic** observation characterised by involuntary detrusor contractions during the filling phase of **cystometry** that may be spontaneous or provoked. See also **urodynamics**.
Diagnostic study	A study to assess the effectiveness of a test or measurement in terms of its ability to accurately detect or exclude a specific disease.
Dominance	A term used in health economics describing when an option for treatment is both less clinically effective and more costly than an alternative option. The less effective and more costly option is said to be 'dominated'.
Double-blind (DB) study	A study in which neither the subject (patient) nor the observer (investigator/clinician) is aware of which treatment or intervention the subject is receiving. The purpose of blinding is to protect against bias.
Economic evaluation	A comparison of alternative courses of action in terms of both their costs and consequences. In **health economic** evaluations the consequences should include health outcomes.
Effectiveness	See **clinical effectiveness**.
Efferent nerve	Nerve carrying motor impulses from the central nervous system to a peripheral effector.
Efficacy	The extent to which a specific treatment or intervention, under *ideally controlled conditions* (e.g. in a laboratory), has a beneficial effect on the course or outcome of disease compared with no treatment or other routine care.
Elective	Name for clinical procedures that are regarded as advantageous to the patient but not urgent.
Electrical stimulation	The application of electrical current to stimulate the pelvic viscera or their nerve supply.
Electromyography (EMG)	Recording of neuromuscular function from an electrode within or in proximity to a muscle. Feedback tool for pelvic floor muscle recruitment.

Empirical	Based directly on experience (observation or experiment) rather than on reasoning alone.
Epidemiology	Study of diseases within a population, covering the causes and means of prevention.
Evidence based	The process of systematically finding, appraising and using research findings as the basis for clinical decisions.
Evidence-based clinical practice	Evidence-based clinical practice involves making decisions about the care of individual patients based on the best research evidence available rather than basing decisions on personal opinions or common practice (which may not always be evidence based). Evidence-based clinical practice therefore involves integrating individual clinical expertise and patient preferences with the best available evidence from research.
Evidence table	A table summarising the results of a collection of studies that, taken together, represent the evidence supporting a particular recommendation or series of recommendations in a guideline.
Exclusion criteria	See **selection criteria**.
Experimental study	A research study designed to test whether a treatment or intervention has an effect on the course or outcome of a condition or disease – where the conditions of testing are to some extent under the control of the investigator. **Controlled clinical trials** and **randomised controlled trials** are examples of experimental studies.
Experimental treatment	A treatment or intervention (e.g. a new drug) being studied to see whether it has an effect on the course or outcome of a condition or disease.
External validity	The degree to which the results of a study hold true in non-study situations, e.g. in routine clinical practice. May also be referred to as the **generalisability** of study results to non-study patients or populations.
Extrapolation	The application of research evidence based on studies of a specific population to another population with similar characteristics.
Focused question	A study question that clearly identifies all aspects of the topic that are to be considered while seeking an answer. Questions are normally expected to identify the patients or population involved, the treatment or intervention to be investigated, what outcomes are to be considered, and any comparisons that are to be made. For example, do insulin pumps (intervention) improve blood sugar control (outcome) in adolescents with type 1 diabetes (population) compared with multiple insulin injections (comparison)? See also **clinical question**.
Frequency	Increased daytime frequency is the complaint by the patient that he/she voids too often by day. See also **nocturia**.
Frequency–volume chart (FVC)	A chart that records voided volumes and times of voiding (day and night) for at least 24 hours. See also **bladder diary**.
Generalisability	The extent to which the results of a study hold true for a population of patients beyond those who participated in the research. See also **external validity**.
Gold standard	A method, procedure or measurement that is widely accepted as being the best available. Also called a reference standard.
Good practice point (GPP)	Recommended good practice based on the expert experience of the guideline development group (and possibly incorporating the expertise

of a wider reference group). A guideline development group may produce a 'good practice point' (rather than an evidence-based recommendation) on an important topic when there is a lack of research evidence.

Grade of recommendation	A code (e.g. A, B, C) linked to a guideline recommendation, indicating the strength of the evidence supporting that recommendation.
Grey literature	Reports that are unpublished or have limited distribution, and are not included in bibliographic retrieval systems.
Guideline	A systematically developed tool that describes aspects of a patient's condition and the care to be given. A good guideline makes recommendations about treatment and care, based on the best research available, rather than opinion. It is used to assist clinician and patient decision making about appropriate health care for specific clinical conditions.
Guideline recommendation	Course of action advised by the guideline development group on the basis of their assessment of the supporting evidence.
Haematuria	The presence of blood in the urine. Macroscopic haematuria is visible to the naked eye, while microscopic haematuria is only visible with the aid of a microscope.
Health economics	A branch of economics that studies decisions about the use and distribution of healthcare resources.
Health technology	Health technologies include medicines, medical devices such as artificial hip joints, diagnostic techniques, surgical procedures, health promotion activities (e.g. the role of diet versus medicines in disease management) and other therapeutic interventions.
Health technology appraisal	A health technology appraisal, as undertaken by NICE, is the process of determining the clinical and cost effectiveness of a **health technology**. NICE health technology appraisals are designed to provide patients, health professionals and managers with an authoritative source of advice on new and existing health technologies.
Heterogeneity	A lack of **homogeneity**. The term is used in **meta-analyses** and **systematic reviews** when the results or estimates of effects of treatment from separate studies seem to be very different – in terms of the size of treatment effects or even to the extent that some indicate beneficial and others suggest adverse treatment effects. Such results may occur as a result of differences between studies in terms of the patient populations, outcome measures, definition of **variables** or duration of follow-up.
Hierarchy of evidence	An established hierarchy of study types, based on the degree of certainty that can be attributed to the conclusions that can be drawn from a well-conducted study. Well-conducted **randomised controlled trials** (RCTs) are at the top of this hierarchy. (Several large statistically significant RCTs that are in agreement represent stronger evidence than say one small RCT.) Well-conducted studies of patients' views and experiences would appear at a lower level in the hierarchy of evidence.
Homogeneity	This means that the results of studies included in a **systematic review** or **meta-analysis** are similar and there is no evidence of **heterogeneity**. Results are usually regarded as homogeneous when differences between studies could reasonably be expected to occur by chance. See also **consistency**.
Idiopathic	Having no defined cause.

Incidence	The probability of developing the disease or condition under study during a defined time period, usually 1 year.
Inclusion criteria	See **selection criteria**.
Information bias	Pertinent to all types of study and can be caused by inadequate questionnaires (e.g. difficult or biased questions), observer or interviewer errors (e.g. lack of **blinding**), response errors (e.g. lack of **blinding** if patients are aware of the treatment they receive) and measurement error (e.g. a faulty machine).
Intention-to-treat (ITT) analysis	An analysis of a clinical trial where patients are analysed according to the group to which they were initially randomly allocated, regardless of whether or not they had dropped out, fully complied with the treatment, or crossed over and received the alternative treatment. Intention-to-treat analyses are favoured in assessments of clinical effectiveness as they mirror the non-compliance and treatment changes that are likely to occur when the treatment is used in practice.
Internal validity	Refers to the integrity of the study design.
International Continence Society (ICS)	Multidisciplinary scientific group concerned with all aspects of urinary and faecal incontinence in all patient groups.
Intervention	Healthcare action intended to benefit the patient, e.g. drug treatment, surgical procedure, psychological therapy, etc.
Interventional procedure (IP)	A procedure used for diagnosis or treatment that involves making a cut or hole in the patient's body, entry into a body cavity or using electromagnetic radiation (including X-rays or lasers). NICE has the task of producing guidance about whether specific interventional procedures are safe enough and work well enough for routine use.
Intrinsic sphincter deficiency (ISD)	Incompetence of the urethral sphincter mechanisms usually associated with severe stress incontinence symptoms, due to inherent weakness of the sphincter itself, as opposed to the more common problem of impaired urethral support (hypermobility).
Introitus	Entrance into the vagina.
Kappa score or rating	A measure of agreement between two individuals or variables, where 1 indicates perfect agreement.
'Knack'	A conscious contraction of pelvic floor muscle preceding rises in intra-abdominal pressure, e.g. with cough. Also called 'counterbracing'.
Level of evidence (evidence level, EL)	A code (e.g. 1++, 1+) linked to an individual study, indicating where it fits into the **hierarchy of evidence** and how well it has adhered to recognised research principles.
Literature review	A process of collecting, reading and assessing the quality of published (and unpublished) articles on a given topic.
Longitudinal study	A study of the same group of people at more than one point in time. (This type of study contrasts with a **cross-sectional study**, which observes a defined set of people at a single point in time.)
Masking	See **blinding**.
Meta-analysis	Results from a collection of independent studies (investigating the same treatment) are pooled using statistical techniques to synthesise their findings into a single estimate of a treatment effect. Where studies are not compatible, e.g. because of differences in the study populations or in the outcomes measured, it may be inappropriate or even misleading

to statistically pool results in this way. See also **systematic review** and **heterogeneity**.

Methodological quality	The extent to which a study has conformed to recognised good practice in the design and execution of its research methods.
Methodology	The overall approach of a research project, e.g. the study will be a **randomised controlled trial**, of 200 people, over 1 year.
Mixed urinary incontinence (MUI)	Involuntary leakage associated with urgency and also with exertion, effort, sneezing or coughing.
Multicentre study	A study where subjects were selected from different locations or populations, e.g. a cooperative study between different hospitals or an international collaboration involving patients from more than one country.
Multivariate analysis	An analysis where the effects of many variables are considered. It can select a subset of variables that significantly contribute to the variable in the outcome.
Negative predictive value (NPV)	The proportion of people with a negative test result who do not have the disease (where not having the disease is indicated by the 'gold' standard test being negative).
Nocturia	The complaint of having to wake at night one or more times to void. See also **frequency**.
Nocturnal enuresis	Urinary incontinence occurring during sleep. The term enuresis itself is synonymous with incontinence and, where it is intended to denote incontinence during sleep, it should always be qualified with the adjective 'nocturnal'.
Nominal group technique	A technique used for the purpose of reaching an agreement on a particular issue. It uses a variety of postal and direct contact techniques, with individual judgements being aggregated statistically to derive the group judgement. See also **consensus methods**.
Non-experimental study	A study based on subjects selected on the basis of their availability, with no attempt having been made to avoid problems of bias.
Non-systematic review	See **review**.
Objective measure	A measurement that follows a standardised procedure that is less open to subjective interpretation by potentially biased observers and study participants.
Observation	Observation is a research technique used to help understand complex situations. It involves watching, listening to and recording behaviours, actions, activities and interactions. The settings are usually natural but they can be laboratory settings, as in psychological research.
Observational study	In research about diseases or treatments, this refers to a study in which nature is allowed to take its course. Changes or differences in one characteristic (e.g. whether or not people received a specific treatment or intervention) are studied in relation to changes or differences in other(s) (e.g. whether or not they died), without the intervention of the investigator. There is a greater risk of **selection bias** than in **experimental studies**.
Odds ratio (OR)	Odds are a way of representing probability, especially familiar for betting. In recent years odds ratios have become widely used in reports of clinical studies. They provide an estimate (usually with a **confidence interval**) for the effect of a treatment. Odds are used to convey the idea of 'risk' and an odds ratio of 1 between two treatment groups would

imply that the risks of an adverse outcome were the same in each group. For rare events the odds ratio and the **relative risk** (which uses actual risks and not odds) will be very similar. See also **relative risk** and **risk ratio**.

Off-label prescribing

When a drug or device is prescribed outside its **specific indication**, to treat a condition or disease for which it is not specifically licensed.

Oxford grading system

A system for assessing pelvic floor muscle contraction, where 0 = no contraction, 1 = flicker, 2 = weak, 3 = moderate, 4 = good, 5 = strong.

Outcome

The end result of care and treatment and/or rehabilitation. In other words, the change in health, functional ability, symptoms or situation of a person, which can be used to measure the effectiveness of care/treatment/rehabilitation. Researchers should decide what outcomes to measure before a study begins; outcomes are then assessed at the end of the study.

Overactive bladder (OAB) syndrome

Urgency, with or without urge urinary incontinence, usually with frequency and nocturia. OAB wet is where (urge) incontinence is present, and OAB dry is where incontinence is absent.

Pad test

A diagnostic method used to detect and quantify urine loss based on weight gain of absorbent pads during a set time period.

Peer review

Review of a study, service or recommendations by those with similar interests and expertise to the people who produced the study findings or recommendations. Peer reviewers can include professional and/or patient/carer representatives.

Pelvic floor muscle training (PFMT)

Repetitive selective voluntary contraction and relaxation of specific pelvic floor muscles.

Pelvic organ prolapse (POP)

Descent of one or more of the anterior vaginal wall, the posterior vaginal wall and the apex, or the vault of the vagina towards or through the vaginal introitus.

Pelvic organ prolapse quantification (POP-Q)

A method for classifying the stage of prolapse, in which six specific vaginal sites (A, Ba, C, D, Bp, Ap) and the vaginal length are measured in centimetres from the introitus.

Performance bias

Systematic differences in care provided apart from the intervention being evaluated. For example, if study participants know they are in the **control group** they may be more likely to use other forms of care; people who know they are in the experimental group may experience **placebo effects**, and care providers may treat patients differently according to what group they are in. Masking (**blinding**) of both the recipients and providers of care is used to protect against performance bias.

Perineometer

A device for measuring the strength of pelvic floor muscle contraction. Used as a form of biofeedback during treatment, or to measure treatment outcome.

Pilot study

A small-scale 'test' of the research instrument. For example, testing out (piloting) a new questionnaire with people who are similar to the population of the study, in order to highlight any problems or areas of concern, which can then be addressed before the full-scale study begins.

Placebo

Placebos are fake or inactive treatments received by participants allocated to the **control group** in a clinical trial that are indistinguishable from the active treatments being given in the experimental group. They are used so that participants are ignorant of their treatment allocation in order to be able to quantify the effect of the experimental treatment over and above any **placebo effect** due to receiving care or attention.

Placebo effect
A beneficial (or adverse) effect produced by a placebo and not due to any property of the **placebo** itself.

Point estimate
A best single estimate (taken from research data) for the true value of a treatment effect or other measurement. For example, researchers in one clinical trial take their results as their best estimate of the real treatment effect – this is their estimate at their point in time. The precision or accuracy of the estimate is measured by a **confidence interval**. Another clinical trial of the same treatment will produce a different point estimate of treatment effect.

Positive predictive value (PPV)
The proportion of people with a positive test result who have the disease (where having the disease is indicated by the 'gold' standard test being positive).

Post-void residual urine (PVR)
The volume of urine left in the bladder immediately after voiding.

Power
See **statistical power**.

Prevalence
The probability of experiencing a symptom or having a condition or disease within a defined population at a defined time point.

Primary care
Health care delivered to patients outside hospitals. Primary care covers a range of services provided by GPs, nurses and other healthcare professionals, dentists, pharmacists and opticians.

Primary care trust (PCT)
A primary care trust is an NHS organisation responsible for improving the health of local people, developing services provided by local GPs and their teams (called **primary care**) and making sure that other appropriate health services are in place to meet local people's needs.

Primary surgery for stress UI
Surgery for stress urinary incontinence undertaken in a woman who has not previously undergone surgery for this condition.

Probability
How likely an event is to occur, e.g. how likely a treatment or intervention will alleviate a symptom.

Prognostic factor
Patient or disease characteristics, e.g. age or **co-morbidity**, that influence the course of the disease under study. In a randomised trial to compare two treatments, chance imbalances in **variables** (prognostic factors) that influence patient outcome are possible, especially if the size of the study is fairly small. In terms of analysis these prognostic factors become **confounding factors**. See also **prognostic marker**.

Prognostic marker
A **prognostic factor** used to assign patients to categories for a specified purpose, e.g. for treatment, or as part of a clinical trial, according to the likely progression of the disease. For example, the purpose of randomisation in a clinical trial is to produce similar treatment groups with respect to important **prognostic factors**. This can often be achieved more efficiently if randomisation takes place within subgroups defined by the most important prognostic factors. Thus if age was very much related to patient outcome then separate randomisation schemes would be used for different age groups. This process is known as stratified random allocation.

Prompted voiding
Prompted voiding teaches people to initiate their own toileting through requests for help and positive reinforcement from carers. It has been used in institutionalised patients with cognitive and mobility problems. They are asked regularly if they wish to void and only assisted to the toilet when there is a positive response.

Prospective study	A study in which people are entered into the research and then followed up over a period of time with future events recorded as they happen. This contrasts with studies that are **retrospective**.
Protocol	A plan or set of steps that defines appropriate action. A research protocol sets out, in advance of carrying out the study, what question is to be answered and how information will be collected and analysed. Guideline implementation protocols set out how guideline recommendations will be used in practice by the NHS, both at national and local levels.
Publication bias	Studies with statistically significant results are more likely to get published than those with non-significant results. **Meta-analyses** that are exclusively based on published literature may therefore produce biased results.
P **value**	If a study is done to compare two treatments then the *P* value is the probability of obtaining the results of that study, or something more extreme, if there really was no difference between treatments. (The assumption that there really is no difference between treatments is called the 'null hypothesis'.) Suppose the *P* value was 0.03. What this means is that if there really was no difference between treatments then there would only be a 3% chance of getting the kind of results obtained. Since this chance seems quite low we should question the validity of the assumption that there really is no difference between treatments. We would conclude that there probably is a difference between treatments. By convention, where the value of *P* is below 0.05 (i.e. less than 5%) the result is seen as statistically significant. Where the value of *P* is 0.001 or less, the result is seen as highly significant. *P* values just tell us whether an effect can be regarded as statistically significant or not. In no way do they relate to how big the effect might be, for which we need the **confidence interval**.
Quality-adjusted life years (QALYs)	A measure of health outcome which looks at both length of life and quality of life. QALYs are calculated by estimating the years of life remaining for a patient following a particular care pathway and weighting each year with a quality of life score (on a zero to one scale). One QALY is equal to 1 year of life in perfect health, or 2 years at 50% health, and so on.
Quantitative research	Research that generates numerical data or data that can be converted into numbers, e.g. clinical trials or the national census which counts people and households.
Quasi experimental study	A study designed to test whether a treatment or intervention has an effect on the course or outcome of disease. It differs from a **controlled clinical trial** and a **randomised controlled trial** in that: (a) the assignment of patients to treatment and comparison groups is not done randomly, or patients are not given equal probabilities of selection; or (b) the investigator does not have full control over the allocation and/or timing of the intervention, but nonetheless conducts the study as if it were an experiment, allocating subjects to treatment and comparison groups.
Random allocation or randomisation	A method that uses the play of chance to assign participants to comparison groups in a research study, e.g. by using a random numbers table or a computer-generated random sequence. Random allocation implies that each individual (or each unit in the case of **cluster randomisation**) being entered into a study has the same chance of receiving each of the possible interventions.

Randomised controlled trial (RCT)	A study to test a specific drug or other treatment in which people are randomly assigned to two (or more) groups, with one (the experimental group) receiving the treatment that is being tested and the other (the comparison or control group) receiving an alternative treatment, a placebo (dummy treatment) or no treatment. The two groups are followed up to compare differences in outcomes to see how effective the experimental treatment was. (Through **randomisation**, the groups should be similar in all aspects apart from the treatment they receive during the study.)
Rectocele	Herniation (protrusion) of the rectum into the vagina.
Relative risk (RR)	A summary measure that represents the ratio of the risk of a given event or outcome (e.g. an adverse reaction to the drug being tested) in one group of subjects compared with another group. When the 'risk' of the event is the same in the two groups the relative risk is 1. In a study comparing two treatments, a relative risk of 2 would indicate that patients receiving one of the treatments had twice the risk of an undesirable outcome than those receiving the other treatment. Relative risk is sometimes used as a synonym for **risk ratio**.
Reliability	Reliability refers to a method of measurement that consistently gives the same results. For example, someone who has a high score on one occasion tends to have a high score if measured on another occasion very soon afterwards. With physical assessments it is possible for different clinicians to make independent assessments in quick succession – and if their assessments tend to agree then the method of assessment is said to be reliable.
Retrospective study	A retrospective study deals with the present/past and does not involve studying future events. This contrasts with studies that are **prospective**.
Review	A summary of the main points and trends in the research literature on a specified topic. A review is considered non-systematic unless an extensive literature search has been carried out to ensure that all aspects of the topic are covered and an objective appraisal made of the quality of the studies.
Risk ratio (RR)	Ratio of the risk of an undesirable event or outcome occurring in a group of patients receiving experimental treatment compared with a comparison (control) group. The term **relative risk** is sometimes used as a synonym for risk ratio.
Royal Colleges	In the UK medical/nursing world the term Royal Colleges, as for example in 'The Royal College of . . . ', refers to organisations that usually combine an educational standards and examination role with the promotion of professional standards.
Sample	A part of the study's target population from which the subjects of the study will be recruited. If subjects are drawn in an unbiased way from a particular population, the results can be generalised from the sample to the population as a whole.
Sampling	Refers to the way participants are selected for inclusion in a study.
Scottish Intercollegiate Guidelines Network (SIGN)	SIGN was established in 1993 to sponsor and support the development of evidence-based clinical guidelines for the NHS in Scotland.
Secondary care	Care provided in hospitals.
Secondary surgery for stress UI	Surgery for stress urinary incontinence undertaken in a woman who has previously undergone surgery for this condition.

Selection bias	Selection bias has occurred if the characteristics of the sample differ from those of the wider population from which the sample has been drawn or if there are systematic differences between comparison groups of patients in a study in terms of prognosis or responsiveness to treatment.
Selection criteria	Explicit standards used by guideline development groups to decide which studies should be included and excluded from consideration as potential sources of evidence.
Sensitivity	In diagnostic testing, this refers to the chance of having a positive test result given that you have the disease. 100% sensitivity means that all those with the disease will test positive, but this is not the same the other way around. A patient could have a positive test result but not have the disease – this is called a 'false positive'. The sensitivity of a test is also related to its **negative predictive value** (true negatives) – a test with a sensitivity of 100% means that all those who get a negative test result do not have the disease. To fully judge the accuracy of a test, its **specificity** must also be considered.
Short form 36 (SF-36)	A generic multipurpose 36-item survey that measures eight domains of health: physical functioning, role limitations due to physical health, bodily pain, general health perceptions, vitality, social functioning, role limitations due to emotional problems, and mental health.
Single-blind (SB) study	A study in which *either* the subject (patient/participant) *or* the observer (clinician/investigator) is not aware of which treatment or intervention the subject is receiving.
Specialist	A specialist is any healthcare professional who has received appropriate training to be able to provide the particular range of specialist services he or she undertakes, and who works within the context of an integrated, multidisciplinary continence team. Particular service profiles will differ from one place to another.
Specific indication	When a drug or a device has a specific remit to treat a specific condition and is not licensed for use in treating other conditions or diseases.
Specificity	In diagnostic testing, this refers to the chance of having a negative test result given that you do not have the disease. 100% specificity means that all those without the disease will test negative, but this is not the same the other way around. A patient could have a negative test result yet still have the disease – this is called a 'false negative'. The specificity of a test is also related to its **positive predictive value** (true positives) – a test with a specificity of 100% means that all those who get a positive test result definitely have the disease. To fully judge the accuracy of a test, its **sensitivity** must also be considered.
Stamey grading of urinary incontinence	Grade 1: urine loss only with coughing/sneezing/lifting heavy objects; Grade 2: urine loss with minimal activities, e.g. walking or rising from sitting position; Grade 3: totally incontinent in upright position.
Standard deviation (SD)	A measure of the spread, scatter or variability of a set of measurements. Usually used with the mean (average) to describe numerical data.
Statistical power	The ability of a study to demonstrate an association or causal relationship between two **variables**, given that an association exists. For example, 80% power in a clinical trial means that the study has a 80% chance of ending up with a P value of less than 5% in a statistical test (i.e. a statistically significant treatment effect) if there really was an important difference (e.g. 10% versus 5% mortality) between

treatments. If the statistical power of a study is low, the study results will be questionable (the study might have been too small to detect any differences). By convention, 80% is an acceptable level of power. See also *P* **value**.

Stress test

A clinical test for the demonstration of stress urinary incontinence. The woman is asked to cough while the observer visualises the external urethral meatus. The test may be undertaken either after filling to a known volume, or prior to micturition, the volume being recorded thereafter. It may be undertaken supine or standing.

Stress urinary incontinence (SUI)

The complaint of involuntary leakage on effort or exertion or on sneezing or coughing.

Structured interview

A research technique where the interviewer controls the interview by adhering strictly to a questionnaire or interview schedule with pre-set questions.

Study checklist

A list of questions addressing the key aspects of the research methodology that must be in place if a study is to be accepted as valid. A different checklist is required for each study type. These checklists are used to ensure a degree of consistency in the way that studies are evaluated.

Study population

People who have been identified as the subjects of a study.

Study quality

See **methodological quality**.

Study type

The kind of design used for a study. **Randomised controlled trials, case–control studies** and **cohort studies** are all examples of study types.

Subject

A person who takes part in an experiment or research study.

Survey

A study in which information is systematically collected from people (usually from a sample within a defined population).

Systematic

Methodical, according to plan; not random.

Systematic error

Refers to the various errors or biases inherent in a study. See also **bias**.

Systematic review

A review in which evidence from scientific studies has been identified, appraised and synthesised in a methodical way according to predetermined criteria. May or may not include a **meta-analysis**.

Systemic

Involving the whole body.

Target population

The people to whom guideline recommendations are intended to apply. Recommendations may be less valid if applied to a population with different characteristics from the participants in the research study – e.g. in terms of age, disease state, social background.

Tertiary centre

A major medical centre providing complex treatments which receives referrals from both primary and secondary care. Sometimes called a tertiary referral centre. See also **primary care** and **secondary care**.

Timed voiding

Timed voiding (scheduled, routine or regular toileting) is a passive toileting assistance programme that is initiated and maintained by a caregiver, e.g. for patients who cannot participate in independent toileting. Toileting is fixed by time or event, on a regular schedule, or a schedule to match the patient's voiding pattern.

Trust

A trust is an NHS organisation responsible for providing a group of healthcare services. An **acute trust** provides hospital services. A **primary care trust** buys hospital care on behalf of the local population, as well as being responsible for the provision of community health services.

Urethral competence The ability of the urethral sphincter mechanisms to retain urine in the bladder at all times other than during normal micturition.

Urethral hypermobility Incompetence of the urethral sphincter mechanisms usually associated with stress incontinence symptoms, due to failure of urethral support.

Urethral pain Pain felt in the urethra and the patient indicates the urethra as the site.

Urge urinary incontinence (UUI) Involuntary urine leakage accompanied by or immediately preceded by urgency.

Urgency The 'complaint of a sudden compelling desire to pass urine which is difficult to defer'.

Urgency-frequency syndrome Another name for **overactive bladder**.

Urinary incontinence (UI) The 'complaint of any involuntary urinary leakage'.

Urodynamics (UD) The term 'urodynamics' encompasses a number of varied physiological tests of bladder and urethral function that aim to demonstrate an underlying abnormality of storage or voiding. The term is often used loosely to mean multichannel cystometry. See also **cystometry** and **uroflowmetry**. Videourodynamics involves synchronous radiographic screening of the bladder with multichannel cystometry and is so called because originally the information was recorded to videotape. Ambulatory urodynamics involves multichannel cystometry carried out with physiological bladder filling rates and using portable recording devices that enable to patient to remain ambulant during the test.

Urodynamic stress urinary incontinence (USI) The demonstration of involuntary leakage of urine during increased abdominal pressure but in the absence of detrusor contraction during filling cystometry.

Uroflowmetry Uroflowmetry entails a free-flow void into a recording device that provides the practitioner with information about the volume of urine passed, and the rate of urine flow.

Validity Assessment of how well a tool or instrument measures what it is intended to measure. See also **external validity** and **internal validity**.

Variable A measurement that can vary within a study, e.g. the age of participants. Variability is present when differences can be seen between different people or within the same person over time, with respect to any characteristic or feature that can be assessed or measured.

Voiding dysfunction The term is not formally defined but is used to indicate objective evidence of abnormal voiding. This is usually based on a combination of diminished urine flow rate, abnormal flow pattern, raised detrusor voiding pressure and the presence of postmicturition residual urine. It is often, but not always, associated with symptoms of voiding difficulty (hesitancy, straining, poor or intermittent urinary stream) and/or post-micturition symptoms (sensation of incomplete emptying, post-micturition dribble).

1. Introduction

1.1   Urinary incontinence

Urinary incontinence (UI) is a common symptom that can affect women of all ages, with a wide range of severity and nature. While rarely life-threatening, incontinence may seriously influence the physical, psychological and social wellbeing of affected individuals. The impact on the families and carers of women with UI may be profound, and the resource implications for the health service considerable.

The International Continence Society (ICS) has standardised terminology in lower urinary tract function: UI is defined as 'the complaint of any involuntary urinary leakage'.[1] This may occur as a result of a number of abnormalities of function of the lower urinary tract, or as a result of other illnesses, and these tend to cause leakage in different situations. Definitions for stress, mixed and urge UI and overactive bladder (OAB) are given in the glossary. Other types of UI may be described by the situations that provoke urine loss, for example during sexual intercourse, or on laughing or giggling. Some patients may simply report being 'wet all the time'. This may be a reflection of the severity of their condition, although may on occasions be due to other pathologies, for example fistula. There are currently approximately 80 cases of fistula between the urinary tract and genital tract treated each year in England and Wales and this condition is not considered further in this guideline. It is recognised that UI may be of a transient nature on occasion, reflecting acute health or environmental factors.

Prevalence and incidence

Urinary incontinence is an embarrassing problem to many women and thus its presence may be significantly underreported. In a UK community study, the prevalence of UI known to the health and social service agencies was 0.2% in women aged 15–64 years and 2.5% in those aged 65 and over.[2] A concurrent postal survey showed a prevalence of 8.5% in women aged 15–64 and 11.6% in those aged 65 and over. Incontinence was described as 'moderate' or 'severe' in one-fifth of those who reported it and, even among these, fewer than one-third were receiving health or social services for the condition.[2]

The Leicestershire MRC Incontinence Study, of individuals over 40 years of age, found that 33.6% of the population reported significant urinary symptoms but only 6.2% found these bothersome, and only 2.4% both bothersome and socially disabling. Of the population surveyed, 3.8% (one in nine of those with clinically significant symptoms) felt the need for help with their symptoms.[3,4] Some women may not see their UI as a major problem. For others, who do perceive a problem with which they would like help, there are often barriers to presentation. Women may take up to 10 years before seeking help.[5] They may be too embarrassed to seek advice, may not wish to bother their general practitioner (GP), may believe UI to be a normal consequence of the ageing process or may not appreciate that treatments are available.[6]

Differences in study populations, the definition and measurement of UI, and the survey method used result in a wide range of prevalence estimates.[7] Where the most inclusive definitions have been used ('ever', 'any', 'at least once in the last 12 months'), prevalence estimates in the general population range from 5% to 69% in women 15 years and older, with most studies in the range 25–45%.[7] There appears to be less variation in the prevalence of more severe UI and estimates in the general population range between 4% and 7% in women under 65 years, and between 4% and 17% in those over 65 for daily UI.[7] The Leicestershire MRC Incontinence Study found that, while 34.2% of women reported UI at times, only 3.5% experienced the symptom on a daily basis, 11.8% weekly, 7.3% monthly and 11.6% yearly.[8]

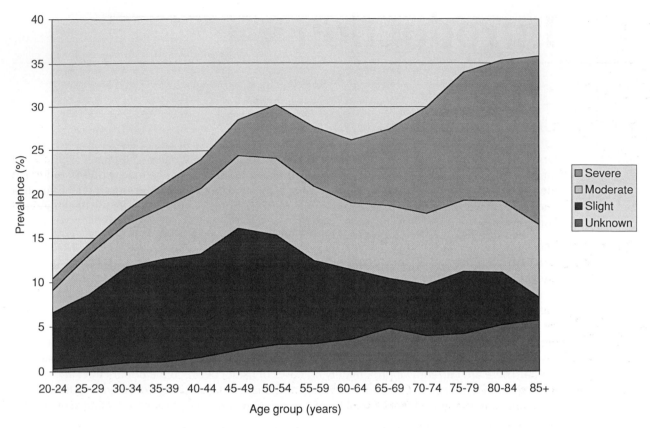

Figure 1.1   Prevalence of incontinence by age group and severity

Several studies have shown that the prevalence of any UI tends to increase up to middle age, then plateaus or falls between 50 and 70 years, with a steady increase with more advanced age. The EPINCONT survey, of women aged over 20 years from Norway, illustrates this point (Figure 1.1). These data also show that slight to moderate UI is more common in younger women, while moderate and severe UI affects the elderly more often.[9,10]

Stress UI appears to be the most common UI type and overall 50% of incontinent women in the EPINCONT survey reported this as their only symptom; 11% described only urge UI and 36% reported mixed UI.[9] This and other studies indicate that the trends in prevalence of UI at different ages reflect a reduction in the complaints of stress UI in those aged 50 years and over, with an increase in urge UI and mixed UI in women aged 60 years and above (Figure 1.2).[9,11] This study also found that the severity of incontinence varied between the different types: the proportion of incontinence that was regarded as being severe was 17%, 28% and 38% in the stress, urge and mixed UI groups, respectively.[9]

There are relatively little epidemiological data on the prevalence of OAB syndrome. A telephone survey from the USA found an overall prevalence of OAB wet of 9.6% in women over 18 years of age, rising from 5% in those aged 18–44 to 19% in those over 65.[12] Survey data from Europe found prevalence of the same order.[13] The Leicestershire MRC Incontinence Study found an overall prevalence of OAB in women aged 40 and over of 21.4%.[14]

It has been estimated that, while not all may need or want help, 20.4% of people aged 40 years and over, representing around 5 million people in the UK, have a healthcare requirement.[8] In women aged 40 and over this figure increases from 20.5% aged 40–49 up to 35.6% at age 80 and over.

Risk factors
In addition to the effect of age, cross-sectional studies suggest other associations and possible risk factors for UI. These include pregnancy, parity, obstetric factors, menopause, hysterectomy, obesity, lower urinary tract symptoms, functional impairment, cognitive impairment, smoking,

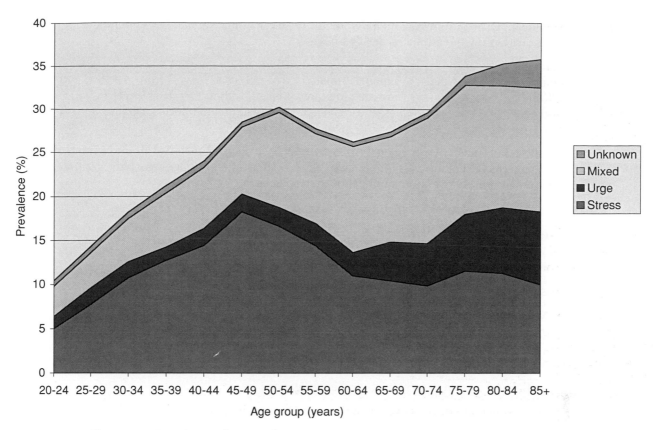

Figure 1.2 Prevalence of UI types by age group

family history, diet and genetics. Urinary incontinence may be a presenting symptom of neuro-logical disease.

Costs and implications for health services

Costs to patients and carers

Urinary incontinence is distressing and socially disruptive. It may be the cause of personal health and hygiene problems. It may restrict employment and educational or leisure opportunities, and lead to embarrassment and exclusion. Furthermore, for some, it may result in abuse of adults in the workplace and older people in residential care or nursing homes. In adult women with UI, 60% avoid going away from home, 50% feel odd or different from others, 45% avoid public trans-port and 50% report avoiding sexual activity through fear of incontinence.[15] Serious psychiatric morbidity has been reported in one-quarter of women attending hospital for investigation of UI.[16] For carers, UI is often a major reason for the breakdown of the caring relationship which can lead to admission to residential or nursing home care; incontinence is second only to dementia as an initiating factor for such moves.[17] Financial costs to patients and carers, including the cost of absorbent products, laundry, etc., may also be considerable.

Costs to the health services

There is limited information on the cost of managing UI in the UK although the estimated total cost in the USA in 1995 was $12.4bn (£7bn), with the vast majority of this relating to community or nursing home care ($8.6bn and $3.8bn [£5bn and £2.2bn], respectively).[18] These costs are of a similar order to those associated with gynaecological cancers, osteoporosis, pneumonia and influenza, and arthritis,[18] and in the USA and Sweden are equivalent to approximately 2% of the total healthcare budget.[19] With current UK health spending of £90bn, this would approximate to £1.8bn annually in England and Wales, or perhaps £600 per incontinent individual. Data from the Leicestershire MRC Incontinence Study estimates the annual cost to the NHS of treating clinically significant UI at £536m (£233m for women). The total annual service costs (including costs borne by individuals) were estimated at £743m.[20]

A recent study of the costs of care for women seeking treatment for UI across Europe (the PURE study), determined that the mean UI-related costs per year ranged from €359 (£248) in the UK/Ireland (where patients were predominantly treated by their GPs) to €515 (£355) in Germany and €655 (£452) in Spain (where the initial referral may sometimes be to specialists and sometimes to GPs).[5]

Health-related costs of managing OAB in the USA have been estimated at around $9bn (£5bn), the cost patterns raising the possibility that treating OAB at an early stage may both improve patient care and minimise overall use of healthcare resources.[21]

1.2 Aim of the guideline

This clinical guideline concerns the management of UI in adult women. It includes:

- stress UI
- OAB (with or without urge UI)
- mixed UI.

It has been developed with the aim of providing guidance on:

- initial and ongoing assessments and investigations
- appropriate use of conservative and surgical treatment options
- the competence required by surgeons performing the primary and subsequent operative procedures.

1.3 Areas outside the remit of the guideline

This guideline does not address:

- the management and treatment of co-morbidities, such as pelvic organ prolapse (POP), except where they relate to the treatment of UI and/or OAB syndrome
- incontinence caused by neurological disease
- incontinence in men
- incontinence in children
- anal incontinence.

1.4 For whom is the guideline intended?

This guideline is of relevance to those who work in or use the NHS in England and Wales, in particular:

- all healthcare professionals who are involved in the care of women who have UI or OAB syndrome (including GPs, nurses, physiotherapists, gynaecologists, urologists and occupational therapists). The healthcare professionals providing care for women with UI or OAB may vary depending on geographical service provision.
- those responsible for commissioning and planning healthcare services, including primary care trust commissioners, Health Commission Wales commissioners, and public health, trust and care home managers
- women with UI and/or OAB syndrome, their families and other carers.

A version of this guideline for the public is available from the NICE website (www.nice.org.uk/CG040publicinfo) or from the NHS Response Line (0870 1555 455); quote reference number N1129).

1.5 Who has developed the guideline?

The guideline was developed by a multi-professional and lay working group (the Guideline Development Group or GDG) convened by the National Collaborating Centre for Women's and Children's Health (NCC-WCH). The membership is listed above. Staff from the NCC-WCH provided support for the guideline development process by undertaking systematic searches, retrieval and appraisal of the evidence and health economic modelling, and wrote successive drafts of the guideline.

All GDG members' potential and actual conflicts of interest were recorded on a declaration form provided by NICE and are shown in Appendix A. The form covered consultancies, fee-paid work, shareholdings, fellowships, and support from the healthcare industry. The GDG leader and NCC-WCH executive director consider that the declarations made did not influence the recommendations developed.

1.6 Other relevant documents

This guideline is intended to complement other existing and proposed works of relevance, including related NICE guidance:

- Guidelines:
  - *Infection Control: Prevention of Healthcare-Associated Infection in Primary and Community Care*[22]
  - *Referral Guidelines for Suspected Cancer*[23]
  - *Routine Postnatal Care of Women and Their Babies*[24]
  - *Faecal Incontinence* (in development – expected date of issue June 2007).
- Cancer service guidance:
  - *Improving Outcomes in Urological Cancer: the Manual.*[25]
- Interventional procedures:
  - *Sacral Nerve Stimulation for Urge Incontinence and Urgency-Frequency.*[26]
  - *Intramural Urethral Bulking Procedures for Stress Urinary Incontinence in Women*[27]
  - *Insertion of Extraurethral (Non-Circumferential) Retropubic Adjustable Compression Devices for Stress Urinary Incontinence in Women*[28]
  - *Insertion of Biological Slings for Stress Urinary Incontinence in Women*[29]
  - *Bone-Anchored Cystourethropexy.*[30]

Other than NICE guidance, relevant works are:

- the third International Consultation on Incontinence (ICI) (2005)[31,32]
- the Royal College of Physicians report on incontinence (1995)[33]
- the Department of Health's *Good Practice in Continence Services* (2000)[34]
- the *National Service Framework for Older People* (2001).[35]

1.7 Guideline method

This guideline was commissioned by NICE and developed in accordance with the guideline development process outlined in the NICE technical manual.[36]

Literature search strategy

Initial scoping searches were executed to identify relevant guidelines (local, national and international) produced by other development groups. The reference lists in these guidelines were checked against subsequent searches to identify missing evidence.

Relevant published evidence to inform the guideline development process and answer the clinical questions was identified by systematic search strategies. The questions are shown in Appendix B. Additionally, stakeholder organisations were invited to submit evidence for consideration by the GDG provided it was relevant to the clinical questions and of equivalent or better quality than evidence identified by the search strategies.

Systematic searches to answer the clinical questions formulated and agreed by the GDG were executed using the following databases via the 'Ovid' platform: Medline (1966 onwards), Embase (1980 onwards), Cumulative Index to Nursing and Allied Health Literature (1982 onwards), British Nursing Index (1985 onwards) and PsycINFO (1967 onwards). The most recent search conducted for the three Cochrane databases (Cochrane Central Register of Controlled Trials, Cochrane Database of Systematic Reviews, and the Database of Abstracts of Reviews of Effects) was Quarter 1, 2006. The Allied and Complementary Medicine Database (AMED) was also used for alternative therapies (1985 onwards via the Datastar platform). Searches to identify economic studies were undertaken using the above databases and the NHS Economic Evaluations Database (NHS EED).

Search strategies combined relevant controlled vocabulary and natural language in an effort to balance sensitivity and specificity. Unless advised by the GDG, searches were not date specific. Language restrictions were not applied to searches. Both generic and specially developed methodological search filters were used appropriately.

There was no systematic attempt to search grey literature (conferences, abstracts, theses and unpublished trials). Hand searching of journals not indexed on the databases was not undertaken.

Towards the end of the guideline development process, searches were updated and re-executed, thereby including evidence published and included in the databases up to 17 March 2006. Any evidence published after this date was not included. This date should be considered the starting point for searching for new evidence for future updates to this guideline.

Further details of the search strategies, including the methodological filters employed, are available on the accompanying CD-ROM.

Synthesis of clinical effectiveness evidence

Evidence relating to clinical effectiveness was reviewed using established guides[37–43] and classified using the established hierarchical system shown in Table 1.1.[36] This system reflects the susceptibility to bias that is inherent in particular study designs.

The type of clinical question dictates the highest level of evidence that may be sought. In assessing the quality of the evidence, each study receives a quality rating coded as '++', '+' or '−'. For issues of therapy or treatment, the highest possible evidence level (EL) is a well-conducted systematic review or meta-analysis of randomised controlled trials (RCTs; EL = 1 ++) or an individual RCT (EL = 1+). Studies of poor quality are rated as '−'. Usually, studies rated as '−' should not be used as a basis for making a recommendation, but they can be used to inform recommendations. For issues of prognosis, the highest possible level of evidence is a cohort study (EL = 2). A level of evidence was assigned to each study, and to the body of evidence for each question.

For each clinical question, the highest available level of evidence was selected. Where appropriate, for example if a systematic review, meta-analysis or RCT existed in relation to a question, studies of a weaker design were not included. Where systematic reviews, meta-analyses and RCTs did not exist, other appropriate experimental or observational studies were sought. For diagnostic tests, test evaluation studies examining the performance of the test were used if the efficacy of the test

Table 1.1 Levels of evidence for intervention studies

Level	Source of evidence
1++	High-quality meta-analyses, systematic reviews of randomised controlled trials (RCTs) or RCTs with a very low risk of bias
1+	Well-conducted meta-analyses, systematic reviews of RCTs or RCTs with a low risk of bias
1−	Meta-analyses, systematic reviews of RCTs or RCTs with a high risk of bias
2++	High-quality systematic reviews of case–control or cohort studies; high-quality case–control or cohort studies with a very low risk of confounding, bias or chance and a high probability that the relationship is causal
2+	Well-conducted case–control or cohort studies with a low risk of confounding, bias or chance and a moderate probability that the relationship is causal
2−	Case–control or cohort studies with a high risk of confounding, bias or chance and a significant risk that the relationship is not causal
3	Non-analytical studies (for example case reports, case series)
4	Expert opinion, formal consensus

was required, but where an evaluation of the effectiveness of the test in the clinical management of patients and the outcome of disease was required, evidence from RCTs or cohort studies was optimal.

The system described above covers studies of treatment effectiveness. However, it is less appropriate for studies reporting diagnostic tests of accuracy. In the absence of a validated ranking system for this type of test, NICE has developed a hierarchy for evidence of accuracy of diagnostic tests that takes into account the various factors likely to affect the validity of these studies (Table 1.2).[36]

For economic evaluations, no standard system of grading the quality of evidence exists. Economic evaluations that are included in the review have been assessed using a quality assessment checklist based on good practice in decision-analytic modelling.[44]

Table 1.2 Levels of evidence for studies of the accuracy of diagnostic tests

Level	Type of evidence
Ia	Systematic review (with homogeneity)[a] of level-1 studies[b]
Ib	Level-1 studies[b]
II	Level-2 studies[c]; systematic reviews of level-2 studies
III	Level-3 studies[d]; systematic reviews of level-3 studies
IV	Consensus, expert committee reports or opinions and/or clinical experience without explicit critical appraisal; or based on physiology, bench research or 'first principles'

[a] Homogeneity means there are minor or no variations in the directions and degrees of results between individual studies that are included in the systematic review.
[b] Level-1 studies are studies that use a blind comparison of the test with a validated reference standard ('gold' standard) in a sample of patients that reflects the population to whom the test would apply.
[c] Level-2 studies are studies that have only one of the following:
• narrow population (the sample does not reflect the population to whom the test would apply)
• use a poor reference standard (defined as that where the 'test' is included in the 'reference', or where the 'testing' affects the 'reference')
• the comparison between the test and reference standard is not blind
• case–control studies.
[d] Level-3 studies are studies that have at least two or three of the features listed above.

Table 1.3 MHRA classification of adverse effect frequency

Classification	Frequency of occurrence
Very common	more than 1 in 10 (>10%)
Common	between 1 in 10 and 1 in 100 ($\geq$1% and $\leq$10%)
Uncommon	between 1 in 100 and 1 in 1000 ($\geq$0.1% and <1%)
Rare	between 1 in 1000 and 1 in 10 000
Very rare	fewer than 1 in 10 000

Evidence was synthesised qualitatively by summarising the content of identified papers in evidence tables and agreeing brief statements that accurately reflected the evidence. Quantitative synthesis (meta-analysis) was performed where appropriate. Where confidence intervals were calculated, this was done in accordance with accepted methods.[45] Summary results and data are presented in the guideline text. More detailed results and data are presented in the evidence tables on the accompanying CD-ROM, where a list of excluded studies is also provided.

Specific considerations for this guideline

It was anticipated that some evidence relevant to this guideline would not be specific to women with UI and thus studies with mixed populations (men and women, and/or with UI of different aetiology) were considered if the majority of the population was women with idiopathic UI or OAB.

Published guidance from the NICE Interventional Procedures (IP) Programme was considered, alongside all relevant evidence in women with UI or OAB when an interventional procedure was approved for use. Where the IP guidance states that an interventional procedure is not for routine use, the procedure was not considered within this guideline.

The NICE health technology appraisal on tension-free vaginal tape (2003) was updated within this guideline by addressing a question on the intervention. The associated NICE guidance will be withdrawn on publication of this guideline.

The classification of adverse effect frequency used by the Medicines and Healthcare products Regulatory Agency (MHRA) was adopted within the guideline, as shown in Table 1.3.

Health economics

The aims of the economic input into the guideline were to inform the GDG of potential economic issues relating to UI in women and to ensure that recommendations represent a cost effective use of healthcare resources.

The health economist helped the GDG by identifying topics within the guideline that might benefit from economic analysis, reviewing the available economic evidence and, where necessary, conducting economic analysis. Reviews of published health economic evidence are presented alongside the reviews of clinical evidence, and modelling is presented in the appendices, with cross references from the relevant chapters.

Outcome measures used in the guideline

For this guideline, treatment has been assessed against a number of outcome domains, as follows:

- the woman's observations, including changes in symptoms and satisfaction

- generic and incontinence-specific aspects of quality of life (QOL)

- the clinician's observations including urodynamic investigation and quantification of incontinence

- harm (adverse effects, surgical complications)

- health economic outcomes, for example quality-adjusted life years (QALYs).

Table 1.4 Classification (grading) of recommendations for intervention studies

Grade	Evidence
A	• At least one meta-analysis, systematic review or randomised controlled trial (RCT) that is rated as 1++, and is directly applicable to the target population, or • a systematic review of RCTs or a body of evidence that consists principally of studies rated as 1+, is directly applicable to the target population and demonstrates overall consistency of results, or • evidence drawn from a NICE technology appraisal.
B	• A body of evidence that includes studies rated as 2++, is directly applicable to the target population and demonstrates overall consistency of results, or • extrapolated evidence from studies rated as 1++ or 1+.
C	• A body of evidence that includes studies rated as 2+, is directly applicable to the target population and demonstrates overall consistency of results, or • extrapolated evidence from studies rated as 2++.
D	• Evidence level 3 or 4, or • extrapolated evidence from studies rated as 2+, or • formal consensus.
D (GPP)	• A good practice point (GPP) is a recommendation for best practice based on the experience of the Guideline Development Group.

Forming and grading recommendations

For each guideline question, recommendations were derived using, and explicitly linked to, the evidence that supported them. In the first instance, informal consensus methods were used by the GDG to agree evidence statements and recommendations. Additionally, in areas where no substantial evidence existed, the GDG considered other guidelines or consensus statements to identify current best practice. Shortly before the consultation period, formal consensus methods were used to agree guideline recommendations (modified Delphi technique) and to select five to ten key priorities for implementation (nominal group technique).

Each recommendation was graded according to the level of evidence upon which it was based, using the established systems shown in Tables 1.4 and 1.5. For issues of therapy or treatment, the best possible level of evidence (a systematic review or meta-analysis or an individual RCT) equates to a grade A recommendation. For issues of prognosis, the best possible level of evidence (a cohort study) equates to a grade B recommendation. However, this should not be interpreted as an inferior grade of recommendation because it represents the highest level of relevant evidence.

In addition, the GDG made research recommendations in areas where evidence is lacking.

External review

This guideline has been developed in accordance with the NICE guideline development process. This has included giving registered stakeholder organisations the opportunity to comment on the scope of the guideline at the initial stage of development and on the evidence and recommendations at the concluding stage. In addition, the guideline was peer reviewed by nominated

Table 1.5 Classification (grading) of recommendations for studies of the accuracy of diagnostic tests

Grade	Level of evidence
A (DS)	Studies with level of evidence Ia or Ib
B (DS)	Studies with level of evidence of II
C (DS)	Studies with level of evidence of III
D (DS)	Studies with level of evidence of IV

individuals. The developers have carefully considered all of the comments during the consultation periods by registered stakeholders with validation by NICE.

1.8 Schedule for updating the guideline

Clinical guidelines commissioned by NICE are published with a review date 4 years from the date of publication. Reviewing may begin earlier than 4 years if significant evidence that affects guideline recommendations is identified sooner. The updated guideline will be available within 2 years of the start of the review process.

5.1 Procedures for overactive bladder

Sacral nerve stimulation is recommended for the treatment of UI due to detrusor over-activity in women who have not responded to conservative treatments. Women should be offered sacral nerve stimulation on the basis of their response to preliminary percutaneous nerve evaluation. Life-long follow-up is recommended.

D

Augmentation cystoplasty for the management of idiopathic detrusor overactivity should be restricted to women who have not responded to conservative treatments and who are willing and able to self-catheterise. Preoperative counselling should include common and serious complications: bowel disturbance, metabolic acidosis, mucus production and/or retention in the bladder, UTI and urinary retention. The small risk of malignancy occurring in the augmented bladder should also be discussed. Life-long follow-up is recommended.

D (GPP)

Urinary diversion should be considered for a woman with OAB only when conservative treatments have failed, and if sacral nerve stimulation and augmentation cystoplasty are not appropriate or are unacceptable to her. Life-long follow-up is recommended.

D (GPP)

Bladder wall injection with botulinum toxin A should be used in the treatment of idiopathic detrusor overactivity only in women who have not responded to conservative treatments and who are willing and able to self-catheterise. Women should be informed about the lack of long-term data. There should be special arrangements for audit or research.

D

The use of botulinum toxin A for this indication is outside the UK marketing authorisation for the product. Informed consent to treatment should be obtained and documented.

Botulinum toxin B is not recommended for the treatment of women with idiopathic OAB.

D

5.2 Procedures for stress urinary incontinence

Retropubic mid-urethral tape procedures using a 'bottom-up' approach with macro-porous (type 1) polypropylene meshes are recommended as treatment options for stress UI if conservative management has failed. Open colposuspension and autologous rectus fascial sling are the recommended alternatives when clinically appropriate.

A

Synthetic slings using a retropubic 'top-down' or a transobturator foramen approach are recommended as alternative treatment options for stress UI if conservative management has failed, provided women are made aware of the lack of long-term outcome data.

D

Synthetic slings using materials other than polypropylene that are not of a macroporous (type 1) construction are not recommended for the treatment of stress UI.

D

Intramural bulking agents (glutaraldehyde cross-linked collagen, silicone, carbon-coated zirconium beads or hyaluronic acid/dextran copolymer) should be considered for the management of stress UI if conservative management has failed. Women should be made aware that:

D

- repeat injections may be required to achieve efficacy

- efficacy diminishes with time

- efficacy is inferior to that of retropubic suspension or sling.

In view of the associated morbidity, the use of an artificial urinary sphincter should be considered for the management of stress UI in women only if previous surgery has failed. Life-long follow-up is recommended.

D

Laparoscopic colposuspension is not recommended as a routine procedure for the treatment of stress UI in women. The procedure should be performed only by an experienced laparoscopic surgeon working in a multidisciplinary team with expertise in the assessment and treatment of UI.

D (GPP)

Anterior colporrhaphy, needle suspensions, paravaginal defect repair and the Marshall–Marchetti–Krantz procedure are not recommended for the treatment of stress UI.

A

Autologous fat and polytetrafluoroethylene used as intramural bulking agents are not recommended for the treatment of stress UI.

D

Chapter 6 Competence of surgeons performing operative procedures for urinary incontinence in women

Surgery for UI should be undertaken only by surgeons who have received appropriate training in the management of UI and associated disorders or who work within a multidisciplinary team with this training, and who regularly carry out surgery for UI in women.

D (GPP)

Training should be sufficient to develop the knowledge and generic skills documented below.

D (GPP)

Knowledge should include the:

- specific indications for surgery

- required preparation for surgery including preoperative investigations

- outcomes and complications of proposed procedure

- anatomy relevant to procedure

- steps involved in procedure

- alternative management options

- likely postoperative progress.

Generic skills should include:

- the ability to explain procedures and possible outcomes to patients and family and to obtain informed consent

- the necessary hand–eye dexterity to complete the procedure safely and efficiently, with appropriate use of assistance

- the ability to communicate with and manage the operative team effectively

- the ability to prioritise interventions

- the ability to recognise when to ask for advice from others

- a commitment to multidisciplinary team working.

Training should include competence in cystourethroscopy.

D (GPP)

Operative competence of surgeons undertaking surgical procedures to treat UI or OAB in women should be formally assessed by trainers through a structured process.

D (GPP)

Surgeons who are already carrying out procedures for UI should be able to demonstrate that their training, experience and current practice equates to the standards laid out for newly trained surgeons.

D (GPP)

Surgery for UI or OAB in women should be undertaken only by surgeons who carry out a sufficient case load to maintain their skills. An annual workload of at least 20 cases of each primary procedure for stress UI is recommended. Surgeons undertaking fewer than five cases of any procedure annually should do so only with the support of their clinical governance committee; otherwise referral pathways should be in place within clinical networks.

D (GPP)

There should be a nominated clinical lead within each surgical unit with responsibility for continence and prolapse surgery. The clinical lead should work within the context of an integrated continence service.

D (GPP)

A national audit of continence surgery should be undertaken.

D (GPP)

Surgeons undertaking continence surgery should maintain careful audit data and submit their outcomes to national registries such as those held by the British Society of Urogynaecology (BSUG) and British Association of Urological Surgeons Section of Female and Reconstructive Urology (BAUS-SFRU).

D (GPP)

2.3 Research recommendations

Chapter 3 Assessment and investigation

3.3 Pelvic floor muscle assessment
The role of clinical pelvic floor muscle assessment prior to PFMT should be investigated to determine whether it enhances the therapeutic effect of the intervention.

3.11 Urodynamic testing
Further research is needed to answer the question of whether the use of urodynamics, prior to initial or subsequent treatments, affects the outcomes and cost effectiveness of interventions in women with UI or OAB.

3.14 Imaging
Further studies are required to clarify the role of ultrasound for the assessment of OAB.

2.3.1 Chapter 4 Conservative management

4.1 Lifestyle interventions
There is a need for prospective interventional studies in all areas of lifestyle interventions to evaluate the effects of modifying these factors on UI and OAB.

4.2 Physical therapies
Studies investigating different pelvic floor muscle training regimens are required to establish the optimum method of delivering and undertaking this intervention.

Research into the optimal electrical stimulation parameters is required, to inform future clinical practice. Studies investigating the role of electrical stimulation in women who cannot contract the pelvic floor muscle are required.

There is a need for a robust evaluation of transcutaneous electrical nerve stimulation and posterior tibial nerve stimulation for the treatment of UI.

4.3 Behavioural therapies
A direct comparison of single-component and multicomponent behavioural therapy is required.

4.4 Drug therapies
There is a need for a comparison of the clinical effectiveness and cost effectiveness of drug therapy compared with other conservative therapy as first-line treatment for women with OAB or mixed UI.

4.7 Preventive use of conservative therapies
Further studies need to be undertaken to evaluate the role and effectiveness of physical and behavioural therapies and lifestyle modifications in the prevention of UI in women. Long-term outcomes in particular should be evaluated.

Chapter 5 Surgical management

5.1 Procedures for overactive bladder
The place of botulinum toxin in the management of detrusor overactivity of idiopathic aetiology deserves further evaluation.

5.2 Procedures for stress urinary incontinence
Newer mid-urethral procedures should be further investigated and compared with pelvic floor muscle training and accepted surgical interventions in the treatment of stress urinary incontinence.

2.4 Algorithm

The management of urinary incontinence in women

Woman with urinary incontinence (UI) or overactive bladder syndrome (OAB)

Initial assessment

- Categorise UI as stress UI, urge UI/OAB or mixed UI. Start treatment on this basis.
- Identify factors that may require referral.
- Ask the woman to complete a bladder diary for at least 3 days, covering variations in usual activities (e.g. working and leisure days).
- Use urine dipstick tests to detect blood, glucose, protein, leucocytes and nitrites.

Lifestyle interventions

Advise women with UI or OAB to:
- modify high or low fluid intake
- lose weight if their body mass index is over 30.

Indications for referral
See Section 3.7.

- Measure post-void residual urine in women with symptoms of voiding dysfunction or recurrent UTI. If available, use a bladder scan in preference to catheterisation.

The following are not recommended:
- urodynamics before conservative treatment
- ultrasound, except to assess residual urine volume
- routine use of pad tests or imaging (MRI, CT and X-ray)
- cystoscopy in the initial assessment of women with UI alone
- Q-tip, Bonney, Marshall and Fluid-Bridge tests.

Dipstick test results

	Positive for leucocytes and nitrites	Negative for either leucocytes or nitrites
Urinary tract infection (UTI)	**Symptoms** Send a mid-stream urine sample for culture and antibiotic sensitivity analysis. Prescribe appropriate antibiotics pending results.	Consider antibiotics pending results.
	No symptoms Do not prescribe antibiotics unless there is a positive urine culture result.	UTI unlikely. Do not send a urine sample for culture.

Mixed UI

- Determine treatment according to whether stress or urge UI is the dominant symptom.

Other treatments for UI or OAB

- Consider desmopressin to reduce troublesome nocturia.[1]
- Consider propiverine to treat frequency of urination in OAB.

The following are not recommended:
- propiverine for the treatment of UI
- flavoxate, imipramine and propantheline
- systemic hormone-replacement therapy
- complementary therapies.

OAB with or without urge UI

- Recommend caffeine reduction.
- First-line treatment for urge or mixed UI should be bladder training lasting at least 6 weeks. If frequency remains troublesome, consider adding an antimuscarinic drug.
- If bladder training is ineffective, prescribe non-proprietary oxybutynin.
  - Counsel the woman about adverse effects of antimuscarinic drugs.
  - If oxybutynin is not tolerated, alternatives are darifenacin, solifenacin, tolterodine, trospium, or different oxybutynin formulations.
  - Carry out an early treatment review after any change in drug.

- In postmenopausal women with vaginal atrophy, offer intravaginal oestrogens for OAB symptoms.
- In women with UI who also have cognitive impairment, prompted and timed toileting programmes may help reduce leakage episodes.
- Do not routinely use electrical stimulation in OAB.

Further assessment

- For the few women with pure stress UI multi-channel cystometry is not routinely necessary before primary surgery.

- Use multi-channel filling and voiding cystometry before surgery for UI if:
  - there is clinical suspicion of detrusor overactivity, or
  - there has been previous surgery for stress UI or anterior compartment prolapse, or
  - there are symptoms of voiding dysfunction.

- Ambulatory urodynamics or videourodynamics may be considered before surgery for UI in the same circumstances as multi-channel filling and voiding cystometry

Stress UI

- First-line treatment for stress or mixed UI should be pelvic floor muscle training (PFMT) lasting at least 3 months.
  - Digitally assess pelvic floor muscle contraction before PFMT.
  - PFMT should consist of at least eight contractions, three times a day.
  - If PFMT is beneficial, continue an exercise programme.
  - During PFMT, do not routinely use:
    - electrical stimulation; consider it and/or biofeedback in women who cannot actively contract their pelvic floor muscles
    - biofeedback using perineometry or pelvic floor electromyography.

- Duloxetine:
  - should not be used as a first-line treatment for stress UI
  - should not routinely be used as a second-line treatment for stress UI
  - may be offered as an alternative to surgical treatment; counsel women about adverse effects.

Stress UI

Discuss the risks and benefits of surgical and non-surgical options. Consider the woman's child-bearing wishes during the discussion.

If conservative treatments have failed, consider:
- retropubic mid-urethral tape procedures using a 'bottom-up' approach with macroporous (type 1) polypropylene meshes,
- open colposuspension or autologous rectus fascial sling
- synthetic slings using a retropubic 'top-down' or a transobturator foramen approach. Explain the lack of long-term outcome data

- intramural bulking agents (glutaraldehyde cross-linked collagen, silicone, carbon-coated zirconium beads, hyaluronic acid/dextran co-polymer). Explain that:
  - repeat injections may be needed
  - the effect decreases over time
  - the technique is less effective than retropubic suspension or sling.
- an artificial urinary sphincter if previous surgery has failed.[*]

The following are not recommended for stress UI:
- routine use of laparoscopic colposuspension
- synthetic slings using materials other than polypropylene that are not of a macroporous (type 1) construction
- anterior colporrhaphy, needle suspensions, paravaginal defect repair and the Marshall–Marchetti–Krantz procedure
- autologous fat and polytetrafluoroethylene as intramural bulking agents.

OAB with or without urge UI

Discuss the risks and benefits of surgical and non-surgical options. Consider the woman's child-bearing wishes during the discussion.

If conservative treatments have failed, consider:
- botulinum toxin A to treat idiopathic detrusor overactivity in those willing and able to self-catheterise; explain the lack of long-term data; special arrangements for audit or research should be in place[2]
- sacral nerve stimulation for UI due to detrusor overactivity; select patients on basis of response to preliminary peripheral nerve evaluation[*]

- augmentation cystoplasty in those willing and able to self-catheterise; explain common and serious complications and the small risk of malignancy in the augmented bladder[*]
- urinary diversion if sacral nerve stimulation and augmentation cystoplasty are not appropriate or unacceptable.[*]

[1] The use of desmopressin for idiopathic UI is outside its UK marketing authorisation. Informed consent to treatment should be obtained and documented. [2] The use of botulinum toxin A for this indication is outside its UK marketing authorisation. Informed consent to treatment should be obtained and documented. Do not use botulinum toxin B. [*] Provide life-long follow-up after this procedure. MRI, magnetic resonance imaging; CT, computed tomography.

3. Assessment and investigation

3.1 Introduction

Initial assessment when a woman comes into first contact with a health professional is important. It forms the basis for counselling, ongoing management and treatment. Categorisation of UI by symptom profile may direct the patient to the most appropriate and effective resources. Further evaluation of severity of the condition, and ultimately the impact of treatment on that severity, will enable the healthcare professional to deliver the optimum care. Co-existing conditions (e.g. prolapse, diabetes, heart failure) or treatments (e.g. drug therapy) must be recognised and clinicians must be aware of their interaction with UI. Investigation should be used appropriately, taking into account the nature of the condition.

Studies considered for the assessment and investigation section

For history taking and physical examination, where primary research data were not available, published consensus statements and narrative reviews that discussed these issues were used as a basis for the GDG's statements and recommendations.[31,33,34]

For each investigation used in the assessment of UI in women, up to five questions were asked (refer to the assessment matrix in Appendix B):

- Does the investigation direct the woman to an alternative pathway?
- What is the diagnostic accuracy of the investigation?
- What is the test–retest reliability of the investigation?
- Does the use of the investigation affect outcomes?
- Does the use of the investigation predict outcomes of treatment?

For questions of diagnostic accuracy, the ideal study is one that makes blind comparison of the test with a validated reference standard in a sample of women reflective of the population to whom the test would apply. Within the clinical area of UI, there is no agreement as to what the reference standard is for the diagnosis of UI and thus studies that consider accuracy are limited by the standard against which they are compared.

3.2 History taking and physical examination

History taking of women with UI or OAB guides the investigation and management by evaluating symptoms, their progression and the impact of symptoms on lifestyle. Taking a history also allows the assessment of risk factors associated with the possible diagnoses. The relevant elements of history follow.

Urinary symptoms

In order to reach a clinical diagnosis, a urinary history is taken to determine storage and voiding patterns and symptoms. The major symptoms to consider include:

- Storage symptoms:

    - frequency (daytime), nocturia, urgency, urge UI
    - stress UI
    - constant leakage (which may rarely indicate fistula).

- Voiding symptoms:

  □ hesitancy, straining to void, poor or intermittent urinary stream.

- Post-micturition symptoms:

  □ sensation of incomplete emptying, post-micturition dribbling.

Accompanying symptoms that may indicate the possibility of a more serious diagnosis and which require referral, such as haematuria, persisting bladder or urethral pain, or recurrent urinary tract infection (UTI), can also be identified when taking a urinary history.

How do urinary symptoms compare with urodynamic findings?
We found no studies in which clinical outcomes in women with UI diagnosed by clinical history alone were compared with those in women with UI diagnosed using urodynamics. However, several studies have evaluated the accuracy of the symptom of stress or urge UI relative to findings on urodynamic (UD) investigations in women undergoing assessment of their urinary symptoms. Most of these studies have been considered in two reviews and a health technology assessment of diagnostic methods for UI.[46-48] Two of the publications included studies of women with symptoms of stress, mixed or urge UI[46,48] and one included only studies evaluating women with stress UI.[47] The reviews that included women with stress, mixed or urge UI calculated and combined sensitivity and specificity data for the symptom of stress (be it with or without mixed symptoms) and for the symptom of urge UI (be it with or without mixed symptoms). The GDG considered that the mixed 'symptom' should be considered separately (because in practice women are categorised into those with stress, mixed or urge UI) and that the important question in relation to the comparison of urinary history with urodynamic findings is whether urodynamics gives additional information to that obtained from the history alone. In considering this question, the GDG took the approach that a clinical history would be taken for every woman, and that a positive history for a particular type of UI would always be followed by treatment appropriate to that type of UI.

Overall, 25 relevant studies that compared the diagnosis based on history with urodynamic findings were considered by the GDG. These studies used cystometry as the reference standard for diagnosis of UI and therefore assumed that history taking had a lower diagnostic value in comparison. Fourteen studies included women with stress, mixed or urge UI, and 11 presented raw data in a way that allowed sensitivity, specificity, positive predictive value (PPV) and negative predictive values (NPV) to be calculated.[49-62] Two of these studies only reported accuracy data for stress and mixed UI.[61,62] Five studies only investigated how a history of urge UI or OAB compared with urodynamic findings of detrusor overactivity (DO).[63-67] Six studies only investigated how a history of stress UI compared with the finding of urodynamic stress incontinence,[68-73] four of which provided some but not all accuracy data.

Multichannel cystometry (with or without uroflowmetry, urethral pressure profilometry, or cystourethrography) was the urodynamic method used in 24 studies. The remaining study used single-channel cystometry for women with urge UI (and suspected DO) and multichannel cystometry for women with stress UI.[50] All except four studies[62-64,70] stated that terminology used for urodynamic findings conformed to ICS standards.

With the exception of one study,[49] which involved primary and secondary care, all studies were conducted in secondary or tertiary care.

The GDG focused on the 11 studies that provided diagnostic accuracy data for stress, mixed and urge UI. Confidence intervals were calculated for each value, as this was considered to be more appropriate than pooling data from individual studies. Pooling the available data (by meta-analysis) or generating receiver operating characteristic curves was not considered to be appropriate because the population in each study varied in terms of the relative proportions of stress, mixed or urge UI, the methods used to obtain a history varied, and the studies were considered to be of poor quality in terms of defining diagnostic accuracy because of unblinded urodynamic testing.

The diagnostic accuracy data for the studies is summarised in Table 3.1. For further details refer to Appendix C.

Table 3.1 Summary of diagnostic accuracy data

UI symptom	Sensitivity median (range)	Specificity median (range)	Positive predictive values median (range)	Negative predictive values median (range)
Stress UI	66% (17–83%)	83% (49–92%)	70% (41–95%)	69% (49–85%)
Mixed UI	68% (42–85%)	77% (34–89%)	35% (18–70%)	90% (80–97%)
Urge UI	45% (14–86%)	96% (81–98%)	73% (25–81%)	91% (79–98%)

The overall conclusions are that the available studies comparing history of stress, mixed or urge UI with findings of stress UI and/or DO on multichannel cystometry have poor internal and external validity. We consider that the NPV is of particular interest in terms of assessing whether urodynamic testing provides additional information compared with clinical history, because this quantity summarises the extent to which a negative history is associated with a negative finding on urodynamics (i.e. whether diagnosis based on urodynamics would alter the findings for women with no history of a particular type of UI). In addressing the question of whether urodynamics gives additional information to that obtained from history alone, with the limitations of the studies in mind, the following conclusions can be drawn:

- If a woman does not report mixed UI (i.e. if she reports pure stress UI or pure urge UI), the probability of finding urodynamic stress incontinence (USI) plus DO on cystometry is small (around 10%), therefore urodynamic testing might be said to offer little additional diagnostic value. It is acknowledged that urodynamic investigation is not simply used to distinguish USI and DO, and that further information may be obtained about other elements of lower urinary tract function, such as the voiding pattern.

- If a woman does not report pure urge UI, the probability of finding DO on cystometry is small (again around 10%), therefore urodynamic testing offers little added diagnostic value.

The situation for pure stress UI is less clear-cut. Here 15–51% (median 31%) of women who do not report pure stress UI may nevertheless be found to have USI on cystometry. However, the lack of consistency between the NPVs in the available studies together with the lack of detailed information about the method of obtaining a history and the poor quality of the studies limit the extent to which the evidence would support urodynamic testing for women who do not report stress UI. However, a limitation of dealing with stress, mixed and urge UI as three separate entities is that the analysis ignores the interdependence between the different diagnoses.

History taking is regarded as the cornerstone of assessment of UI. Current practice is that women with UI are categorised according to their symptoms into those with stress, mixed or urge UI; women with mixed UI are treated according to the symptom they report to be the most troublesome. In the absence of evidence that urodynamic testing improves the outcome of women treated conservatively (see Section 3.11), and without robust evidence that urodynamic testing provides additional valuable information to the history alone in the initial assessment of women with UI, the GDG concluded that urodynamic testing is not required before initiating conservative treatment.

Bowel symptoms

Constipation or problems with defecation may predispose to UI and adversely affect the outcome of any continence surgery. Straining can contribute to loss of bladder control by weakening pelvic floor muscles (refer to lifestyle interventions, Section 4.1). Faecal incontinence in association with UI or OAB may suggest the presence of cognitive impairment, neurological and/or anatomical damage. Women with faecal incontinence may require referral for management of that condition (a NICE guideline on faecal incontinence is in development, with an expected date of issue of June 2007).

Medical history

Conditions that may exacerbate or co-exist with UI or OAB can be identified by taking a general history and are important contributory factors to exclude. These include mental health, cognitive impairment and disorders of the:

- neurological system (e.g. multiple sclerosis, spinal cord injury, Parkinson's disease, cerebrovascular accident, cauda equina syndrome, pelvic plexus injury)
- metabolic system (e.g. diabetes)
- cardiorespiratory system
- renal system.

Surgical history

Previous surgery for UI or for POP may complicate treatment and make diagnosis more difficult because of its interference with the normal support mechanisms of the vagina and urethra. Any surgery that might have interfered with normal nerve supply to the bladder or urethra may also be relevant; this could include low spinal surgery, radical hysterectomy, low rectal surgery, sympathectomy or complex pelvic surgery.

Obstetric and gynaecological history

The number and type of deliveries and their outcome would normally be documented. The woman's desire for further childbearing should also be established as this may have implications for the most appropriate treatment options. The menstrual history and menopausal status should be determined, and enquiry made into symptoms of uterovaginal prolapse. The woman's sexual function and her expectations from this point of view should also be considered.

Drug history

Some medications may be associated with UI and their use may need to be reviewed. These include drugs that affect:

- the central nervous system, for example sedatives, hypnotics, anxiolytics and smooth muscle relaxants
- the autonomic nervous system, for example drugs with antimuscarinic action, sympathomimetics and sympatholytics
- fluid balance, for example diuretics and alcohol.

A drug history should consider previous medication for UI symptoms, and any known allergies, which may affect future treatment choices.

Does history taking affect outcome?

No evidence was identified that addressed this question. Nevertheless, the fundamental importance of history taking within all aspects of clinical practice cannot be overemphasised.

Test–retest reliability of history taking

No evidence was identified that addressed this question.

General assessment

Assessment of the social and functional impact of UI, desire for treatment, expectations and motivation are important as these help to establish the woman's goals, and may influence the type and degree of intervention offered.

Social circumstances to consider include home environment, personal relationships, occupational history and lifestyle factors such as smoking and body mass index (BMI). Adjustment of these lifestyle factors may form part of the management of the condition in some women (refer to Section 4.1).

Functional assessment, which may include consideration of access and ease of use of toileting aids, mobility and dexterity, is important. Assessment of the home environment may be undertaken, for example by an occupational therapist.

Physical examination

Physical examination is carried out to guide the diagnosis and management of incontinence and the identification of any underlying, modifying or serious conditions that require treatment outside the scope of this guideline.

The assessment of cognitive impairment allows the effect of disease to be taken into account and allows modification of treatment. The Abbreviated Mental Test Score (AMTS) and the Mini Mental State Examination (MMSE) should be undertaken for women aged over 75 years with complex co-morbidities. These scales should also be considered for younger women if clinically appropriate.

Abdominal examination can detect a significantly enlarged bladder or palpable pelvic mass. A palpable bladder may indicate the presence of chronic urinary retention. Palpation may detect a volume of 300 ml or more.[74] Urinary incontinence may occur in association with urinary retention (often called overflow incontinence).

Pelvic assessment is important and should include vaginal examination, and possibly also rectal examination if clinically indicated. Vaginal examination can assess POP and identify atrophic changes, infection and excoriation. Uterine and ovarian enlargement may be determined by bimanual examination. When rectal examination is undertaken, it is used to further evaluate posterior vaginal wall prolapse and, where indicated by a history of constipation, prolapse or faecal incontinence. Assessment of pelvic floor, prolapse and residual urine are considered in more detail in Sections 3.3, 3.4 and 3.6.

Neurophysiology
Neurophysiological tests include assessments of nerve conduction and electromyography (EMG). The former include sacral reflex latencies, pudendal terminal motor latencies and evoked potentials, which test the integrity of nerve pathways relating to voiding and continence. Abnormal results might indicate underlying neurological dysfunction. Electromyography tests the end organ function of somatic muscles of the pelvic floor, or sphincter complexes, but cannot be used to record activity from smooth muscle. No evidence was identified that addressed diagnostic accuracy of neurophysiological testing in relation to idiopathic UI. Where history suggests evidence of neurological disease, examination of lower limbs together with sacral sensation and sacral reflexes is required.

Evidence statements for history taking and physical examination

The reporting of stress, urge or mixed UI is commonly used to direct treatment decisions. [EL = 4]

The diagnostic value of history taking has been compared with urodynamic testing in women with UI or OAB. In general, there is a low level of agreement between a history of urinary symptoms and urodynamic findings. [EL = DS III]

However, women who do not report mixed or urge UI are unlikely to have findings of mixed UI or DO on urodynamics. [EL = DS III]

Recommendations for history taking and physical examination

At the initial clinical assessment, the woman's UI should be categorised as stress UI, mixed UI, or urge UI/OAB. Initial treatment should be started on this basis. In mixed UI, treatment should be directed towards the predominant symptom. [D (GPP)]

The clinical assessment should seek to identify relevant predisposing and precipitating factors and other diagnoses that may require referral for additional investigation and treatment. [D (GPP)]

3.3 Pelvic floor muscle assessment

Methods used to assess pelvic floor muscle contraction include digital palpation, EMG and perineometry. For digital palpation, grading scales have been used to quantify the strength of contraction, for example the Oxford grading system.[31]

Does pelvic floor muscle assessment affect outcome?

In RCTs that evaluated pelvic floor muscle training (PFMT) for the treatment of UI, both those studies that did and those that did not assess pelvic floor muscle contraction prior to treatment showed efficacy of active treatment compared with control (refer to physical therapies, Section 4.2). [EL = 3] No further evidence was identified in relation to the effects of undertaking pelvic floor assessment on outcomes of women with UI.

Test–retest reliability

Two case series evaluated the test–retest reliability of grading systems for digital assessment.[75,76] One assessed the test–retest and inter-rater reliability of a four-item pelvic floor muscle rating scale (covering pressure, duration of contraction and displacement; $n = 37$, about two-thirds of whom had urinary symptoms). Retest was done after 1–4 weeks. Significant inter- and intra-rater correlations were reported for the rating scale, and for EMG, which was also performed.[75] [EL = 3] The second case series evaluated test–retest reliability of digital assessments of pelvic floor muscle power and endurance in women with UI, with power being assessed on a modified Oxford grading system. Retest was undertaken after 2–5 weeks. Significant correlations between test and retest results were reported for both parameters, with agreement seen in nine cases ($n = 20$).[76] [EL = 3]

Two case series considered the inter-rater (not test–retest) reliability of a modified Oxford grading system. In the first study ($n = 20$, seven of whom had stress UI), poor inter-rater reliability was found for the grading system undertaken by physiotherapists, with agreement in nine cases ($r = 0.7$, Kappa score 0.37).[77] [EL = 3] The second case series in women with UI compared results of three clinicians' assessments with that of an expert clinician's assessment. No agreement was found between one of the clinicians and the expert prior to training. After training, the percentage agreement between the three clinicians and the expert was 70%, 78% and 80% ($n = 30$).[78] [EL = 3]

Evidence statements for pelvic floor muscle assessment

There is a lack of evidence as to whether digital assessment of pelvic floor muscle contraction affects the outcome of PFMT in women with UI. [EL = 3] Inter- and intra-observer reliability of grading systems for digital assessment of pelvic floor muscle contraction is poor. [EL = 3]

From evidence to recommendations
The GDG recognises that there is a lack of evidence for clinical utility of digital pelvic floor muscle assessment. However, expert opinion is that the determination of whether a woman can contract pelvic floor muscles will direct treatment decisions. [EL = 4]

Recommendation for pelvic floor muscle assessment

Routine digital assessment of pelvic floor muscle contraction should be undertaken before the use of supervised pelvic floor muscle training for the treatment of UI. [D (GPP)]

Research recommendation for pelvic floor muscle assessment

The role of clinical pelvic floor muscle assessment prior to PFMT should be investigated to determine whether it enhances the therapeutic effect of the intervention.

3.4 Assessment of prolapse

Several grading systems for POP have been described, including the Baden and Walker halfway method and the Pelvic organ prolapse quantification (POP-Q) system. The POP-Q system was designed to measure the type and severity of prolapse. In practice, the extent to which symptoms are bothersome is also an important factor to consider.

Women who present with symptoms of prolapse and UI should have an abdominal examination to exclude other pathology. Inspection of the genitalia may reveal the degree of uterine descent. On vaginal examination, the position of the cervix is determined and, at this point, the clinician can make an assessment of the strength of the pelvic floor. Bimanual examination will reveal any pelvic masses. The woman can be asked to cough and bear down, which may demonstrate stress UI or the presence of cystocele or rectocele.

Diagnostic accuracy

In considering the question of diagnostic accuracy in relation to POP assessment, the GDG considered that the important issue is how symptoms correlate with the prolapse grading systems available. Three cross-sectional studies considered the correlation of POP symptoms with the degree of pelvic organ support.[79–81] POP-related symptoms and/or their bother factor were not significantly associated with the stage of prolapse, as defined by the POP-Q classification system in one study. However, women reported a mean of more than one symptom when the prolapse extended beyond the hiatus, compared with a mean of less than one symptom when the leading edge of the prolapse did not reach the hiatus ($n = 477$).[79] [EL = 3] In a survey of women attending a gynaecological examination, the prevalence of POP was 31%, with 2% having prolapse that reached the introitus. Although no significant differences in the prevalence of certain symptoms (sense of heaviness in the abdomen, difficulty voiding or emptying bowel) were found in women with or without POP, cystocele or rectocele, respectively, the symptom prevalence was higher in women with prolapse ($n = 487$).[80] The third study found that seeing or feeling a bulge was reported by all women who had prolapse beyond the hiatus. However 21% of women who had this level of prolapse did not report this symptom.[81] [EL = 3]

Does assessment of prolapse affect outcome?

No evidence was identified that addressed this question.

Evidence statement for assessment of prolapse

Prolapse visible at or beyond the introitus is commonly associated with symptoms. [EL = 3]

> **Recommendation for assessment of prolapse**
>
> Women with UI who have symptomatic prolapse that is visible at or below the vaginal introitus should be referred to a specialist. [D (GPP)]

3.5 Urine testing

Urinalysis is used to detect infection, protein, blood and glucose in the urine. Protein may indicate infection and/or renal impairment, blood may indicate infection or malignancy, and glucose may indicate diabetes mellitus. Some findings on urine testing indicate referral (see Section 3.7).

Diagnostic accuracy of urine testing for urinary tract infection

One study evaluated the accuracy of urine reagent strips for the diagnosis of UTI in women with UI. Identification of leucocytes and/or nitrites on a reagent strip was indicative of a positive test for infection. Using urine culture as the reference standard, the reagent strips had sensitivity of 29%, specificity of 99%, and positive and negative predictive values of 82% and 92%, respectively ($n = 265$).[82] [EL = DS II]

Does urine testing affect outcome?

No evidence was identified that addressed this question. The GDG also considered whether treating a UTI affects UI symptoms. While no evidence was found in relation to treating an infection, one study in nursing home residents considered the impact of treating bacteriuria on UI. Half the patients had bacteriuria at baseline, which was removed in 81% of patients by antibiotic treatment. Eradication of bacteriuria appeared to have no effect on incontinence ($n = 191$; 71% women).[83] [EL = 2+]

Evidence statements for urine testing

Urine dipstick testing for leucocytes and nitrites has low sensitivity and high specificity for the diagnosis of UTI in women with UI. A negative urine dipstick test therefore excludes a UTI with a high degree of certainty. Only one-third of positive tests are associated with bacteriologically proven UTIs. [EL = DS II]

From evidence to recommendations

Although urine testing for leucocytes and nitrites has a high specificity, false negatives can arise when infection occurs with organisms that do not convert nitrates to nitrites. Hence, in symptomatic patients with a negative test, the clinician may wish to consider prescribing antibiotics once a urine sample has been collected but before results of midstream urine culture are available.

In patients with symptoms of UTI and a positive urine test for leucocytes and nitrites, infection is highly likely and immediate prescription of antibiotics is therefore justified. In single uncomplicated UTI it might be argued that this should be done without sending urine for laboratory analysis, depending on local knowledge of antibiotic resistance. In recurrent or complicated cases, however, this would not be appropriate. We therefore recommend that a midstream urine specimen be sent for culture and antibiotic sensitivities before prescribing in all cases.

Recommendations for urine testing

A urine dipstick test should be undertaken in all women presenting with UI to detect the presence of blood, glucose, protein, leucocytes and nitrites in the urine. [D (GPP)]

Women with symptoms of UTI whose urine tests positive for both leucocytes and nitrites should have a midstream urine specimen sent for culture and analysis of antibiotic sensitivities. An appropriate course of antibiotic treatment should be prescribed pending culture results. [D (GPP)]

Women with symptoms of UTI whose urine tests negative for either leucocytes or nitrites should have a midstream urine specimen sent for culture and analysis of antibiotic sensitivities. The healthcare professional should consider the prescription of antibiotics pending culture results. [D (GPP)]

Women who do not have symptoms of UTI, but whose urine tests positive for both leucocytes and nitrites, should not be offered antibiotics without the results of midstream urine culture. [D (GPP)]

Women who do not have symptoms of UTI and whose urine tests negative for either leucocytes or nitrites are unlikely to have UTI and should not have a urine sample sent for culture. [B (DS)]

3.6 Assessment of residual urine

Some findings on physical examination or from history taking in relation to emptying may indicate referral because of suspected voiding dysfunction. Abdominal examination can detect a significantly enlarged bladder, which may indicate the presence of chronic urinary retention. Palpation may detect a volume of 300 ml or more.[74] Large post-void residual urine may indicate the presence of underlying bladder outlet obstruction, neurological disease or detrusor failure. These would be a reason for referral to a specialist rather than progression through a path of conservative treatments. Large residual urine – in effect chronic retention of urine – may also present with renal failure although this is much less likely in women than in men. However, there is no accepted definition for what constitutes a high or large residual volume in women with UI. Residual urine volumes may vary and thus repeat measurements may be required.

Methods used to measure post-void residual urine are abdominal palpation, ultrasound scanning and catheterisation.

Diagnostic accuracy

The diagnostic accuracy of bladder ultrasound for the measurement of post-void residual urine was evaluated in three studies, using a bladder scanner (portable bladder ultrasound).[84–86] The accuracy of bimanual examination was evaluated in one study.[87] Catheterisation was used as the reference standard in each. The residual urine volume indicative of a positive test result ranged from 50 to 200 ml across the studies.

Portable ultrasound (bladder scanner) versus catheterisation

Two studies enrolled men and women.[84,86] The first study, in nursing home residents, reported sensitivities of 90–95% with a portable bladder ultrasound device at residual volume cut-off of less than 50 or 100 ml, and 59–69% for residual volumes of more than 100, 150, or 200 ml. Specificity values were 63–71% and 95–99%, respectively. It was not possible to calculate positive and negative predictive values from the data given ($n = 201$; 74% women).[86] [EL = DS Ib] The second study reported sensitivities of 90% for a post-void residual of 100 ml or more, and 92% for 200 ml or more. Specificities were 88% and 83%, PPV 91% and 76%, and NPV 86% and 95%, respectively ($n = 46$; 74% women).[84] [EL = DS Ib]

One study evaluated only women with UI. Based on a residual urine volume of 100 ml being a positive result, ultrasound had a sensitivity of 67% and specificity of 97%. It was not possible to calculate PPV or NPV from the data given ($n = 95$).[85] [EL = DS II]

Bimanual examination versus catheterisation

The diagnostic accuracy of bimanual examination relative to catheterisation in women was assessed in one study. Based on a residual urine volume of 50 ml being a positive result, bimanual examination had a sensitivity of 14%, specificity of 67%, PPV 7% and NPV 82% ($n = 47$).[87] [EL = DS Ib]

Does assessment of residual urine affect outcome?

No evidence was identified that addressed this question.

Test–retest reliability

One study reported test–retest reliability of portable ultrasound scanner measurements, with good correlation reported for both observers ($r = 98$ for one [187 pairs measured] and $r = 97$ for the second [143 pairs]).[86] [EL = DS Ib]

Evidence statements for assessment of residual urine

The sensitivity and specificity of ultrasound (using a bladder scanner) in the detection of post-void residual urine volume, in comparison with catheterisation, is within clinically acceptable limits. [EL = DS II] The former is less invasive with fewer adverse effects. [EL = 4] The sensitivity of bimanual examination to detect small post-void residual volumes is poor. [EL = DS Ib]

From evidence to recommendations

The GDG considers that the lack of evidence for what constitutes a clinically significant residual volume in women with UI precludes making a recommendation other than in women who have signs or symptoms suggestive of voiding dysfunction.

Recommendations for residual urine

The measurement of post-void residual volume by bladder scan or catheterisation should be performed in women with symptoms suggestive of voiding dysfunction or recurrent UTI. [B (DS)]

A bladder scan should be used in preference to catheterisation on the grounds of acceptability and lower incidence of adverse events. [D (GPP)]

Women who are found to have a palpable bladder on bimanual or abdominal examination after voiding should be referred to a specialist. [D (GPP)]

3.7 Referral

Evidence statement

Certain signs or symptoms on assessment indicate referral for further investigation by an appropriate specialist. The NICE guideline on referral for suspected cancer covers some indications for referral that are relevant to this guideline.[23] [EL = 4]

From evidence to recommendations

There are other women for whom referral for further advice or specialist intervention may be considered, because of either co-existent conditions or a history of prior interventions. The GDG recognises that not all such women may wish to be referred. However, referral should be considered in these cases. Owing to variations in service configuration, it is not possible to state to which service or healthcare professional women should be referred. Similarly, timescales are not specified for referral priorities because NICE recommends that trusts should work to local definitions of maximum waiting times. [EL = 4]

Recommendations for referral

Women with UI who have any of the following should receive an urgent* referral:

- microscopic haematuria[†] in women aged 50 years and older

- visible haematuria

- recurrent or persisting UTI associated with haematuria in women aged 40 years and older

- suspected malignant mass arising from the urinary tract.

Indications for referral are:

- symptomatic prolapse that is visible at or below the vaginal introitus (Section 3.4)

- the finding of a palpable bladder on bimanual or abdominal examination after voiding (Section 3.6). [D (GPP)]

In women with UI, further indications for consideration for referral to a specialist service include:

- persisting bladder or urethral pain

- clinically benign pelvic masses

- associated faecal incontinence

- suspected neurological disease

- symptoms of voiding difficulty

- suspected urogenital fistulae

---

* NICE's *Referral Guidelines for Suspected Cancer* (www.nice.org.uk/CG027) define urgent referral as the patient being seen within the national target for urgent referrals (currently 2 weeks).

† Haematuria visible with the aid of a microscope.

- previous continence surgery
- previous pelvic cancer surgery
- previous pelvic radiation therapy

3.8 Symptom scoring and quality of life assessment

Symptom and quality of life scoring is used to give some quantification of the impact of urinary symptoms and provides a measure that can be used to assess outcomes of treatment at a later stage. The International Consultation on Incontinence (ICI) uses three grades of recommendation for symptom scoring and QOL scales, based on the evidence available to support their use, as listed below:[31]

- highly recommended – validity, reliability and responsiveness established with rigour in several data sets ('Grade A'), or in one dataset with UI ('Grade A[new]')

- recommended ('Grade B') – validity, reliability and responsiveness indicated but not with rigour; validity and reliability established with rigour in several data sets

- with potential ('Grade C') – questionnaires in early development.

The test–retest reliability of ICI 'Grade A' or 'Grade A[new]' condition-specific scales for use in women are considered within this guideline because these are the questionnaires validated to the highest level. These are:[31]

- ICIQ, BFLUTS and SUIQQ (for combined evaluation of symptoms and QOL impact of UI)

- I-QOL, SEAPI-QMM, KHQ, IIQ, IIQ-7, UISS and CONTILIFE (for evaluation of QOL impact of UI)

- OAB-q, UDI, UDI-6, ISI and BFLUTS (for combined evaluation of symptoms and QOL impact of OAB).

Test–retest reliability of symptom scoring and quality of life scales

Test–retest reliability was generally reported within validation studies for these questionnaires, although in the case of CONTILIFE,[88] and the short forms of UDI and IIQ (UDI-6, IIQ-7),[89] no test–retest reliability data were presented. The available studies generally quoted correlation of test and retest findings, with some publications reporting actual scores or differences in test–retest scores. [EL = 3]

The results are shown in Table 3.2. For ICIQ, BFLUTS, I-QOL, SUIQQ, UISS, SEAPI-QMM, ISI and KHQ, either significant agreement or significant correlation between test and retest scores was reported (correlation was assessed using Spearman's, Pearson's, Cronbach's alpha, or the intraclass correlation coefficients). Few studies reported the actual test and retest scores. The available evidence for UDI, IIQ and OAB-q showed either a significant difference between test and retest scores and/or poor correlation between test and retest scores. [EL = 3]

Evidence statement for symptom scoring and quality of life

The test–retest reliability of ICIQ, BFLUTS, I-QOL, SUIQQ, UISS, SEAPI-QMM, ISI and KHQ is good. For other scores, the evidence is weak or absent. [EL = 3]

Recommendation for symptom scoring and quality of life

The following incontinence-specific quality of life scales are recommended when therapies are being evaluated: ICIQ, BFLUTS, I-QOL, SUIQQ, UISS, SEAPI-QMM, ISI and KHQ. [D (GPP)]

3.9 Bladder diaries

Bladder diaries are used to document each cycle of filling and voiding over a number of days and can provide information about urinary frequency, urgency, diurnal and nocturnal cycles,

Table 3.2 Test–retest reliability of quality of life and symptom scoring scales

Questionnaire	Population	Test–retest interval	Level of agreement between test and retest
International Consultation on Incontinence Questionnaire (ICIQ)[90]	144 men and women (84% women); several samples in clinics and in the community	2 weeks	Significant agreement reported for each of the nine symptom items (percentage agreement ranging from 85% to 96%)
Bristol Female Lower Urinary Tract Symptoms (BFLUTS)[91]	50 women with UI	2 weeks	78% of answers identical on both occasions; Spearman's rank correlation for total symptom and problem scores 0.86 and 0.90
Stress and Urge Incontinence and Quality of Life Questionnaire (SUIQQ)[92]	59 women with stress or mixed UI	Mean 22 days	No retest value significantly different from test value; Cronbach's alpha ranged from 0.72 to 0.77 for components
Incontinence Quality of Life (I-QOL)[93–95]	288 women with stress or mixed UI[93]	2 weeks	Cronbach's alpha 0.95, scores not reported
	62 patients (68% women)[94]	Mean 18 days	Intraclass correlation 0.93, scores not reported
	1901 women with stress UI enrolled in duloxetine trials	2 weeks	Median intraclass correlation score 0.87
SEAPI-QMM[96]	315 men and women with UI (68% women)	5 days	Cronbach's alpha correlation ranging from 0.73 to 0.88 for the three domains
King's Health Questionnaire (KHQ)[97]	110 women referred to a tertiary urogynaecology unit for urodynamic investigations	Mean 9 days (2–16)	Cronbach's alpha ranging from 0.73 to 0.89 for each domain
Urogenital Distress Inventory (UDI) and Incontinence Impact Questionnaire (IIQ)[98]	237 women with UI; 3 samples (community-dwelling with stable, unspecified UI; undergoing assessment for conservative treatment; on waiting list for colposuspension)	Median 3 days	A significant difference seen between test and retest scores for both UDI and IIQ, with poor agreement (Kappa ratings) for one question on UDI and for two questions on IIQ
IIQ[99]	69 women with UD stress UI or DO	1 week and 6 weeks	Pearson's correlation $r = 0.73$ at 1 week and $r = 0.65$ at 6 weeks; test–retest scores not reported
Urinary Incontinence Severity Score (UISS)[100]	51 women with UI	1 week	Spearman's rank correlation 0.88; no test–retest scores presented
Overactive Bladder Questionnaire (OAB-q)[101]	47 men and women (75% women) with a clinical diagnosis of OAB	2 weeks	Symptom bother scale scores fell significantly from test to retest; no significant differences in other items; Spearman's rank correlation between 0.8 and 0.93 for all items of the questionnaire
Incontinence Severity Index (ISI)[102]	237 women with UI	3 days	Kappa scores for the two questions of the instrument (leakage episodes and quantity) were significant (0.69 and 0.83); severity index scores not reported

r = correlation coefficient

functional bladder capacity and total urine output. They also record leakage episodes, fluid intake and pad changes and give an indication of the severity of wetness. They may also be used for monitoring the effects of treatment.

Test–retest reliability of bladder diaries

Five studies evaluated the test–retest reliability of bladder diaries or frequency–volume charts. One study evaluated a 1 day diary,[103] one a 3 day diary,[104] and three studies evaluated a 7 day diary.[105–107] Data captured in the charts were: frequency and voided volume;[103] frequency, leakage and urgency episodes, and voided volume;[104] frequency and leakage episodes;[105,106] and leakage episodes only.[107]

1 day diary

A case–control study reported some reproducibility data for the 1 day charts in women with stress UI. The 95% limits of agreement between the first and second days of measurement lay between 0.5 and 2.1 for frequency, and for total, mean and largest single voided volume measures ($n = 80$).[103] [EL = 3]

3 day diary

In a case series of men and women with stress, mixed or urge UI, or OAB, the retest reliability of a 72 hour bladder diary and pad test was evaluated after an interval of 1 week ($n = 106$; 84% women). The authors' predefined minimum correlation coefficient for test–retest reliability of 0.7 was met for overall frequency, day frequency, leakage episodes, urgency episodes and mean voided volume (correlation coefficient 0.70–0.87), but not for night frequency (0.605). Correlation, but not actual results, was also reported for 24 and 48 hour results; the correlation appeared to improve at 72 hours compared with 24 hours for urgency episodes. Compliance with recording voided volume data fell with time.[104] [EL = 3]

Diaries of 7 days or longer

A case series evaluated the reproducibility of leakage episode and frequency data from a 7 day diary repeated after 4 weeks in women with urodynamic stress UI ($n = 138$). Minimal differences in test–retest results were seen for leakage episodes (mean 1.7/week, $r = 0.906$) and frequency (mean 0.03/(24 hours), $r = 0.831$). Correlation coefficients for the first 3 and last 4 days of the diary were also reported, which were 0.887 for leakage episodes and 0.908 for frequency.[105] [EL = 3]

A second case series reported test–retest variability and correlations of leakage episodes, and diurnal and nocturnal frequency, based on a 7 day diary in women aged 55 years or over ($n = 50$; 68% USI, 32% DO with or without stress UI). The test–retest reliability was reported to be significant for the three parameters, with correlation coefficients of 0.86–0.91. No significant differences were seen between any test and retest results.[106] [EL = 3]

The third case series investigated the reliability of a 14 day diary for the measurement of leakage episodes in women. Significant correlation was reported between the diary findings of weeks one and two, with 5 days' recording being necessary for internal consistency, for women with predominant urge UI and 7 days for women with predominant stress UI ($n = 214$).[107] [EL = 3]

Does the use of bladder diaries affect outcome?

A considerable placebo effect has been reported in many placebo-controlled trials evaluating the effectiveness of conservative interventions for the treatment of UI or OAB, with this placebo effect being reflected in self-reported changes in voiding pattern, using bladder diaries. This placebo effect usually decreases over time. Several investigators suggest that completion of these diaries, together with the close monitoring, placebo medication, and therapeutic attention via interaction between them and their patients, induces a bladder training/retraining effect. However, none of the trials were designed to examine whether bladder diaries affect outcomes of women with UI or OAB, and therefore the conclusion that the diaries are the cause of a placebo effect is not proven. In addition, sufficient duration will be needed to allow the initial 'beneficial' placebo response to run its course so that true effects of interventions can be observed.

Evidence statements for bladder diaries

Bladder diaries are a reliable method of quantifying urinary frequency and incontinence episodes. [EL = 3] They are useful as a measure of outcome of treatments. The optimum duration of bladder diaries is unclear. [EL = 4]

> **Recommendation for bladder diaries**
>
> Bladder diaries should be used in the initial assessment of women with UI or OAB. Women should be encouraged to complete a minimum of 3 days of the diary covering variations in their usual activities, such as both working and leisure days. [D (GPP)]

3.10 Pad testing

Pad tests are used to detect and quantify urine loss. Pad tests of varying duration have been evaluated: 1 hour or less, 24 hours, and 48 hours or longer.

Does pad testing affect outcome?

No studies were identified that addressed this question.

Test–retest reliability

Short pad tests
Fourteen studies considered the test–retest reliability of pad testing: eight studies considered short pad tests (1 hour or less), and six considered tests of longer duration (24–72 hours). The data reported generally were correlation of test and retest findings, with some publications reporting actual scores or differences in test–retest scores. Correlation was assessed using Spearman's, Pearson's or Lin's concordance correlation coefficients in five studies; the remaining nine studies did not state which test was used.

The results for the short pad tests are shown in Table 3.3. One study considered the reliability of a test of 12–15 minutes' duration.[108] The standardised 1 hour pad test was used in four studies.[109–113] Another three studies used a modified version where the test differed in the method of filling the bladder, or in the quantity of fluid instilled or consumed.[114–116] Across these studies, significant correlation or agreement was reported between test and retest urine loss, although the differences between test and retest results across studies varied widely (means of 2–23 g).

24, 48 and 72 hour pad tests
Six case series reported test–retest reliability for pad tests of 24–72 hours.[104,117–121] The results are shown in Table 3.4. These studies also reported significant correlation between test and retest results. One study noted that the number of pad-test days required for optimal reliability was 3 days (data only shown in graph in publication).[119] Another found that correlation appeared to improve at 72 hours compared with 24 hours, but compliance fell.[104] [EL = 3]

Evidence statements for pad testing

The evidence supporting the use of pad testing is contradictory and of poor quality. However, there appears to be good group correlation with test–retesting even though the amounts leaked may differ in individuals. It is possible that pad tests of longer duration (24 hours or longer) are more sensitive for measuring incontinence than a short standardised 1 hour test. There is a lack of evidence in relation to whether pad testing in the assessment of women with UI affects outcomes. [EL = 3]

While there is no evidence of diagnostic value or clinical utility for pad testing, the GDG's view is that pad tests may be useful for evaluating therapies for incontinence. [EL = 4]

> **Recommendation for pad testing**
>
> Pad tests are not recommended in the routine assessment of women with UI. [D]

Table 3.3 Test–retest reliability of short pad tests

Pad test duration	Population and any relevant test conditions	Test–retest interval	Level of agreement between test and retest
12–15 minutes[108]	33 women with stress UI; testing undertaken as part of cystometry, with the bladder filled to 75% of cystometric capacity	Same day	Significant correlation ($r = 0.74$) reported between test and retest; no numerical data reported
Standardised 1 hour test[109]	56 women with an unspecified type of UI; study aimed to ensure bladder volume at retest was similar to that at the first test, although median volumes were significantly different	3–10 days	Significant difference of 9.7 g between test and retest
Standardised 1 hour test[110,111]	18 women with stress or mixed UI	1–15 days	Mean test–retest difference of 23 g (median 4 g); significant correlation reported ($r = 0.68$)
Standardised 1 hour test[113]	20 women with stress, mixed or urge UI	1 week	Difference in median pad weight gain of 3 g between tests; significant correlation $r = 0.77$
Standardised 1 hour test[112]	19 men and women with stress, mixed or urge UI	1–36 days	Correlation of 0.96 reported for difference in urine loss; differences in test–retest results not reported
Modified standardised 1 hour test[114]	67 women with stress and mixed UI; bladder filled to capacity with normal saline	Immediate	Significant test–retest difference in urine loss of 9 g and 12 g; correlations $r = 0.97$ and $r = 0.84$, respectively
Modified standardised 1 hour test[115]	16 women referred for PFMT; 1 litre rather than 500 ml fluid consumed	1–7 days	Mean difference in urine loss of 2 g on pad test; significant correlation $r = 0.73$
Modified standardised 1 hour test[116]	25 women with stress or mixed UI; bladder instillation of fluid to 50% of maximum cystometric capacity	1–85 days	Mean test–retest differences of up to 24 g; significant correlation $r = 0.97$

3.11   Urodynamic testing

The term 'urodynamics' encompasses a number of varied physiological tests, of bladder and urethral function, which aim to demonstrate an underlying abnormality of storage or voiding. The term is often used loosely to mean multichannel cystometry.

Cystometry is the measurement of intravesical pressure, which can be carried out through a single recording channel (simple cystometry) or, more commonly, by multichannel cystometry, which involves the synchronous measurement of both bladder and intra-abdominal pressures by means of catheters inserted into the bladder and the rectum or vagina. The aim is to replicate the woman's symptoms by filling the bladder and observing pressures changes or leakage caused by provocation tests.

Uroflowmetry entails a free-flow void into a recording device, which provides the practitioner with information about the volume of urine passed and the rate of urine flow.

Table 3.4 Test–retest reliability of pad tests of at least 24 hours' duration

Pad test duration	Population and any relevant test conditions	Test–retest interval	Level of agreement between test and retest
24 hours[117]	13 women with stress or mixed UI	Consecutive days	Non-significant mean difference of 5 g between test and retest; retest results differed approximately three-fold from the first test
24 hours[118]	31 women with stress or urge UI	Consecutive days	Significant correlation ($r = 0.82$)
24 hours[119]	104 women with UI; urodynamic finding: 65% stress UI, 29% mixed UI, 6% DO and 'others'	Consecutive days	Significant correlation between the first 24 hours and 7 days of data; authors also claimed that 3 pad-test days optimal for reliability (data only shown in graph)
24 and 48 hours[120]	15 women with unspecified type of UI	6–28 days	Significant correlation for both tests: 24 hour ($r = 0.66$), 48 hour ($r = 0.9$)
24 and 48 hours[121]	112 women with lower urinary tract symptoms	1 week	Significant correlation for 24 hour ($r = 0.9$) and 48 hour ($r = 0.94$) tests; test–retest differences (percentage of the mean) 7% and 2%, respectively
72 hours[104]	106 patients (84% women) with stress, mixed or urge UI or OAB	1 week	Mean test–retest difference 13 g; the predefined minimum correlation coefficient for test–retest reliability of 0.7 was met for pad weight gain ($r = 0.935$)

There are also numerous tests of urethral function, including urethral pressure profilometry and leak point pressure measurement. These are used to derive values that reflect the ability of the urethra to resist urine flow, expressed most commonly as maximum urethral closure pressure (MUCP), or as abdominal, cough or Valsalva leak point pressures (ALPP, CLPP, VLPP).

Videourodynamics involves synchronous radiographic screening of the bladder with multichannel cystometry and is so called because originally the information was recorded to videotape. Ambulatory urodynamics involves multichannel cystometry carried out with physiological bladder filling rates and using portable recording devices, which enable the woman to remain ambulant during the test.

Diagnostic accuracy

The agreement between urinary history and urodynamic findings is considered in Section 3.2.

Does urodynamic testing affect outcome?

A systematic review considering this question has been published but it only included one fully published RCT.[122] The RCT was considered alongside other relevant, fully published data.[123]

The RCT compared conservative treatment tailored to urodynamic findings (PFMT or bladder retraining) with a multicomponent conservative treatment regimen (PFMT and bladder retraining), without prior urodynamic investigation in women with symptoms of UI or OAB ($n = 60$; 48 analysed). After 3 months of treatment, no significant differences were seen between groups in any outcome (leakage episodes, frequency, nocturia, subjective assessment, short pad test). Since the uninvestigated trial arm received both treatments, the outcomes from treatment may be uninformative about the value of urodynamics.[123] [EL = 1−]

Two observational studies reported outcomes of continence surgery for stress UI in women who had preoperative urodynamic investigations (61% or 71%), compared with those who did not. Neither found significant differences between groups in cure/success rates or symptom severity scores at mean follow-up of 25 months ($n = 109$)[124] [EL = 2−] or at 1 year ($n = 279$).[125,126] [EL = 2+]

Do preoperative urodynamic findings predict post-surgical outcomes?

In a few case series of surgical interventions for stress UI in women, authors retrospectively explored whether certain preoperative findings on urodynamic testing (urethral pressure profilometry or uroflowmetry) predicted surgical success or complications. These studies cover a range of surgical procedures (suspension procedures, slings, intramural bulking agents), with some studies evaluating more than one procedure. Data were presented in various ways, with some studies comparing the mean urethral pressures in successful or failed groups and others considering the success or failure rates above certain urethral pressure thresholds. Generally, small numbers of women were involved in the individual studies (n range 45–375, with most studies including fewer than 100 women). Cure rates were reported at varying durations of follow-up, ranging from 3 to 26 months (most under 1 year). The impact of possible confounding factors was not generally considered within the study reports. The studies were neither designed nor powered to show differences in the outcomes evaluated. [EL = 3]

The majority of the identified studies considered whether urethral closure pressures or leak point pressures predicted success of surgical procedures.[127–139] Other studies considered whether urine flow rates or urethral closure pressures predicted complications (voiding dysfunction or *de novo* DO).[129,140–144]

Success
Five of eight case series reported that the urethral closure pressure was statistically significantly lower in women who failed surgery (colposuspension, tension-free vaginal tape [TVT], vaginal wall sling), or that the failure rate was higher in women with maximum urethral closure pressure (MUCP) of 20 cmH$_2$O or less.[127,131–133,139] Two case series found no significant association between preoperative MUCP and surgical success or failure.[128,129] One case series reported varying results according to the procedure undertaken, with mean MUCP significantly lower in women who failed colporrhaphy, with no differences found for MUCP in women who had successful or unsuccessful needle suspension or colposuspension procedures.[134]

A further two studies considered different pressure measurements. One reported that preoperative opening detrusor pressure and urethral pressure at closure were significantly lower in women who had objective failure of colposuspension.[129] Another reported that the preoperative 'index of urethral relaxation at stress' (ratio of highest intraurethral pressure between coughs in the stress urethral pressure profilometry to the MUCP at rest) in women undergoing a suspension procedure was significantly lower in cases of objective failure.[128]

Four studies considered success according to abdominal or Valsalva leak point pressures (VLPP). Three reported no difference in success rates after surgery (vaginal wall sling, polypropylene sling, polytetrafluoroethylene bulking) according to baseline leak point pressures.[130,131,135] One of these studies reported that the failure rate was significantly higher in women with both VLPP less than 50 cmH$_2$O and MUCP less than 30 cmH$_2$O, compared with both values above these thresholds.[131] The fourth case series reported a significantly lower cure rate with TVT in women with low VLPP (less than 60 cmH$_2$O).[138]

Complications
The preoperative maximum urine flow rate was significantly lower in women who had delayed voiding in three of four studies that considered this.[140,142,144] One reported that a maximum flow rate of less than 20 ml/second was associated with delayed voiding.[140] The third study found no significant association between preoperative peak urine flow rate or residual volume and delayed voiding.[141] The procedures undertaken were a fascia lata sling, TVT and colposuspension.

No association was found between preoperative MUCP or VLPP values and voiding dysfunction in the studies that considered this.[140,142,143]

Two studies considered factors associated with the development of *de novo* DO, following colposuspension. Preoperative opening detrusor pressure, urethral pressure at closure and acceleration of flow rate were significantly higher in women with *de novo* DO in one study, while preoperative MUCP was not found to be associated with *de novo* DO ($n = 209$).[129] The second study did not report an association between uroflowmetry and *de novo* DO ($n = 77$).[144] [EL = 3]

Different methods of urodynamic investigation

Single-channel versus multichannel cystometry
The findings of single-channel ('simple') and multichannel cystometry were compared in four studies (n range 70–179).[145–148] Two studies included elderly men and women, with data reported separately for women.[145,146] The tests were conducted on the same day in three studies[146–148] (in random order in one[147]) and after an interval of 1–4 weeks in the fourth study.[145] Assessments or interpretation of the traces were performed blind in two of the studies[146,147] [EL = DS II] but not in the other two.[145,148] [EL = DS III] The diagnostic accuracy results, for simple compared with multichannel cystometry, for a diagnosis of DO (or detrusor hyperreflexia[145]) in the four studies were: sensitivity range 59–100%, specificity 68–89%, PPV 17–84%, NPV 79–100%.

A fifth study reported accuracy of single-channel cystometry with cough stress test, relative to multichannel cystometry, for a diagnosis of stress UI. The sensitivity, specificity, PPV and NPVs found were 84%, 84%, 87% and 81%, respectively ($n = 145$).[149] [EL = DS III]

Stress test versus multichannel urodynamics
Three studies evaluated the accuracy of a simple stress test for a diagnosis of stress UI.[150–152] In the first, the stress test was conducted with a fixed bladder volume (which requires catheterisation). Compared with videocystometry and leak point pressure findings, the stress test had sensitivity of 94%, specificity 90%, PPV 97% and NPV 82%.[150] [EL = DS II] In the second study, the stress test was conducted with an empty bladder and found sensitivity of 49%, specificity 95%, PPV 98% and NPV 29% compared with multichannel cystometry. These values changed to 65%, 76%, 66% and 76%, respectively, when the stress test was compared with MUCP of 20 cmH_2O or less.[151] [EL = DS III]

The third study compared the accuracy of urethral closure pressure profilometry during multichannel cystometry for a diagnosis of stress UI, relative to a diagnosis based on a clinical stress test. Urethral closure pressure profilometry had sensitivity of 93%, specificity of 83%, PPV 92% and NPV 86% ($n = 981$).[152] [EL = DS III]

Ambulatory versus conventional multichannel urodynamics
Six case series compared ambulatory urodynamics with conventional multichannel cystometry or videocystometry (n range 20–22).[153–158] In three studies, the populations evaluated were those in whom a diagnosis had not been reached on conventional cystometry or whose symptoms did not match the cystometric findings.[153,156,158] Three of the studies included men and women, the majority being women.[153,156,157]

The studies differed in the duration of ambulatory monitoring (3–24 hours) and in the interval between tests (from 1 week to a mean of 37 weeks in those that reported this). The studies considered agreement between the two methods with none reporting data in a way that allows calculation of sensitivity, specificity, PPV or NPV. Two studies reported the agreement for any type of UI,[153,154] and four for urge UI or DO.[155–158]

The studies reported the following:

- 63% had additional findings on ambulatory urodynamics[153]

- significant difference in the proportions with DO or with normal findings on ambulatory versus conventional urodynamic testing[154]

- more patients were found to have DO on ambulatory than conventional urodynamic testing[155–158] [EL = 3]

Videocystourethrography versus other methods

Videocystourethrography (VCU) was compared with multichannel cystometry in one study ($n = 159$). VCU had sensitivity of 61%, specificity 70%, PPV 56% and NPV 74% for a diagnosis of stress UI, and 14%, 97%, 87% and 45%, respectively, for urge UI.[159] [EL = DS III]

Compared with clinical assessment ($n = 37$), the accuracy of VCU was: [160]

- sensitivity of 74%, specificity 78%, PPV 78% and NPV 74% for stress UI

- 0, 91%, 0 and 91%, respectively, for mixed UI (zero sensitivity and PPV because no women had both a clinical and urodynamic finding of mixed UI)

- 50%, 89%, 20% and 97%, respectively, for urge UI.[160] [EL = DS III]

No studies were identified that compared the accuracy of leak point pressures with MUCP for the diagnosis of intrinsic sphincter deficiency.

Test–retest reliability of urodynamic testing

One case series evaluated the intra- and inter-observer reliability of voiding measurements (pressure flow parameters) in women. Repeat cystometry was done after 1 week. Differences in intra- and inter-rater findings for the parameters measured (opening and closure detrusor pressure, maximum flow rate, detrusor pressure at maximum flow rate) were reported to be small although no statistical analysis was reported ($n = 554$).[161] [EL = 3]

No studies were identified in relation to the test–retest reliability of the filling phase of cystometry.

In a series of men and women with OAB, cystometry was performed at baseline and repeated after 2–4 weeks' placebo treatment within an RCT. All parameters (volume at first desire to void, volume at first involuntary contraction, and maximum pressure of involuntary contraction) increased significantly at the second measurement, and therefore it seems this study evaluated the effects of placebo on cystometric parameters rather than reproducibility ($n = 30$; 40% women).[162] [EL = 3]

Health economics of urodynamic testing

Resource scarcity provides the rationale for undertaking any health economic analysis. Finite resources mean that expenditure on preoperative urodynamic testing, or anything else for that matter, carries an opportunity cost – that is, other possible uses of those resources and benefits from them are foregone. The efficiency issue is then whether that expenditure represents the best use of those scarce resources: could greater patient benefit be obtained if the resources used for preoperative urodynamic testing were employed elsewhere? The health economics of preoperative urodynamic testing is especially important to consider because its impact on outcomes has been questioned and yet it currently represents routine clinical practice, using actual NHS resources. Therefore, an economic analysis of preoperative urodynamic testing in women who failed conservative treatment has been undertaken for this guideline and the details are given in Appendix D.

Evidence statements for urodynamic testing

There is often inconsistency between the clinical history and the urodynamic findings. [EL = DS III] Multichannel cystometry, when it reproduces the woman's symptoms, may reveal the underlying pathophysiological explanation of incontinence. Single-channel cystometry is less reliable, although a simple clinical stress test may be as accurate as multichannel cystometry in the diagnosis of stress UI. [EL = 3] Although videocystourethrography has the benefit of simultaneous structural and functional assessment, it is not clear whether this adds any relevant diagnostic accuracy, compared with multichannel cystometry. Ambulatory monitoring demonstrates functional abnormalities more often than multichannel cystometry, but the significance of this is unclear. [EL = 3]

There is no evidence that pretreatment multichannel cystometry will improve the outcomes of treatments for incontinence. [EL = 2–] Although some urodynamic parameters have been found to correlate with adverse outcomes of surgery such as voiding difficulty and OAB, no test has been shown to reliably predict beneficial or adverse outcomes of surgery. [EL = 3] Nevertheless, it is recognised that preoperative urodynamic testing is firmly established in clinical practice and widely believed to contribute to improved patient counselling with regard to the likely outcomes of surgery. [EL = 4]

Economic modelling shows the cost effectiveness of preoperative urodynamic testing to be highly sensitive to the proportion of women with pure stress incontinence who failed conservative treatment, but this is not clearly established.

From evidence to recommendations
The GDG considers that urodynamic testing does not assist in the assessment of a woman prior to conservative treatment. The GDG also maintains the view that urodynamics investigation is not essential in every woman prior to primary surgery for stress UI, and therefore is not routinely recommended.

While the evidence suggests that preoperative urodynamics are not necessary for women with pure stress incontinence, the GDG accepts that these tests may help where the clinical diagnosis is not clear or in those women where initial surgical therapy has failed. Complex reconstructive urological procedures such as augmentation cystoplasty have been developed for use in specific urodynamic abnormalities; they should only be undertaken where these abnormalities are shown to be present.

Recommendations for urodynamic testing

The use of multichannel cystometry, ambulatory urodynamics or videourodynamics is not recommended before starting conservative treatment. [D]

For the small group of women with a clearly defined clinical diagnosis of pure stress UI, the use of multichannel cystometry is not routinely recommended. [D]

Multichannel filling and voiding cystometry is recommended in women before surgery for UI if:

- there is clinical suspicion of detrusor overactivity, or

- there has been previous surgery for stress incontinence or anterior compartment prolapse, or

- there are symptoms suggestive of voiding dysfunction.

Ambulatory urodynamics or videourodynamics may also be considered in these circumstances. [D (GPP)]

Research recommendation for urodynamic testing

Further research is needed to answer the question of whether the use of urodynamics, prior to initial or subsequent treatments, affects the outcomes and cost effectiveness of interventions in women with UI or OAB.

3.12 Other tests of urethral competence

Other than urodynamic studies, the Q-tip, POP-Q, Bonney, Marshall and Fluid-Bridge tests can assess urethral competence (hypermobility of the urethrovesical junction). The Q-tip test involves placing a sterile Q-tip in the urethra and the woman is asked to bear down. If the Q-tip moves more than 30°, the test is considered positive. The Bonney and Marshall tests involve pressing either the index and middle finger of the examiner's hand (Bonney test) or the jaws of a forceps (Marshall test) against the anterior vaginal wall, without pressing on the urethra. The stress provocation test is repeated and if no leakage occurs the Bonney or Marshall test is said to be positive. The Fluid-Bridge test is designed to test bladder neck competence by testing for the presence of fluid within the urethra, by demonstrating continuity between two channels of a pressure-recording catheter (one in the bladder and the other in the urethra).

Diagnostic accuracy

Q-tip test

One study compared the accuracy of the Q-tip test for evaluating urethrovesical junction mobility against ultrasound, as the reference standard in women with prolapse or UI (93% UI). It reported that the Q-tip test (change of 30° or more between rest and straining angles from the horizontal) had sensitivity of 25%, specificity 78%, PPV 67% and NPV 37%, relative to a positive test on ultrasound (more than 10 mm movement, $n = 114$).[163] [EL = DS III]

Three studies compared visual assessment of the urethrovesical junction (POP-Q) with the Q-tip test.[164–166] One of these studies reported the accuracy of the POP-Q system for diagnosing urethral hypermobility, using the Q-tip test as the reference standard, in women with symptoms of prolapse (70%) and/or UI (30%). Results were presented for different cut-off points of Aa descent. As the Aa point became more distal, specificity and PPV of visual assessment increased (from 36% to 100% and 80% to 100%, respectively), and sensitivity and NPV fell (from 94% to 2% and 67% to 26%, respectively) ($n = 111$).[164] [EL = DS III] The other studies evaluated the correlation between Q-tip and POP-Q measurements in women who had urethral hypermobility (maximum straining angle of 30° or more on Q-tip test). The proportions with urethral hypermobility for each stage of the POP-Q classification were:

- 62% for stage 0, 83% stage I, 95% stage II, 100% for stages III and IV, correlation coefficient $r = 0.47$ ($n = 274$)[165] [EL = 3]

- 6% for stage 0, 91% for stage II, 100% for stages II to IV, correlation coefficient $r = 0.79$.[166] [EL = 3]

Bonney and Marshall tests

Three studies reported findings of urodynamic testing with or without the Bonney test in women with stress UI.[167–169] None were truly diagnostic accuracy studies in that they did not report sensitivity, specificity, PPV or NPV.

One case series found that none of the women who had demonstrable leakage during urodynamic investigation leaked during the Bonney test (hence all had a positive Bonney test). Urethral closure pressure was approximately three-fold higher when conducting the test than when not ($n = 61$).[167] [EL = 3]

In a similar study, outcomes were measured at rest, when conducting the Bonney test, and with direct compression of the urethra and bladder neck. Urethral closure pressure, pressure profile area and cough pressure profile area increased significantly compared with resting profiles, when conducting the Bonney test, and when urethra and bladder neck were directly compressed. No significant differences in pressures were seen between the Bonney test and urethral compression. All women had urine leakage when coughing at rest; none leaked during the Bonney test or with urethral/bladder neck compression ($n = 12$).[168] [EL = 3]

A third study did not report complete numerical results for the outcomes assessed (urethroscopic observations, proximal urethral pressure changes, pressure transmission ratio). The authors noted that there was no overlap between the Bonney test and direct urethral compression in proximal urethral pressure changes ($n = 37$).[169] [EL = 3]

One study reported urethral closure pressure profile and cough pressure profile measurements in women with stress UI when undertaking the Marshall test, and with intentional urethral occlusion.

The urethral closure and cough pressure profiles were not significantly different during the Marshall test or with urethral occlusion ($n = 16$).[170] [EL = 3]

Fluid-Bridge test

Three studies evaluated the accuracy of the Fluid-Bridge test for the diagnosis of stress UI in women.[171–173] In each study, fluid reaching a point 0.5 cm from the urethrovesical junction indicated a positive test. In two studies, the reference standards used were a clinical and a urodynamic diagnosis of stress UI.[171,172] The test was conducted with women in the supine position in both studies, and additionally in the erect position in one.[172] With women in the supine position, the Fluid-Bridge test had:

- sensitivity 74–86%, specificity 42–62%, PPV 66–72% and NPV 64–70% relative to urodynamic findings

- sensitivity 72–89%, specificity 35–53%, PPV 43–54%, and NPV 71–85% relative to a clinical diagnosis ($n = 67$, $n = 76$).[171,172] [EL = DS III]

With women in the erect position, the Fluid-Bridge test had:

- sensitivity 100%, specificity 24%, PPV 37% and NPV 100% relative to a urodynamic diagnosis ($n = 76$)[172]

- sensitivity 100%, specificity 16%, PPV 40% and NPV 100% relative to a clinical diagnosis ($n = 76$).[172] [EL = DS III]

A third study evaluated the accuracy of a 'modified' Fluid-Bridge test relative to a diagnosis of stress UI due to bladder neck incompetence based on findings on history or on the Marshall test ($n = 66$). The Fluid-Bridge test had:

- sensitivity 86%, specificity 87%, PPV 79% and NPV 93% relative to the Marshall test

- sensitivity 73%, specificity 88%, PPV 85% and NPV 80% relative to history.

Urethral pressure profilometry had sensitivity 50%, specificity 88%, PPV 69% and NPV 78% relative to the Marshall test.[173] [EL = DS III]

Do tests of urethral competence predict outcome?

Only one study reported any data relevant to this question. In a case series of women undergoing colposuspension or needle suspension, the failure rate was significantly higher in women with a negative Q-tip test, who formed 4% of the study population ($n = 406$).[174] [EL = 3]

Evidence statements for tests of urethral competence

The Q-tip, Bonney, Marshall and Fluid-Bridge tests have been developed to evaluate the mobility or competence of the urethrovesical junction. [EL = DS III] However, there is no evidence to support their role in the clinical assessment of UI. [EL = 4]

Recommendations for tests of urethral competence

The Q-tip, Bonney, Marshall and Fluid-Bridge tests are not recommended in the assessment of women with UI. [D]

3.13 Cystoscopy

Cystoscopy is the direct visualisation of the bladder and urethral lumen using either a rigid or flexible cystoscope. Examination is used to identify areas of inflammation, tumour, stones and diverticula, all of which are findings that will require management within a different clinical pathway.

Alternative pathway

One study aimed to determine whether multichannel cystometry, in combination with urethro-cystoscopy, improved the 'diagnostic accuracy' of cystometry alone in women, 93% of whom presented with UI, the remainder with prolapse (6%) or retention (1%). The women's history as reported did not indicate that cystoscopy was necessary. Urethrocystoscopy indicated a new diagnosis, of different pathology, in six women (n = 84).[175] [EL = 3]

Diagnostic accuracy

Two studies evaluated the accuracy of dynamic urethroscopy (urethroscopy with simultaneous supine cystometry) relative to multichannel cystometry with or without urethral pressure profilometry, for the diagnosis of stress UI (one study)[176] or DO (one study).[148] For a diagnosis of stress UI, urethroscopy had sensitivity of 60%, specificity 79%, PPV 75% and NPV 66% (n = 99).[176] [EL = DS III] For a diagnosis of DO, urethrocystoscopy had sensitivity of 25%, specificity 94%, PPV 65% and NPV 74% (n = 218).[148] [EL = DS III]

Evidence statement for cystoscopy

The available evidence does not support the role of cystoscopy in the assessment of women with UI. [EL = 3]

From evidence to recommendation

The GDG felt that cystoscopy may be of value in women with pain or recurrent UTI following previous pelvic surgery, or where fistula is suspected; its place in recurrent stress UI without these additional features is less clear.

> **Recommendation for cystoscopy**
>
> Cystoscopy is not recommended in the initial assessment of women with UI alone. [D (GPP)]

3.14 Imaging

Imaging techniques that can be used in the assessment of the urinary tract include ultrasonography, X-ray, computed tomography (CT) and magnetic resonance imaging (MRI). Confirmation of alternative pelvic pathology, by means of cross-sectional imaging or ultrasound, would be an indication for referral to a specialist. In addition, imaging may be used to characterise the extent and anatomical contents of a POP, especially in the standing position with MRI.

Diagnostic accuracy

The use of ultrasound for the diagnosis of post-void residual urine is considered in Section 3.6.

Diagnosis of UI

No evidence was identified that considered the use of MRI or CT scanning in the assessment of women with UI. Studies considering the use of ultrasound and X-ray imaging are described below.

The sensitivity and specificity of ultrasound and the Q-tip test, relative to a urodynamic finding of stress UI in women, was reported in one case series. Ultrasound (a positive test defined as a 1 cm or greater drop in urethrovesical junction) had a sensitivity and specificity of 86% and 91%, respectively. The values were 90% and 55%, respectively, for a positive Q-tip test (change in angle of 35° or more) (n = 67).[177] [EL = DS II]

Other studies have investigated whether certain parameters that could be measured by imaging might be used in the assessment of women with UI. These parameters include bladder wall thickness, bladder neck positioning, specific urethral measurements and the posterior urethrovesical angle.

Bladder wall thickness for DO diagnosis

Two studies focused on bladder wall thickness measured by transvaginal ultrasound for the diagnosis of DO.[178,179] One reported significantly greater bladder wall thickness in women with DO than with any other diagnosis, and that bladder wall thickness of more than 5 mm had sensitivity of 84%, specificity 89% and PPV 94% for diagnosing DO, using videocystourethrography with or without ambulatory urodynamics as the reference standard ($n = 180$).[178] [EL = 3] The second study investigated bladder wall thickness in women in whom urodynamic findings and clinical diagnoses were equivocal. Compared with women with stress UI, and compared with women without UI on urodynamic testing, the bladder wall thickness in women with DO appeared to be significantly greater ($n = 128$).[179] [EL = 3]

Studies investigating correlation of anatomical shape or movement with stress UI

Another four studies considered whether anatomical shape or movement correlates with reporting of UI, or with urodynamic findings, but the clinical significance of the findings reported in these studies is not clear. The studies considered the following (see evidence tables for findings).

- A case series investigated whether urethral measurements, taken by intraurethral ultrasonography, could distinguish women with intrinsic sphincter deficiency (ISD) from those with urodynamic stress UI ($n = 39$).[180]

- Two studies considered whether the posterior urethrovesical angle measured using bead chain urethrocystography could be used to diagnose stress UI.[181,182] One of the studies aimed to determine how bladder neck descent and posterior urethrovesical angle correlated with urodynamic findings ($n = 84$).[181] [EL = 3] The other study considered the prevalence of several parameters, including posterior urethrovesical angle of 115° or more, in continent and incontinent groups ($n = 59$).[182] [EL = 3]

- One study evaluated two parameters measured on bead chain cystography (the urethra at the most dependent position in the bladder, and descent of the urethrovesical junction below the posterior edge of the symphysis pubis) compared with a 1 cm or greater drop in urethrovesical junction, measured on ultrasound in women with stress UI ($n = 85$).[183] [EL = 3]

Does imaging affect women's outcomes?

No evidence was identified that addressed this question.

Evidence statement for imaging

There is a lack of evidence regarding the use of MRI or CT scanning in the assessment of women with UI. The available data do not support the use of ultrasound or X-ray imaging in the assessment of UI. The correlation between anatomy and function is unclear. [EL = 3]

Recommendation for imaging

Imaging (magnetic resonance imaging, computed tomography, X-ray) is not recommended for the routine assessment of women with UI. Ultrasound is not recommended other than for the assessment of residual urine volume. [D]

Research recommendation for imaging

Further studies are required to clarify the role of ultrasound for the assessment of OAB.

3.15   Information provision

No evidence was identified in relation to whether providing information to a woman has an impact in terms of her satisfaction with the outcomes of treatment for UI or OAB.

While there is a lack of evidence in relation to the information given to women with UI, women need the right information, at the right time, with the support they need to use it. It is well recognised in the healthcare community that clear communication, the involvement of service users and the provision of timely evidence-based information are key elements in moving towards a genuinely patient-centred service. Improving information for patients was a commitment in the NHS Plan[184] and part of the recommendations in the Kennedy Report.[185] There are NHS guidelines on the importance of patient information and a toolkit to help develop these can be downloaded from www.nhsidentity.nhs.uk/patientinformationtoolkit/index.htm.

Patients' desire for information may be underestimated in the majority of cases, although it is also recognised that individual patients' desire for information varies.[186] Information 'seekers' may cope better with more information, and information 'avoiders' cope better with less.

Women presenting with symptoms of UI need information that helps them to understand the various types of UI, their symptoms, investigations and the treatments recommended. They need to feel confident that the information provided is based on valid, systematic research into which clinical procedures, drug therapies and medical devices are most effective. However, patients and their families need information that is both scientifically valid and understandable. Since patients make important medical decisions with their clinicians (not separately from them), information provided must be designed for use by patients with their clinicians.

Women with UI should also be given information on where else to go for help and support, for example patient organisations such as Incontact (www.incontact.org) and the Continence Foundation (www.continence-foundation.org.uk).

4. Conservative management

In this chapter we refer to those therapies used for UI that do not involve surgery. These include lifestyle interventions, physical, behavioural, drug and complementary therapies, and non-therapeutic interventions (products that collect or contain leakage). The preventive use of physical and behavioural therapies and of lifestyle interventions is also considered.

4.1 Lifestyle interventions

Studies considered for the lifestyle interventions question

Evidence described in this section is derived from studies that investigated the effects of modifying the specified lifestyle factors on UI- or OAB-related outcomes. Where no such interventional studies were identified, other study designs investigating how these lifestyle factors may affect the prevalence, or incidence, of UI or OAB were considered. Several observational studies have considered the possible association between lifestyle factors and UI, many of which include both men and women.

4.1.1 Bowel habit

No studies were identified that addressed the effects of modifying bowel habit on UI in women. Three observational studies in women considered whether bowel habit is a risk factor for UI.

One observational study compared the history of bowel function in women with uterovaginal prolapse ($n = 23$, ten of whom had 'minor' stress UI symptoms), women with stress UI ($n = 23$) and a control group ($n = 27$). Straining at stool as a young adult was reported by significantly more women with prolapse or stress UI than the control group (61% versus 30% versus 4%), as was bowel frequency of less than twice a week as young adults in women with prolapse compared with control (48% versus 8%).[187] [EL = 2+]

Another cohort study reported that bowel urgency was associated with risk of OAB at 1 year ($n = 12\,570$).[14] [EL = 2+]

A cross-sectional study considered the effects of constipation and straining at stool on lower urinary tract symptoms. Stress UI, urgency and hesitancy were associated with both constipation and straining at stool. Sensation of incomplete emptying, post-void dribble and straining were associated with straining at stool ($n = 487$).[188] [EL = 3]

A further cross-sectional survey reported that constipation was associated with a risk of stress and urge UI, although constipation was not defined ($n = 6006$).[189] [EL = 3]

4.1.2 Dietary factors

No studies were identified that addressed the effects of modifying dietary factors, including alcohol consumption. A cohort study investigated the association between the intake of certain foods, energy, minerals and vitamins and the 1 year incidence of stress UI or OAB in women aged 40 years or above. The data indicate that certain quantities of some foods may be associated with reduced risk of new-onset OAB (chicken, vegetables, bread, protein, vitamin D and potassium) or new-onset stress UI (bread), and some quantities may be associated with an increased risk of new-onset OAB or stress UI (carbonated drinks) or stress UI (high fat, cholesterol, vitamin B12 and zinc intake) $n = 6424$.[190–192] [EL = 2+]

A cross-sectional study did not find an association between alcohol use and urgency ($n = 1059$; 50% women).[193] [EL = 3]

4.1.3 Caffeine

One RCT evaluated the effects of reducing caffeine intake to a maximum of 100 mg/day in addition to bladder training compared with bladder training alone in men and women with OAB with or without UI ($n = 74$). At 1 month, significantly greater reductions in urgency episodes and frequency were seen in the caffeine reduction group, with no significant differences between groups in reductions in urge UI episodes.[194] [EL = 1+]

Four observational studies investigated the relationship between caffeine consumption and UI or OAB.[195–198] Two of these studies evaluated the effects of caffeine on urodynamic parameters in women, as follows:

- A case–control study reported that the risk of DO was significantly higher with high versus minimal caffeine intake (OR 2.4, 95% CI 1.1 to 6.5). The risk with moderate versus minimal caffeine intake was not statistically significant (OR 1.5 , 95% CI 0.1 to 7.2, $n = 259$).[195] [EL = 2+]

- A significant increase in detrusor pressure rise on bladder filling was seen after 200 mg caffeine intake in women with DO. No significant changes were identified in other urodynamic parameters in either group (women with DO or asymptomatic women, $n = 30$).[196] [EL = 3]

The other two studies reported the effects of modifying caffeine intake on subjective or objective outcomes:[197,198]

- During the initial 2–4 week self-monitoring phase of a behaviour management programme in women,[199] daily intake of caffeine, urine loss, daytime leakage episodes, and frequency fell and daily fluid intake increased. None of the changes in outcomes was significantly associated with reduced caffeine intake ($n = 34$).[197] [EL = 3]

- In a series of older people with psychiatric conditions who underwent a 13 week programme of alternating caffeine intake or abstinence, day and night leakage episodes were higher during periods of caffeine intake ($n = 14$; eight women).[198] [EL = 3]

Four cross-sectional studies investigated the association between caffeine intake and UI or OAB.[193,200–202] The findings in the individual studies were as follows:

- no association between coffee intake and urgency ($n = 1059$; 50% women)[193]

- increased risk of UI with tea intake ($n = 6876$)[200]

- nocturia was more common in women who drank tea in the evening (no numerical data presented; $n = 3669$)[201]

- the risks for difficulty in emptying the bladder and having a weak urinary stream were higher in women who drank coffee ($n = 297$).[202] [EL = 3]

4.1.4 Fluid intake

In one RCT in women with UI (type unspecified), no significant changes in leakage episodes were reported after modifying daily fluid intake for 5 weeks. Adherence to fluid intake protocols was reported to be poor ($n = 32$).[203] [EL = 1−]

A further crossover RCT considered the effects of fluid manipulation over a 3 week period in women with stress UI or idiopathic DO. Fluid manipulation consisted of caffeine restriction for 1 week followed by increased or decreased fluid intake in association with continued caffeine restriction for 2 weeks. Caffeine restriction alone did not lead to statistically significant reductions in any outcome (leakage or urgency episodes, frequency, 24 hour pad test). Increasing fluid intake led to a significant increase in urgency episodes in women with DO, with no significant effects on other outcomes. After reducing fluid intake, significant reductions in leakage and urgency episodes, and in frequency, were seen ($n = 84$; 69 analysed).[204] [EL = 1−]

Based on women with stress UI or DO enrolled in a study of behaviour management,[205] weak correlation between fluid intake and diurnal and nocturnal frequency and leakage episodes was reported over a 1 week period ($n = 126$).[206] [EL = 3]

4.1.5 Smoking

No studies were identified that addressed the effects of smoking cessation on UI in women. One cohort study found significantly increased incidence of stress UI or OAB in current smokers compared with never smokers at 1 year ($n = 6424$).[190] [EL = 2+] A case–control study reported significantly higher prevalence of smoking among women with UI than women who were continent (OR 4.2, 95% CI 2.2 to 8.2). In women with UI, the prevalence of urge UI was significantly higher among smokers than non-smokers ($n = 160$).[207] [EL = 2−]

Six cross-sectional surveys considered the relationship between smoking and UI in women. Three surveys reported no association ($n = 297$, $n = 486$, $n = 6037$; 56% women).[202,208,209] The others reported a positive association between current smoking and UI (one study, $n = 6876$)[200] or nocturia (one study, $n = 3669$),[201] and between former smoking and UI (two studies, $n = 6876$; 1059 [50% women]).[193,200] [EL = 3]

4.1.6 Weight

One RCT evaluated the effects of a 3 month weight reduction programme in overweight women with UI. Reductions in weight and leakage episodes and improvements in QOL were significantly greater in the group assigned weight reduction compared with no intervention. Beyond the randomisation phase, women were offered continued intervention for 6 months, after which symptoms were still improved compared with baseline ($n = 48$; 40 analysed).[210] [EL = 1−]

Three case series reported the effects of surgically induced weight loss on UI in morbidly obese women:

- In 12 women with stress, urge or mixed UI who had mean weight loss of 33% following gastric bypass surgery, nine were subjectively cured of UI with no significant change in frequency at mean follow-up of 14 months.[211] [EL = 3]

- In women who had lost 50% or more of their excess weight following bariatric surgery, the prevalence of stress UI fell from 61% to 12% after stabilisation of weight loss (2–5 years) ($n = 138$).[212] [EL = 3]

- In men and women who lost 46% of their excess bodyweight following laparoscopic adjustable gastric banding, 64% reported that their stress UI was better. Symptoms were unchanged in the remainder ($n = 195$; 83% women).[213]

A fourth case series evaluated the effects of a 3 month weight reduction programme on leakage episodes in ten women with UI (six urge, three mixed, one stress). Seven women reported at least 50% reduction in leakage episodes (all those who lost at least 5% of their weight, and one-quarter of those who lost less than 5% of their weight).[214] [EL = 3]

Two cohort studies[190,215] and five cross-sectional studies[188,200,201,208,209] investigated the relationship between BMI and UI or OAB. One cohort study found significantly increased 1 year incidence of stress UI or OAB in women with BMI more than 30, compared with a BMI of 20–25 ($n = 6424$).[190] [EL = 2+] The second cohort study, which investigated the prevalence of stress or urge UI in participants of high- or low-impact exercise, reported that BMI was associated with risk for regular stress and urge UI but gave no specific detail ($n = 104$).[215] [EL = 2+]

The cross-sectional studies found that the prevalence or risk of UI or OAB was higher with increased BMI, specifically:

- increased risk of UI with BMI greater than 25 ($n = 6876$)[200]

- women with regular UI had the highest mean BMI ($n = 486$)[208]

- significantly higher prevalence of UI in women with BMI greater than 29 ($n = 6037$; 56% women)[209]

- increased risk of two or more nocturia episodes versus one episode for women with BMI of 30 or more versus less than 20 ($n = 3669$)[201]

- increased risk of UI or urgency with increasing BMI, although BMI thresholds were not defined ($n = 487$)[188]

- increased risk of urge UI and a trend towards increased risk of urgency in women within the highest versus lowest BMI quartiles ($n = 297$)[202]

- increased risk of both stress and urge UI in women within the highest BMI quartile ($n = 6006$).[189] [EL = 3]

4.1.7 Physical exercise

No controlled studies were identified that addressed the effects of physical exercise on UI in women. A cohort study investigated the prevalence of stress or urge UI in past US Olympians who had participated in long-term high-impact exercise (gymnastics or track and field) in the past compared with low-impact exercise (swimming). No significant difference in the prevalence of stress or urge UI was identified between high- or low-impact exercise groups ($n = 104$).[215] [EL = 2+] Another cohort study evaluated the effects of physical activity before, during and after first childbirth; the analysis suggested that prepregnancy high-impact activity may be associated with risk of UI ($n = 665$).[216] [EL = 2+]

Three cross-sectional studies investigated the prevalence of UI in women who exercise compared with those who do not. The three studies found that the overall prevalence of UI was not significantly different between groups (total $n = 1677$).[217–219] [EL = 3] A further cross-sectional study reported that urgency was less likely in women who exercise at least weekly ($n = 6006$).[189] [EL = 3]

Evidence statements for lifestyle interventions

There is a lack of high-quality prospective controlled trials evaluating the effects of modifying lifestyle factors in women with UI or OAB. [EL = 4]

Observational studies suggest that an increased caffeine intake may be associated with OAB and UI. [EL = 3] There is some evidence that caffeine reduction leads to less urgency and frequency when used in addition to bladder training. [EL = 1+]

Only RCTs of poor quality exist for modifying fluid intake, which were inconclusive. [EL = 1−] There is evidence of an association between obesity and UI or OAB, and in obese women weight reduction of at least 5% is associated with relief of UI symptoms. [EL = 3]

Constipation (bowel frequency of less than twice a week), and increased straining at stool in early adult life, may be associated with an increased tendency to prolapse and UI but no evidence on the effect of modifying bowel habit on continence was identified. [EL = 2+] Some dietary factors may increase the risk of developing UI or OAB although there is no evidence in relation to the effects of modifying these factors. [EL = 2+] Most observational studies suggest that smoking is associated with an increased risk of UI and OAB although there is no evidence relating to smoking cessation in the management of these symptoms. [EL = 3] There are conflicting data in relation to the association between physical exercise and UI prevalence. [EL = 3]

From evidence to recommendations
Where there is consistent evidence that a lifestyle factor appears to increase the risk of UI or OAB, or where there is consistent evidence of benefit from modifying a lifestyle factor, the GDG has recommended interventions in relation to these (caffeine, weight). Both excessive and inadequate fluid intake may lead to lower urinary tract symptoms; this should be considered on an individual basis. The overall lack of consistency in findings indicates a need for further research in this area.

Recommendations for lifestyle interventions

A trial of caffeine reduction is recommended for the treatment of women with OAB. [D]

Consider advising modification of high or low fluid intake for the treatment of women with UI or OAB. [D (GPP)]

Women with UI or OAB who have a body mass index greater than 30 should be advised to lose weight. [D]

Research recommendation for lifestyle interventions

There is a need for prospective interventional studies in all areas of lifestyle interventions to evaluate the effects of modifying these factors on UI and OAB.

4.2 Physical therapies

A variety of physical therapies are used in the management of UI in women. Pelvic floor muscle training (PFMT) involves recruiting pelvic floor muscles for muscle strengthening and skill training. Contraction of pelvic floor muscles causes inward lift of the muscles, with resultant increase in urethral closure pressure, stabilisation and resistance to downward movement.[220] Biofeedback can promote awareness of the physiological action of pelvic floor muscles by visual, tactile or auditory means, for example by manometry or electromyography (EMG).[221,222] Weighted vaginal cones are cone-shaped appliances of various weights that can be used to facilitate strengthening of pelvic floor muscles. Passive and active contraction of the pelvic floor muscles prevent the cones from slipping out of the vagina.[222] Electrical stimulation involves the application of electrical current, usually via vaginal electrodes, to stimulate the pelvic floor muscles via their nerve supply, or to aim to normalise reflex activity.[221,223]

Studies considered for the physical therapies question

Evidence described in this section is derived from RCTs. Two systematic reviews published on the Cochrane library (PFMT, and weighted vaginal cones) in women with UI collate much of the RCT data identified in the systematic searches.[224,225] Owing to overlap of studies within Cochrane reviews, and because they include abstracts that have not subsequently been published, the studies were considered individually alongside all other relevant primary data.

Overall, the studies of physical therapies are heterogeneous in terms of the treatment programmes used, duration of treatment and/or follow-up, the populations and number of individuals enrolled and the outcomes measured. Several studies considered more than one intervention.

4.2.1 Pelvic floor muscle training

A wide range of different PFMT programmes was used across the RCTs, varying in duration, in number and type of contractions and repetitions. Daily PFMT was used in most. Further detail of the PFMT programmes used is provided in the relevant subsections.

PFMT versus no treatment or sham PFMT

Six RCTs compared PFMT with no treatment in a total of 422 women (211 having either treatment). Four enrolled women with stress UI,[226–229] and one included women with stress or mixed UI (8.9%).[230] The remaining study included women with stress, mixed or urge UI (urge UI in 16%), in which those with urge UI were treated with bladder training and those with mixed UI with bladder training plus PFMT; this study is considered in the behavioural therapies section (4.3).[231,232] Some results for the 60% of women from this study who had stress UI were reported separately and are considered here.[232] Other than one quasi-RCT,[231,232] the studies were considered to be of good quality. [EL = 1+]

Women were advised to undertake daily PFMT in five studies. The number of contractions instructed varied, other than one study that only evaluated the 'knack' over a 1 week period.[227]

The lowest number of contractions across the other studies was 8–12 contractions three times a day (plus an exercise class every week) and the highest was 20 contractions four times a day, increasing to 200 per day.[226,228,230,231] In a comparison with duloxetine, PFMT involved a target of 200 contractions per week (over 4 days), and the 'knack'. Half the studies provided other support, including an audiotape plus group training once a week[226] or a leaflet in addition to initial instruction.[230,231] The woman's ability to contract the pelvic floor muscle (PFM) was checked by vaginal palpation in five studies,[226–229,231,232] one of which excluded women unable to contract the PFM.[227]

Duration of treatment was 3 months in most studies, although this varied from 1 week to 6 months. Most studies considered cure rates and changes in leakage episodes at the end of treatment, which showed significantly greater improvements with PFMT compared with no treatment, in the five studies that recommended daily PFMT. The results for PFMT groups versus no treatment were:

- subjective cure rates of 16% and 56% versus 3% (two studies)[226,230]

- success (combined subjective cure and improvement) in 85% versus 0% (one study)[232]

- objective cure rates (1 hour pad test or negative stress test) of 44% and 65% versus 0% and 7% (two studies)[226,232]

- reductions in leakage episodes of 54% or 72% versus 6% and an increase of 10% (three studies; no numerical data in one).[226,230,232]

Three studies also considered short pad test results, each of which showed significantly less leakage in women undergoing PFMT.[226–228] One RCT used a 24 hour pad test where no difference was identified.[226] Both those studies that did[226–228,231,232] and those that did not[230] assess PFM contraction prior to treatment showed efficacy of active treatment groups over control. [EL = 3]

Five year follow-up has been reported of women from a 3 month study during which the control group was offered PFMT.[233] At 5 years in women with stress, mixed or urge UI (those with stress or mixed undergoing PFMT), 69% reported improvement or dryness compared with pretreatment. However, a non-significant increase in leakage episodes was seen in women with stress UI ($n = 110$).[233] [EL = 3]

In a comparison of PFMT with sham PFMT (and with duloxetine 80 mg with or without PFMT), sham PFMT involved contracting hip abductor muscles. No significant differences were reported between PFMT and sham PFMT groups in any outcome (leakage episodes, global improvement, QOL) after 12 weeks' treatment. It is unique to this trial that PFMT apparently gave no significant benefit over sham treatment.[229] [EL = 1+]

Adverse effects

The majority of studies comparing PFMT with no treatment did not consider adverse effects. One RCT reported isolated adverse effects (pain, and an 'uncomfortable feeling' during exercise).[231] Another RCT reported that no adverse effects occurred.[226] Adverse effects occurring in the PFMT and no treatment arms of the duloxetine study were pooled, and therefore a distinction between these interventions is not possible.[229]

Different pelvic floor muscle training regimens

Several RCTs compared different PFMT regimens, or different methods of delivering PFMT.

Intensive versus standard regimens

Four RCTs compared 'intensive' with 'standard' PFMT. The PFMT programmes and the populations evaluated were as follows:

- an exercise class every week in addition to standard PFMT (individual instruction, clinic biofeedback, 8–12 contractions three times a day, contraction checked by palpation) versus standard PFMT alone; 6 months' treatment, women with stress UI ($n = 52$)[234,235] [EL = 1+]

- a program of PFMT with bladder training for women with frequency and urgency (PFMT consisting of individualised instruction, target 80–100 contractions/day) versus standard postnatal care (which could include information on pelvic floor exercises); in women with stress, urge (15%) or mixed UI (31%) 3 months postpartum, assessed after 1 year's treatment,[236] and at 6 years (n = 747)[237] [EL = 1++]

- PFMT with or without vaginal cones versus standard PFMT (antenatal and postnatal instruction) in women with UI 3 months postpartum, assessed after 1 year's treatment and at 24–44 months postpartum; awareness of contraction checked by perineometry (n = 145)[238] [EL = 1−]

- one-to-one instruction while in hospital postnatally, with an option to attend two postnatal pelvic floor exercise classes, versus standard care (verbal promotion of exercises, plus explanatory leaflet); effects assessed at 6 months postpartum (n = 190)[239] [EL = 1+]

The rate of subjective cure or improvement was significantly higher in the intensive group in the study that considered this outcome (96% versus 66%; cure rates alone 9% versus 0%).[234,235] Two of three studies in postpartum women found significantly lower UI prevalence in the intensive groups (60% versus 69% and 50% versus 76%),[236,238] while the third reported no significant difference (60% versus 46%).[239] The findings of pad tests were inconsistent (two studies).[234,235,238]

Longer term follow-up is available from two studies. At 6 years, no significant differences were found between 'intensive' and 'standard' groups in UI prevalence, severity or leakage episodes in the 69% of women followed up.[236,237] [EL = 1++] Five year follow-up of the intensive PFMT arm (23 women) of one RCT[234,235] has also been published,[240] and a 15 year follow-up of both treatment arms.[241] Data at 15 years show no differences in urinary outcomes or satisfaction between groups in the 91% of women followed up.[241]

Group versus individual training
Two RCTs of 3 months' duration compared groups with individual PFMT in women with stress, mixed or urge UI (n = 530, n = 44).[242] [EL = 1+] [243] [EL = 1−] Group sizes were eight to ten[242] or four to twelve.[243] In the smaller of the two RCTs (n = 44), women also underwent bladder training. Neither study found significant differences between the two methods in the outcomes evaluated (leakage, UI severity, self-reported change in symptoms, pad test, QOL or frequency).

None of the RCTs comparing different PFMT methods considered adverse effects.

PFMT and drug treatment

One RCT compared PFMT with intravaginal oestrogen in women with stress UI (3 months' treatment with follow-up at 12 months) but no between-group analyses were reported.[228] [EL = 1+] Three RCTs evaluated combined PFMT and drug therapy (estriol, tolterodine and duloxetine).[229,244,245]

The PFMT regimen varied across these studies: five contractions per hour,[228] 75 contractions per day,[245] 15 minutes per day,[244] and a target of 200 contractions per week over a 4 day period.[229] Pelvic floor muscle contraction was checked by vaginal palpation in two studies.[228,229]

Oral estriol 1 mg plus PFMT was compared with PFMT alone in postmenopausal women with stress UI (n = 73; 66 analysed). A higher cure rate was reported with estriol plus PFMT compared with PFMT alone, at 2 years (78% versus 68%); no other outcomes were reported.[244] [EL = 1−]

The effects of adding PFMT to tolterodine 2 mg b.d. compared with tolterodine alone was considered in men and women with frequency, urgency and urge UI (n = 480; 75% women). After 6 months' treatment, no significant differences were seen between tolterodine plus PFMT versus tolterodine alone in changes in any outcome. The reductions in symptoms with combined therapy versus tolterodine alone were: urge UI episodes 64% versus 70%, frequency 23% versus 27%, and urgency 79% versus 83%. Overall 82% versus 86% considered themselves improved. Adverse effects reported with tolterodine (with or without PFMT) were dry mouth, headache, constipation, nausea, dry eyes and dizziness.[245] [EL = 1++]

Duloxetine 80 mg daily (with or without PFMT) was compared with PFMT and with no active treatment (sham PFMT and placebo drug) in women with stress UI (n = 201). Significantly greater reductions in leakage episodes were reported with duloxetine (with or without PFMT) compared with PFMT alone after 3 months' treatment. Global improvement and I-QOL scores indicated greater improvement with duloxetine plus PFMT compared with no active treatment. Discontinuation and adverse effect rates (nausea, dizziness, dry mouth, constipation, insomnia, somnolence, asthenia) were significantly higher in duloxetine-treated groups compared with PFMT or no active treatment combined.[229] [EL = 1+]

4.2.2 Vaginal cones

Ten RCTs evaluated the use of weighted vaginal cones in women with UI compared with PFMT or electrical stimulation, or in combination with PFMT.[226,238,246–253] Other than one study that enrolled women with stress, mixed or urge UI (postnatally),[238] all studies included women with stress UI. Between 37 and 145 women were evaluated in each study.

The protocol for cone use differed across studies. Seven used a range of weights, increasing according to ability to retain the cone (20–70 g,[226,247,252,253] 20–100 g,[238,250] or 50–100 g[246]). One study used a fixed weight of 150 g,[251] while two studies did not specify weights used.[248,249] In five studies, women were instructed to hold the cones in place twice or three times a day for 10–15 minutes.[238,246–248,250] Once daily use for between 5 and 25 minutes was advised in another five studies.[226,249,251–253]

In studies involving PFMT, daily PFMT was undertaken. The number of contractions ranged from 24 (eight contractions three times a day) to 100 where specified.[226,238,246–248] PFMT was individually tailored in three studies,[247,249,252] and included the 'knack' in two.[247,252] Seven studies stated that ability to contract PFM was checked at baseline.[226,238,246–248,252,253]

Cones versus no active treatment
Cones were compared with no treatment within one RCT (total $n = 107$). Significantly greater improvement in leakage and social activity indices were seen with cones after 6 months' treatment. No significant differences were seen between groups in other outcomes (subjective or objective cure, leakage episodes).[226] [EL = 1+]

Cones versus PFMT
Cones were compared with PFMT in four studies of 3–6 months' duration.[226,246,247,249] Two of these studies had other treatment arms (electrical stimulation and an untreated control,[226] biofeedback[249]). A further study, also described under the intensive versus standard PFMT section, compared 'intensive' PFMT (PFMT/cones/PFMT plus cones) with standard postnatal care but only analysed results for women who completed the study. Results were presented for the intensive group as a whole, except for the proportion cured, where there was no significant difference between cone and PFMT groups at 1 year postpartum.[238] [EL = 1–]

Two studies of 3 months' duration reported no significant differences between cones and PFMT in improvements in outcomes evaluated: leakage episodes, subjective improvement, subjective or objective cure rates ($n = 60$);[247] [EL = 1+] or leakage episodes, PFM strength or QOL (KHQ) ($n = 101$).[249] [EL = 1–]

The third study found significantly greater improvement with PFMT versus cones in the short pad test, leakage episodes, leakage index and PFM strength, and a significant difference in subjective and objective cure rates (56% versus 7% and 44% versus 15%). No significant differences were seen in 24 hour pad test results after 6 months' treatment ($n = 107$).[226] [EL = 1+] The fourth study, which only analysed results for those who completed 4 months' treatment, found a significantly greater reduction in leakage on the stress pad test with cones versus PFMT. No significant differences were found in other outcomes (PFM strength and subjective assessment) ($n = 37$).[246] [EL = 1–]

Cones versus electrical stimulation
Cones were compared with electrical stimulation in three studies, none of which reported significant differences between groups in any outcome, whether assessed at 1 or 6 months. Women in one study also undertook PFMT.[250] Outcomes evaluated across two studies were: short and 24 hour pad tests, subjective cure, leakage episodes, leakage and social activity indexes, and pelvic floor

muscle strength.[226,250] [EL = 1+] The remaining study only considered urethral pressure and pad test results, and gave inadequate data and detail of methods for evaluation ($n = 20$).[253] [EL = 1−]

Cones in combination with PFMT

Cones and PFMT in combination were compared with PFMT alone in a 3 month study. Limited results were given (urodynamics only available for 59%), with no between-group analysis for subjective assessments; however, a similar proportion of women in both groups reported cure or improvement ($n = 46$).[252] [EL = 1+]

Cones and PFMT in combination were compared with electrical stimulation in two studies of 6 weeks' duration. One reported no differences between groups in leakage episodes or frequency, while no between-group analyses were reported for other outcomes ($n = 40$).[248] [EL = 1−] The other study found no significant differences between groups in any outcome (urethral or vaginal pressures, PFM contraction and subjective assessment) ($n = 120$).[251] [EL = 1+]

Adverse effects

One study reported adverse effects, which were four reports in 27 cone users (one abdominal pain, one bleeding, two vaginitis) and two reports in the electrical stimulation group (tenderness and bleeding; discomfort).[226] No adverse effects were reported in the PFMT or untreated control groups. Motivation problems were very common in the cone and electrical stimulation groups in one study (52% and 32%).[226]

The withdrawal rate from cone therapy was 47% in a study that noted this, compared with none with PFMT.[247] Differences in withdrawal rates between groups were not apparent in other studies.

4.2.3 Biofeedback

Most data regarding biofeedback relate its use in conjunction with PFMT, rather than as an isolated intervention. A variety of biofeedback methods were used across these studies, differing in the probes used (vaginal probes with EMG electrodes, pressure-sensitive intravaginal devices), in the feedback provided (visual and/or auditory) and the setting in which biofeedback was undertaken (home or clinic). Additionally, a few studies used electrodes/rectal catheters to monitor muscle activity or abdominal pressure.

Only one study compared biofeedback alone with PFMT (and with cones, $n = 101$). No significant differences were found between the three groups in improvements in outcomes evaluated at 3 months: leakage episodes, PFM strength and QOL (KHQ).[249] [EL = 1−]

Eleven RCTs compared biofeedback-assisted PFMT with PFMT alone, in women with stress UI (eight studies),[254–263] stress or mixed UI (one study),[230] stress or urge UI (one study)[264] or OAB (one study).[265] Treatment duration ranged from 4 weeks to 6 months, with the number of women per study ranging from 22 to 103; most included fewer than 50 women. Of the 11 studies, four were considered to be of poor quality [EL = 1−][255,258,261–263] and seven of good quality.[230,254,256,257,259,260,264,265] [EL = 1+]

The majority of the studies found no significant differences between biofeedback-assisted PFMT groups and PFMT alone in the outcomes measured (subjective or objective cure, QOL [BFLUTS] or social activity index scores).[230,256,258–265] Cure rates in the seven studies that reported this outcome (though variously defined) ranged from 16% to 69% (median 30%) with PFMT and from 15% to 73% (median 50%) with biofeedback-assisted PFMT.[230,254,256,258,261,264,265] Significant additional benefit, in terms of leakage episodes, was reported in one study that alternated biofeedback with electrical stimulation,[262,263] and in PFM parameters in two studies.[259,260,262,263]

A further two RCTs evaluated different methods of biofeedback. One compared biofeedback by palpation with EMG in women with stress UI. There were no significant differences between the biofeedback methods in urinary outcomes after 8 weeks' treatment ($n = 50$).[266] [EL = 1+] The second study compared the use of a vaginal plus abdominal probe with a vaginal probe only, for 4 weeks. Greater improvement in QOL was seen using a vaginal probe only, with no differences reported in other outcomes (leakage, pelvic floor muscle strength or endurance) ($n = 38$).[267] [EL = 1+]

Two RCTs considered adverse effects. None were reported in one,[261] and another noted that two women (13%) found the vaginal probe uncomfortable, and that 17% from PFMT or biofeedback-assisted groups reported pain while training.[259,260]

4.2.4   Electrical stimulation

A range of various electrical stimulation methods and protocols were used across the RCTs, although the protocol used was poorly reported in some studies. Various types of current were used (interferential therapy, faradic stimulation, alternating pulse currents), with various current intensities. The setting (home or clinic), duration (15 to 30 minutes) and frequency (two to three times per week) of individual treatments also varied. Electrical stimulation parameters were generally tailored to the woman's tolerance.

Electrical stimulation versus sham stimulation

Eight RCTs compared electrical stimulation with sham stimulation. Treatment duration ranged from 4 to 15 weeks, with the number of women recruited in each study ranging from 24 to 121.[248,268–274] Four studies included women with stress UI,[248,268,270,271] two included women with stress, mixed or urge UI,[272,273] and two included women or men and women (57% women) with urge or urge-predominant UI.[269,274] One study was of poor quality,[248] [EL = 1−] and the others were of good quality.[268–273] [EL = 1+]

The outcomes reported across these studies were leakage episodes, UI prevalence, pad tests, subjective cure or improvement, PFM strength, urodynamic parameters and QOL (SF-36, IIQ, UDI). The findings across these studies were inconsistent, with significant benefit with electrical stimulation versus sham stimulation reported for some but not all outcomes, and not across all studies. Not all studies reported between-group comparisons.

A further RCT compared electrical stimulation with 'lower urinary tract exercises' (PFMT and bladder training), and with both interventions combined, in women with DO ($n = 68$). At 9–11 weeks, no significant differences were found between groups in any outcome (detrusor activity index, leakage episodes, PFM strength).[275] [EL = 1−]

PFMT versus electrical stimulation

Eight RCTs compared PFMT with electrical stimulation in women (six in women with stress UI,[226,228,248,276–278] one in those with stress, mixed or urge UI,[279] and one in those with OAB with urge UI[265]).

The RCTs involving women with stress UI recruited between 18 and 51 patients. Duration of treatment ranged from 6 weeks to 12 months. The PFMT group also used vaginal cones in one study.[248] The quality of two studies was poor,[248,278] [EL = 1−] while four were of good quality.[226,228,276,277] [EL = 1+] None of the studies reported significant differences between groups in subjective or objective cure rates. The subjective cure rates ranged from 10% to 56% with PFMT, and from 4% to 12% with electrical stimulation, and objective cure rates from 10% to 54% versus 4% to 40%. Several other outcomes were reported in one study, where improvements in PFM parameters, short pad test results, leakage and social activity indexes were significantly greater in the PFMT group compared with electrical stimulation.[226] No significant differences were reported between groups in leakage episodes or leakage frequency (three studies),[226,248,277] or in 48 hour pad test results (one study).[226] One of the studies also compared propantheline with electrical stimulation, which reported no significant differences between groups in subjective or objective cure or improvement.[277]

The RCT involving women with stress or mixed or urge UI (66% mixed) found no significant differences between PFMT and electrical stimulation groups in any outcome (subjective assessment, 48 hour pad test results, improvements in PFM strength or DO prevalence) after 8 weeks' treatment ($n = 35$).[279] [EL = 1+]

The RCT in women with OAB and urge UI reported significantly greater improvements in PFM parameters and QOL (KHQ) with PFMT compared with electrical stimulation, but no significant differences in self-reported cure or improvement after 12 weeks' treatment ($n = 103$).[265] [EL = 1+]

Electrical stimulation in combination with PFMT

Four RCTs evaluated electrical stimulation in combination with PFMT versus PFMT alone in women with stress UI (stress or urge in one RCT).[278,280–282] The duration of treatment ranged from 1 to six months, with the number of women enrolled ranging from 14 to 57. One RCT also compared the combination with electrical stimulation alone.[278] Three studies were of poor quality,[278,280,282] [EL = 1−] and one of good quality.[281] [EL = 1+]

Across these RCTs, electrical stimulation did not confer additional benefit to PFMT alone in the outcomes measured (self-reported cure or improvement, pad test, PFM parameters). No significant differences in self-reported cure or improvement were seen with electrical stimulation plus PFMT compared with electrical stimulation alone.

Adverse effects

Of all studies that considered the effectiveness of electrical stimulation, five considered adverse effects. None were reported in one study.[275] Across the others, adverse effects or complications noted were: vaginal irritation (12–22%), pain (6–9%), and cases of faecal incontinence, discomfort, and tenderness and bleeding.[226,268,269,277] One study reported difficulty in maintaining motivation in 32% of the electrical stimulation group.[226]

4.2.5 Transcutaneous electrical nerve stimulation and posterior tibial nerve stimulation

Transcutaneous electrical nerve stimulation (TENS) is a form of electrical nerve stimulation in which the electrodes are placed over the dermatomes of S2 to S4 for long periods of time, daily. The Stoller afferent nerve stimulator (SANS) involves inserting a fine gauge needle into the posterior tibial nerve just above the ankle. The tibial nerve then carries an electrical stimulation in an afferent direction to the sacral spine.

TENS

One 12 week crossover RCT compared TENS with oxybutynin in men and women (70% women) with idiopathic DO ($n = 43$). Significant improvements in functional capacity and frequency were reported with both treatments. No significant changes in SF-36 parameters were seen. Adverse effects reported were dry mouth, blurred vision and dry skin; these all had a lower incidence in the TENS group.[283] [EL= 1+]

Two case series reported findings of TENS over the short term (1–3 weeks) in men and women with OAB (total $n = 103$, with 84 analysed). These generally indicated improvements in frequency, nocturia and urgency,[284,285] and in urge UI.[285] [EL = 3]

Posterior tibial nerve stimulation

Posterior tibial nerve stimulation was considered in one RCT,[286] and in five case series of patients with OAB.[287–293] Except for one study that included only women, others also included men (predominantly women). Patient numbers ranged from 15 to 90 (total 282).

Posterior nerve stimulation was delivered via a SANS device. The stimulation protocol involved a fixed pulse width and frequency, with amplitude tailored to individual patients. The treatment regimen varied from 30 minutes three or four times a week for 3 or 4 weeks, to 30–60 minutes once weekly for 8–12 weeks. End of treatment results were reported except for one study that had follow-up to 3 years (mean 21 months).[292]

The RCT evaluated the effects of oxybutynin 5 mg daily in addition to PTNS compared with PTNS alone in men and women ($n = 43$; 88% women). Improvements in frequency, urgency and urge UI episodes were noted with both treatments, with no significant difference between groups in 'response rates'.[286] [EL = 3]

The smallest case series noted that two-thirds of patients achieved cure or partial response ($n = 15$).[290] Across the others, significant improvements in all outcomes were seen (leakage episodes, frequency and voided volumes).[287–289,291–293] Quality of life (I-QOL and SF-36) was improved (two studies).[287–289,293] In 11 patients from one case series,[293] in whom treatment was maintained for a mean of 13 months, treatment was withheld for 6 weeks and then re-introduced. This study showed that symptoms deteriorated when treatment was withdrawn and that the majority of patients reported some improvement in symptoms 4 weeks after re-introducing treatment.[294]

There were case reports of adverse effects across the studies. Those related to site of needle insertion were haematoma, minor bleeding, temporary painful/numb feeling, throbbing and transient local tenderness. Systemic effects noted were diarrhoea, cramps, headache, lower back pain, moderate right foot pain and stomach discomfort (no numerical data). Adverse effects reported in the group treated with PTNS and oxybutynin were dry mouth and blurred vision.[286]

4.2.6 Magnetic therapy

Magnetic therapy aims to stimulate the pelvic floor muscles and/or sacral roots by placing them within an electromagnetic field.

Two RCTs compared magnetic stimulation therapy with sham stimulation delivered via a portable device for the treatment of UI for 8 weeks. In the first study, in women with stress, mixed or urge UI, significantly more women in the magnetic therapy group reported improvement in symptoms. No significant differences in improvements in other outcomes were seen (pad weight, PFM contraction, leakage episodes or nocturia). Two reports of a pulsating sensation in users of magnetic stimulation were noted.[295] [EL = 1+] The second study, in women with urge-predominant mixed UI, reported a significantly higher 'success' rate with magnetic stimulation; between-group comparisons for other outcomes were not reported (frequency, nocturia). No women experienced adverse effects ($n = 39$).[296] [EL = 1−]

Two case series considered the effects of 6 or 8 weeks of magnetic therapy using a special chair (two 20 minute sessions a week). Women in one had stress UI (a minority having urge-predominant mixed UI), and urge or mixed UI in the other. Results for 74 patients have been reported, which showed significant improvement in all outcomes considered (leakage episodes, pad test results, frequency and satisfaction). Adverse effects were not considered in one study, while none were reported in the other.[297,298] [EL = 3]

4.2.7 Economic evidence for physical therapies

There is a lack of good-quality evidence about the clinical and cost effectiveness of conservative therapies for UI. In the absence of evidence of a difference in efficacy between treatment options, cost minimisation analysis may be used to determine the most cost effective. Cost minimisation was undertaken for the physical therapies PFMT, cones, biofeedback and electrical stimulation. Estimates of the costs of the conservative therapies and an explanation of how these estimates were derived are given in Appendix E.

Additionally, because the other conservative treatment option for stress UI is duloxetine (see Section 4.4.4), a decision tree model was developed to compare the cost effectiveness of PFMT and duloxetine, as a first-line treatment for women with moderate to severe stress UI (assumed to be 14 or more leakage episodes per week). Treatment effects and costs were based on a 52 week time frame. This is described in detail in Appendix F. Under baseline assumptions, PFMT 'dominates' duloxetine. This means that it is both more effective and less costly. The sensitivity analyses undertaken (and detailed in Appendix F) did not change this conclusion.

Evidence statements for physical therapies

Daily PFMT is an effective treatment for stress or mixed UI compared with no treatment over the short term. Other than occasional cases of pain or discomfort, no other adverse effects were noted. [EL = 1+] Women's pelvic floor contraction was assessed at baseline in the majority of studies. Studies that did or did not assess pelvic floor muscle contraction prior to treatment both showed efficacy of active treatment compared with control. [EL = 3]

In studies of up to 1 year, higher intensity PFMT regimens confer greater subjective cure or improvement than lower intensity regimens. Over the longer term, differences between these groups are not sustained. [EL = 1+] There is a lack of evidence for optimum training regimens for PFMT. [EL = 4]

There is no additional benefit from the use of PFMT in women undergoing treatment with tolterodine for OAB. [EL = 1++]

In women with stress UI, vaginal cones are more effective than no treatment over the short term. There is no evidence of a difference in effectiveness between cones and PFMT. Compared with PFMT, cones are associated with more adherence problems. [EL = 1+] One study suggested that the training time for using vaginal cones is one-third of that for PFMT, which would make vaginal cones cheaper than PFMT. However, it is not clear what the appropriate training regimen should be for women using vaginal cones. Vaginal cones are not suitable for all women. Cones are inappropriate for use in some circumstances, such as when there is a moderate to severe prolapse, too narrow or too capacious a vagina causing difficulty with insertion or misplacement of the cone, untreated atrophic vaginitis, vaginal infection, or during menstruation or pregnancy. [EL = 4]

Evidence does not indicate additional benefit from biofeedback with PFMT in comparison with PFMT alone in treating UI. [EL = 1+] Biofeedback with PFMT is more costly than PFMT alone and therefore is not cost effective given a lack of additional benefit.

There is lack of consistency in the electrical stimulation protocols employed in available studies. There is limited evidence for the benefit of electrical stimulation versus sham electrical stimulation in the treatment of urge UI. [EL = 1+] There is no evidence of additional benefit of electrical stimulation in combination with PFMT compared with PFMT alone. [EL = 1−]

Case series of up to 3 weeks' duration show improvements in frequency and nocturia with TENS, although the available data do not allow conclusions to be drawn as to the efficacy of TENS in women with UI. [EL = 3]

Data on posterior tibial nerve stimulation are mainly derived from case series of men and women with OAB, which show improvement in leakage episodes, frequency, voided volume and QOL with treatment for up to 3 months. Symptoms recur on treatment withdrawal. Adverse effects reported relate to needle insertion site (pain, tenderness, haematoma). Combining oxybutynin treatment with posterior tibial nerve stimulation did not lead to additional benefit. Overall the available data are inadequate to define the place of posterior tibial nerve stimulation for UI or OAB. [EL = 3]

There are limited data on the use of magnetic therapy for UI, and its role in the treatment of women with UI is unclear. [EL = 3]

An economic model constructed for the purposes of this guideline suggested that PFMT is more cost effective than duloxetine alone, as first-line treatment for stress UI. This result was generally not affected by making plausible changes to model parameters in favour of duloxetine. While the model was based on the best available clinical evidence, there is a lack of long-term effectiveness data for either treatment.

From evidence to recommendations

While there is no evidence of effectiveness for either biofeedback or electrical stimulation, the GDG considered that the information and support generated by biofeedback may assist motivation for some women, and that electrical stimulation may be of value for those who are unable to initiate a pelvic floor muscle contraction. [EL = 4]

In recommending the use of PFMT, the GDG considered that guidance should be given on the number of pelvic floor contractions to be undertaken within such a programme. Without clear evidence on optimal training regimens, the minimum number of daily pelvic floor muscle exercises advised across the studies was adopted by the GDG as the minimum number of contractions that women should be aiming for, that is 24 (eight contractions three times a day). Most studies evaluate 3 months' treatment and, in the view of the GDG, this is an appropriate period of time to recommend PFMT before assessing its effectiveness.

Recommendations for physical therapies

A trial of supervised pelvic floor muscle training of at least 3 months' duration should be offered as first-line treatment to women with stress or mixed UI. [A]

Pelvic floor muscle training programmes should comprise at least eight contractions performed three times per day. [A]

If pelvic floor muscle training is beneficial, an exercise programme should be maintained. [D (GPP)]

Perineometry or pelvic floor electromyography as biofeedback should not be used as a routine part of pelvic floor muscle training. [A]

Electrical stimulation should not routinely be used in the treatment of women with OAB. [D]

Electrical stimulation should not routinely be used in combination with pelvic floor muscle training. [A]

Electrical stimulation and/or biofeedback should be considered in women who cannot actively contract pelvic floor muscles in order to aid motivation and adherence to therapy. [D (GPP)]

Research recommendations for physical therapies

Studies investigating different pelvic floor muscle training regimens are required to establish the optimum method of delivering and undertaking this intervention.

The role of clinical pelvic floor assessment prior to PFMT should be investigated to determine whether it enhances the therapeutic effect of the intervention (Section 3.3).

Research into the optimal electrical stimulation parameters is required, to inform future clinical practice. Studies investigating the role of electrical stimulation in women who cannot contract the pelvic floor muscle are required.

There is a need for a robust evaluation of transcutaneous electrical nerve stimulation and posterior tibial nerve stimulation for the treatment of UI.

4.3   Behavioural therapies

Behavioural therapy involves an individual learning new patterns of response or re-establishing previously learnt behaviour to fit in with what is considered usual. Women with OAB (wet or dry) usually void more frequently than usual due to urgency. Women with stress UI also often void more frequently in the belief that they will pre-empt an involuntary urine loss associated with any increase in intra-abdominal pressure.

Various toileting programmes have been used. Bladder training (also described as bladder retraining, bladder drill, bladder re-education or bladder discipline) actively involves the individual, in attempting to increase the interval between the desire to void and the actual void.[299] This may occur by mandatory schedules in which the individual may not use the toilet between set times for voiding, or a self-scheduled regimen where the patient gradually increases their inter-voiding times, and may use the toilet between times if the urge becomes unbearable.[300]

Studies considered for the behavioural therapies question

Evidence described in this section is derived from RCTs. Four systematic reviews of various toileting regimens have been published on the Cochrane library.[299,301–304] The RCTs within these systematic reviews were considered individually. Further RCTs identified are also included here. Several studies included both men and women, none of which reported data separately by gender.

4.3.1 Bladder training

Bladder training versus control

Two RCTs compared bladder training with control in women ($n = 60$, $n = 123$).[205,305] In the first study, supervised bladder training as inpatients towards a target voiding interval of 4 hours was compared with unsupervised training at home, in women with frequency, urgency and urge UI (two-thirds of whom also had stress UI). At 6 months follow-up (duration of intervention unclear), more women in the supervised group were continent or symptom-free.[305] [EL = 1+] The second RCT in women with UI (type unspecified) compared bladder training (target voiding interval of 2.5–3 hours) with an untreated control group. Urine loss, leakage episodes and QOL (IIQ) were improved in the bladder training group after 6 weeks' treatment.[205] [EL = 1+] Neither study considered adverse effects.

Bladder training versus drug treatment

Two RCTs compared bladder training with drug treatment in women with urge or mixed UI (one oxybutynin,[306] one a combination of flavoxate and imipramine[307]).

In women with urge UI, similar self-reported cure rates (about 73%) were seen with a 6 week bladder training programme (target voiding interval of 3–4 hours) and with oxybutynin ($n = 81$). Relapse occurred in 4% of the bladder training group, and in 44% of the oxybutynin group, at 6 months. About half of the oxybutynin group required dose reduction owing to adverse effects. No between-group comparisons were made for other outcomes.[306] [EL = 1+]

No details of the bladder training programme were provided for the comparison with flavoxate plus imipramine ($n = 50$). Significantly more women were subjectively or objectively cured after 4 weeks' bladder training than with drug therapy.[307] [EL = 1+]

Bladder training in combination with drug treatment

Three double-blind (DB) RCTs evaluated the addition of antimuscarinic drug treatment to bladder training (one oxybutynin,[308] one terodiline[309] [no longer available in the UK], and one imipramine[310]). Bladder training aimed to reduce frequency by delaying voiding for as long as possible in two studies,[308,309] and aimed at a 4 hourly voiding target in one.[310] A further RCT compared tolterodine plus bladder training with tolterodine alone.[311] All studies included men and women; two included elderly people,[308,309] and two included a broader age group.[310,311]

In individuals with symptoms of urinary frequency, urgency and urge UI, a significant reduction in daytime frequency was seen with oxybutynin plus bladder training compared with placebo plus bladder training, after 6 weeks' treatment ($n = 60$; 93% women). No significant differences were reported in other outcomes (daytime leakage episodes, nocturia, nocturnal enuresis, self-reported benefit, adverse effects).[308] [EL = 1+]

No significant differences in frequency, leakage episodes or self-reported improvement were seen between terodiline or placebo in addition to bladder training in individuals with urinary frequency and urge UI, after 6 weeks' treatment ($n = 37$; 88% women). Two adverse effects were noted with terodiline (one oesophagitis, one dry mouth).[309] [EL = 1+]

In individuals with incontinence and 'unstable bladders', no significant differences were seen between imipramine plus bladder training and bladder training alone, in cure or urodynamic parameters with follow-up to 11 months. Dry mouth and constipation were reported with imipramine, with no adverse effects reported with bladder training ($n = 33$).[310] [EL = 1−]

Bladder training in addition to tolterodine was compared with tolterodine alone in men and women ($n = 501$; 75% women) with urinary frequency, urgency, with or without urge UI (61% with). The aim of bladder training was five to six voids per day while maintaining the same fluid intake. Combined treatment resulted in reduced frequency and increase in volume voided versus tolterodine alone, with no differences between groups in leakage or urgency episodes, patient's perception of change or adverse effects after 6 months' treatment.[311] [EL = 1++]

Bladder training versus PFMT

Two RCTs compared bladder training with biofeedback-assisted daily PFMT in women.[312,313] One did not report the type of UI or report between-group comparisons for bladder training, PFMT or no treatment ($n = 50$).[312] [EL = 1−]

The other RCT compared bladder training, biofeedback-assisted PFMT and the interventions in combination in women with stress, urge or mixed UI who had palpable pelvic floor contraction on vaginal examination.[313] After 3 months' treatment, a significantly greater reduction in leakage episodes was seen with combination treatment compared with monotherapy; this was not sustained after a further 3 months follow-up. No other significant differences were reported between groups ($n = 204$).[313] [EL = 1+]

4.3.2 Multicomponent behavioural therapy

Eight RCTs evaluated the use of a multicomponent behavioural programme that included bladder training and PFMT.[199,231,314–324] The bladder training methods used were urge strategies in three studies,[314–319] bladder training in three studies (one also included fluid management),[199,231,320] education in one study,[321,322] and one study allocated PFMT or prompted voiding depending on the cognitive status of individuals.[323,324] In four of the RCTs, biofeedback-assisted PFMT was used.[199,314,315,317–319] PFMT involved daily exercises in six studies, and the programme was not described in two.[320–322] Six studies checked the ability of individuals to contract the pelvic floor muscle at baseline.[231,314–320,323,324] Seven RCTs enrolled women only, while one enrolled men and women.[323,324]

Compared with no active treatment or usual care

In four of the RCTs, the comparison group was no active treatment or usual care. Owing to the variety of behavioural methods used, each study is described individually. One RCT in women aged 55 years or above with stress, urge or mixed UI compared a 6 month sequential programme of behavioural management (self-monitoring including fluid management, bladder training, EMG-assisted PFMT) with no active treatment. The behavioural management group achieved significantly greater improvement in leakage episodes, 24 hour pad test, QOL (IIQ) and subjective severity assessment compared with control. Only 21% were followed up to 2 years, in whom improvements seemed to be maintained. No significant differences between groups were reported in voiding frequency or interval ($n = 218$).[199] [EL= 1++]

Another RCT compared 3 months of behavioural therapy with untreated control in women with any type of incontinence. The behavioural strategies used were PFMT for stress UI, bladder training for urge UI and bladder training followed by PFMT for mixed UI. Overall, the results showed significant reduction in leakage episodes with behavioural therapy, and a higher proportion reporting improvement versus control ($n = 110$).[231] [EL = 1+] Results for the 60% of women with stress UI were reported separately, which also showed significant reduction in leakage episodes.[232]

The third RCT, in women with any type of UI, reported significant reductions in leakage episodes with 6 weeks' behavioural therapy (bladder training and PFMT) compared with no active treatment. No significant differences were reported in frequency ($n = 152$).[320] [EL = 1+]

The fourth RCT compared a 10 week behavioural therapy programme (education, PFMT), with usual care in women with stress or urge UI. Significantly greater reductions in leakage episodes were reported with behavioural therapy, with no differences between groups in QOL ($n = 145$).[321,322] [EL = 1+]

Compared with other active interventions

Two RCTs in women with urge or mixed UI compared a sequential 8 week programme of behavioural training (PFMT with anorectal biofeedback, urge strategies, repeat PFMT if needed, review and reinforcement) with oxybutynin, or self-help.[314–318] Significant reductions in leakage episodes and in nocturia were seen with behavioural training versus oxybutynin, and oxybutynin versus placebo tablets, and significantly more reported satisfaction and improvement with behavioural training versus oxybutynin. Dry mouth and inability to void were significantly more frequent with oxybutynin than control groups ($n = 197$).[314,315,317] [EL = 1+] In the study evaluating the same behavioural training programme with a group receiving biofeedback (vaginal palpation), and a self-help group receiving written instructions of the programme only, no significant differences were reported in satisfaction, improvement, QOL (IIQ, SF-36) or bladder capacity (n = 222).[318] [EL = 1++]

After the initial 8 week period of one of these RCTs,[314] women initially treated with behavioural therapy or oxybutynin who were not cured or not completely satisfied were offered the other treatment option in addition to the initial therapy for a further 8 weeks. Significant additional improvement in leakage episodes was seen in those who took oxybutynin in addition to continued behavioural treatment (n = 8) and in those who continued with oxybutynin and, in addition, underwent behavioural treatment (n = 27).[325] [EL = 2+]

A further RCT in women with predominant stress UI also compared an 8 week sequential programme of behavioural training (PFMT with anorectal biofeedback, the 'knack', managing urgency, repeat PFMT if needed, review and reinforcement), with or without the addition of electrical stimulation, with a self-help group who received written instructions of the programme (n = 200). Leakage episodes were significantly reduced in both behavioural training groups versus self-help, and significantly more of the behavioural training (electrical stimulation) group reported 'much better' improvement (versus anorectal feedback) or satisfaction with treatment (versus self-help). No differences were reported in QOL (IIQ, SF-36), or bladder capacity. Vaginal irritation was reported in 6% of the electrical stimulation group.[319] [EL = 1++]

One RCT assigned homebound adults with UI (type unspecified) to different treatment strategies depending on cognitive status: biofeedback-assisted PFMT versus control for the cognitively intact (n = 93; 91% women), or prompted voiding versus control for the cognitively impaired (n = 19; 68% women). Although reported as one trial, this was effectively two separate 8 week trials.[323,324] PFMT was significantly more effective than control in reducing leakage episodes (the only outcome reported).[323] [EL = 1+]

4.3.3 Prompted voiding

Prompted voiding and timed voiding are toileting programmes used in people who are not capable of independent toileting, such as the cognitively impaired. Prompted voiding teaches people to initiate their own toileting through requests for help and positive reinforcement from carers.[303] It has been used in institutionalised patients with cognitive and mobility problems. They are asked regularly if they wish to void and only assisted to the toilet when there is a positive response.[326]

Five RCTs compared 1 hourly prompted voiding (three studies[326–329]) or 2 hourly prompted voiding (two studies[324,330]) with usual care, or 'wet checks' only. Four studies were conducted in cognitively impaired elderly nursing home residents,[326–330] and one in homebound adults.[324] One study enrolled women only,[327] while the remainder enrolled both genders although predominantly women.

The findings of the RCTs of prompted voiding were as follows:

- significant benefit with 'functional incidental training', which included daytime 2 hour prompted voiding, in terms of leakage and urine toileting ratio compared with usual care in a 32 week study (n = 190; 84% women)[330] [EL = 1+]

- significant reduction in wet episodes versus usual care after 13 weeks' intervention, which appeared to be sustained after a further 22 weeks follow-up; no differences were reported between groups in improvement or self-initiated requests (n = 143; all women)[327] [EL = 1+]

- reductions in leakage and an increase in requests for toileting assistance during the 3 week intervention period versus wet checks only (n = 21; 71% women)[328] [EL = 1+]

- reductions in leakage and an increase in toileting into a receptacle over an intervention period of 10–20 days versus usual care (n = 126; 75% women)[326,329] [EL = 1+]

- No differences versus usual care in any outcome (leakage episodes, % wet, or self-initiated toileting) (n = 19; 68% women).[324] [EL = 1+]

None of the studies evaluating prompted voiding considered adverse effects.

A placebo-controlled RCT evaluated the effects of oxybutynin in non-responders to prompted voiding ($n = 75$; 78% women).[331] Significant improvement in leakage episodes was reported with oxybutynin after 20 days' treatment (40% versus 18% had one or fewer episodes per day). No other outcomes were significantly different (change in leakage episodes, continent voids, volume voided).[331] [EL = 1+]

4.3.4 Timed voiding

Timed voiding (scheduled, routine or regular toileting) is a passive toileting assistance programme that is initiated and maintained by a caregiver, for example for patients who cannot participate in independent toileting. Toileting is fixed by time or event, on a regular schedule or on a schedule to match the patient's voiding pattern. The aim is to avoid incontinence episodes rather than restore bladder function.[302]

Three RCTs evaluated timed voiding in cognitively impaired elderly men and women (predominantly women) who were nursing home residents (two studies),[332,333] or had caregiver support at home (one study).[334] The comparator was no active treatment.

One 6 month RCT reported significant reduction in leakage episodes in the intervention group (scheduled toileting according to voiding pattern, mostly about 2 hours, and advice on fluid intake and environment; $n = 118$, 69% women).[334] [EL = 1+] A cluster RCT of 36 weeks' duration reported limited results indicating greater reductions in leakage episodes, with scheduled toileting (toileting within 30 minutes prior to an individual's mean voiding time) but no differences between groups in volume voided ($n = 113$; 82% women).[332] [EL = 1−]

The third RCT compared timed voiding (2 hourly) in combination with antimuscarinic drugs for urge UI, or PFMT for stress UI, with no active intervention for 8 weeks ($n = 278$; 83% women). Significant improvements in night-time leakage episodes were reported in the active intervention group, but not in daytime leakage or pad test findings.[333] [EL = 1+]

None of the studies evaluating timed voiding considered adverse effects.

Evidence statements for behavioural therapies

Bladder training is more effective than no treatment in women with urge or mixed UI, at 6 months follow-up. In women with urge UI, bladder training had a similar subjective cure rate to oxybutynin after a 6 week programme but adverse effects and relapse rates were lower with bladder training. The combination of oxybutynin or tolterodine and bladder training programmes results in greater reduction in frequency of micturition but has not been shown to lead to further improvements in incontinence. Combination treatment of bladder training together with PFMT may confer a greater short-term benefit to women with stress, urge or mixed UI, but in the long term combination and monotherapies are equally effective. [EL = 1+]

A wide range of behavioural therapies have been used within multicomponent treatment regimens in women with stress, mixed or urge UI. All appear to show improvements in leakage episodes over comparators (no active treatment, drug therapy, written instructions, usual care) within a 6 week to 6 month time frame. [EL = 1+] No direct comparisons of single-component behavioural therapy with multicomponent behavioural therapies were identified.

Prompted voiding and timed voiding strategies lead to reduced leakage episodes in cognitively impaired men and women. [EL = 1+]

From evidence to recommendations
Bladder training is less costly than most antimuscarinic drug treatment and is not associated with adverse effects. [EL = 4]

Recommendations for behavioural therapies

Bladder training lasting for a minimum of 6 weeks should be offered as first-line treatment to women with urge or mixed UI. [A]

If women do not achieve satisfactory benefit from bladder training programmes, the combination of an antimuscarinic agent with bladder training should be considered if frequency is a troublesome symptom. [A]

In women with UI who also have cognitive impairment, prompted and timed voiding toileting programmes are recommended as strategies for reducing leakage episodes. [A]

Research recommendation for behavioural therapies

A direct comparison of single-component and multicomponent behavioural therapy is required.

4.4 Drug therapies

4.4.1 Antimuscarinic drugs

Drugs with antimuscarinic action are used to treat OAB. They block muscarinic receptors in the bladder, which reduces the ability of bladder muscle to contract and affects bladder sensation. The drugs differ in their selectivity for various muscarinic receptors, and some drugs have additional actions such as direct smooth muscle effects.

Several systematic reviews of antimuscarinic drugs for the treatment of UI and/or OAB were identified.[335–340] These reviews included studies conducted only in men, and in patients with neurogenic bladders, both of which are outside the scope of this guideline. The fully published RCTs included in these reviews were thus considered individually, together with other relevant RCTs. In addition, because of the relatively short duration of most RCTs, case series (so-called 'extension studies') were also considered as these provide longer term data.

The use of antimuscarinic drugs with bladder training was considered in the behavioural section (4.3.1). Studies evaluating imipramine, oxybutynin and tolterodine in this context were identified, which showed that the combination of antimuscarinic drugs and bladder training programmes resulted in greater reduction in frequency but did not lead to further improvements in incontinence.[308–311]

In the following section, placebo-controlled studies of antimuscarinic drugs are considered first, followed by comparisons of the drugs.

Placebo-controlled trials of antimuscarinic drugs

Darifenacin
Two DB RCTs compared darifenacin extended release (ER) with placebo in men and women ($n = 398$, $n = 561$; ~85% women) with urge UI, frequency and urgency. In both studies, significantly greater improvement in leakage episodes, frequency, urgency episodes and severity were seen with darifenacin 7.5–15 mg compared with placebo after 12 weeks' treatment. Reductions in leakage episodes of 62–73% were reported with darifenacin compared with 49–56% with placebo, the reductions in frequency episodes were in the range 15–19% versus 8–10%, and for urgency 28–29% versus 11–13%. No significant differences were seen between darifenacin and placebo groups in changes in nocturnal awakening due to OAB. Adverse effects occurring more frequently with darifenacin included constipation (14–21% versus ~7%), dry mouth (19–31% versus 9%) and headache (4–7% versus 2–5%).[341,342] One of the studies also had a darifenacin 3.75 mg treatment arm, for which no formal comparisons were made against placebo.[341] [EL = 1+]

A further two placebo-controlled RCTs of 2 and 12 weeks' duration were designed to evaluate the effects of darifenacin ER 30 mg on the outcome of warning time in men and women with urgency ($n = 72$; 71% women) or urge UI ($n = 439$).[343,344] One study was of poor quality[343] [EL = 1−] while the other was of good quality.[344] [EL = 1+] Neither study reported significant differences between groups in this outcome, nor in urgency episodes. Urge UI episodes were significantly reduced with darifenacin compared with placebo in the larger study.[343]

Flavoxate

Two DB placebo-controlled crossover RCTs evaluated 2 weeks' treatment with flavoxate for idiopathic DO.[345,346] The first RCT in men and women ($n = 41$; only 25 analysed; 48% women) found no significant differences between flavoxate 200 mg t.d.s. and placebo in any urodynamic parameters. Complete results were not given for frequency, the only other outcome.[345] [EL = 1−] The second RCT, in women only, found no significant differences between flavoxate 200 mg q.d.s. and placebo in frequency (median per three days 25 versus 23), nocturia (medians 3 versus 0), or leakage episodes (medians 1 versus 0) after treatment ($n = 20$). The most common adverse effects reported across all treatment groups were dry mouth (5–7%), and nausea or heartburn (2–7%).[346] [EL = 1+]

A DB randomised study compared two different daily doses of flavoxate (600 or 1200 mg), given for 4 weeks to women with sensory and/or motor urge syndrome or incontinence ($n = 27$). Symptoms were scored on a scale of 0 to 2; no results were provided for individual symptoms although it was reported that total scores fell from baseline in both groups. Of the urodynamic variables evaluated, greater benefit was seen with the 1200 mg dose in volume at first desire to void and in bladder volume at capacity. Nausea was reported by about 22% of the women.[347] [EL = 1−]

A further RCT compared a combination of flavoxate and imipramine with bladder training. Significantly more women were subjectively or objectively cured after 4 weeks' bladder training than with drug therapy ($n = 50$).[307] [EL = 1+]

Imipramine and other tricyclic antidepressants

No placebo-controlled RCTs evaluating the use of imipramine for UI were identified. A DB placebo-controlled crossover RCT involving 3 week treatment periods evaluated doxepin (50–75 mg at night) in women with DO and frequency, urgency or urge UI, who had failed to respond to other drugs, mainly antimuscarinics ($n = 19$). Significantly greater reduction in night leakage episodes and frequency were seen with doxepin compared with placebo, and a greater increase in maximum cystometric capacity. No significant differences were reported between groups in day leakage episodes, frequency or the 1 hour pad test. More doxepin-treated women reported adverse effects than those treated with placebo (68% versus 16%).[348] [EL = 1+]

Oxybutynin

Four RCTs of 8–12 weeks' duration compared various formulations and/or doses of oxybutynin (oral in three, transdermal in one) and tolterodine, in studies that also included placebo arms. The studies generally showed greater benefit in efficacy outcomes with oxybutynin and tolterodine compared with placebo, although with varying statistical significance. Reductions in frequency of 15–21% were seen with oxybutynin and tolterodine compared with 10–11% with placebo, reductions in leakage episodes were 46–77% versus 19–46%, and subjective improvement rates were 38–73% versus 22–53%.[349–352]

Another placebo-controlled crossover RCT evaluated immediate release (IR) oxybutynin 2.5–5 mg t.d.s. in cognitively impaired elderly nursing home residents who had not responded to 2 hourly prompted voiding ($n = 75$; 78% women). Significant improvement in leakage episodes was reported with IR oxybutynin after 20 days' treatment (40% versus 18% had one or fewer episodes per day). No other outcomes were significantly different (change in leakage episodes, continent voids).[331] [EL = 1+]

Transdermal oxybutynin was evaluated in a DB placebo-controlled RCT in women with urge UI and frequency, 66% of who had mixed UI ($n = 520$). Three doses were assessed: 1.3, 2.6 and 3.9 mg. Significantly greater improvement in outcomes was seen with oxybutynin 3.9 mg compared with placebo after 12 weeks' treatment (leakage episodes, frequency and IIQ scores) but not with other dosages. Of the 22% previously treated with antimuscarinics, 'similar trends' in results were reported.[353] [EL = 1+] A further 12 weeks' open use of transdermal oxybutynin by 411 patients generally showed sustained improvement in leakage episodes, frequency, and QOL (IIQ) with all doses. Application-site reactions and dry mouth were common with oxybutynin.[353] [EL = 3]

One RCT evaluated 12 days' treatment with intravesical oxybutynin (20 mg) compared with placebo in women with frequency and DO ($n = 56$; 43 analysed). Nine women withdrew from treatment, three from the active group owing to the need for daily catheterisation and six from the placebo group owing to lack of improvement; all were excluded from the analyses. In the remaining women who were assessed 2 weeks after treatment, improvements in frequency and bladder capacity were seen in both groups, with no between-group analyses reported.[354] [EL = 1−]

Propantheline
No placebo-controlled studies were identified for propantheline.

Propiverine
A DB placebo-controlled RCT was conducted to evaluate the cardiac effects of propiverine in men and women with frequency, urgency, and mixed or urge UI during 4 weeks' treatment ($n = 107$; 98 analysed; 79% women). Urinary outcomes were reported although the groups were not balanced at baseline for these outcomes. Additionally, no between-group comparisons were made. Of the cardiac monitoring undertaken, the only difference noted between groups was a greater increase in minimum heart rate on a 24 hour electrocardiogram with propiverine than with placebo.[355] [EL = 1−]

A randomised study evaluated four dosages of propiverine (15, 30, 45 and 60 mg daily) given for 3 weeks to men and women with urge UI (43%) or urgency (57%) ($n = 185$; 98% women). Improvements from baseline were seen in all dosage groups in frequency and in urodynamic parameters. Blurred vision was the most common adverse effect (8–26%), followed by dry mouth (6–27%). A dose–response effect was evident for adverse effects. Subjective efficacy and tolerability showed optimum effects with the 30 mg dose.[356] [EL = 1+]

Solifenacin
One DB dose-finding RCT evaluated solifenacin daily doses of 2.5, 5, 10 and 20 mg compared with tolterodine 2 mg b.d. and placebo in men and women with idiopathic DO ($n = 225$; ~60% women). After 4 weeks' treatment, reduction in frequency was significantly greater with 5, 10 and 20 mg solifenacin compared with placebo (18–23% versus 9%). No significant differences were seen between solifenacin and placebo groups in leakage and urgency episodes. QOL (CONTILIFE) was significantly improved in all solifenacin groups compared with placebo. Adverse effects seen with solifenacin (dry mouth, constipation, blurred vision) showed a dose–response relationship.[357] [EL = 1+]

Two DB RCTs of 12 weeks' duration compared solifenacin 5 mg o.d. and 10 mg o.d. with placebo in men and women with OAB (the proportions of women were 75% and 82%).[358,359] Overall, 57% had UI in one study (47% urge UI),[358] and 93% in the other (63% urge UI).[359] One study also had a tolterodine 2 mg b.d. treatment arm.[359] About 33% in both studies had had prior drug treatment for OAB; treatment response in these patients was not considered separately. In one of the studies, reductions in frequency, leakage and urgency episodes were significantly greater with solifenacin 5 and 10 mg compared with placebo. Reduction in nocturia was significantly greater with solifenacin 10 mg versus placebo ($n = 857$).[358] In the second study, significantly greater reductions in frequency were seen with both solifenacin doses and with tolterodine compared with placebo. Reductions in urgency and leakage episodes were significantly greater with solifenacin 5 and 10 mg compared with placebo ($n = 1033$).[359]

Across the studies, the improvements in each outcome with solifenacin, tolterodine and placebo were: frequency 17–22% versus 15% versus 8–13%; leakage episodes 47–61% versus 59% versus 28–29%; urgency episodes 51–55% versus 38% versus 33%; nocturia 25–39% solifenacin versus 16% placebo. Adverse effects reported in both studies were dry mouth, constipation and blurred vision, which occurred in more solifenacin-treated patients than with placebo.[358,359] [EL = 1+]

A total of 1633 (91%) of the patients from the two 12 week RCTs took solifenacin 5 or 10 mg for up to 1 year. The results indicate continued benefit. Dry mouth was the most common adverse effect, reported by 21%.[360] [EL = 3]

Results for QOL (KHQ) during both RCTs[358,359] and the case series[360] have been published separately. Pooled results from the RCTs show significantly greater improvements in nine of ten domains (except personal relationships) with solifenacin 5 mg or 10 mg compared with placebo. The longer term study suggested sustained improvement.[361] [EL = 3]

Tolterodine

Three DB RCTs compared 4 weeks' treatment with tolterodine 1 mg and 2 mg b.d. with placebo in men and women with frequency, urgency and/or urge UI (72–75%). The majority of patients were women (65–79% of $n = 670$).[362–364] One enrolled patients aged at least 65 years.[362] In one study, significantly greater reductions in frequency, urgency and leakage episodes were seen with tolterodine 2 mg b.d., although groups were not balanced at baseline in frequency or leakage. Dry mouth was significantly more common in tolterodine-treated patients. Response to treatment in patients who had previously received drug treatment for OAB was not considered separately.[362] [EL = 1−]

In the second study, significantly greater reductions in leakage episodes were seen with both tolterodine doses compared with placebo (41% versus 17%), with no significant differences between tolterodine and placebo in improvements in frequency (13% versus 10% reporting reductions). Of the 75% of patients who had poor efficacy response to prior drug treatment, 37–51% across the groups in this study had a 'good response'. Dry mouth was significantly more common in the tolterodine 2 mg b.d. group compared with placebo (34% versus 6%).[364] [EL = 1+] The third RCT only reported urodynamic outcomes, with no bladder diary data or patients' perception of change. Increases in volume at first contraction and maximum cystometric capacity were significantly greater with tolterodine 2 mg b.d. compared with placebo.[363] [EL = 1+]

Following completion of these three studies, patients were offered continued treatment with tolterodine 2 mg b.d. for a further 12 months.[365] Overall, 62% continued treatment for this duration, with 23% reducing the dose to 1 mg b.d. Reasons stated for withdrawal were adverse events (15%), loss to follow-up or withdrew consent (17%). The results for bladder diary variables indicate sustained benefit in those who continued treatment. Dry mouth was the most common adverse effect.[365] [EL = 3]

One DB placebo-controlled RCT evaluated 12 weeks' treatment with tolterodine 1 mg and 2 mg b.d. in men and women with DO ($n = 316$; 75% women). Significantly greater reductions in frequency were seen with both tolterodine groups compared with placebo (~20% versus 12%). More patients treated with tolterodine 2 mg b.d. reported improvement compared with other groups. No other significant differences were seen (leakage episodes, cure or adverse effects). Overall, 46% had had prior drug treatment for OAB; results in these patients were not considered separately.[366] [EL = 1+]

Four RCTs of 8–12 weeks' duration that compared oxybutynin (oral in three, transdermal in one) with tolterodine also had placebo arms. The studies generally showed greater benefit in efficacy outcomes with oxybutynin and tolterodine compared with placebo, although with varying statistical significance. Reductions in frequency of 15–21% were seen with oxybutynin and tolterodine, compared with 10–11% with placebo; reductions in leakage episodes ranged from 46% to 77% versus 19–46%, and subjective improvement rates ranged from 38% to 73% versus 22–53% (see later).[349–352]

Extended release tolterodine

Two formulations of tolterodine (2 mg b.d. and 4 mg ER o.d.) were compared in a 12 week placebo-controlled DB RCT in men and women with frequency and urge UI ($n = 1529$; 81% women). Two-thirds of the population were aged at least 65 years. Significantly greater improvements in outcomes were seen in both tolterodine groups compared with placebo (reductions in frequency of 15% versus 17% versus 11%; leakage episodes 46% versus 53% versus 30%). QOL was assessed using KHQ and SF-36 questionnaires. In both tolterodine groups, improvements in six or seven of the ten KHQ domains were greater than with placebo. No differences were seen between groups in the SF-36. Dry mouth was reported by significantly fewer patients treated with ER than standard tolterodine (23% versus 30%, compared with 8% placebo).[367–373] [EL = 1+] No differences in efficacy or tolerability were seen in older (65 years or above) compared with younger patients.[369]

Following completion of this study, patients were offered continued treatment with ER tolterodine 4 mg for 12 months.[374] Overall, 71% continued treatment ($n = 1077$; 82% women). Reasons stated for withdrawal included adverse events (10%) and loss to follow-up or withdrawal of consent (8%). The results for bladder diary variables indicated sustained benefit for those who continued treatment. Dry mouth was the most common adverse effect.[374] [EL = 3]

A further DB placebo-controlled RCT compared ER tolterodine 4 mg o.d. with placebo in women with urge-predominant mixed UI, frequency and urgency over 8 weeks (n = 854). Significantly greater improvements were seen with tolterodine compared with placebo in frequency, urge leakage episodes, urgency, subjective improvement and QOL (KHQ). In women with predominant stress UI (25%), improvements in leakage episodes were not significantly different between groups. Significantly more tolterodine-treated women reported dry mouth.[375] EL = 1++]

Trospium

Results from two placebo-controlled RCTs[376,377] that evaluated 3 weeks' treatment with trospium 20 mg b.d., in men and women with DO were pooled in a meta-analysis (n = 508; 69% women). The main outcomes were urodynamic parameters, with greater improvement reported with trospium in maximum cystometric capacity and volume at first contraction. More trospium-treated patients reported subjective cure or marked improvement of symptoms.[378] [EL = 1+]

Three further placebo-controlled RCTs evaluated trospium.[379–381] Two evaluated trospium 20 mg b.d. in men and women with symptoms of OAB (total n = 1170; 78% women). Improvements in efficacy outcomes were significantly greater with trospium after 12 weeks' treatment (frequency, urgency, urge UI episodes, QOL [IIQ]). Dry mouth was reported by more trospium-treated patients (21% versus 6%).[380,381] [EL = 1+] A smaller RCT of 4 weeks' duration compared trospium 15 mg t.d.s. with placebo in men and women with urge UI. No differences in adverse effects or in maximum cystometric capacity were found between groups, although groups were not balanced at baseline for cystometric capacity (n = 46; ~92% women).[379] [EL = 1−]

Comparisons of antimuscarinic drugs

Immediate release oxybutynin versus flavoxate
A DB crossover RCT compared flavoxate 400 mg t.d.s. with IR oxybutynin 5 mg t.d.s. in women with urgency (n = 50; only 41 analysed). No significant differences were found between groups in urodynamic findings or subjective cure or improvement after 4 weeks' treatment. Bladder diary outcomes were assessed using a scoring system of 0 to 2, with no between-group analyses reported. Significantly more oxybutynin-treated women reported adverse effects (90% versus 27%).[382] [EL = 1−]

Immediate release oxybutynin versus propantheline
A single-blind crossover RCT compared propantheline 15 mg t.d.s. with IR oxybutynin 5 mg t.d.s. in women with OAB (n = 23). Significantly greater increases in cystometric capacity were seen with oxybutynin compared with propantheline after 4 weeks' treatment (36% versus 17%), with no differences between treatments in frequency, subjective improvement or adverse effects.[383] [EL = 1+]

Immediate release oxybutynin versus propiverine
One DB placebo-controlled RCT compared 4 weeks' treatment with IR oxybutynin 5 mg b.d. and propiverine 15 mg t.d.s. in men and women with urgency or urge UI (n = 366; 310 analysed; 93% women). Physician's assessment of improvement, and incidence of adverse effects, was significantly higher with both drugs than with placebo. No other significant differences were identified between the three groups (frequency, urgency or cystometric capacity). Results for only 85% were analysed, with no explanation for withdrawals.[384] [EL = 1−]

Oxybutynin versus tolterodine
Oxybutynin and tolterodine were compared in ten RCTs, six of which were DB comparisons of standard (immediate release) formulations of both drugs (oxybutynin 5 mg b.d. or t.d.s. with tolterodine 2 mg b.d.).[349,350,385–388] The four other comparisons were: transdermal oxybutynin versus ER tolterodine;[351] IR oxybutynin versus ER tolterodine;[352] ER oxybutynin versus IR tolterodine;[389,390] and ER formulations of both drugs.[391–393]

Immediate release oxybutynin versus tolterodine
Four DB studies compared the effectiveness of oxybutynin and tolterodine, in men and women (predominantly women; 67–77%) with OAB. Duration of treatment ranged from 8 to 12 weeks.[349,350,385,386] Across the studies, between 27% and 60% of the study populations had previously received drug treatment for OAB or urge UI. The response to treatment in these groups was not considered separately in the study reports.

Two of the four RCTs compared tolterodine 2 mg b.d. with oxybutynin 5 mg b.d. (starting at a lower dose of 2.5 mg b.d.). The primary outcome of dry mouth occurred in significantly more oxybutynin-treated patients than with tolterodine (61% versus 37%). No significant differences were seen between groups in efficacy outcomes (*n* = 378).[386] [EL = 1+] A study in Asian patients reported similar findings (*n* = 228).[385] [EL = 1+]

Two placebo-controlled RCTs of identical design compared tolterodine 2 mg b.d. with oxybutynin 5 mg t.d.s., although one only reported efficacy data for completers (53% of those randomised). Both found no significant differences between treatments in frequency or in leakage episodes, while significantly more people treated with oxybutynin reported dry mouth. Improvements in efficacy outcomes were significantly greater with tolterodine and oxybutynin compared with placebo (*n* = 293),[349] [EL = 1+] (*n* = 277; 147 analysed).[350] [EL = 1−] Following completion of these two studies (and two other RCTs), patients were offered continued open treatment with tolterodine 2 mg b.d. for a further 9 months.[394] Overall 70% continued treatment, with 13% reducing the dose to 1 mg b.d. Reasons stated for withdrawal were adverse events (9%), lack of efficacy (6%), loss to follow-up or withdrew consent (10%). Bladder diary variables indicated sustained benefit in those who continued treatment. Dry mouth was the most common adverse effect (28%).[394] [EL = 3]

Two open RCTs with specific objectives provide further comparative data for tolterodine and oxybutynin in women with OAB. Duration of treatment was 10–12 weeks; one was a crossover study.[387,388] The main objective of one study was to assess whether urodynamic grade predicts response to treatment; this also reported no differences between tolterodine 2 mg b.d. and oxybutynin 5 mg t.d.s. in frequency or cystometric capacity (*n* = 128; 107 analysed).[387] [EL = 1−] The other RCT evaluated the impact of dry mouth with tolterodine 2 mg b.d. and oxybutynin 5 mg b.d. using a 'Xerostomia Questionnaire.' The authors reported no significant differences between groups in this outcome, but no numerical results were presented.[388] [EL = 1+]

Transdermal oxybutynin versus extended release tolterodine
Transdermal oxybutynin 3.9 mg was compared with ER tolterodine 4 mg o.d. in a placebo-controlled DB RCT in men and women with frequency and urge UI (*n* = 361; 93% women). No significant differences were seen between active treatments in any outcome (frequency, leakage episodes, QOL, adverse effects) after 12 weeks' treatment. Improvements in frequency were significantly greater with tolterodine compared with placebo, and significantly greater benefit was seen in leakage episodes and subjective cure or improvement with both active drugs compared with placebo.[351] [EL = 1+]

Immediate release oxybutynin versus extended release tolterodine
Extended release tolterodine 4 mg o.d. was compared with IR oxybutynin 3 mg t.d.s. in a placebo-controlled DB RCT in men and women with urgency, frequency, and urge UI (*n* = 605; 70% women). No differences in efficacy measures were seen between tolterodine or oxybutynin, but fewer people treated with tolterodine experienced dry mouth after 12 weeks' treatment. Improvements in leakage episodes and frequency were significantly greater with active treatment compared with placebo. No significant differences were seen between the three groups in the proportion of people reporting improvement. Overall, 24% had received prior drug treatment for OAB; the response in these patients was not considered separately.[352] [EL = 1+] Treatment was continued in 31% of patients for up to 12 months; the results available indicate continued efficacy.[395] [EL = 3]

Extended release oxybutynin versus immediate release tolterodine
One DB RCT compared IR tolterodine 2 mg b.d. with ER oxybutynin 10 mg o.d. in men and women with urge UI, of whom 40% had previously been treated with antimuscarinic drugs (*n* = 378; 83%

women). Results were presented for study completers only (88%), with statistical analysis quoted for all patients randomised, which indicated consistent effects. Significantly greater reductions in leakage episodes (urge and total) and in frequency were seen with ER oxybutynin compared with IR tolterodine after 12 weeks' treatment. No significant differences were identified between groups in adverse effects reported.[389,390] [EL = 1+]

Extended release oxybutynin versus extended release tolterodine

One DB RCT compared ER formulations of both tolterodine and oxybutynin in women with OAB, 47% of whom had previously received antimuscarinic treatment. No significant differences were found between ER tolterodine 4 mg o.d. and ER oxybutynin 10 mg o.d. in changes in leakage episodes (urge or total), while reductions in frequency were reported to be significantly greater with ER oxybutynin (mean reductions of 28% versus 25%) with 12 weeks' treatment. Dry mouth occurred in significantly more women in the oxybutynin group (30% versus 22%) ($n = 790$).[391–393] [EL = 1+]

Immediate release oxybutynin versus trospium

One DB RCT compared IR oxybutynin 5 mg b.d. with trospium 20 mg b.d. in men and women with urge syndrome ($n = 357$; 86% women). After 1 year, improvements in frequency, urgency and cystometric capacity were seen in both groups, with between-group analysis only reported for cystometric capacity. The incidence of dry mouth and gastrointestinal effects was significantly higher with oxybutynin (50% versus 33% and 51% versus 39%, respectively).[396] [EL = 1+]

Solifenacin versus extended release tolterodine

In men and women ($n = 1200$; 87% women) with OAB, solifenacin 5 to 10 mg (dose increased on patient request in 48%) was compared with ER tolterodine 4 mg daily in a 3 month study. The proportion of patients with UI was not reported. The aim of the study was to demonstrate non-inferiority of solifenacin to ER tolterodine in frequency of micturition, which was proven. The two drugs were not significantly different in terms of improvements in nocturia, but improvements in leakage and urgency episodes were significantly greater with solifenacin, as was the reduction in pad usage. The patients' perception of their bladder condition was also reportedly improved to a greater extent with solifenacin than with tolterodine. The adverse effects listed occurred with both drugs: dry mouth (30% solifenacin versus 24% tolterodine), constipation (6% versus 3%) and blurred vision (1% versus 2%). Discontinuation rates were 6% versus 7%.[397] [EL = 1+]

Different formulations of the same drug compared

Transdermal versus immediate release oral oxybutynin

Transdermal oxybutynin (2.6–5.2 mg) and IR oral oxybutynin (5 mg b.d. to 7.5 mg t.d.s.), were compared in a 6 week RCT in men and women (92% women) with DO, all of whom had urge UI and who were currently responding to oral oxybutynin ($n = 76$). No significant differences were identified in efficacy (leakage episodes, cure) between treatment groups. Significantly more patients reported dry mouth with oral oxybutynin (39% versus 82%).[398] [EL = 1+]

Extended versus immediate release oxybutynin

Four DB RCTs compared ER and IR oral oxybutynin formulations in men and women with urge UI,[399–402] (with frequency in two studies[399,401]). In three RCTs, the population had previously responded to oxybutynin or to other antimuscarinic treatment.[400–402] Treatment duration ranged from 4 to 6 weeks. Three of the studies allowed dose titration of oxybutynin; the daily doses taken were within 5–30 mg (ER) or 5–20 mg (IR formulation).[399,400,402] One study compared 10 mg given as a single ER daily dose or a twice daily dose of IR oxybutynin.[401] Each study included men and women (n range 105 to 226), with the majority in each study being female (68–92%).

In both 6 week studies, only adverse effects were reported for all patients; efficacy outcomes were only reported for those who completed treatment,[400] or who completed at least 2 weeks' treatment and followed the protocol.[399] [EL = 1–] The other two studies were of higher quality.[401,402] [EL = 1+] Two of the studies reported no significant differences in efficacy or adverse effects between ER and IR oxybutynin.[399,401] One study reported that the incidence of dry mouth was significantly lower with ER oxybutynin (68% versus 87%).[400] One found no significant differences between ER and IR oxybutynin in incidence of dry mouth, although the cumulative rate of the first report of dry mouth, at a given dose, was significantly lower with ER oxybutynin.[402]

A case series evaluated treatment with ER oxybutynin 5–30 mg for 1 year in men and women with urge or mixed UI ($n = 1067$; 85% women). Overall, 46% continued treatment to 1 year; the main reasons for withdrawal were adverse effects (24%) and lack of efficacy (10%). Significant improvement was seen in impact on sleep and in the effects of leakage on lifestyle at 1 year (measured using the IIQ questionnaire).[403] [EL = 3]

Extended versus immediate release tolterodine

In one placebo-controlled DB RCT, the reduction in leakage episodes was significantly greater with ER tolterodine 4 mg o.d. compared with IR tolterodine 2 mg b.d. (median reductions 71% versus 60% at 12 weeks) in men and women with frequency and urge UI ($n = 1529$; 81% women). Dry mouth was reported by significantly fewer patients treated with ER than IR tolterodine (23% versus 30%, compared with 8% placebo).[367–373] [EL = 1+]

Economic evidence

From the health economics literature review, a total of seven articles were included as being relevant to the question of which is the most cost effective drug treatment for OAB. The design and the results of all included studies are presented in the evidence tables. All the studies included economic models, and the efficacy data used to populate these models was derived from a number of sources – trial data, literature review and expert opinion. All but two of the studies made some comparison between one or more of the formulations for oxybutynin and tolterodine. Two of the studies were based exclusively on a UK setting.[404,405] One other study also considered the UK context, in addition to France and Austria.[406]

In the studies that considered oxybutynin, the general conclusion was that ER oxybutynin was cost effective. Two studies reported that it dominated IR tolterodine, being at least as cheap and more efficacious.[404,407] In addition, a further two studies reported that ER oxybutynin dominated IR oxybutynin in addition to ER tolterodine.[406,408] One UK study noted that IR oxybutynin was cheaper than ER oxybutynin and all formulations of tolterodine.[405] It reported that IR oxybutynin and ER formulations of oxybutynin and tolterodine might all be considered cost effective contingent on the willingness of the NHS to pay for an additional incontinent-free week. However, it noted that IR tolterodine did not appear cost effective as it was more expensive but no more efficacious than ER formulations.

One Canadian study reported that tolterodine appeared cost effective in a population who had discontinued initial oxybutynin therapy.[409] The comparison was against no further treatment and they argued that the incremental cost effectiveness ratio (ICER) fell within cost effectiveness thresholds for willingness to pay. Finally, a Swedish study compared the cost effectiveness of tolterodine against no treatment.[410] They reported that the incremental cost per quality-adjusted life year (QALY) with tolterodine fell within the threshold generally accepted as cost effective.

Where treatments are of equivalent efficacy, the cheapest treatment will generally be the most cost effective. Since we did not find consistent evidence of greater efficacy of one antimuscarinic over another, a cost minimisation analysis has been adopted in this guideline. One possible criticism of such a cost minimisation approach is that it does not sufficiently take into account the differences between drugs and formulations in terms of their adverse effects and tolerability profile. While recognising a certain validity in this criticism, we believe that the cost minimisation approach was justified because of a lack of head-to-head trials, the difficulties of comparing across studies using different study designs, and evidence from actual practice showing low persistence with all antimuscarinic therapy.[403,412] Furthermore, good prescribing practice requires that patients be reviewed when starting on new pharmacological treatment and therefore the costs of switching from a poorly tolerated drug are, at least partly, subsumed within this review process. The costs (see Appendix E) were based on a typical dose, as determined by the GDG, taken for 12 months and using prices published in BNF 50. Based on this, non-proprietary oxybutynin is the most cost effective.

Evidence statements for antimuscarinic drugs

Treatment with darifenacin, oxybutynin, solifenacin, tolterodine and trospium in women with OAB is associated with improvements in frequency, leakage episodes and quality of life. [EL = 1+] There is no evidence of a clinically important difference in efficacy between antimuscarinic drugs. Based on the cost minimisation analysis undertaken, non-proprietary immediate release oxybutynin is the most cost effective antimuscarinic drug.

Propiverine may be associated with an improvement in frequency. [EL = 1+] There is limited evidence that doxepin reduces night-time leakage episodes and nocturia. [EL = 1+] There is no evidence of efficacy for the use of flavoxate, propantheline or imipramine for the treatment of UI or OAB. [EL = 4]

Antimuscarinic adverse effects are common with all antimuscarinic drugs, and dry mouth is more likely with oral IR oxybutynin than tolterodine, trospium, ER or transdermal oxybutynin, but skin reactions are very common with the latter. [EL = 1+] In view of the high incidence of adverse effects and the time to maximum benefit the GDG believes that early treatment review is good practice. [EL = 4]

Recommendations for antimuscarinic drugs

Immediate release non-proprietary oxybutynin should be offered to women with OAB or mixed UI as first-line antimuscarinic drug treatment, if bladder training has been ineffective. If immediate release oxybutynin is not well tolerated, darifenacin, solifenacin, tolterodine, trospium or an extended release or transdermal formulation of oxybutynin should be considered as alternatives. Women should be counselled about the adverse effects of antimuscarinic drugs. [A]

An early treatment review should be undertaken following any change in antimuscarinic drug therapy. [D (GPP)]

Propiverine should be considered as an option to treat frequency of urination in women with OAB, but is not recommended for the treatment of UI. [A]

Flavoxate, propantheline and imipramine should not be used for the treatment of UI or OAB in women. [A]

Research recommendation for antimuscarinic drugs

There is a need for a comparison of the clinical effectiveness and cost effectiveness of drug therapy compared with other conservative therapy as first-line treatment for women with OAB or mixed UI.

4.4.2   **Desmopressin**

Desmopressin (also known as DDAVP) is a synthetic analogue of vasopressin or antidiuretic hormone, which acts by inhibiting diuresis while avoiding vasopressive effects. Used at night, it decreases nocturnal urine production.

Nocturia

Three DB placebo-controlled RCTs evaluated the use of desmopressin for nocturia. One evaluated 3 weeks' treatment in women ($n = 144$),[413] who were then offered continued desmopressin treatment for up to 1 year.[414] The two other RCTs were smaller crossover studies that evaluated 2 weeks' treatment ($n = 17$, $n = 25$),[415,416] one of which enrolled men and women.[415] An oral formulation of desmopressin was used in two studies (dose ranging from 100 to 400 μg),[413–415] and an intranasal formulation in the third (dose 20 μg).[416]

In the 3 week RCT in women, significantly greater improvements were seen with desmopressin in all nocturia-related outcomes (nocturia episodes, volume of nocturnal voids, duration of sleep to first nocturnal void, diuresis, ratio of day/night to 24 hour urine volume), and a reduction in the 'bothersome factor' of nocturia (assessed using BFLUTS).[413] [EL = 1+] Follow-up of women who took desmopressin for up to 1 year indicated sustained benefit in the outcomes measured (50% or greater reduction in nocturia, duration of sleep to first nocturnal void, 'bothersome factor').[414] [EL = 3]

In the crossover study in men and women, nocturia episodes and nocturnal diuresis were significantly lower with desmopressin compared with placebo, with no significant change in either group in 24 hour diuresis.[415] [EL = 1+] Nocturnal frequency and urine output were significantly reduced with desmopressin (from baseline and compared with placebo) in the crossover study in women only, with no significant change in diurnal outcomes.[416] [EL = 1+]

Urinary incontinence

A placebo-controlled 'pilot' RCT evaluated the use of desmopressin in the treatment of women with daytime UI. Four sequences of desmopressin 40 μg (seven doses) or placebo (three doses) were evaluated, with treatment administered intranasally when required. At both 4 and 24 hours after dose administration, the number of periods with no leakage was greater with desmopressin compared with placebo, and the volume voided or leaked during a UI episode lower with active treatment, although the confidence intervals for all mean values overlapped, indicating that differences were not statistically significant.[417] [EL = 1+]

Adverse effects

Adverse effects reported across the short-term studies included headache, nausea, hyponatraemia, abdominal pain, frequency, dry mouth, dizziness, fatigue, peripheral oedema and earache.[415–417] In the longer term study (up to 1 year), the most frequent adverse effects related to treatment in women were: hyponatraemia 12% (none required treatment, none with sodium below 125 mmol/l); headache 7%; frequency, peripheral oedema and UTI (each 3%); and nausea and dizziness (each 2%).[414]

Evidence statements for desmopressin

The use of desmopressin significantly reduces nocturia. There is insufficient evidence that desmopressin reduces incontinence in adult women. A reduction in serum sodium is very common (more than 10%). [EL = 1+]

Symptomatic hyponatraemia due to therapy with desmopressin may be more common in elderly women, and is more likely to occur soon after treatment initiation. Pretreatment and early post-treatment (72 hours) serum sodium monitoring is recommended. Where there are new symptoms or a change in medication, further measurement of serum sodium is recommended. [EL = 4]

Recommendations for desmopressin

The use of desmopressin may be considered specifically to reduce nocturia in women with UI or OAB who find it a troublesome symptom. [A]

However, the use of desmopressin for nocturia in women with idiopathic UI is outside the UK marketing authorisation for the product. Informed consent to treatment should be obtained and documented.

4.4.3 Diuretics

Only one RCT involving women was identified. This was a small DB placebo-controlled crossover study that evaluated bumetanide 1 mg for the treatment of nocturia in men and women (*n* = 33; 28 completed; 13 women). Treatment was given 4–6 hours before bedtime for 2 weeks. Weekly nocturia episodes were significantly fewer after bumetanide treatment compared with placebo (10 versus 14).[418] [EL = 1−] No studies evaluating furosemide in women were identified.

Evidence statement for diuretics

There is insufficient evidence to support the use of diuretics for the treatment of nocturia in women with UI. [EL = 1−]

4.4.4   **Duloxetine**

Duloxetine is a serotonin and noradrenaline reuptake inhibitor that acts chiefly in the sacral spinal cord. It is thought that the resultant increase in pudendal nerve activity increases urethral sphincter contraction and closure pressure. It is licensed for use in moderate to severe stress UI.

A systematic review has considered the effectiveness of serotonin and noradrenaline reuptake inhibitors (duloxetine) for the treatment of stress UI.[419] Because some of the studies included in the review were only published as abstracts, and because some relevant studies were not included in the review, all relevant studies are considered individually.

Six DB placebo-controlled RCTs evaluated the effectiveness of duloxetine for the treatment of predominant stress UI in women, five of which were considered to be of good quality.[420–424] [EL = 1+] A further RCT compared duloxetine (with or without PFMT) with PFMT alone or no active treatment (placebo drug and sham PFMT) in women with stress UI, 11% of whom had had prior continence surgery (n = 201).[229]

Of the six placebo-controlled RCTs, one was a 12 week dose-ranging study, comparing 20, 40 and 80 mg daily doses of duloxetine in women with at least four leakage episodes per week (n = 553).[420] Three other 12 week studies, identical in design, evaluated duloxetine 80 mg in women with at least seven (mean about 17) leakage episodes per week (total n = 1635).[421–423] The fifth study considered the impact of duloxetine 80 mg on QOL after 9 months' treatment (n = 451).[424] [EL = 1+] One study evaluated duloxetine use in women awaiting surgery for stress UI (n = 92).[425] [EL = 1−] Across the six studies, between 8% and 18% had had prior continence surgery. Up to 35% of women across four studies performed PFMT.[420–423]

The outcomes evaluated across the 12 week studies were leakage episodes, voiding interval, QOL (I-QOL) and patient global impression of improvement (PGI-I). The findings for duloxetine 80 mg per day (40 mg b.d.) compared with placebo were as follows:

- leakage episodes: significantly greater median reductions with duloxetine in each study (range of median reductions 50–64% versus 28–41% placebo)[420–423]

- voiding interval: significantly greater increases with duloxetine in each study (range of mean increases 15–24 minutes versus 4–9 minutes)[420–423]

- QOL: significantly greater improvement (I-QOL) with duloxetine in three studies;[420–422] no significant difference between groups in one[423]

- PGI-I: significantly more women reported improvement with duloxetine in three studies;[420–422] no significant difference between groups in one.[423] [EL = 1+]

The lower daily duloxetine dose of 20 mg b.d. (40 mg daily) was associated with significantly greater reductions in leakage episodes and in frequency compared with placebo, but not in QOL or PGI-I.[420] [EL = 1+]

The RCT that focused on QOL as an outcome after 9 months' treatment found no significant differences between duloxetine 80 mg and placebo in increases in I-QOL scores or in PGI-I at 3 or 9 months. About one-quarter of the women had dropped out of the study at the endpoint.[424] [EL = 1+]

In the study of women awaiting surgery, significantly greater improvements in leakage episodes, I-QOL and PGI-I scores were seen with duloxetine compared with placebo. A 'willingness to consider surgery' questionnaire indicated that a greater proportion of women treated with duloxetine versus placebo would change their mind about having surgery, although seven women (one duloxetine, six placebo) were excluded from this analysis.[425] [EL = 1−]

In the comparison of duloxetine 80 mg (with or without PFMT) with PFMT alone or no active treatment (sham PFMT and placebo drug), PFMT involved a target of 200 contractions a week (over 4 days), and the 'knack'. Sham PFMT involved contracting hip abductor muscles. Significantly greater reductions in leakage episodes were reported with duloxetine (with or without PFMT) compared with PFMT alone after 12 weeks' treatment. Global improvement and I-QOL scores indicated greater improvement in the duloxetine plus PFMT group compared with no active treatment.[229] No significant differences were reported between the PFMT and placebo groups in any outcome (leakage episodes, global improvement, I-QOL scores) after 12 weeks' treatment.[229] [EL = 1+]

Adverse effects

Across all studies, significantly more women in all duloxetine dosage groups discontinued treatment owing to adverse effects compared with placebo (range 15–33% versus 0–6%). Nausea was significantly more common with all daily dosages of duloxetine (range 13–46% versus 2–13% placebo), and accounted for a significant proportion of withdrawals compared with placebo in one study.[422] Other adverse effects that occurred significantly more commonly with duloxetine in two or more studies were dry mouth, constipation, fatigue, insomnia, dizziness, increased sweating, vomiting and somnolence.[229,421–423,425] Adverse effects occurring in the PFMT and no active treatment arms of the duloxetine study were pooled, and thus a distinction between duloxetine and PFMT or no active treatment is not possible.[229]

Cost effectiveness of duloxetine

Duloxetine is the only drug therapy currently available for stress UI. As part of this guideline, we considered the cost effectiveness of duloxetine in order to inform recommendations about the sequencing of conservative therapies, something that could potentially have a large impact on clinical practice.

One published article considered the cost effectiveness of duloxetine.[426] This described a state transition (Markov) model to evaluate the cost effectiveness of duloxetine alone or in combination with PFMT against 'standard' treatment (PFMT and surgery), either as a first-line treatment or as second line to PFMT for stress UI, over 2 years. The Markov approach was adopted so as to capture the effect of waiting times on access to services, with a concomitant effect on deferred costs and benefits. The results of the model suggested that, using a willingness to pay threshold of £30,000 per QALY, duloxetine was a cost effective treatment for stress UI. Using baseline assumptions, the authors reported that the ICER of duloxetine alone when used first-line was £8,730 per QALY and £5,854 per QALY when used first-line in combination with PFMT.[426] When used second-line to PFMT, duloxetine dominates standard treatment.

The health economics model of the use of duloxetine as a first-line treatment for stress UI in women used in this study factored in delays for access to services.[426] Clinical trials would normally try to eliminate differential timings of treatment, to ensure a like-for-like comparison. Similarly, it could be argued that economic evaluation should be neutral with respect to treatment timing so that the results are not contingent on a particular service configuration. Indeed, it seems that service delivery should be configured to produce cost effective health care rather than be a driver of what is deemed cost effective. Therefore, two additional health economics models, which did not consider access times to health services, were developed for this guideline. The first sought to compare the cost effectiveness of PFMT versus duloxetine as a first-line treatment for women with moderate to severe stress UI, which is assumed to be 14 or more leakage episodes per week. In this model, treatment effects and costs were based on a 52 week time frame. A second model, based on a 2 year follow-up, assessed the cost effectiveness of duloxetine versus surgery as a second-line treatment for women with moderate to severe stress UI in whom first-line treatment with PFMT had been unsuccessful. These models are described in detail in Appendix F.

Under baseline assumptions, PFMT 'dominates' duloxetine as a first-line treatment. This means that it is both more effective and less costly. The sensitivity analyses undertaken (and detailed in Appendix F) did not change this conclusion. The second-line treatment model suggests that surgery is more cost effective than duloxetine. Surgery is more costly but the ICER, in the baseline analysis, falls below the £20,000 per QALY threshold used by NICE as a willingness to pay benchmark for cost effectiveness.

Evidence statements for duloxetine

Short-term studies (up to 12 weeks) suggest that the use of duloxetine is associated with a reduction in leakage episodes, an increased voiding interval and improved quality of life in women with stress UI or mixed UI where stress-related leakage is the predominant symptom. Between-group differences are clinically small. Adverse effects, particularly nausea, and discontinuation rates are very common (more than 10%). There is a lack of long-term safety data. The combination of duloxetine and PFMT is more effective than no treatment. It remains unclear whether the combination is better than either treatment alone. [EL = 1+]

An economic model constructed for the purposes of this guideline suggested that PFMT is more cost effective than duloxetine alone as first-line treatment for stress UI. This result was generally not affected by making plausible changes to model parameters in favour of duloxetine. While the model was based on the best available clinical evidence, there is a lack of long-term effectiveness data for either treatment. A second model suggested that surgery was cost effective relative to duloxetine as a second-line treatment to PFMT. However, duloxetine was the lower cost treatment option and therefore its use does not necessarily impose opportunity costs on the NHS relative to surgery.

> **Recommendation for duloxetine**
>
> Duloxetine is not recommended as a first-line treatment for women with predominant stress UI. Duloxetine should not routinely be used as a second-line treatment for women with stress UI, although it may be offered as second-line therapy if women prefer pharmacological to surgical treatment or are not suitable for surgical treatment. If duloxetine is prescribed, women should be counselled about its adverse effects. [A]

4.4.5 Oestrogens

Oestrogens help to maintain health of the tissues that are essential for normal pressure transmission in the urethra. This includes the sphincter muscles, urothelium and vascular tissues, as well as the urethral secretions that may help to create a 'seal'. Oestrogen replacement has been promoted as a solution to UI in postmenopausal women, although its chief mode of action is unclear.

Four systematic reviews of oestrogens for the treatment of UI and/or OAB were identified, which were completed at different times and which considered different questions.[427–430] Therefore, studies included in these reviews were considered individually, together with other relevant RCTs.

Ten RCTs evaluated the use of oestrogens for the treatment of postmenopausal women with stress UI[228,431–434] or other types of UI or OAB.[435–439] Four further RCTs that primarily evaluated the effects of oestrogen on symptoms of vaginal atrophy reported some data for urological symptoms.[440–443] Additionally, secondary analyses of data from three RCTs that were designed to evaluate the benefits and risks of hormone replacement therapy (HRT) provide data on UI and/or OAB.[444–449]

The comparator group was placebo in all except two studies. One of these two studies is also considered in the physical therapies section and involved a comparison of PFMT with oestrogen, electrical stimulation and no treatment.[228] The second study compared two oestrogen preparations.[436]

Intravaginal oestrogens

Five RCTs evaluated the use of intravaginal oestrogens for UI and/or other urological symptoms. Two RCTs enrolled women with stress UI ($n = 100$). One reported significantly greater subjective improvement of incontinence with intravaginal estriol compared with placebo at 6 months (68% versus 16%, $n = 88$).[431] [EL = 1+] No comparisons were made between the conjugated oestrogen cream and control groups in the 3 month RCT; cure rates were 12% versus 0.[228] [EL = 1+]

One RCT compared two intravaginal oestrogen preparations (the estradiol vaginal ring with estriol pessaries) in women with urgency, frequency, stress or urge UI. No significant differences were seen between groups in any outcome after 6 months' treatment (subjective improvement; responder or cure rates for urgency, frequency, nocturia, urge or stress UI). Responder rates across all outcomes ranged from 51% to 61%, and cure rates from 27% to 44% ($n = 251$).[436] [EL = 1+]

Two placebo-controlled RCTs, in which an intravaginal oestrogen preparation was used to treat urogenital symptoms, reported the following:[439,443] [EL = 1+]

- The prevalence of UI and frequency/nocturia fell to a greater extent with an intravaginal estradiol tablet than with placebo at 1 year (UI prevalence 18% versus 10%; frequency/nocturia 38% versus 10%) but no between-group analyses were reported. At baseline, 28% of women had UI and 43% frequency or nocturia ($n = 1612$).[439]

- Significantly more women who had urological symptoms (41–53%) reported improvement in symptoms (frequency, dysuria, urge or stress UI) with intravaginal 17β-estradiol versus placebo after 3 months' treatment (63% versus 32%, $n = 164$).[443]

Systemic oestrogens

Systemic oestrogens for UI or OAB

Three RCTs evaluated oral oestrogens for the treatment of stress UI for 3 or 6 months.[432–434] The oestrogens evaluated were conjugated equine oestrogen (CEE) with medroxyprogesterone acetate (MPA), given for 10 days a cycle;[432] estradiol;[433] and estrone.[434] No significant differences were seen between oestrogen and placebo groups in any outcome across the studies (leakage episodes, pad tests, frequency, QOL, perception of improvement, objective cure).[432–434] [EL = 1+]

Two RCTs evaluated systemic oestrogens for the treatment of stress or urge UI.[435,438] One reported no differences between a subcutaneous estradiol or placebo implant in subjective outcomes (self-reported cure, leakage episodes, frequency) after 6 months' treatment ($n = 40$).[438] [EL = 1+] In the second RCT, improvements in leakage episodes, frequency and urgency were seen after 3 months' treatment with oral estriol and placebo, but no between-group differences were reported ($n = 56$).[435] [EL = 1−]

A further RCT evaluated CEE+MPA in female nursing home residents who were incontinent. No significant differences were found between CEE+MPA and placebo groups in any outcome (leakage, bladder capacity), although only data from 21 of the 32 women randomised, who completed 6 months' treatment, were analysed.[437] [EL = 1−]

Systemic oestrogens for urogenital symptoms

Three RCTs that primarily evaluated the effects of systemic oestrogen on symptoms of vaginal atrophy reported some continence data.[440–442] One of these studies compared oral estradiol and estriol with placebo in women with stress or mixed UI. At 4 months, a higher cure rate was reported for women on active treatment compared with placebo, although no baseline data were given ($n = 29$).[440] [EL = 1−] A second RCT comparing oral estriol with placebo in women with stress, urge or mixed UI was of unclear duration (3 or 6 months) and only reported that symptoms were alleviated in the majority of women with urge or mixed UI ($n = 34$).[441] [EL = 1−] No significant changes in frequency were reported with oral estriol or placebo in a 10 week RCT investigating the effects of oestrogen on vaginal flora, cytology and urogenital symptoms ($n = 35$).[442] [EL = 1+]

Studies evaluating HRT for other indications

Data from two RCTs that were designed to evaluate the benefits and risks of HRT have been analysed with respect to continence outcomes. In the 'HERS' RCT,[445] which compared CEE+MPA with placebo, 55% of women had UI (stress, mixed or urge) at baseline ($n = 1525$).[444] After 4 years' treatment, significantly fewer women in the HRT group reported improvement and significantly more reported worsening of UI symptoms, compared with the placebo group. Leakage episodes were increased in the HRT group compared with placebo.[444] In women who did not have UI at baseline, the risk of reporting any type of UI at study end was also significantly higher in the HRT group.[450] [EL = 1++]

In women enrolled in the Women's Health Initiative (WHI) RCTs (CEE+MPA versus placebo[447] or CEE versus placebo[448]), 85% had continence data at baseline and at 1 year ($n = 23\,296$). In women who were continent at the beginning of the study (35%), the relative risk of incident UI of any type at 1 year was significantly higher in the CEE+MPA and CEE groups compared with placebo. When the relative risk of each type of UI was considered separately, all results remained significant except for the risk of urge UI in the CEE+MPA versus placebo study. The relative risk of worsening prevalent UI (leakage quantity and episodes, limitations of daily activities, bother factor) was also significantly higher with HRT compared with placebo.[446] [EL = 1++]

A further placebo-controlled RCT, which evaluated both CEE and raloxifene for the prevention of osteoporosis in postmenopausal women, reported a significantly higher incidence of UI with CEE compared with other treatment groups at 3 years. Fewer women treated with oestrogen reported improvement of pre-existing UI ($n = 619$).[449] [EL = 1+]

Adverse effects

Adverse effects reported across the studies of intravaginal oestrogens (mostly uncommon) included vaginal irritation or discomfort, burning and itching,[431,436] breast pain,[436] and vaginal spotting or discharge.[439] One study reported that no systemic adverse effects occurred.[431]

Adverse effects reported with systemic oestrogens included breast tenderness,[437,438] vaginal spotting[437] and increased vaginal discharge.[439] No adverse effects were reported in two RCTs.[435,440] Adverse effects were not considered in four RCTs.[432,433,441,442] In the HERS study, the risk of venous thromboembolism was significantly higher with CEE+MPA compared with placebo.[445] In the WHI studies, the risk of stroke was significantly higher with CEE+MPA (mean follow-up 5.2 years) and with CEE (mean follow-up 6.8 years), compared with placebo.[447,448] The risk of coronary heart disease, venous thromboembolism and invasive breast cancer was also significantly higher with CEE+MPA compared with placebo.[447]

Evidence statements for oestrogens

Short-term studies (up to 6 months) of intravaginal oestrogens suggest some improvement in symptoms of incontinence and frequency in postmenopausal women who have urogenital symptoms secondary to vaginal atrophy. There is a lack of evidence to support the use of intravaginal oestrogens for the treatment of UI. [EL = 1+]

Systemic oestrogen does not confer any benefit in women with UI and there is evidence that it may increase the likelihood of developing incontinence in postmenopausal women. Systemic oestrogens are associated with increased risk of systemic adverse effects such as thromboembolism. [EL = 1+]

Recommendations for oestrogens

Systemic hormone replacement therapy is not recommended for the treatment of UI. [A]

Intravaginal oestrogens are recommended for the treatment of OAB symptoms in postmenopausal women with vaginal atrophy. [A]

4.5 Non-therapeutic interventions

This section covers the use of products that collect or contain leakage (e.g. absorbent products, urinals and toileting aids, catheters) and products used to prevent leakage (e.g. devices that support the bladder neck, intra- or extraurethral devices).

Studies considered for the non-therapeutic interventions section

Little primary research evidence was identified that addressed the guideline questions. No studies were identified that evaluated the effects of containment on maintenance of independent living, rates of institutionalism, or return to work, and only one study considered QOL (an evaluation of pessaries for UI, described below). Published consensus statements and narrative reviews that discussed issues relevant to the circumstances of use of containment products, or catheterisation, were used as a basis for the recommendations.[32,451–453] [EL = 4]

4.5.1 Absorbent products, urinals and toileting aids

One RCT compared a conservative management strategy with the use of absorbent products (pads and pants) for 6 months ($n = 90$). Conservative management involved providing estriol (depending on oestrogen status), PFMT (six training sessions), bladder training (for urge or mixed UI), electrical stimulation, and pads and pants. Significantly greater reductions in UI severity and impact, and leakage episodes, were seen with conservative management compared with the control group. No significant differences were seen between groups in frequency. The pads and pants arm showed no change in incontinence impact at 6 months.[454] [EL = 1+]

Evidence statement for absorbent products, urinals and toileting aids

Pads and pants are ineffective in the treatment of UI. [EL = 1+] There is no evidence to support the use of hand-held urinals and toileting aids in the treatment of UI. There is a variety of such products available. There is a lack of evidence for their use in management. However, they are used by women in maintaining social continence. [EL = 4]

From evidence to recommendation
The GDG recognises that some women may not wish to pursue active interventions for UI and that absorbent products, urinals and toileting aids are an alternative management option in such circumstances. However, the GDG felt that women must be fully aware of all possible treatment options before adopting this course of action. In addition, the GDG agreed that the use of these products should be considered for women awaiting definitive treatment.

Recommendation for absorbent products, urinals and toileting aids

Absorbent products, hand-held urinals and toileting aids should not be considered as a treatment for UI. They should be used only as:

• a coping strategy pending definitive treatment

• an adjunct to other ongoing therapy

• long-term management of UI only after treatment options have been explored. [D (GPP)]

4.5.2 Catheters

The care of patients with long-term urinary catheters is covered within the NICE clinical guideline *Infection Control: Prevention of Healthcare-Associated Infection in Primary and Community Care*.[22] Within that guideline, the recommendation that intermittent catheterisation is preferred to indwelling catheterisation was informed by a systematic review of risk factors for UTI, in adults with spinal cord dysfunction. The GDG's view is that the evidence relating to adults with spinal cord dysfunction is relevant to the use of catheters in women with idiopathic UI.[455] The systematic review found eight cohort studies that considered risk of infection according to type of catheter used by men and/or women with spinal cord injuries. In seven of eight studies, patients using intermittent catheters, had fewer infections or lower prevalence of bacteriuria than those who used indwelling catheters (follow-up ranging from about 1 to 2.5 years). However, none of the primary studies adjusted for baseline differences between groups (total $n = 1153$). [EL = 2+]

Evidence statement for catheters

Intermittent catheterisation is associated with reduced risk of UTI compared with indwelling catheterisation. [EL = 2+]

From evidence to recommendations
In the absence of evidence on long-term catheterisation in women, but alongside the systematic review described, the GDG considered that suprapubic catheterisation is preferable to indwelling urethral catheterisation owing to reduced risk of urethral and other complications (symptomatic UTI, and 'bypassing'). Suprapubic catheterisation is not without risk, particularly at initial insertion, although the benefits and risks of this approach have not been fully established. Long-term medical management of suprapubic catheterisation may be problematic if healthcare providers lack knowledge and expertise in this area, and if the homebound patient lacks rapid access to medical care if a problem arises.

The population for whom catheterisation is recommended was also determined by GDG consensus.

The GDG feels that the use of an indwelling catheter in a woman with OAB may be associated with an increase in detrusor activity and therefore an increased tendency to 'bypassing' (urine leakage around the catheter). Assuming they empty their bladder completely, as most patients with idiopathic DO will, a catheter is unlikely to achieve continence.

Recommendations for catheters

Bladder catheterisation (intermittent or indwelling urethral or suprapubic) should be considered for women in whom persistent urinary retention is causing incontinence, symptomatic infections or renal dysfunction, and in whom this cannot otherwise be corrected. Healthcare professionals should be aware, and explain to women, that the use of indwelling catheters in urge UI may not result in continence. [D (GPP)]

Intermittent urethral catheters
Intermittent urethral catheterisation should be used for women with urinary retention who can be taught to self-catheterise or who have a carer who can perform the technique. [C]

Indwelling urethral catheters
Careful consideration should be given to the impact of long-term indwelling urethral catheterisation. The practicalities, benefits and risks should be discussed with the patient or, if appropriate, her carer. Indications for the use of long-term indwelling urethral catheters for women with UI include:

- chronic urinary retention in women who are unable to manage intermittent self-catheterisation

- skin wounds, pressure ulcers or irritations that are being contaminated by urine

- distress or disruption caused by bed and clothing changes

- where a woman expresses a preference for this form of management. [D (GPP)]

Indwelling suprapubic catheters
Indwelling suprapubic catheters should be considered as an alternative to long-term urethral catheters. Healthcare professionals should be aware, and explain to women, that they may be associated with lower rates of symptomatic UTI, 'bypassing', and urethral complications than indwelling urethral catheters. [D (GPP)]

4.5.3 Products to prevent leakage

Studies reporting the use of the following products were identified:

- intravaginal devices: Continence Guard (also known as the Conveen Contiguard),[456–462] Contrelle® continence tampon,[462] Contiform®,[463] bladder neck support prosthesis (Introl)[464]

- meatal devices: FemAssist®,[465,466] CapSure® shield,[467] Miniguard[468–470] (also called 'continence control pad'/Impress Softpatch[471])

- intraurethral devices: a urethral plug[472,473] (the ViVa Plug, also called Alive[474]), FemSoft® insert,[475] Reliance®[476,477] (one of the studies was a controlled trial versus NEAT).[478]

Two of these products are known to be available or could be obtained by women in the UK (Contrelle® Activgard [formerly known as Conveen Contiguard, or Continence Guard], and FemSoft®). Neither product can be provided on NHS prescription. The Rocket® incontinence device is also available, but no studies were found regarding its use. Many of the other products listed are known to have been withdrawn from the UK market for commercial reasons (Contiform®, FemAssist®, CapSure®,[479] Reliance®).

While there is no evidence to support the use of menstrual tampons in the management of UI, GDG members are aware that menstrual tampons are used by many women to support the bladder neck and to prevent leakage. Manufactures of these products do not recommend this usage and state that they should be used only during menstruation.

Evidence relating to the use of the available products

A case series of women with stress or mixed UI who used FemSoft® (mean follow-up 15 months), reported that leakage episodes were fewer and more pad tests were negative with the device in place, compared with without the device. Symptomatic UTI was very common (47%), and the incidence of insertion trauma, haematuria, spotting, cystoscopic evidence of bladder or urethral irritation or trauma and device migration were common (*n* = 150).[480] [EL = 3]

Four case series[456–459,461] (patient numbers ranging from 15 to 38) and one crossover RCT[462] (*n* = 94; 62 completed and analysed) found that the majority of users of the Continence Guard reported cure or improvement (57–89%) after 3–5 weeks' treatment (up to 1 year in one study). Adverse effects reported were expulsion of the device (8–47%),[456,457,462] voiding difficulties (11–14%),[456,457,462] UTI (11%)[458] and vaginal irritation (23%).[462] Three studies found no vaginal irritation or erosion on gynaecological examination.[456–459] No adverse effects were reported in two studies.[459,461]

Evidence statement for products to prevent leakage

There is limited evidence of efficacy for Contrelle® Activgard (formerly known as the Continence Guard or Conveen Contiguard) and FemSoft® in the management of UI. Adverse effects, in particular UTI, are very common. [EL = 3]

From evidence to recommendation
In the GDG's view, some women find these products beneficial for occasional use in certain circumstances as a preventive strategy.

Recommendation for products to prevent leakage

Intravaginal and intraurethral devices are not recommended for the routine management of UI in women. Women should not be advised to consider such devices other than for occasional use when necessary to prevent leakage, for example during physical exercise. [D (GPP)]

4.5.4 Pessaries

A small case series reported that QOL improved (IIQ) in women with stress or mixed UI and POP who used a ring pessary with diaphragm for 1 year (six of 38 women enrolled).[481] [EL = 3]

Evidence statement for pessaries

The limited evidence available does not support the use of ring pessaries for the treatment of UI in women whether or not there is prolapse present. [EL = 3]

4.6 Complementary therapies

Women who do not find conventional treatments acceptable often explore the use of complementary therapies for UI, and as adjuncts to conventional treatments.

Studies considered for the complementary therapies section

Most of the articles identified reported the use of acupuncture or hypnotherapy for UI, or were narrative reviews regarding the use of complementary therapies for UI. Use of traditional Chinese medicines was also mentioned in a narrative review, but no further references to their use for UI were found. [482]

4.6.1 Acupuncture

Three RCTs[483–486] and three case series[487–490] evaluated the use of acupuncture for UI or OAB in women. Across these studies, the acupuncture points and duration of stimulation used varied. Duration of treatment ranged from 2 to 4 weeks. All were considered to be of poor quality because of lack of information or for only analysing results for women who completed treatment.

One RCT assessed the effects of daily acupuncture at acupoints Sp-6 and St-36 on nocturnal frequency in elderly people on long-stay hospital wards. The median reduction in frequency in the acupuncture group after 2 weeks' treatment (20 minutes per day) was −2.0 (95% CI −1.0 to −3.0). No significant change was seen in the placebo group, who received mock TENS. Two publications of this RCT were identified; one stated that 15 of the 20 studied were women, another stated that 17 were women.[483,484] [EL = 1−]

The acupuncture treatment given in the second RCT, to women with stress UI, depended on what the deficiency was considered to be. A total of 30 sessions were given every other day. Significantly more women treated with acupuncture than placebo were improved (assessed clinically and urodynamically) after treatment.[485] [EL = 1−]

An RCT in women with OAB with urge UI reported significant improvements in frequency, urgency and QOL (UDI and IIQ) after 4 weeks' acupuncture treatment compared with placebo acupuncture (designed for relaxation). Changes in leakage episodes were not significantly different between groups. Adverse effects reported were bruising or bleeding from acupuncture sites (23%) and minor discomfort on needle placement (25%) ($n = 85$; 74 analysed).[486] [EL = 1−]

Case series
Three case series evaluated acupuncture for UI or OAB in a total of 87 patients (84 women).[487–489,491] The symptoms being treated were frequency, urgency and dysuria,[487] 'lower urinary tract symptoms'[489] and urge or mixed UI.[491] Treatment consisted of a single session, or 6 or 12 weeks' regular treatment. The acupuncture points used also varied across studies.

Symptomatic improvement was reported in 53–60% of patients (assessed at 3 or 8 months).[487–489,491] No adverse effects were reported. Longer term follow-up (about 5 years) of 21 patients show that symptoms recur, and that repeated treatment may be necessary.[488] [EL = 3]

4.6.2 Hypnosis

The studies identified in relation to hypnotherapy in women with UI consisted of case series and case reports.

In the largest case series of women with incontinence due to DO, they underwent 12 sessions of hypnotherapy over 1 month, which involved symptom removal by direct suggestion and 'ego strengthening'. At the end of the 12 sessions, the majority of women were subjectively cured or improved, with the remainder unchanged ($n = 50$). Objective cure or improvement (on cystometry) was seen in the majority at 3 months ($n = 44$).[492] Limited follow-up data at 2 years for 30 of the women have been reported. Of the women who were subjectively or objectively cured at 3 months, fewer than half remained cured ($n = 30$).[493] [EL = 3]

In another publication, four cases (three women) of hypnotherapy for DO were reported. Hypnotherapy involved three 1 hour sessions, including anxiety control methods, ego strengthening, training in self-hypnosis, age progression, explanation of stable bladder function and 'hand-on-abdomen technique'. Two of the three women reported remission of symptoms at 6 months.[494] [EL = 3] A report of two women with UI who were 'successfully' treated with hypnotic techniques and waking counselling was also identified.[495] [EL = 3]

4.6.3 Herbal medicines

One report described the use of a tablet preparation containing crataeva (*Crataeva nurvala*, a herb used in traditional Hindu science of medicine) and equisetum (horsetail) to treat women with symptoms of urge and/or stress UI for 12 weeks ($n = 8$). Quality of life (UDI) showed significant positive change to perceptions of frequency, leakage related to urgency or activity and difficulty emptying the bladder. All parameters of the IIQ questionnaire except physical recreation and household chores improved significantly.[496] [EL = 3]

Evidence statements for complementary therapies

Poor-quality evidence shows that acupuncture may reduce nocturia and both stress and urge incontinence in the short term (up to 4 weeks) but it is unclear whether any particular acupuncture treatment is more effective than others. [EL = 3]

There is limited evidence that hypnotherapy for women with UI secondary to detrusor overactivity offers some benefit over the short term (up to 6 months). About half of women relapsed over a 2 year period. [EL = 3] There is a lack of evidence on herbal medicines for UI or OAB.

The GDG recognises that, despite the limited and poor-quality evidence available, some women may wish to explore complementary therapies for their incontinence [EL = 4].

> **Recommendation for complementary therapies**
>
> Complementary therapies are not recommended for the treatment of UI or OAB. [D]

4.7 Preventive use of conservative therapies

Studies considered for this section

Evidence described in this section is derived from RCTs. Two systematic reviews of the use of physical therapies for prevention of UI were identified.[497,498] The RCTs within these systematic reviews were considered individually if they addressed effectiveness. Any further RCTs identified are also included here.

No studies were identified that evaluated the use of lifestyle interventions for prevention of UI or OAB.

4.7.1 Behavioural therapy

One RCT evaluated a multicomponent behavioural modification programme comprising initial education, PFMT and bladder training in older women who had no UI (39%) or minimal UI (defined as one to five wet days in the previous year) ($n = 480$ randomised; 359 analysed). At 1 year follow-up, significantly more women maintained or improved their continence status compared with an untreated control group. Significantly greater improvements in frequency and voiding interval were also seen in the behavioural modification group versus control. Adverse effects were not considered.[499,500] [EL = 1−]

4.7.2 Physical therapies

Preventive use during pregnancy

Four RCTs compared more structured PFMT with usual care during pregnancy (from weeks 18 or 20) in women in their first pregnancy.[501–504] One study enrolled women with increased bladder neck mobility,[501] which has been shown to be predictive of postnatal stress UI.[505] Women with UI were excluded from one study,[501] whereas in two studies between 25% and 32% had UI at baseline.[503,504] Between 72 and 1169 women were enrolled in these studies (total $n = 1810$); the proportion completing follow-up or responding to questionnaire follow-up was noted to be low in three studies (64–86%).

The PFMT programmes involved daily exercises with between 42 and 72 contractions.[501–504] The individual's ability to contract the pelvic floor muscle was checked at baseline. The comparison group was 'usual care' in each study, which comprised: 'usual' information from midwife or GP;[503] routine antenatal care (likely to have received verbal advice on pelvic floor exercises);[501] and routine care, no systematic PFMT programme.[502,504] Two of the studies reported that women in the control group also undertook PFMT regularly (20%[502] and 51%[501]).

In the first study, significantly fewer women who had been randomised to a 12 week PFMT programme reported UI at the end of treatment, and at 3 months postpartum, compared with those receiving usual care. Greater benefit was seen with PFMT in the number of leakage episodes and in pelvic floor muscle strength. No adverse effects were reported.[503] [EL = 1++]

In a study of women with increased bladder neck mobility, significantly fewer reported stress UI or had a positive 1 hour pad test at 3 months postpartum, after a structured PFMT programme, compared with those receiving usual care. No significant differences were seen between groups in changes in bladder neck mobility, pelvic floor muscle strength or in QOL (KHQ). Women in the PFMT group had significantly higher scores in the general health domain of SF-36 compared with the usual care group.[501] [EL = 1+]

No numerical data were reported in the third RCT, although the authors noted that no significant differences were seen between groups in UI or pelvic floor muscle strength at 12 months postpartum (n = 46). Adverse effects were not considered.[502] [EL = 1−]

The largest study considered risk of urinary outcomes during the antenatal period and up to 6 months postpartum. At antenatal week 36, there was a trend towards reduced risk of any type of UI and of fewer leakage episodes in the PFMT group, although no difference between groups was statistically significant. At 6 months postpartum, differences between groups were less, again with none being significant (n = 1169).[504] [EL = 1+]

Preventive use after pregnancy

Four controlled trials evaluated PFMT for the prevention of UI in postpartum women. UI was reported by 17–32% of women across all studies at baseline.[506–509] The intervention was started 24 or 48 hours after delivery in primi- or multiparous women in two RCTs.[506,507] A more structured 4 or 8 week PFMT programme was compared with usual care in both studies. At 3 months postpartum, the following results were seen:

- significantly lower prevalence of UI in the PFMT group following the 8 week treatment programme (n = 676); this difference was not sustained at 1 year (n = 569)[510] [EL = 1+]

- no significant differences in UI prevalence between groups following the 4 week treatment programme (n = 1609; 89% of those randomised).[507] [EL = 1−]

A further two studies (one RCT,[509] one cohort[508]) recruited women 8 weeks postpartum. The RCT compared a 6 week programme of PFMT with biofeedback and electrical stimulation, with usual care in primiparous women (n = 107). Stress UI prevalence was not significantly different between groups at 10 months postpartum. However, the prevalence of stress UI differed between groups at baseline (31% PFMT versus 16% control), which was not accounted for in the analysis at 10 months.[509] [EL = 1−]

The cohort study reported a significantly lower stress UI prevalence in women (41% of whom had UI at baseline) who had undergone a structured 8 week PFMT programme compared with usual care, both at the end of the intervention (n = 198)[508] and at 1 year postpartum (n = 162).[511] No significant differences were found between groups in leakage index or social activity index. [EL = 2+]

Evidence statement for preventive use of physical therapies

There is evidence that PFMT used during a first pregnancy reduces the prevalence of UI at 3 months following delivery. [EL = 1+] The effects in the longer term are inconsistent and the impact of subsequent pregnancies unknown. [EL = 4]

Recommendation for preventive use of physical therapies

Pelvic floor muscle training should be offered to women in their first pregnancy as a preventive strategy for UI. [A]

Research recommendation for preventive use of conservative therapies

Further studies need to be undertaken to evaluate the role and effectiveness of physical and behavioural therapies and lifestyle modifications in the prevention of UI in women. Long-term outcomes in particular should be evaluated.

4.8 Optimal sequence and timescales for conservative therapies

The GDG's view was that conservative management should be pursued prior to surgical procedures in the treatment of UI. The factors affecting the GDG's decisions regarding first-line conservative therapies are summarised below.

For stress UI, the GDG considered the cost effectiveness of PFMT and duloxetine as first-line treatment. The conclusion was that PFMT dominated and it was therefore recommended as the first-line intervention for stress UI.

For OAB (with or without urge UI), cost minimisation was used to determine whether bladder training or antimuscarinic drug treatment should be offered as first-line treatment. Bladder training was recommended as the first-line intervention as it is less costly and not associated with adverse effects.

In the GDG's view, the management of mixed UI depends upon which symptom predominates (i.e. stress or urge UI).

In the absence of evidence for optimal duration of treatment, the GDG considered that a 3 month trial period of PFMT is sufficient to determine whether treatment is effective and tolerated. A shorter trial period of 6 weeks would usually be appropriate for bladder training.

5. Surgical management

When conservative treatment of UI, whether for stress UI or OAB symptoms, has failed it is usual to consider surgical therapy. The objective of all surgery for UI should be to restore the woman's lower urinary tract function as closely as possible to normal, with the minimum short- and long-term morbidity and for this improvement to be durable; indeed, this is the expectation of most patients. Such ideal outcomes are, however, unusual, and women should be given relevant information and realistic expectations about anticipated outcomes, including potential perioperative complications and long-term adverse effects. This is especially true of the operations for OAB, which comprise the first part of this chapter.

The range of procedures is wide but, in principle, all operations for UI aim either to reduce bladder filling pressures in the case of OAB symptoms or to augment urethral closure in the case of stress UI. The best chance of long-term success lies with the primary procedure and therefore this chapter should be read in conjunction with the chapter on surgical competence. Well over a hundred surgical procedures have been described to treat UI over the last century; this guideline addresses only those procedures that are currently in common clinical practice.

Recommendation for surgical management

Any woman wishing to consider surgical treatment for UI should be informed about the benefits and risks of surgical and non-surgical options. Counselling should include consideration of the woman's childbearing wishes. [D (GPP)]

5.1 Procedures for overactive bladder

Currently accepted practice is to offer lifestyle or behavioural modifications or antimuscarinic medications as initial treatments. Where these are unsuccessful, a range of surgical interventions may be considered. In contrast to procedures used for the treatment of stress UI (aimed at stabilising the bladder neck or urethra, or augmenting sphincter pressure), these procedures aim to increase the capacity of the bladder, alter or modulate its nerve supply and contractility, or to bypass the lower urinary tract completely. It is inherent in several of these procedures that contractility of the detrusor is reduced; hence difficulty voiding is a very common adverse effect. Women might only be considered suitable for such procedures if they are both willing and demonstrably able to undertake clean intermittent self-catheterisation (CISC).

Studies considered for this section

Evidence described in this section is derived where possible from controlled trials. Where data were lacking, case series were considered. The procedures considered are not specific to women with idiopathic UI; the majority of evidence is in relation to treatment of neurogenic bladders. Interpretation and extraction of available data, relevant to the population within this guideline, is difficult owing to heterogeneity of populations included, both in terms of gender and aetiology of UI.

5.1.1 Sacral nerve stimulation

The principle of neuromodulation is that appropriate electrical stimulation of the sacral reflex pathway will inhibit the reflex behaviour of the bladder. Permanently implantable sacral root stimulators have been developed to provide chronic stimulation directly to the S3 nerve roots. Patients first undergo a percutaneous nerve evaluation (PNE) in which a needle is inserted through the sacral foramina under local anaesthetic. This is connected to an external stimulation source and left in place for a few days. Those who show satisfactory response to the PNE may then proceed to a permanent implant.

Guidance on sacral nerve stimulation (SNS) for urge incontinence and urgency-frequency was issued by the Interventional Procedures Programme of NICE, in 2004.[26] It states that: 'Current evidence on the safety and efficacy of sacral nerve stimulation for urge incontinence and urgency-frequency appears adequate to support the use of this procedure provided that the normal arrangements are in place for consent, audit and clinical governance.'

The systematic review conducted to inform the NICE interventional procedures (IP) guidance aimed to evaluate the efficacy and safety of SNS for urge UI and urgency-frequency (of any aetiology) in men and women.[512] In considering the effectiveness of SNS within this guideline, studies of any design that were conducted in women with idiopathic UI or OAB are of relevance. Studies that only reported results for PNE ('test stimulation') are not considered, as these do not address effectiveness of the implanted device. One additional case series to those considered by NICE IP was identified.[513]

All studies considered SNS in the S3 foramen via an implanted device. Most studies included men and women. The majority also included patients with urinary retention as well as urge UI or OAB; only a few reported data separately for patients with urge UI or OAB. Overall, the proportions who responded to PNE, in studies that reported this, ranged from 28% to 63% (median 42%).

Randomised controlled trials

Three RCTs evaluated SNS in men and women (mostly women) who had failed prior conservative and/or surgical treatment for urge UI[514,515] or urgency-frequency.[516] Two of the three RCTs were conducted by the Sacral Nerve Stimulation Group.[515,516]

The RCTs had a 6 month controlled phase after which patients in the control groups were offered the implant. The quality of the RCTs was considered to be poor: of the urge UI studies, some only analysed data from patients who completed treatment; others did not state whether intention-to-treat analysis was undertaken; none provided sufficient data to determine whether groups were similar at baseline, other than in the intervention given. [EL = 1−]

After 6 months' treatment in patients with urge UI, leakage episodes, leakage severity and pad usage were significantly lower with SNS compared with control (continued prior treatment).[514,515] Scores on the SF-36 physical health status domain were significantly higher in the SNS group.[515] Following crossover of patients in the control groups to receive sacral nerve stimulation, the following results were reported:

- treatment failure in 21% of patients followed up (median 18 months, range 6–36 months); very common adverse effects were pain at implant site, lead migration and leg pain; common effects were leg stimulation, disturbed bowel function, urinary retention, vaginal cramps, anal pain and skin irritation at implant site ($n = 44$; 91% women)[514] [EL = 3]

- 52% of patients were dry at 18 months and a further 24% reported at least 50% reduction in leakage episodes ($n = 58$); at 3 years, 46% were dry and 13% improved ($n = 41$, of 98 originally randomised).[515,517]

In the RCT of patients with urgency-frequency, after 6 months' treatment, frequency was significantly reduced, mean voided volume and bladder volume at first sensation to void were significantly increased in the SNS group compared with control, with improvements in several SF-36 domains in the active treatment group ($n = 51$; 90% women).[516] [EL = 1−] At 2 years follow-up of 21 patients, 43% had at least 50% reduction in frequency and 62% had at least 50% increase in voided volume.[517] [EL = 3]

Of 157 patients enrolled across the Sacral Nerve Stimulation Group studies, 33% had adverse events that required surgical revision. Pain at stimulator or implant sites was very common, and lead migration, infection or skin irritation requiring removal of the implant were common.[515,516] [EL = 3]

Case series
The Italian National Register[518] and twelve case series[513,519–529] reported the outcomes of sacral neuromodulation in patients with urge UI or OAB resistant to conservative treatment. All except one study[527] included men and women and did not report results separately for women. The majority of studies included people with urinary retention or voiding difficulty, as well as OAB and/or urge UI.[518–521,523,525,526,529] Four studies reported results of patients with idiopathic UI or OAB separately.[518,520,521,523] Some studies included a minority of patients with neurogenic bladder.

The number of patients included in each study ranged from 12 to 113 (total 550), with eight considering fewer than 50 patients. The mean duration of follow-up ranged from 8 months to 5 years; reasons for withdrawal or missing data were not generally given. The Italian National Register included both retrospective and prospective data, which were considered separately (total $n = 196$). The outcomes considered were bladder diary variables, continence status, satisfaction, QOL, urodynamic variables and adverse effects and complications.

Bladder diary
These outcomes were considered in nine studies, with significant reduction in leakage episodes and frequency reported in five studies with up to 5 years follow-up.[513,521,522,524,529] Another two studies found variable reductions in leakage episodes and frequency at various time points.[518,523] No significant change was seen in these outcomes in one study ($n = 12$),[527] and a significant change in frequency only in one other ($n = 15$).[525]

Continence status
Subjective or objective cure or improvement was considered in eight studies, with varying definitions of cure, success or improvement used.[518–522,524,528,529] Across the studies, at least some improvement was reported in 39–77% of patients (median 63%). In a study with follow-up to 41 months, cure rates fell to 39% from 59% at 12 months.[518]

Satisfaction and quality of life
A satisfaction rate of 68% was reported at mean follow-up of 2 years in one study.[519] Three studies found significant improvement in QOL (IIQ at mean 8 months[527] or I-QOL at 18 months[518,523]).

Adverse effects and complications
Complications relating to the device were reported across 11 studies.[513,518–522,525–527,529] These were:

- pain or discomfort: median 11% (range 2–34%)

- technical device problems, e.g. current-related problems, device malfunction: median 11% (3–42%)

- lead problems: median 6% (3–11%).

Surgical intervention for these complications was reported in between 7% and 66% (median 22%) of patients, across seven studies.[513,518,520–522,528,529] Removal of the implant was required in 4–11% (median 7%) in three studies.[518,524,528]

Other adverse effects were cases of seroma formation,[521,528] disturbed bowel function (1–7%),[519,524,525,528] wound dehiscence or infection (3–15%),[513,521,526] infection (2–9%),[519–521] toe flexion (8%)[519] and pain (abdominal, leg, pelvis and gluteal incision) (2–20%).[513,525]

A cost–consequence analysis was undertaken for sacral nerve stimulation – see Appendix G for further details.

Evidence statements for sacral nerve stimulation

Up to two-thirds of patients achieve continence or substantial improvement in symptoms after SNS, and the available data show that beneficial effects appear to persist for up to 3–5 years after implantation. Around one-third of patients may require re-operation, most often owing to pain at the implant site, infection, or the need for adjustment and modification of the lead system.

Permanent removal of the electrodes may be required in one in ten patients. [EL = 3] Developments in the devices and leads have resulted in reduced rates of complications since introduction of the technique. [EL = 4]

From evidence to recommendation
The recommendation for SNS was made a key priority for implementation by the GDG. The treatment options for women who have not responded to conservative treatments are all costly and associated with significant morbidity. There is a stronger body of evidence to support the use of sacral nerve stimulation than augmentation cystoplasty, urinary diversion or botulinum toxin A. The need for lifelong clinical supervision for procedures for OAB has been highlighted in the recommendations.

> **Recommendation for sacral nerve stimulation**
>
> Sacral nerve stimulation is recommended for the treatment of UI due to detrusor overactivity in women who have not responded to conservative treatments. Women should be offered sacral nerve stimulation on the basis of their response to preliminary percutaneous nerve evaluation. Life-long follow-up is recommended. [D]

5.1.2 Augmentation cystoplasty

Augmentation cystoplasty aims to increase functional bladder capacity by bivalving the bladder wall and incorporating a segment of bowel into the resultant defect. Most commonly, this has been a segment of ileum but ileocaecal and sigmoid segments are occasionally used. Other vascularised bowel segments have been used, with and without their surface epithelium, but these techniques have been largely experimental or applied to children.

No prospective controlled trials were identified that evaluated augmentation cystoplasty for the treatment of UI or OAB in women. One case series reported outcomes of the intervention in women with idiopathic urge UI who had not responded to prior treatment (conservative and surgical). About half the women also had evidence of interstitial cystitis on cystoscopy. Additionally, about half underwent Burch colposuspension for stress UI. At mean follow-up of about 5 years, 53% were continent, 53% were satisfied with treatment, 25% had occasional leaks and 18% were incontinent. One-quarter required treatment with antimuscarinics, and about one-quarter patch revision or further surgery. Very common adverse effects were recurrent UTI (49%), mucus retention requiring intermittent catheterisation (20%) and chronic diarrhoea (12%). Other adverse effects were partial bowel obstruction (8%) and cases of incisional hernia, bladder calculus and augmentation necrosis (*n* = 51).[530] [EL = 3]

Another five case series reported outcomes of augmentation cystoplasty in men and women with neurogenic or idiopathic DO.[531–535] Concomitant surgery was performed in 15–33% of patients in three studies.[531,532,535] One study reviewed patients who had either cystoplasty or detrusor myectomy, but did not report the time point of the outcomes considered and it is thus not considered further.[534] One only reported satisfaction with surgery, which was noted in 78%.[535] The other three studies reported the following effects on urinary symptoms:

- significant reduction in urgency and urge UI; 53% cured or much improved at mean follow-up 20 months (*n* = 45)[533]

- about 90% of patients had improved frequency; significant reduction in urinary symptom scores at 12 months (*n* = 48)[531]

- 90% cured at 12 months mean follow-up (*n* = 40).[532]

Two of the studies also considered urodynamic outcomes: one reported no significant change in the parameters measured,[533] while the other reported significant increase in total bladder capacity.[531]

Across these studies, adverse effects or complications reported were:

- recurrent UTI (median 37%, range 5–58%)[531–533,535]

- voiding dysfunction (18–39%),[532,533,535] problems with CISC 11%[531]

- disturbed bowel habit: increased bowel frequency (22–25%),[531,535] faecal incontinence (17%), diarrhoea (11%), constipation (4%).[531]

Other complications included mucus plug retention (3%),[532] anastomotic leak (2%),[531] persistent urine leak (3%),[532] incisional hernia (4–6%),[531,533] calculus formation (2%),[531] and urethral stricture (2–4%).[531,533]

A narrative review on augmentation cystoplasty included complications of the procedure in a series of 267 patients at 5–17 years follow-up. However, the indications for the procedure were not clear. Short-term complications were small intestine obstruction (2%), infection (1.5%), thromboembolism (1%), bleeding (0.75%) and fistula (0.4%). Long-term complications were CISC (38%), UTI (20% symptomatic), stones (13%), metabolic disturbance (16%), deterioration in renal function (2%) and bladder perforation (0.75%).[536] [EL = 3]

Evidence statements for augmentation cystoplasty

Data on augmentation cystoplasty in women with UI or OAB are limited to case series. Cure or improvement has been reported in at least half of patients with idiopathic DO. Postoperative complications such as bowel disturbance, metabolic acidosis, mucus production and/or retention in the bladder, UTI and urinary retention are common or very common. There is a high incidence of recurrent UTI postoperatively, and many patients will need to self-catheterise. [EL = 3] Malignant transformation in the bowel segment or urothelium has been reported in a small number of cases. [EL = 4]

Recommendations for augmentation cystoplasty

Augmentation cystoplasty for the management of idiopathic detrusor overactivity should be restricted to women who have not responded to conservative treatments and who are willing and able to self-catheterise. Preoperative counselling should include common and serious complications: bowel disturbance, metabolic acidosis, mucus production and/or retention in the bladder, UTI and urinary retention. The small risk of malignancy occurring in the augmented bladder should also be discussed. Life-long follow-up is recommended. [D (GPP)]

5.1.3   Urinary diversion

Urinary diversion implies that urine drainage has been rerouted away from the urethra. This is most commonly achieved by means of transposing the ureters to an isolated segment of ileum, which is used to create a permanent cutaneous stoma (ileal conduit). Urine, which drains continuously, is collected in a stoma bag, which is attached to the skin of the abdominal wall. Other bowel segments can be used including jejunum and colonic segments but these are unusual. Continent urinary diversion may be achieved by creation of a catheterisable abdominal stoma, or by formation of a rectal bladder. These techniques are largely employed in children and patients with neurogenic bladder dysfunction and rarely in adult women with UI.

Little information on the outcomes of urinary diversion in women with idiopathic UI or OAB was identified. Some data on the complications of urinary diversion, for benign conditions, are provided in a case series of men and women with neurogenic disease (76%), or intractable UI or interstitial cystitis (24%). After a minimum of 2 years follow-up, very common complications were vesical infection (52%), stoma problems – including parastomal hernia – and upper tract dilatation ($n = 93$; 63% women).[537] [EL = 3]

A retrospective study of women with stress UI who underwent ileal loop diversion also reported complications relating to the procedure ($n = 18$; minimum 1 year follow-up). Overall, eight women required surgical revisions of the loops/stomas and eight required formation of a vesicovaginal fistula arising from complications related to the defunctioned bladder.[538]

Evidence statement for urinary diversion

There are limited data on the outcomes of urinary diversion in women with UI or OAB. Where the procedure has been used in men and women with benign conditions, vesical infection, stoma-related problems and the need for surgical revisions occur very commonly. [EL = 3]

> **Recommendation for urinary diversion**
>
> Urinary diversion should be considered for a woman with OAB only when conservative treatments have failed, and if sacral nerve stimulation and augmentation cystoplasty are not appropriate or are unacceptable to her. Life-long follow-up is recommended. [D (GPP)]

5.1.4 Detrusor myectomy

Detrusor myectomy aims to improve the functional bladder capacity by excising bladder muscle from the fundus of the bladder while leaving the mucosa intact, thus creating a permanent wide-necked diverticulum. The defect is usually covered with a segment of mobilised omentum. Theoretically, this should avoid the complications associated with bowel interposition.

No prospective controlled trials were identified that evaluated detrusor myectomy for the treatment of UI or OAB in women. One case series reported the outcomes of detrusor myectomy in men and women with idiopathic or neurogenic DO, resistant to antimuscarinic drug treatment ($n = 30$; 20 women). Improvement was reported in 19 of 24 patients with idiopathic DO, with minimum follow-up of 2 years (median 6.5 years, maximum ~12). Three patients underwent further treatment (two ileal conduit, one colposuspension for stress UI). Other outcomes were not reported separately for patients with idiopathic DO. There was one case of bowel perforation. Overall, one-third of patients required intermittent self-catheterisation (ISC).[539,540] [EL = 3]

Evidence statement for detrusor myectomy

All case series on detrusor myectomy include patients with both neurogenic bladder dysfunction and those with idiopathic detrusor overactivity. While urodynamic parameters may improve in some patients, the clinical outcomes are unclear; hence the role of detrusor myectomy in the treatment of detrusor overactivity is not yet established. [EL = 3]

5.1.5 Botulinum toxin

Botulinum toxin is a potent neurotoxin derived from the bacterium *Clostridium botulinum*. Two strains are available for clinical use, types A and B. Botulinum toxin is known to block the release of acetylcholine and it will temporarily paralyse any muscle into which it is injected. However, the precise mechanism of action when injected into the detrusor muscle is unknown. It can be injected directly into the bladder wall and performed as a day case procedure using a flexible cystoscope. There are currently two preparations of botulinum toxin A available in the UK, BOTOX® (Allergan Ltd) and Dysport® (Ipsen Ltd). These have different formulations and molecular structures, and safety and efficacy may also not be the same for both products. All the evidence for botulinum toxin A in this guideline refers to BOTOX®.

Botulinum toxin A

No controlled studies evaluating the use of botulinum toxin A for idiopathic OAB were identified. Six case series evaluated botulinum toxin (type A) for the treatment of OAB or DO refractory to conservative treatments (specifically antimuscarinic drugs in two studies). Patient numbers in these studies were small; three studies included men and women, which did not report results separately for women (total $n = 99$),[541–543] and three studies included women only (total $n = 48$).[544–547] Duration of follow-up ranged from 3 to 12 months. One case series considered duration of response following a single dose of botulinum toxin.[547]

The doses injected varied, ranging from 100 to 300 units into 10–40 sites in the detrusor wall. Outcomes considered were bladder diary variables, continence status, satisfaction, QOL and complications.

The findings were:

- improvements in frequency in four of five studies that considered bladder diary variables;[543,544,546,547] initial improvement in leakage episodes that did not persist in one[545]

- cure or improvement rates of 60–75% at varying follow-up (3 weeks to 6 months) across three studies[541,542,546]

- 'subjective response' rate of 86% in one study[543]

- improvement in QOL (IIQ-7, UDI-6, KHQ, BFLUTS), in all studies.

In the study that considered duration of response to a single dose, frequency returned to baseline values after a mean of 24 weeks (range 10–52 weeks).[547]

Adverse effects and complications reported, which occurred in more than 10% of patients (very common), were haematuria,[541,542] pelvic pain,[541] transient dysuria,[541] transient retention,[542] difficulty urinating,[542] feeling of incomplete emptying,[542] and UTI.[542,546] Three studies noted that there were no adverse effects.[543,545,547]

Botulinum toxin B

A crossover placebo-controlled RCT evaluated botulinum toxin B in men and women with refractory DO, most of idiopathic origin. After treatment periods of 6 weeks, a statistically significant increase in mean voided volume, and reductions in leakage episodes and frequency, were seen, together with improvements in five of nine domains of KHQ. Transient adverse effects were urinary retention, constipation and dry mouth ($n = 20$; 17 women).[548] [EL = 1+]

A case series evaluated several doses of botulinum toxin B (between 2500 and 15 000 units) in women with OAB. Women were followed for the duration of response. Except for one woman, significant reduction from baseline in frequency was reported with all doses in all women, with duration of response significantly related to dose (19–25 days at lower dose, 80–98 days at the higher dose). Adverse effects were reported to be mild, which were transient injection site discomfort, and mild general malaise and dry mouth ($n = 15$).[549] [EL = 3]

Evidence statements for botulinum toxin

Data on the use of botulinum toxin A in the management of idiopathic detrusor overactivity are limited. The available data show cure or improvement in about half of patients, with duration of benefit between 3 and 12 months. [EL = 3] Botulinum toxin B appears to be effective only in the short term (up to 6 weeks). [EL = 3]

From evidence to recommendations

Despite the limited available evidence, the GDG recognises that the use of botulinum toxin A is rapidly becoming accepted in clinical practice. They feel that a recommendation is appropriate, provided that its use is limited to a point in the treatment pathway where otherwise only very major surgical interventions with high morbidity are available. Nevertheless, the GDG also feels that there is an urgent need for further data on this treatment modality, and hence has made both clinical and research recommendations.

Recommendations for botulinum toxin

Bladder wall injection with botulinum toxin A should be used in the treatment of idiopathic detrusor overactivity only in women who have not responded to conservative treatments and who are willing and able to self-catheterise. Women should be informed about the lack of long-term data. There should be special arrangements for audit or research. [D]

The use of botulinum toxin A for this indication is outside the UK marketing authorisation for the product. Informed consent to treatment should be obtained and documented.

Botulinum toxin B is not recommended for the treatment of women with idiopathic OAB. [D]

Research recommendation for botulinum toxin

The place of botulinum toxin in the management of detrusor overactivity of idiopathic aetiology deserves further evaluation.

5.1.6 Vanilloid receptor agonists

Resiniferatoxin is a derivative of capsaicin (chilli pepper). Intravesical instillation of resiniferatoxin was considered in two case series of patients with OAB, one in women ($n = 30$)[550] and another in men and women ($n = 41$; 20 women).[551] The duration of follow-up is unclear in one study, making interpretation of the results presented difficult.[551] In the other study, in women refractory to antimuscarinic treatment, urgency and urge UI were significantly reduced 1 month after resiniferatoxin treatment. Adverse effects were not considered.[550] [EL = 3]

No relevant studies of sufficient quality regarding the use of capsaicin were identified.

Reduction in urge UI and urgency in women has been reported in one case series, 1 month after intravesical instillation of resiniferatoxin. [EL = 3]

5.2 Procedures for stress urinary incontinence

The large number of different procedures described for the surgical management of stress UI reflects the numerous theories proposed to explain the pathophysiology of the condition and the continuing search for a procedure that can successfully deal with all cases. Although the range of procedures described is bewildering, a recent proposal for a new surgical classification simplifies them into those that aim to augment urethral closure and those that aim to support or stabilise the bladder neck or urethra.[552]

In 1997–98 approximately 8000 operations for stress UI were carried out in England (over a 12 month period). By 2004–05 the annual number had increased by 16% since that time, despite an approximately 90% reduction in the numbers of colposuspension and needle suspension procedures, and a 30–50% reduction in bladder neck buttress, sling and periurethral injection procedures. The increase was entirely made up by the rapid introduction of tension-free vaginal tape and similar mid-urethral tape procedures (see Figure 5.1).[553]

These trends in surgical techniques applied in the treatment of stress UI appear to be having a substantial impact on resource utilisation within acute hospital trusts. The average length of hospital stay for women undergoing surgical treatment has reduced by over 50% since the introduction of mid-urethral tapes in 1998. As a result, the number of hospital bed days used in the treatment of stress UI has reduced by a similar amount (see Figure 5.2).[553]

5.2.1 Operations to augment sphincter closure

Procedures in this section include injection of urethral bulking agents and implants that aim to occlude the urethra.

Studies considered for this section

Evidence described in this section is derived where possible from RCTs; where RCTs were not identified or had only short duration of follow-up, case series were considered. A systematic review of periurethral injection therapy for UI has been published on the Cochrane library.[554] Because most of the studies included in the review were published only as abstracts, and owing to publication of further studies, all relevant studies were considered individually. A further systematic review considered studies evaluating the silicone implantable product, which are considered individually in this section.[555]

The Interventional Procedures Programme of NICE has published guidance on two procedures of relevance to this area of practice:

- *Intramural Urethral Bulking Procedures for Stress Urinary Incontinence in Women* (2005). The guidance states that 'current evidence on the safety and short-term efficacy of intramural urethral bulking procedures for stress urinary incontinence is adequate to support the use of these procedures provided that normal arrangements are in place for clinical governance and for audit and research' and that 'clinicians should ensure that patients understand that the benefits of the procedures diminish in the long-term and provide them with clear written information'.[27]

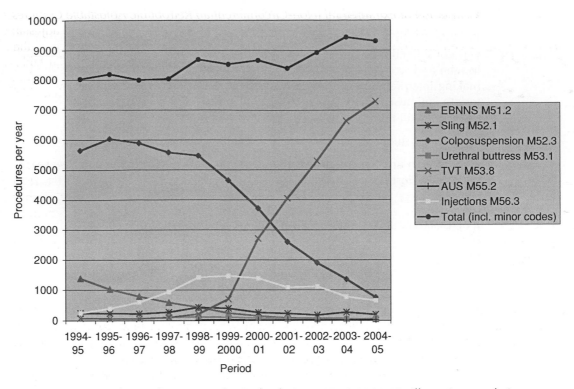

Figure 5.1 Hospital episode statistics for England, 1994–95 to 2004–05, illustrating trends in surgery for stress UI;[553] EBNNS = endoscopic bladder neck needle suspension, TVT = tension-free vaginal tape, AUS = artificial urinary sphincter, injections = periurethral bulking agents

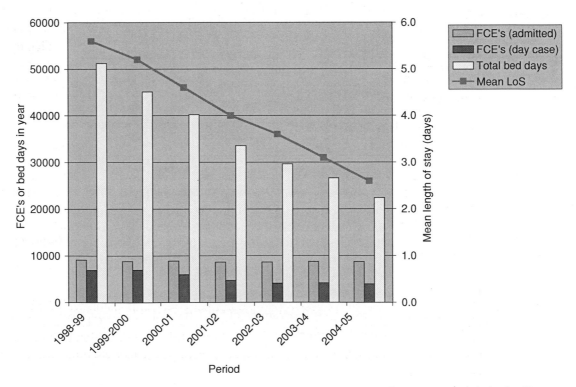

Figure 5.2 Hospital episode statistics for England, 1998–99 to 2004–5, illustrating trends in bed utilisation for women with a diagnosis of stress UI;[553] FCE's = finished consultant episodes, LoS = length of stay

- *Insertion of Extraurethral (Non-Circumferential) Retropubic Adjustable Compression Devices for Stress Urinary Incontinence in Women* (2005), which applies to the adjustable compression therapy balloon. The guidance states that 'current evidence on the safety and efficacy of insertion of extraurethral (non-circumferential) retropubic adjustable compression devices for stress urinary incontinence in women does not appear adequate for this procedure to be used without special arrangements for consent and for audit or research'.[28] Such devices are therefore not considered further in this guideline.

Intramural urethral bulking agents

The injection of a pliable bulking agent into the submucosal tissues of the urethra, or bladder neck, may increase the resistance to flow within the urethra, so preventing stress UI. The injections may be undertaken transurethrally, either using a needle passed down the operating channel of a cysto-scope under direct vision, or blind, using specifically developed injection systems. Alternatively, a paraurethral approach may be taken, inserting the needle through the skin, alongside the external urethral meatus and then passing it parallel to the urethra, while visualising the area around the bladder neck by cystoscope. A variety of biological and synthetic materials are available.

Controlled trials

Six RCTs[556–561] and two cohort studies[562,563] compared the effectiveness of a urethral bulking agent with other bulking agents, surgical interventions or placebo in women with stress UI. A further RCT and cohort study compared different routes of urethral injection of the same products (collagen[564] or hyaluronic acid/dextran copolymer[565]).

Silicone versus sling

One RCT compared periurethral silicone injection with an autologous rectus fascial sling in women with stress UI secondary to ISD in whom conservative treatment had failed. At 6 months, no signifi-cant differences were seen between groups in subjective cure or satisfaction, QOL (UDI-6, IIQ) or on a 1 hour pad test. Significantly fewer women undergoing injection therapy were objectively cured (no leakage on urodynamic assessment), but duration of the procedure, catheterisation, inpatient stay, and time to return to normal activities were significantly shorter compared with the sling. No significant differences in other adverse effects were noted (voiding dysfunction, *de novo* DO, UTI). A telephone survey of two-thirds of the women at 5 years found no significant differences between groups in urinary symptoms or in satisfaction with surgery, although fewer women in the silicone group were satisfied (29% versus 69%) (*n* = 45).[557] [EL = 1+]

Collagen versus continence surgery

Collagen was compared with surgery (46% suspension procedure, 54% fascial sling) in women with stress or mixed UI, in one RCT. No differences in satisfaction or QOL (SF-36, IIQ) were seen between groups at 1 year. Using intention-to-treat analysis (where treatment was considered to have failed in women with missing data), there was no significant difference in continence rates at 1 year (52% collagen versus 55% surgery). If only the 89% of women who underwent the randomised intervention were considered, the continence rate with collagen was significantly lower (53% versus 72%). Adverse effects were significantly higher in the surgery group (urinary retention, transient voiding difficulty, UTI) (*n* = 133).[560] [EL = 1+]

Silicone versus porcine dermal collagen implant

One RCT compared silicone with porcine dermal collagen implant, with 6 months follow-up. No statistical analysis was reported for the outcomes evaluated (QOL, change in Stamey grade, cure or improvement on pad test); this, together with lack of definition of improvement on pad test, makes interpretation of the results difficult. Adverse events were not considered (*n* = 50).[556] [EL = 1−]

Carbon-coated zirconium beads versus collagen

Two RCTs compared carbon-coated zirconium beads with collagen in women with stress UI due to ISD in whom prior treatment had failed. Duration of follow-up was 14 months and 2.7 years. In both studies, fewer women were followed up than were randomised, with no explanation for the missing data. Neither study found significant differences between groups in continence outcomes (changes in Stamey grading, cure rates, 1 hour pad test results). Only one study[559] reported adverse effects; both urgency and acute retention occurred in significantly more women treated with carbon-coated zirconium beads ($n = 52$, $n = 355$).[558,559] [EL = 1−] A cohort study that compared the same interventions also found no differences between groups in outcomes (time to treatment failure and satisfaction) with minimum of 8 months follow-up ($n = 86$).[562] [EL = 2+]

Autologous fat versus placebo (saline) or collagen

One RCT compared periurethral injection of autologous fat with saline in women with stress UI. A course of three injections was given to all women in the control group and to 82% of women treated with autologous fat. The rate of cure or improvement was about 21% in both groups 3 months after the final injection, with no significant change from baseline in UI score or in pad weight. Complications noted for all women were short-term urgency (very common [more than 10%]), and UTI and acute retention (common [1% or more]). One woman died from fat embolism ($n = 68$).[561] [EL = 1+]

A cohort study compared autologous fat with collagen in women who had failed prior continence surgery. At mean 7 months follow-up, the failure rate was significantly higher in women treated with autologous fat (57% versus 14%), and subjective improvement was lower. One woman treated with autologous fat had a subcutaneous abdominal wall haematoma. Other complications were not reported separately for the two treatment groups ($n = 67$).[563] [EL = 2+]

Different injection routes of the same product

One RCT compared outcomes of transurethral and paraurethral placement of hyaluronic acid/dextran copolymer in women with stress UI who had failed conservative treatment. Up to three injections were given within 3 months (mean 1.7 months). No significant differences were seen between groups in subjective cure or improvement at follow-up to 1 year. Significantly more women in the paraurethral group experienced postoperative urinary retention (30% versus 5%) ($n = 40$).[565] [EL = 1+]

A retrospective review of women who had either trans- or paraurethral collagen injections for stress UI also found no differences between groups in any outcome (continence status, pad usage, transient haematuria or UTI), although mean duration of follow-up differed between groups (6 versus 9 months) ($n = 45$).[564] [EL = 2−]

Case series of silicone bulking agent

Nine case series evaluating the outcomes of silicone were evaluated (total $n = 379$; range 21–102).[566–575] Eight studies included 60 women or less. Duration of follow-up ranged from 3 months to 3 years, with most between 1 and 2 years. All included women with stress UI, some of whom had had prior continence surgery (median 62%, range 19–100% across all studies).

Silicone was injected transurethrally in most studies. A single injection was given to women in two studies, while between 10% and 45% (median 18%) of women received a second injection after 3 months in the other studies. A third injection was given to 3% of women in one.[570] Each study reported continence status although the way in which this was reported varied widely across the studies. Given the difference in definitions, the results at maximum duration of follow-up in individual studies were:

- success rates (three studies): median 48% (range 48–74%)[566,567,569]

- objective cure (two studies): range 48–59%[571,572,574]

- cure or improvement in four studies that reported both: cure median 30% (range 10–45%), improvement median 28% (range 17–39%).[568,570,573,575]

Continence rates reduced over the duration of follow-up.[567–569,573,574] One study considered QOL, which reported significant improvements in all domains of KHQ.[571,572]

In one study, no complications were seen during or after treatment.[573] In other studies, adverse effects reported were transient. These were:

- dysuria (six studies, combined with report of haematuria in two): median 90% (range 53–100%)[566–569,571,572,575]

- haematuria (four studies, combined with report of dysuria in two): median 58% (range 45–100%)[566–569]

- frequency (two studies): mean 74% (range 72–76%)[568,569]

- acute retention (six studies): median 11% (range 3–18%)[566–572]

- UTI (two studies): 6%.[570,574]

Case series of glutaraldehyde cross-linked collagen bulking agent

Sixteen case series of injectable collagen in women with stress UI were evaluated.[139,576–594] Patient numbers ranged from 28 to 337 (total 1573). Duration of follow-up ranged from a mean of 5 months to a maximum of 5 years, the majority having follow-up to 2 years. One publication was an analysis of results in women aged over 65 years, within a study population of broader age range.[581] Women in one study had failed conservative treatment:[579] in ten studies, between 9% and 100% (median 67%) of women had had prior continence surgery. A skin test to collagen was performed 2–4 weeks prior to injection therapy, in each study.

The number of treatments required to achieve initial benefit was reported in two ways: as mean or median number of injections (which ranged from 1.7 to 2.2), or as the proportion of women who had two or more injections (which ranged from 8% to 74%, median 50%).

Subjective and objective cure rates were reported across the studies, although the definitions varied, for example changes in Stamey grading or pad usage. Given the difference in definitions, the results were:

- subjective cure (11 studies): median 38% (range 7–49%)

- subjective improvement (ten studies): median 40% (range 20–65%)

- subjective cure and improvement combined (two studies): 47% and 74%

- objective cure (two studies): 48%.

Other outcomes assessed also indicated improvement (pad test,[591] frequency and nocturia[589]). Continence rates reduced over the duration of follow-up.[139,578–580,584,585,594] Two studies considered time to treatment failure: one reported that this occurred at mean 13 months,[594] and another found that 50% were considered failures at 5 months.[590]

The complications reported across the studies were:

- de novo DO, urgency or urge UI (four studies): median 21% (range 10–39%)

- retention (nine studies, transient in five): median 6% (range 0–23%)

- UTI (six studies): median 5% (range 0.5–26%)

- transient haematuria (four studies): median 2% (range 0.7–5%).

Other effects reported were abscess at injection site (1%),[579] transient flu-like symptoms (2%)[139,580] and cystitis (1%).[593]

Case series of hyaluronic acid/dextranomer copolymer bulking agent

Three case series of the hyaluronic acid/dextranomer copolymer in women with stress UI were identified (total $n = 204$). Women in two studies had failed conservative treatment. One reported subjective cure or improvement by about 80% of the women at 3–6 months. Of 80% followed up to 5–6 years, 56% had continued response. Overall, 55% had two or three injections ($n = 20$; 16 followed up to 5–6 years).[595,596] [EL = 3] In the other two studies, women were followed for 1 year. A repeat injection was given to 43%. In the smaller study, 69% of women reported improvement, while objective cure or improvement was seen in 82% of those assessed ($n = 22$). Significant improvement in QOL (seven of ten KHQ domains) was reported ($n = 42$).[597,598] [EL = 3] In the larger study, 77% reported at least 50% improvement, with significant reductions in leakage episodes and in 24 hour pad weight, and improvements in six of nine domains of the KHQ (n = 142).[599] [EL = 3]

No adverse effects were reported in one study.[595,596] Adverse effects reported across the other two, which were mainly transient, included UTI (12%), urgency (12%), haematuria (10%), dysuria (8%), urethral disorder, reduced urine flow, vaginal discomfort (all 7%), urinary retention (7–20%) and injection-site pain (4%) or infection (2%) (n = 42).[597–599] [EL = 3]

Case series of carbon-coated zirconium beads bulking agent
Two case series reporting the use of carbon-coated zirconium beads were identified, which had mean follow-up duration of 9 or 10 months. One study that included men and women reported efficacy data for women separately (n = 20; 13 women).[600] The other included women only, with follow-up data for only 66% of those treated (n = 46).[601] Across both studies, 65% and 77% of women reported subjective cure or improvement: in the study that reported this outcome at 6 and 12 months, the proportion improved fell to one-third at 12 months.[600] No cases of urinary retention were seen in one study.[601] The other reported transient effects (skin reactions, urine retention in one case each).[600] [EL = 3]

Case series of polytetrafluoroethylene bulking agent
Only case series studies evaluating the use of para- or transurethral PTFE in women with stress UI were identified. The outcomes considered were subjective cure or improvement, and complications.[135,602–607] Mean duration of follow-up ranged from 1 to 5 years. Across the seven studies, 14–73% had had prior continence surgery. Between 22 and 56 patients were included in each study; one included men and women with results reported separately for women.[604]

In six studies the median subjective cure rate was 36% (range 7–70%), and median improvement rate 19% (range 11–41%).[135,602–607] The remaining study reported a combined cure or improvement rate of 32% at 1 year, which fell to 18% at 5 years.[607]

Five of the studies considered complications. Those reported in two or more studies were:

- acute retention (three studies): median 11% (range 3–31%)[135,603,605]

- UTI (two studies): 3% and 4%[135,605]

- voiding difficulties (two studies): 2% and 'common'.[135,604]

Other adverse effects were burning around urethral injection site (32%),[607] paraurethral infection (14%),[607] dysuria or urethral discomfort (38%),[603] foreign body granuloma (one case)[607] and passage of PTFE plug via the urethra (12%).[603]

Case series of hydroxylapatite bulking agent
A case series described as a preliminary evaluation of transurethral injection of hydroxylapatite (also referred to as hydroxyapatite) was identified, which enrolled ten women with stress UI. A second injection was given in seven cases. At 1 year, seven women were not using any pads or were using 'many fewer' pads. At about 3 years, six women were satisfied with the outcome (telephone follow-up). Complications reported were transient UTI and retention in three and five women.[608] [EL = 3] No other studies evaluating this material were identified.

Artificial urinary sphincters

The artificial urinary sphincter is a complex device that comprises an occlusive cuff inserted around the urethra which, while inflated, will exert a constant closure pressure. Pressure is maintained by means of an inflated pressure-regulating balloon. A small pump located in the labium is manually operated by the woman whenever she wishes to pass urine.

Most studies evaluating the AUS were conducted in populations outside the scope of this guideline (men and/or patients with neurogenic bladder), or studies included a mixed population but did not report data separately for women with idiopathic UI.

Six case series reported the outcomes of AUS in women with idiopathic stress UI. Across the studies 51–100% had failed prior continence surgery. The largest study included 206 women,

82% of whom had idiopathic UI, with results reported separately for this group.[609] The other studies included between 25 and 55 women.[610–613] The AUS device used was stated in five studies; except for a minority of women in two studies who received AS 791/792 or AS 742/761 sphincter, all received AS 800.

Duration of follow-up varied, with most being about 2–3 years (minimum 4 months, maximum about 9 years). Between 84% and 100% of women were subjectively cured. The largest study noted peri-operative complications, which were injuries to the vagina, bladder neck or urethra (all common) ($n = 168$).[609]

One series reported the duration and aetiology of device failure. At mean follow-up of about 9 years, 56% of women still had the same device *in situ*, 35% had revisions, and the median duration of the implanted device was 11 years ($n = 55$).[614]

Mechanical problems were reported in 4–22% of patients across the studies, including cuff or connector leaks and pump malfunction. Device removal or revision was common (five studies) with a median of 9% (range 8–17%),[609,611–614] as was urinary retention (two studies, 1.2% and 6%).[609,610] Other complications were incisional hernia (7%),[609] urgency with or without leakage (5%),[609] haematoma of labia majora and scar (4%),[609] phlebitis (1%),[609] superficial wound dehiscence (3%),[610] pelvic abscess (3%; device removed)[610] and the need for ISC (12%).[612]

5.2.2 Procedures to suspend the vaginal wall

Many procedures have been devised that share the common objective of preventing the downward displacement of the urethra which plays a part in the pathogenesis of stress UI. These include retropubic suspension procedures such as the Burch colposuspension, Marshall–Marchetti–Krantz (MMK) and vagino-obturator shelf procedure, each of which secures the paraurethral or vaginal tissues to a fixed structure by means of sutures.

A separate group of procedures was devised to be minimally invasive and suspend the paraurethral tissues by means of a suspensory suture, usually inserted under endoscopic control and secured to the rectus sheath to provide support. These include the Raz, Pereyra, Stamey and Gittes procedures.

Sling operations aim to stabilise the urethra by placing a strip of material around the underside of the urethra and securing the ends to a fixed structure above. These differ in numerous ways but could be classified according to the following framework:

- the tissues to which they are fixed (pubic arch or rectus sheath)

- the route by which they are inserted:

  □ traditional open surgery:

    – abdominal
    – combined abdomino-vaginal

  □ minimally invasive:

    – retropubic space (from bottom upwards or from top downwards)
    – obturator foramen (from outside inwards or from inside outwards)

- the materials used:

  □ synthetic – the various materials used in hernia repair were classified as follows;[615] this classification has been adopted to describe materials used in surgery for UI and POP:

    – type I – macroporous with pore size greater than 75 μm (allowing macrophages, fibroblasts, blood vessels, collagen fibres to penetrate pores), for example Prolene®, Marlex®, Trelex Natural®
    – type II – microporous with pore size less than 10 μm, for example Gore-Tex®, DualMesh®
    – type III – macroporous, but with multifilamentous or microporous components, for example PTFE mesh (Teflon®), braided Dacron® mesh (Mersilene®), braided polypropylene mesh (Surgipro®)

    – type IV – submicron pore size, for example Silastic, Cellgard, Preclude® Pericardial Membrane, Preclude® Dura-substitute

    ▫ moulded
    ▫ woven tapes
    ▫ biological:

        – autograft, for example autologous rectus fascia, vaginal wall
        – allograft, for example cadaveric dura mater
        – xenograft, for example porcine dermis, porcine small bowel submucosa.

The emphasis on recent innovations in sling surgery has been for slings to be placed with 'no tension' under the urethra while this may not have been the case with early surgical reports of sling techniques.

Other procedures such as anterior colporrhaphy and abdominal paravaginal repair are aimed primarily at treating POP but may have a secondary effect in preventing associated stress UI.

Studies considered for this section

Evidence on relative effectiveness of procedures described in this section is derived from RCTs. Due to the relatively short duration of follow-up in RCTs of surgical interventions, studies of other designs, notably cohort studies or case series, were considered if they provided information on outcomes over the longer term. Four systematic reviews of relevance have been published on the Cochrane library, considering open retropubic colposuspension,[616] laparoscopic suspension[617] (also published elsewhere),[618] bladder neck needle suspension[619] and anterior vaginal repair.[620] Further, earlier reviews evaluating surgery for stress UI have been published.[621–623] Owing to the substantial overlap of studies included in the Cochrane reviews, and because the reviews included abstracts that have not subsequently been published, the primary data, and further studies published, were considered alongside the reviews. Where pooling of studies and outcomes within the Cochrane reviews was deemed to be appropriate, the results are described in this section.

Other related guidance
The Interventional Procedures Programme of NICE issued guidance on bone-anchored cystourethropexy in 2003, stating that 'current evidence of the safety and efficacy of bone-anchored cystourethropexy does not appear adequate to support the use of this procedure without special arrangements for consent and for audit or research'.[30] Therefore, this procedure is not considered further within this guideline.

Colposuspension

Within the literature on suspension procedures, open colposuspension is the procedure against which others have most often been compared. Overall, most of the women included across all the studies considered were undergoing their primary surgical procedure for stress UI.

Open versus laparoscopic colposuspension
Six RCTs compared open (Burch) colposuspension with laparoscopic colposuspension in women with stress UI.[624–629] Two studies included women with mixed UI (proportion not stated[624] and 22%[626]). The studies compared open Burch colposuspension with laparoscopic colposuspension using sutures. One study had a third treatment arm, which was laparoscopic colposuspension using mesh and staples.[624] A further three studies compared different suturing methods for laparoscopic suspension.[630–635]

Between 52 and 291 women were randomised in these studies (fewer than 100 in four studies). Duration of follow-up ranged from 6 months to 2 years. One study only analysed results for women available at the 1 year follow-up with no attempt to consider the impact of losses to follow-up.[624] [EL = 1−] One study randomised women except where they expressed a preference for one of the interventions.[628] [EL = 1−] The remaining studies were of better quality.[625–627,629] [EL = 1+] Varying proportions of women (0–100%) underwent additional concomitant surgery across these studies.

Each study considered objective cure rates, using varying methods, including pad testing, stress test or urodynamic assessment. Four studies found no significant differences between open and laparoscopic colposuspension in this outcome,[624,626–629] one found a significantly higher cure rate with open colposuspension at 6 months (96% versus 80%; provocative testing on urodynamics),[628] and the other a higher cure with laparoscopic suspension at 18 months (78% versus 85%; stress test), with no difference between groups if objective and subjective cure were considered together.[625] Three studies considered subjective success and satisfaction, which were similar with both interventions.[624,626,629] In the study that evaluated open colposuspension, and laparoscopic suspension with sutures or mesh and staples, objective cure rates were significantly higher at 1 year with open than laparoscopic colposuspension with mesh and staples by the stress test (92% versus 63%), with no difference between groups when assessed by a 48 hour pad test (92% versus 91% versus 76%) (n = 211).[624] [EL = 1−]

Peri- and postoperative complications were reported for each study. Significantly fewer women in the laparoscopic colposuspension group using mesh and staples had urinary retention for longer than 5 days.[624] No other significant differences in complications were seen with open and laparoscopic colposuspension, which were bladder injury, urinary obstruction, de novo DO, haematuria, UTI, wound complications, haematoma, dyspareunia, urinary retention and enterocele.[625–628]

Operating time was significantly shorter in the open colposuspension group in four studies,[624–627] with one not identifying a significant difference between groups.[628] Conversion to open colposuspension was required in 1% and 5% of women undergoing the laparoscopic procedure in two studies.[624,626] Duration of hospital stay was longer in the open group in three studies,[624,625,627] and not significantly different in two.[626,629] The UK MRC study also reported no significant difference between open and laparoscopic groups in the time to return to work, which applied to about half of the women studied.[629]

Studies comparing different suturing methods for laparoscopic suspension
Four RCTs compared different suturing methods for laparoscopic suspension.[624,630–635] Sutures were compared with mesh and staples in three studies,[624,631–635] while the remaining study compared the use of double- with single-bite sutures.[630]

In the study that evaluated open colposuspension, and laparoscopic suspension with sutures or mesh and staples, objective cure rates were significantly higher at 1 year with open than laparoscopic suspension with mesh and staples by the stress test (92% versus 63%), with no difference between groups when assessed by a 48 hour pad test (92% versus 91% versus 76%). No other significant differences were identified (subjective cure, 'quality of life' assessed on a visual analogue scale, or satisfaction). Duration of hospital stay and bladder drainage were significantly shorter in the mesh and staples group and fewer people had retention; no other differences in complication rates were noted (n = 211).[624] [EL = 1−] While another RCT found no significant differences in objective cure rates at 1 year (n = 69),[631] the third study comparing sutures with mesh and staples reported significantly higher objective and subjective cure rates at 1, 2 and 3 years in the sutures group; cure rates declined with time in both groups. No significant differences were noted in operating time or hospital stay or in complications (bladder injury or DO) (n = 60).[632–635] [EL = 1+]

Recruitment to the RCT comparing double- with single-bite sutures was terminated early because of a notably higher cure rate in the double-grip group. Those who were treated were all evaluated at 1 year; both objective and subjective cure rates were significantly higher in the double-grip suture group. No significant differences in immediate or subsequent postoperative complications were reported between groups (n = 161).[630] [EL = 1−]

Open colposuspension versus the MMK procedure
Four RCTs compared the open colposuspension and MMK procedures in women with stress UI; 22% of women in one study had mixed UI.[636–639] One study also had an anterior colporrhaphy arm.[639] The study with three treatment arms was of poor quality, with no baseline data provided and no definition of objective cure.[639] [EL = 1−] The other studies were of better quality. The number of women randomised ranged from 30 to 170, with minimum follow-up of 6 months, up to 4 years. In three of the studies, other procedures were undertaken concomitantly in varying

proportions of women; these procedures included posterior colporrhaphy, paravaginal defect repair and culdoplasty.[636,637,639] One study noted that 23% had had prior vaginal surgery for prolapse and stress UI.[638]

Objective and/or subjective cure or improvement rates were reported in each study. In the study with three treatment arms, the rate of combined objective and subjective cure (not precisely defined) at 4 years was significantly higher with colposuspension than with MMK or anterior colporrhaphy ($n = 170$; 91% analysed).[639] [EL = 1−] A study that only reported subjective cure or improvement also found that significantly more women failed MMK than colposuspension at mean follow-up of 2 years (range 6 months to 5 years), when analysed using intention-to-treat (36% versus 15%) or for completers only (25% versus 7%) ($n = 138$).[636] [EL = 1+]

The remaining two studies both reported objective cure by negative stress test.[637,638] [EL = 1+] One found no significant differences between colposuspension and MMK in objective (80% versus 65%) or subjective cure rates (92% versus 85%), at a minimum of 2 years follow-up (mean ∼3 years) ($n = 80$).[637] The second study, in women with stress UI with low urethral pressure and hypermobility, reported significantly higher objective (53% versus 93%) and subjective (66% versus 100%) cure rates in the MMK group at 1 year ($n = 30$).[638]

Three of the four studies reported complications.[637–639] *De novo* DO and urge UI were common with both procedures, and with anterior colporrhaphy.[637,639] Time to normal voiding was significantly longer with MMK in one study (mean 21 versus 7 days),[638] as were hospital stay and duration of catheterisation in another.[637]

Colposuspension or vagino-obturator shelf versus bladder neck needle suspension or anterior colporrhaphy

Open colposuspension was compared with anterior colporrhaphy in two RCTs[640,641] and in a further two which also had a Pereyra needle suspension treatment arm.[642–645] Four studies compared open colposuspension or the vagino-obturator shelf procedure with needle suspension alone,[646–649] one of which also had a transvaginal colposuspension arm.[648]

Open colposuspension or vagino-obturator shelf versus anterior colporrhaphy
The four studies that compared open colposuspension with anterior colporrhaphy included women with stress UI without prior continence surgery; two specifically included women with prolapse.[640,642,643] In women with stress UI and prolapse, one study found significantly higher objective (74% versus 42%, negative stress test) and subjective cure rates (86% versus 52%) in the colposuspension group, compared with colporrhaphy after a minimum of 8 years follow-up. Recurrence of cystocele was significantly higher in the colposuspension group (34% versus 3%). Hysterectomy was also undertaken in all women in this study ($n = 71$; 96% analysed).[640] [EL = 1+] The second study compared colposuspension with the Pereyra procedure and with anterior colporrhaphy. Only women with complete data were analysed at 1 year, with only limited information on baseline characteristics of the women across groups. This study also reported significantly higher combined objective and subjective cure rates with colposuspension compared with Pereyra and anterior colporrhaphy; 87% versus 70% versus 69%, defined as negative stress test with no history of UI, and no urine loss observed at any post-surgical assessment ($n = 298$).[642,643] [EL = 1−]

Both other studies reported significantly higher objective and subjective cure rates at 1 year with colposuspension compared with anterior colporrhaphy[641,644,645] or Pereyra.[644,645] The study that combined objective and subjective data reported cure rates of 89% colposuspension versus 65% Pereyra versus 63% colporrhaphy at 1 year; this study only analysed results for women with complete follow-up data and gave no description of the women's baseline characteristics ($n = 127$; 84% analysed). Five year follow-up data of the women cured at 1 year also showed significantly higher cure rates with colposuspension compared with both other procedures.[644,645] [EL = 1−] In the second RCT, the objective and subjective cure rates with colposuspension and colporrhaphy at 1 year were 89% versus 31% (stress test), 83% versus 40% (20 minute pad test) and 95% versus 19% (subjective). Quality of life scores (IIQ) were significantly different in favour of Burch at 1 year. There were significant differences between groups in concomitant procedures undertaken in this RCT: anterior colporrhaphy for cystocele (16% versus 100%) or paravaginal defect (42% versus 6%) (n = 35).[641] [EL = 1+]

Other than urgency symptoms, which were very common in both colposuspension and colporrhaphy arms of one study, no other results were reported.[641] Data on hospital parameters were also lacking.

Open colposuspension or vagino-obturator shelf procedure versus bladder neck needle suspension

Four RCTs compared open colposuspension or the vagino-obturator shelf procedure with needle suspension in women with stress UI,[646–649] one of which also had a transvaginal colposuspension arm.[648] One study noted that 42% had had prior continence surgery.[649] Three of the four studies, which compared Burch with Stamey procedures, were considered to be of poor quality because of the use of alternate allocation rather than true randomisation, or not describing randomisation, and were additionally lacking in baseline data to enable consideration of whether groups were similar other than in the intervention.[646,647,649] [EL = 1–] Patient numbers were 50 or 51 in the three studies; all reported higher cure rates (subjective in two, objective in one) with colposuspension at varying durations of follow-up (minimum 8–12 months). The remaining study was of better quality, although only 74% of the women were followed up to 3 years. No significant differences in objective (urodynamics) or subjective cure rates were reported between retropubic Burch, transvaginal Burch or Raz procedures at 1, 2 or 3 years follow-up (n = 204).[648] [EL = 1+]

One RCT noted that there were no complications.[647] Common complications were haematoma, retention, abscess,[646] urgency or *de novo* DO,[646,648,649] wound infection, and postoperative pain in both groups, and voiding problems (not defined) in the vagino-obturator shelf procedure group.[649] Hospital stay was longer with colposuspension compared with Stamey needle suspension in two studies.[646,649]

Data from six RCTs were pooled in the Cochrane review[642,644,646–648,650] to calculate risk of failure with colposuspension (open or laparoscopic) compared with needle suspension (any).[616] The relative risk (RR) of subjective failure was significantly lower with colposuspension compared with needle suspension both up to and after 5 years follow-up (RR 0.56, 95% CI 0.39 to 0.81 after the first year and up to 5 years, and RR 0.32, 95% CI 0.15 to 0.71 after 5 years[616]).

Other colposuspension RCTs

One RCT compared Burch colposuspension with abdominal paravaginal defect repair in women with stress UI and grade 1 urethrocystocele. At mean follow-up of about 2 years, objective (negative stress test) and subjective cure rates were significantly higher in the colposuspension group (100% versus 61% and 100% versus 72%, respectively). The majority of women in both groups also underwent hysterectomy and culdoplasty. Recruitment to the trial was stopped after 36 women as it was considered that paravaginal defect repair was no longer ethical in the treatment of stress UI. Persisting voiding difficulties were very common, and recurrent urethrocystocele common in both groups; *de novo* DO was common in the colposuspension group (n = 36).[651] [EL = 1+]

Open colposuspension and pubococcygeal repair were compared in one RCT in women undergoing primary surgery for stress UI. Women with poor or absent pelvic floor contraction were excluded from the pubococcygeal repair group. At 1 year, objective cure rates were 67% with colposuspension versus 47% with repair. Subjective cure rates were 73% and 80% at 1 year, and 43% and 60% at between 5 and 7 years. Postoperative UTI was common. The median hospital stay was longer in the pubococcygeal repair group although the range of durations was similar in both groups (n = 45).[652–654] [EL = 1–]

Other needle suspension RCTs

One RCT compared the Raz suspension procedure with anterior colporrhaphy in women with grade 3 or 4 cystocele, about half of whom also had urge UI. Hysterectomy was undertaken in the majority of women alongside the continence procedure. At follow-up (between 10 months and about 4 years) the failure rate was significantly higher in the anterior colporrhaphy group (27% versus 14%). Postoperative urinary retention of between 5 and 10 days was common in both groups. No other complications were reported (n = 80).[655] [EL = 1+]

One RCT compared the Stamey suspension procedure with a porcine dermis suburethral sling in women with stress UI who were considered unsuitable for colposuspension; overall 60% had had prior continence surgery. At 2 years, subjective cure rates were 70% versus 90%. Intraoperative blood loss and postoperative infection were significantly more common in the sling group. Other common complications in both groups were bladder injury and *de novo* DO (*n* = 20).[656] [EL = 1+]

Colposuspension versus slings or synthetic tapes

Open colposuspension versus biological slings
Open colposuspension was compared with dura mater sling in one RCT of women with recurrent stress UI after hysterectomy.[657] The combined objective and subjective cure rates were 86% with colposuspension versus 92% with dura mater sling at follow-up of about 3 years (*n* = 72). Significantly more women in the sling group had voiding difficulty or retention postoperatively, both of which were common; and more in the colposuspension group developed rectocele. Bladder perforation and *de novo* urgency were common in both groups. Time to spontaneous voiding was significantly longer in the sling group.[657] [EL = 1+]

One RCT compared colposuspension with autologous rectus fascial sling and TVT.[658] Higher cure rates (negative stress test and symptom-free) were reported in the sling group at 1 year (93%) compared with open colposuspension or TVT (88% versus 87%). *De novo* DO and hesitancy were common in the colposuspension group, and retention common in the other groups (*n* = 92).[658] [EL = 1+]

Colposuspension versus synthetic slings
As well as the study of colposuspension, TVT and rectus fascial sling described above,[658] a further seven RCTs compared colposuspension with TVT: open colposuspension in four studies[659–663] and laparoscopic colposuspension in three.[664–667] Another RCT compared open colposuspension with a polypropylene soft tissue patch sling.[668,669]

Open colposuspension versus tension-free vaginal tape
Five RCTs studies compared open colposuspension with TVT in women undergoing primary surgery for urodynamic stress UI.[658–663] Overall, 627 women were randomised to either intervention (range of numbers across studies 50–344). One study also evaluated an autologous fascial sling.[658] [EL = 1+] Duration of follow-up ranged from 1 to a maximum of 3 years and was mostly about 2 years, although one study only provided results at 3–6 months.[663] In the largest study, 8% of the women withdrew consent after randomisation. Further losses to follow-up occurred by the 2 year analysis, the impact of which was considered in the analysis of results.[659,660] [EL = 1 + +] A second study also lost 17% of the women from the colposuspension arm before the end of follow-up.[662] [EL = 1+] The other two studies did not use true randomisation[661] or did not describe randomisation or consider whether groups were balanced at baseline in key parameters.[663] [EL = 1−]

The study with 3–6 months follow-up reported that 72% were subjectively 'completely' cured at that time point.[663] Of the other studies, each considered objective cure as an outcome, which was defined as less than 1 g[659–661] or 2 g[662] change in pad weight during a 1 hour pad test. The individual studies reported objective cure rates for colposuspension versus TVT of 80% versus 81%[659,660] and 86% versus 84%[661] at 2 years, with the third study reporting 76% versus 82% at median follow-up of 22 months.[662] While none of the trials identified significant differences between groups when women with complete data were analysed at follow-up, the impact of losses to follow-up were considered in the largest study. Assuming that all losses were failures or with the last observation carried forward (LOCF), the cure rate would be significantly higher with TVT. If all losses were assumed to be cured, or both presurgery withdrawals cured, and LOCF used for post-surgery withdrawals, there would be no significant difference between the interventions. In these analyses, the best and worst case cure rates were 51–87% for colposuspension and 63–85% with TVT.[659,660] [EL = 1 + +]

Other outcomes evaluated were QOL,[659,660] satisfaction[659,660] and subjective success.[662] Significant improvements in two-thirds of questions on the BFLUTS questionnaire were seen in both groups, and similar proportions were satisfied with treatment (82% versus 85%). The rate of subjective cure or improvement was not significantly different between groups (93% versus 92%).

Complications were reported in the four studies, although one only noted that there were no 'significant' complications.[662] Bladder injury or perforation* was common with the TVT procedure in each study, and was noted to be significantly higher than with colposuspension in one.[659] No other significant differences in complications were reported (de novo DO, wound infection, fever, sensory urgency). Complications reported with TVT were vaginal perforation, retropubic haematoma, vascular injury and tape erosion, and in the colposuspension arm were incisional hernia, haematoma, retention and pain at incision site.

During the 2 year follow-up period of the largest study, significantly more women in the colposuspension group required surgery for uterovaginal prolapse (5% versus none).[659] No other significant differences were identified in further procedures required (surgery for stress UI, cystoscopy, hysterectomy, urethral dilatation). Division or trimming of the tape was undertaken in 2% of the TVT group, and incisional hernia repair in 3% of the colposuspension group.[660]

Time to return to work[659,660] and to normal activities[659–661] was significantly longer with colposuspension, as were hospital stay, operating time and duration of catheterisation.[659–661,665]

Laparoscopic colposuspension versus tension-free vaginal tape
Three studies compared laparoscopic colposuspension with TVT in women with stress UI.[664–667] Prior continence surgery was an exclusion criterion in two studies (except colporrhaphy in one); the third reported that 17% in the TVT group had had prior continence surgery.[667] The numbers of women randomised were 46, 72 and 128. Duration of follow-up in two studies was 1 year, and a mean of 11 months in the third. In two studies, one or more women withdrew after randomisation (1% and 5%),[664–666] and only 88% of those treated in one study were followed-up to 1 year.[666] One study had sparse methodological data, and had different mean duration of follow-up in groups, which was not adjusted for in the analysis of results.[667] [EL = 1−]

Objective cure at 1 year was reported in two studies, with the third reporting combined subjective and objective cure. Within one study, the significance of the results depended on the definition of cure, with cure in significantly more women in the TVT group assessed by a stress test (86% versus 57%), but not with a 48 hour pad test (73% versus 59%).[664] Severity and KHQ scores were significantly lower with TVT at 1 year, and satisfaction higher. In the second study, objective cure rates (urodynamics) were 97% versus 81% in the TVT and colposuspension groups at mean follow-up of 21 months. No significant differences were found in UDI or IIQ scores, in leakage episodes or in satisfaction at 1 or 2 years. The majority of women in the study underwent another gynaecological procedure at the same time as the continence surgery.[666] In the third study, 83% of women in both groups were cured at mean follow-up of 11 or 13 months (minimum 3 months).

Intra- or postoperative complications common in both groups across the studies were bladder perforation, prolonged retention, wound infection, UTI, haematoma and pelvic abscess.[665,666] In two studies 9% of the women required conversion from laparoscopic to open colposuspension.[666,667] Other complications occurring less commonly were de novo DO,[667] vaginal erosion of mesh,[666] transection for voiding[666] and urge symptoms[665] with TVT, and port-site infection,[665] postoperative ileus, pulmonary embolism and pyelonephritis with laparoscopic colposuspension.[666]

Hospital stay, duration of catheterisation and operating time were significantly longer with laparoscopic colposuspension than TVT.[665–667]

Open colposuspension versus polytetrafluoroethylene soft tissue patch sling
One RCT compared Burch colposuspension with a PTFE soft tissue patch sling in women with stress UI and urethral hypermobility. At baseline, the proportion of women with DO was significantly higher in the colposuspension group (95% versus 41%). Subjective and objective cure rates were

---

* Bladder injury during a TVT procedure is a relatively minor complication resulting from bladder perforation by the introducing needle, and can be identified by a cystoscope used during the procedure. Although practices vary considerably, it has been managed by bladder drainage for periods of 12–48 hours and no long-term sequelae have been reported. Bladder injury during colposuspension requires formal closure and drainage for up to 5 days.

not significantly different at 3 months or after minimum follow-up of about 2.5 years (objective 100% versus 90% and 100% versus 85%, respectively; subjective 100% versus 95% and 84% versus 93%, respectively). *De novo* DO was common in both groups (24% versus 5%). Common events over the longer term in the sling groups were erosion, and urethrolysis for retention. No significant differences were found between groups in hospital stay or in time to catheter removal ($n = 36$).[668,669] [EL = 1+]

Long-term follow-up of suspension procedures

Cohort studies and case series were reviewed for long-term follow-up data because of the relatively short duration of RCTs.

Eleven cohort studies comparing long-term outcomes with colposuspension (Burch or MMK) and anterior colporrhaphy or needle suspension were identified.[670–681] Most were retrospective reviews of cases undertaken, some with questionnaire follow-up. The duration of follow-up of these studies ranged from a minimum of 2 years to a maximum of 17 years; most had follow-up of within 5–10 years. Losses to follow-up were noted in most studies, ranging from 2% to 76% (median 40%). Patient numbers ranged from 90 to 742, with a total of 3306. Procedures were selected for specific indications, typically with colporrhaphy undertaken in women with stress UI and prolapse of a higher grade. Those who underwent colposuspension usually had more severe stress UI. None of the studies considered the impact of potential confounding factors on the statistical significance of continence outcomes. Owing to losses to follow-up, and because of differences between groups in terms of patient characteristics, comparative outcome data derived should be viewed with caution and are not considered here. [EL = 2−]

Of the 18 case series identified for retropubic suspension procedures, most were in the form of retrospective reviews of case notes, with telephone or mailed questionnaires used for further follow-up (total $n = 2568$, range 48–374).[682–702] The majority of the studies evaluated the Burch colposuspension procedure, with the others being laparoscopic colposuspension or the MMK procedure. The duration of follow-up ranged from a minimum of 1 year to a maximum of 18 years; two-thirds had 5 years follow-up or more. Between 32% and 91% of those originally treated provided follow-up data. Concomitant procedures were undertaken alongside colposuspension in many of the studies, such as hysterectomy or correction of prolapse.

Long-term complications noted with colposuspension across the cohort and case series studies were:

- prolapse (cystocele, rectocele or enterocele; 16 studies): median 4% (range 0–60%)
- voiding difficulties/chronic retention (13 studies): median 6% (range 4–43%)
- *de novo* urgency or urge UI (nine studies): median 22% (range 3–40%)
- dyspareunia (seven studies): median 3% (range 1–12%)
- recurrent UTI (five studies): median 5% (range 4–11%)
- suprapubic pain/pain at site of suture (five studies): median 2% (range 0–12%).

Case series of needle suspension procedures

Twelve case series reporting long-term complications of needle suspension procedures were considered.[703–715] Patient numbers ranged from 55 to 206 (total treated 1346), with the majority including fewer than 100 women. Two described the Raz procedure,[703,704,706] one study each the Pereyra[707] and Gittes[708] procedures, and seven the Stamey procedure.[709–715] The duration of follow-up was about 4–5 years in most studies, ranging from 1 year to over 8 years.

Long-term complications reported with needle suspension procedures across the cohort and case series studies were:

- suprapubic pain/pain at site of suture (nine studies): median 6% (range 2–10%)
- surgery to release or remove sutures (eight studies): median 3% (range 1–10%)
- *de novo* urgency or urge UI (seven studies): median 13% (range 0–30%)

- recurrent UTI (five studies): median 2% (range 1–13%)

- voiding difficulty (four studies): median 6% (range 2–17%)

- dyspareunia (four studies): median 9% (range 2–16%)

- POP (cystocele, rectocele or enterocele; three studies): median 2% (range 0–8%)

- ISC due to retention (two studies): 2%.

Synthetic slings

Other relevant guidance
The NICE technology appraisal programme issued guidance on tension-free vaginal tape in February 2003. The technology appraisal is updated within this guideline by addressing a question on the procedure. The HTA informing the NICE guidance identified five RCTs (three published as abstracts), nine non-randomised comparative studies (all published only as abstracts), 66 case series (44 published as abstracts) and two population-based registries evaluating TVT.[716] The fully published data identified for TVT, and considered within this guideline, are as follows.

- eight RCTs comparing TVT with colposuspension

- two RCTs comparing TVT with an autologous fascial sling

- ten RCTs or non-randomised controlled trials comparing TVT with other slings or tapes (porcine dermal collagen sling, transobturator tape, suprapubic arc sling, intravaginal slingplasty and polypropylene mesh sling)

- one cohort study comparing different surgical approaches to TVT insertion (caudocranial or craniocaudal)

- 83 case series, the majority published subsequent to the HTA.

Where the TVT abbreviation is used in the text, this indicates the Gynecare TVT™ device.

Controlled trials comparing tension-free vaginal tape with colposuspension
Tension-free vaginal tape has been compared with open and laparoscopic colposuspension in eight RCTs.

Tension-free vaginal tape versus open colposuspension
Five RCTs studies compared TVT with open colposuspension in women undergoing primary surgery for urodynamic stress UI.[658–663] Overall, 627 women were randomised to either intervention. One study also evaluated an autologous fascial sling.[658] [EL = 1+] Duration of follow-up ranged from 1 to a maximum of 3 years and was mostly about 2 years, although one study only provided results at 3–6 months.[663] In the largest study, 8% of the women withdrew consent after randomisation. Further losses to follow-up occurred by the 2 year analysis.[659,660] [EL = 1 + +] A second study also lost 17% of the women from the colposuspension arm before the end of follow-up.[662] [EL = 1+] The other two studies did not use true randomisation[661] or did not describe randomisation or consider whether groups were balanced at baseline in key parameters.[663] [EL = 1–]

The study with 3–6 months follow-up reported that 72% were subjectively 'completely' cured at that time point.[663] Objective cure was reported in four studies; three defined this as less than 1 g[659–661] or 2 g[662] change in pad weight during a 1 hour pad test. The individual studies reported objective cure rates for TVT versus colposuspension of 81% versus 80%[659,660] and 84% versus 86%[661] at 2 years, with the third study reporting 82% versus 76% at median follow-up of 22 months.[662] The fourth study reported cure rates (negative stress test and symptom-free) of 87%, 88% and 93%, with TVT, open colposuspension and rectus fascial sling at 1 year. ($n = 92$).[658]

While none of the trials identified significant differences in cure rates with TVT and colposuspension when women with complete data were analysed at follow-up, the impact of losses to follow-up were considered in the largest study. Assuming that all losses were failures or with the last observation carried forward (LOCF), the cure rate would be significantly higher with TVT. If all losses were assumed to be cured, or both presurgery withdrawals cured and LOCF used for post-surgery withdrawals, there would be no significant difference between the interventions. In these analyses, the best and worst case cure rates were 63–85% with TVT, and 51–87% for colposuspension.[659,660] [EL = 1 + +]

Other outcomes evaluated were QOL[659,660] satisfaction,[659,660] and subjective success.[662] Significant improvements in two-thirds of questions on the BFLUTS questionnaire were seen in both groups, and similar proportions were satisfied with treatment (85% TVT versus 82% colposuspension). The subjective cure or improvement rates were 92% versus 93%.

Complications were reported in the four studies, although one only noted that there were no 'significant' complications.[662] Bladder injury or perforation[†] was common with TVT, and noted to be significantly higher than with colposuspension in one study.[659] No other significant differences in complications were reported (de novo DO, wound infection, fever, sensory urgency). Complications reported with TVT were vaginal perforation, retropubic haematoma, vascular injury and tape erosion, and in the colposuspension arm were incisional hernia, haematoma, retention and pain at incision site.

During the 2 year follow-up period of the largest study, significantly more women in the colposuspension group required surgery for uterovaginal prolapse (5% versus 0%).[659] No other significant differences were identified in further procedures required (surgery for stress UI, cystoscopy, hysterectomy, urethral dilatation). Division or trimming of the tape was undertaken in 2% of the TVT group, and incisional hernia repair in 3% of the colposuspension group.[660]

Time to return to work[659,660] and to normal activities[659–661] was significantly longer with colposuspension, as were hospital stay, operating time and duration of catheterisation.[659–661,665]

Tension-free vaginal tape versus laparoscopic colposuspension

Three studies compared TVT with laparoscopic colposuspension in women with stress UI.[664–667] Prior continence surgery was an exclusion criterion in two studies (except colporrhaphy in one); the third reported that 17% in the TVT group had had prior continence surgery.[667] The numbers of women randomised were 46, 72 and 128. Duration of follow-up in two studies was 1 year, and a mean of 11 months in the third. In two studies, one or more women withdrew after randomisation (1% and 5%),[664–666] and only 88% of those treated in one study were followed up to 1 year.[666] [EL = 1+] The third study had sparse methodological data, and had different mean duration of follow-up in groups that was not adjusted for in the analysis of results.[667] [EL = 1–]

Objective cure at 1 year was reported in two studies, the third reporting combined subjective and objective cure. Within one study, the significance of the results depended on the definition of cure, with cure in significantly more women in the TVT group assessed by a stress test (86% versus 57%), but not with a 48 hour pad test (73% versus 59%).[664] Severity scores, and KHQ scores were significantly lower with TVT at 1 year, and satisfaction higher. In the second study, objective cure rates (urodynamics) were 97% versus 81% in the TVT and colposuspension groups at mean follow-up of 21 months. No significant differences were found in QOL (UDI, IIQ), leakage episodes or satisfaction at 1 or 2 years. The majority of women in the study underwent another gynaecological procedure at the same time as continence surgery.[666] In the third study, 83% of women in both groups were cured at mean follow-up of 11 or 13 months (minimum 3 months).

Intra- or postoperative complications that were common in both groups across the studies were bladder perforation, prolonged retention, wound infection, UTI, haematoma and pelvic abscess.[665,666] In two studies, 9% of the women required conversion from laparoscopic to open colposuspension.[666,667] Other complications were de novo DO,[667] vaginal erosion of mesh,[666]

[†]   Bladder injury during a TVT procedure is a relatively minor complication resulting from bladder perforation by the introducing needle, and can be identified by a cystoscope used during the procedure. Although practices vary considerably, it has been managed by bladder drainage for periods of 12–48 hours and no long-term sequelae have been reported. Bladder injury during colposuspension requires formal closure and drainage for up to 5 days.

transection for voiding[666] and urge symptoms[665] with TVT, and port-site infection,[665] postoperative ileus, pulmonary embolism and pyelonephritis with laparoscopic colposuspension.[666]

Hospital stay, duration of catheterisation and operating time were significantly shorter with TVT than with laparoscopic colposuspension.[665–667]

Tension-free vaginal tape versus autologous fascial sling

Two small RCTs compared TVT with an autologous rectus fascial sling, one of which also had a colposuspension arm (total $n = 145$). In the study with three arms, cure rates (negative stress test and symptom-free) were 87%, 88% and 93%, with TVT, open colposuspension and rectus fascial sling, respectively, at 1 year ($n = 92$).[658] [EL = 1+] The second study reported cure rates (using the same criteria) of 92% in both groups at 6 months. Complications reported were *de novo* DO (0% with TVT versus 0% or 4% with rectus fascial sling), wound pain (7% versus 28%) and urinary retention (13% versus 7%).[658,717] [EL = 1+]

Comparison of different surgical techniques for tension-free vaginal tape

Results for the caudocranial (bottom-up) and craniocaudal (top-down) approach to TVT were compared in a retrospective review of women with stress UI who had undergone either procedure. No significant differences in subjective continence status, operating time or hospital stay were identified between groups. Bladder and vaginal perforation rate appeared to be higher (2% versus 7% and 0% versus 4%, respectively) with the craniocaudal approach ($n = 90$).[718] [EL = 2−]

Controlled trials comparing TVT and synthetic slings

Most synthetic slings available are made of polypropylene but they differ in the composition of the sling mesh and in the way by which they are inserted. Tension-free vaginal tape and suprapubic arc sling (SPARC) are made of monofilament threads, and the intravaginal slingplasty (IVS) of multifilament polypropylene threads. The slings are introduced via retropubic (TVT, IVS, SPARC), or transobturator (transobturator tape [TOT]) approaches. Prior to the TVT procedure being introduced, other synthetic materials had been used (PTFE, silicone, polyester and self-fashioned polypropylene).

TVT has been compared with porcine dermal collagen sling, TOT, SPARC, IVS and polypropylene mesh in studies of varying design and quality.

Tension-free vaginal tape versus porcine dermal collagen sling

In an RCT of women who had failed conservative treatment, no significant differences were seen between TVT and porcine dermal collagen in subjective cure or improvement at 1 or 3 years, nor in satisfaction at 3 years (assessed by mailed questionnaire). Operating time, hospital stay and complication rates were not significantly different. The complications seen were haemorrhage (3% TVT versus 4% porcine dermal sling), infection (0% versus 2%), the need for sling release or urethral dilatation (5% versus 10%), ISC (3% versus 3%), *de novo* urgency or urge UI (15% versus 18%) and dyspareunia (3% versus 0%) ($n = 142$).[719,720] [EL = 1+]

Tension-free vaginal tape versus transobturator tape

One RCT with 12 months follow-up found no significant differences in objective or subjective cure rates between the TVT and TVT-O (tension-free vaginal tape obturator) procedures ($n = 89$). Duration of hospital stay was similar following both procedures, although duration of the transobturator procedure was significantly shorter (17 versus 27 minutes). *De novo* instability or urgency, UTI and urinary retention were common in both groups, and bladder perforation occurred in 7% of the TVT group compared with none in the TVT-O group.[721] [EL = 1+]

The outcomes of TVT and TOT were also compared in two cohort studies, which were both retrospective analyses of cases ($n = 633$). [EL = 2−] No significant differences in cure, improvement or satisfaction rates between the interventions were identified. The duration of follow-up was longer with TVT (mean 19 versus 13 months; 75% followed up by telephone) in one study,[722] and about 1 year in the second.[723] Complications common in both groups were haemorrhage[722] and persisting or *de novo* urgency.[722,723] Other complications with TVT were bladder or vaginal perforation (14%) and haematoma (2%), and in the TOT group were bladder perforation (0.5%), vaginal erosion (1%), urethral perforation (1%) and difficulty with needle passage (1%).[722,723] Data for the TOT group in one study were stated to reflect the learning curve of the surgeon.[722] [EL = 2−]

Tension-free vaginal tape versus intravaginal slingplasty or suprapubic arc sling
Two RCTs compared TVT with intravaginal slingplasty (IVS), one of which also evaluated the suprapubic arc sling (SPARC), in women with urodynamic stress UI, a minority of whom had had prior continence surgery.[724,725] One specifically included women who had failed conservative treatment or required prophylactic continence surgery during prolapse repair for occult stress UI (no symptoms, but stress UI found on urodynamics); follow-up in this study was for 3 months only.[725] The other study had longer follow-up (median 13 months) but was a quasi-RCT.[724] [EL = 1−] Neither study found statistically significant differences between groups in cure or improvement rates (objective and/or subjective). One study evaluated satisfaction, which was similar across groups. Other than retention, which occurred in more TVT-treated women,[724] no other significant differences in complications were identified between TVT and IVS (n = 195; 93% analysed).[725] [EL = 1+] Other complications, with both TVT and IVS, were bladder perforation, haemorrhage and *de novo* urgency.[724,725]

In addition to the RCT mentioned above, two further RCTs compared TVT with SPARC in women with urodynamic stress UI, with or without POP (n = 84, n = 62).[726,727] Minimum duration of follow-up was 1 year,[726] and the median was 25 months.[727] Neither study reported significant differences in objective cures rates (pad testing), which ranged from 81% to 95%. Quality of life scores (IIQ) in the single study that evaluated this were similar.[726] Sling protrusion occurred in significantly more women in the SPARC group compared with TVT or IVS (13% versus 3% versus 2%).[725] No other significant differences were seen between TVT and SPARC in complications reported (bladder perforation, retention, voiding difficulties, tape release/erosion/rejection, haematoma, defective vaginal wound healing, protrusion of tape edge),[726,727] even though the bladder injury incidence was 13% with SPARC in one study, compared with no cases with TVT. However, the surgeon who performed all procedures had 700 case experience with TVT compared with none for SPARC.[727]

A survey of members of the Urological Society of Australasia reported the incidence of urethral and vaginal erosions following use of polypropylene slings (TVT, SPARC, IVS or other synthetic material) and the management of these complications. The questionnaire response rate was 61% (n = 198); 39% of respondents performed sling procedures which were TVT and SPARC (993 versus 466 cases). Vaginal erosions were reported for 1.2% of women treated, the majority presenting within 3 months. Removal of part of, or the entire sling, was undertaken in all cases. Urethral erosion was reported for 0.6%, the majority within 3 months, with one-third of cases presenting after 1 year. Half were treated conservatively, and removal of part of the sling was required in the other half. Urinary retention was reported for 6.5%, two-thirds of which required intermittent or indwelling catheterisation, and the remaining one-third required corrective surgery.[728] [EL = 3]

Tension-free vaginal tape versus polypropylene mesh sling
A cohort study compared the outcomes of TVT (n = 23) and a polypropylene mesh sling (n = 57) in women with stress UI, at mean of 23 or 20 months follow-up. No significant differences were found between groups in cure (negative cough stress test and no reports of leakage), improvement, or in QOL (IIQ-7, UDI-6), although preoperative UDI-6 scores were significantly different between groups. Transient urinary retention, and voiding difficulty was reported in both groups, *de novo* DO, dyspareunia and vaginal or suprapubic pain in the polypropylene mesh group, and bladder perforation with TVT (n = 80).[729] [EL = 2−]

Case series of tension-free vaginal tape
Over 100 case series reporting the outcomes of TVT in women with stress UI were identified, some of which represent multiple reports from the same institutions or by the same authors. Within these multiple reports it is not always possible to determine whether some or all of the same patients are included in these studies, and thus duplication of some data cannot be ruled out. Data were extracted from 83 studies involving over 15 000 women, about 30% of whom were included in

the national registries of Austria and Finland, which gathered data on complications. Two-thirds of the studies had mean, median or fixed follow-up of up to 2 years, the longest duration of follow-up being about 8 years.

Women with stress UI were included in all studies, with 23 including those with mixed UI, the proportion varying from 5% to 79% (median 25%). Overall, 70% of the studies included women with urodynamic findings of stress (or mixed) UI. In the majority of studies, a proportion of women had undergone prior continence surgery. Two studies only included women who had failed prior continence surgery.[730,731] Four studies either stated that none of the women had had prior continence surgery or excluded such women.[732–735] Concomitant pelvic surgery such as prolapse repair or hysterectomy was undertaken in combination with TVT, in varying proportions of women, in most studies. In three studies, the TVT procedures were undertaken with other pelvic surgery in all women enrolled.[736–738] Another three studies specifically stated that no other procedure was undertaken concomitantly.[136–138,739,740]

The quality of reporting in these studies varied. Although similar outcomes were reported across the studies, the definitions and terminology for cure, improvement and failure varied. The duration of follow-up was not always clearly stated, with most studies reporting mean or median follow-up durations. Drop-out rates were high in some studies.

The outcomes considered in most studies were continence status and/or complications. A minority reported other outcomes, predominantly satisfaction and QOL. Some studies had specific objectives, for example to consider predictors of urinary retention or of voiding function,[741,742] haemorrhagic complications,[743] bladder perforation,[744] sexual function,[745,746] or outcomes in subgroups (those with recurrent stress UI, with ISD, or with mixed UI).[747–749]

Twenty studies ($n = 3621$) had follow-up to less than 1 year (range 6 weeks to 10 months),[136–138,739–741,746,750–764] six of which did not report continence status.[741,753,756,760,762,763] Thirty-nine case series ($n = 4017$) reported follow-up of between 1 and 2 years;[730,731,733,735–738,743,765–795] other than four studies,[743,770,774,784] all reported continence status. Eleven studies ($n = 2173$) had follow-up of between 2 and 3 years.[732,742,744,796–806] The two largest studies, accounting for 61% of patients, only considered complications,[744,804] and another only considered voiding function.[742] Nine series reported outcomes with at least 3 years follow-up, up to about 8 years.[734,745,747–749,807–812] Apart from one, which only considered sexual function, the other studies considered continence status and complications.

The findings of these studies, other than complications, are summarised in Table 5.1.

In one study that considered whether cure rates declined with time, the rates were 85% and 81% at 5 and 7 years (69% follow-up) compared with 91% at 1 year.[735,810,811] In the 16% of women in one study who had mixed UI symptoms, there was a statistically significant reduction in cure rate from 60% at 3 years to 30% at 6–8 years.[812] [EL = 3]

Complications
Across the case series, most complications reported were intra-operative and thus results of all case series are considered together rather than by duration of follow-up.

The following intra-operative complications were reported:

- bladder perforations (63 studies): median 4% (range 0–23%, IQR 3–7%)

- haematoma (32 studies): median 1.5% (range 0–10%)

- haemorrhage (21 studies): median 1.2% (range 0–4%)

- urethral perforation (seven studies): median 0.5% (range 0–2%)

- nerve injury (four studies): median 0.7% (range 0–1.6%).

Postoperative complications reported across the case series were:

- voiding problems/urinary retention (53 studies): median 11% (range 1.6–60%, IQR 5–17%)

- *de novo* urgency, urge UI or DO (40 studies): median 6% (range 0–26%)

Table 5.1 Outcomes of TVT case series by duration of follow-up

Outcomes	Duration of follow-up, number of studies and patients			
	Up to 1 year (range 6 weeks to 10 months) 20 studies 3621 women	**1–2 years 39 studies 4017 women**	**2–3 years 11 studies 2173 women**	**More than 3 years (up to mean of 8 years) 9 studies 1504 women**
Subjective cure	10 studies: median 88% (range 76–97%, IQR 87–89%)	18 studies: median 87% (range 59–95%, IQR 83–91.5%)	6 studies: median 80% (range 67–90%)	2 studies:[a] 79% and 90% 2 studies 7/8 year follow-up: 80% and 90%
Objective cure	1 study: 87%	14 studies: median 87% (range 42–95%, IQR 83–91.5%	4 studies: median 90% (range 83–91%)	3 studies: range 81–95%
Cure that included subjective and objective elements	2 studies: 91% and 93%	8 studies: median 87% (range 81–94%, IQR 83.5–91%)	2 studies: 83% and 91%	4 studies: median 85% (range 81–90%)
Satisfaction	3 studies: median 87% (range 85%–91%)	8 studies: median 80% (range 72–96%, IQR 76–93%)	2 studies: 82% and 88%	1 study: 95%
Quality of life	3 studies: improvements in KHQ (2 studies) and IIQ and UDI (1 study)	3 studies: improvements in UDI and IIQ in each study (UDI-6 and IIQ-7 used in 2 studies)	2 studies: improvements in IIQ-7 and UDI-6	Not evaluated
Other outcomes	2 studies: sexual function of 58% returned to normal after TVT; 15% reported dyspareunia; 5% loss of libido. 34% improved sexual function, 62% unchanged, 4% worse; coital UI cured in 87%[b]	None reported	None reported	1 study: improvement in sexual function reported in 50% of women who no longer had UI during intercourse ($n = 19$); reduced libido was common

[a] the largest study ($n = 256$) only had data for about one-quarter of patients at 2 years, and 6% at 3 years[807]
[b] of those who reported the symptom at baseline
IQR = interquartile range

- UTI (31 studies): median 7% (range 0–19%)

- healing problems/wound infection (25 studies): median 0% (range 0–2%)

- tape rejection (25 studies): median 0% (range 0–3%)

- tape trimmed or removed (18 studies): 1.2% (range 0–8%)

- tape erosion (16 studies, 11 with up to 2 years follow-up): median 1.1% (range 0–6%)

- voiding difficulty described as long-term or requiring intermittent self-catheterisation (eight studies): median 1.8% (range 0–5%)

- pain relating to surgery, such as inguinal, loin or suprapubic (six studies): median 3.4% (range 0–12%)

- cystitis (five studies): median 11% (range 2–25%).

Asymptomatic POP was reported in 8% of women in one of the studies with longest follow-up (mean 7 years).[811]

National registry data

Two national registries (Austria and Finland) provide data on intra- and postoperative complications related to TVT; these gave a similar profile of complications to those listed above ($n = 4250$). Complications were: bladder injuries (~3–4%); bleeding, haematoma (each 2%); vesicovaginal fistula, thrombosis, seroma formation around tape, injury to epigastric vessel, injury to obturator nerve, vaginal haematoma, urethral lesion (each 0.07%); urinary retention (2%); UTI (4% and 17%); surgery (mainly for tape loosening/division/removal) (~3%); and *de novo* urgency (0.3%).[813–816] [EL = 3]

Survey of surgeons

In a survey of UK surgeons who performed TVT procedures ($n = 7336$) in the UK in 2001, 44% reported that they had had cases of bladder perforations, 37% cases of *de novo* DO and 28% cases of voiding difficulties persisting for more than 6 weeks. Tape erosion was uncommon (reported by 0.3%).[817] [EL = 3]

Studies considering TVT in specific patient groups

A few cohort studies evaluated whether TVT outcomes differed in women of different age, BMI, or in those undergoing concomitant surgical procedures, without attempting to address potential confounding factors. In addition, some case series attempted to determine whether certain preoperative urinary factors such as urgency or prior continence surgery, or demographic factors such as age or weight, predicted or affected outcome. [EL = 3]

The cohort studies found no consistent differences between older women (aged 65 or 70 years or older) and younger women in continence outcomes or complications with TVT.[818–820] [EL = 2–] Three of four case series studies reported no association between age or menopausal status and successful continence outcome;[732,761,787] the fourth study reported lower cure rates for women aged over 55 years.[785] Others reported fewer postoperative complications in pre- versus postmenopausal women,[804] or that increasing age was associated with greater delay in resuming voiding.[741] [EL = 2–]

In cohort or case–control studies that compared outcomes according to BMI, one reported that significantly more women with a BMI greater than 30 had postoperative urge UI, although more women in this group had urgency preoperatively; no other differences between groups in continence status or complications were reported.[821] Another found no differences in cure rates, but all cases of bladder perforation occurred in women with lower BMI, though this may have reflected the surgeon's learning curve for the procedure.[822] [EL = 2–] Two case series studies reported conflicting findings regarding cure rates and BMI,[752,799] as did two case series that considered postoperative complications in these subgroups.[741,769] [EL = 3]

In two cohort studies and one case series with follow-up to 3 years, concomitant surgery did not appear to affect TVT cure rate.[769,823,824] Fewer women undergoing the TVT procedure alone had retention, bladder injury or infections.[823,824] Another reported that concomitant vault suspension surgery was associated with postoperative voiding dysfunction.[758] Two case series reported no association between concomitant surgery and intra-operative complications[804] or prolonged voiding problems.[741] [EL = 3]

Seven studies reported continence outcomes for women who had preoperative mixed UI (range 8–36% [median 21%], observed on urodynamics in five of the seven studies). The cure rates for mixed UI were lower than for pure stress UI in five of six studies.[765,766,769,788,800,812] The risk of TVT failure was higher in women with mixed UI in one study, although the confidence intervals were wide.[138] [EL = 3]

Women undergoing primary stress UI surgery were more likely to be cured than those who had had prior surgery in one case series,[799] while another reported no significant difference in subjective cure rates between these groups.[751] Four reported a higher risk of complications (bladder injury, voiding dysfunction, or intra-operative complications) in women who had had prior surgery (hysterectomy, prolapse or continence),[759,760,800,804] while three others did not find an association between prior surgery and postoperative complications or specifically voiding dysfunction.[751,761,769]

A further four studies considered whether urinary flow rate,[758] maximum urethral closure pressure[138] or urethral hypermobility[740,825] predicted outcome and reported that voiding dysfunction was more likely in women with a maximum flow rate of less than 15 ml/second, that the procedure was more likely to fail in women with MUCP less than 20 cmH$_2$O, and that the results for women with or without hypermobility were similar. [EL = 3]

Economic evaluation of tension-free vaginal tape

An HTA of the clinical and cost effectiveness of TVT used economic modelling to compare the cost effectiveness of TVT with other common surgical procedures for the treatment of stress UI (open colposuspension, laparoscopic colposuspension, biological slings, injectable agents).[716]

Effectiveness data for the model were derived from the systematic review. One large RCT of TVT and open colposuspension did provide a direct comparison of the cure rates for these two techniques, but systematic differences in losses to follow-up between the two arms complicate the interpretation of these results.[659,660]

There are few trials of the different surgical procedures and most of the literature is from case series. In particular, there was a lack of studies directly comparing TVT with surgical procedures other than open colposuspension. Therefore, comparisons between open colposuspension and these other techniques were used to infer an estimate of their effectiveness relative to TVT.

Costs were analysed from an NHS perspective, with resource use identified from existing studies, manufacturer reports and expert opinion. Unit costs for resource items were obtained from the literature, manufacturer's price lists and NHS Reference Costs. The primary outcome measure in the model was QALYs.

A number of sensitivity analyses were undertaken to reflect trial-based uncertainty in the relative cure rates for TVT compared with open colposuspension, and the likelihood that TVT would be considered cost effective at different cost per QALY willingness to pay thresholds was estimated. Sensitivity analysis was additionally undertaken on a number of model parameters.

The modelling suggested that at baseline TVT dominates open colposuspension at 5 years. It costs £267 less per patient and produces an additional 0.00048 QALYs. This dominance result was driven by the assumptions that the women who withdrew from the trial were missing completely at random, that re-treatment colposuspension is less effective than primary colposuspension and that the failure rate of TVT will not deteriorate over time. Analysis which took account of sampling data variation suggested that there was a 93% chance that TVT would be considered cost effective if the willingness to pay for a QALY was £30,000. Sensitivity analysis suggested that changes in a number of parameters could reduce the likelihood of TVT being considered cost effective at different cost per QALY thresholds. For example, assumptions about hospital length of stay are an important driver of cost effectiveness results as it accounts for a substantial proportion of the procedure costs. The review reasoned that TVT was likely to be cost effective when compared with other surgical techniques on the assumption that it was at least as effective and cheaper.

A two-year follow-up of women in an RCT of TVT versus open colposuspension has shown that prolapse is more prevalent in those who had open colposuspension.[660]

Other synthetic slings

Slings made of polypropylene, that are not tension-free vaginal tape

Suprapubic arc sling (SPARC)
As well as the three RCTs comparing SPARC with TVT,[725–727] and a survey of complications,[728] three case series of the suprapubic arc sling were also identified.[826–828] One provided no information on the patients, nor details of the procedure ($n = 140$).[827] The second reported objective and subjective cure rates of 90% and 69%, respectively.[826] The third series focused on QOL, but only reported mean scores from 46% of the women treated.[828] Two studies reported complications: bladder injury (4–7%), transient UTI (9%), retention requiring sling release (3–4%), voiding difficulties (11%) and *de novo* urge symptoms (6–12%).[826,828] [EL = 3]

Intravaginal slingplasty sling (IVS)
Other than the RCTs comparing IVS with TVT,[724,725] four case series of IVS were identified.[829–832] [EL = 3] Only one series considered cure rate, which was 86% at median 18 months follow-up ($n = 49$).[830] Complications noted in this series were haematoma (2%), temporary ISC (18%) and voiding difficulties (10%). The other case series reported specific complications, as follows:

- 7% sling infection, requiring sling removal in ten of the 11 cases; women presented at median 9 months (range 4–17 months) with either vaginal discharge or vaginal/abdominal fistula ($n = 149$)[829]

- 19 cases requiring sling removal owing to retropubic abscess, vesico-vaginal fistula, voiding difficulties, pain syndrome or mesh infection[831]

- 17% vaginal mesh extrusion, presenting at mean 9 months ($n = 35$).[832]

Self-anchoring polypropylene mesh
One case series reported the outcomes of a self-anchoring polypropylene mesh sling (Safyre™) inserted retropubically in women with stress UI, of whom 60% had had prior continence surgery. At mean follow-up of 18 months, the subjective cure rate was 92% and improvement 2%. Transient *de novo* urgency was very common (21%). Bladder perforation, retention requiring loosening of sling tension, and vaginal erosion of tape all occurred in between 2–5% of the women ($n = 126$).[833] [EL = 3]

The same authors also retrospectively compared outcomes when the sling had been inserted vaginally, through the retropubic space or through the obturator foramen. Duration of follow-up was a mean of 18 and 14 months, respectively. Subjective cure rates were similar (92–94%) but complications higher with the transvaginal route: bladder injury 10% versus 0%, transient voiding symptoms 21% versus 10%, and sling infection 3% versus 1% ($n = 226$).[834] [EL = 2−]

Transobturator tape (TOT)
Other than the cohort studies that compared a TOT procedure with TVT,[722,723] ten case series reported outcomes of the TOT procedure (total $n = 504$).[835–844] One of these considered the inside-out technique for passage of the tape.[835] The mean/median follow-up period ranged from 7 weeks to 17 months. Cure rates ranged from 55% to 92% (median 81%), and improvement from 5% to 15%. Complications reported across the studies describing the 'outside-in' technique were:

- bladder perforation (eight studies): median 0.5% (range 0–1%)

- *de novo* urgency (six studies): median 4% (range 1.6–14%)

- urethral perforation (five studies): median 1% (range 0–2.5%)

- voiding difficulty or retention (five studies): median 2.1% (range 1–16%)

- vaginal erosion (five studies); median 2.5% (range 0–14%)

- vaginal perforation (four studies): median 0.7% (0.3–2%).

Other complications reported in fewer studies included haemorrhage, haematoma and dyspareunia (all uncommon), and dysuria and UTI (both common).

The study that focused on vaginal erosion following TOT insertion (incidence 14%) reported that women presented with persistent vaginal discharge a mean of 9 months (range 2–19 months) after the procedure. Tape removal or trimming was required in all cases ($n = 65$).[845] [EL = 3]

The case series in which the transobturator inside-out technique was described reported complications. Immediately postoperatively, 16% experienced pain or discomfort in thigh folds, and at 1 month, vaginal erosion and complete urinary retention occurred in 1% and 3%, respectively ($n = 107$).[835] [EL = 3]

A cohort study compared the outside-in and inside-out approach to inserting a transobturator sling. No significant differences were found in objective cure or satisfaction rates or in complications at 12 months ($n = 100$).[846] [EL = 2+]

Additionally, one RCT compared a retropubic sling with the transobturator route of inserting a similar sling. Subjective cure rates were 93% in both groups and changes in QOL (UDI and IIQ) were also similar at 1 month. Bladder injury during the procedures was significantly higher with retropubic insertion (10% versus 0%), and vaginal injury higher with transobturator insertion (0% versus 11%) ($n = 88$).[847] [EL = 1+]

Comparative complication rates with retropubic and transobturator slings
Data from all studies that reported bladder injury, urethral injury or voiding difficulties with retropubic slings (TVT, IVS, SPARC, Safyre™) were pooled and the incidence compared with pooled data from studies evaluating transobturator slings. While bladder and urethral injury are consistently defined across the studies, the definition of voiding difficulties varied, with some including transient voiding problems. Allowing for these factors, the RR of each complication with retropubic compared with transobturator slings were as follows:

- bladder injury: RR 6.29 (95% CI 3.78 to 10.45)

- urethral injury: RR 0.30 (95% CI 0.12 to 0.77)

- voiding difficulties: RR 2.71 (95% CI 1.97 to 3.73).

These show that the risk of bladder injury and voiding difficulties is significantly higher with retropubic compared with transobturator slings, and that the risk of urethral injury is significantly lower with retropubic slings. When comparing TVT alone with the TOT procedure, the same pattern is seen:

- bladder injury: RR 6.14 (95% CI 3.69 to 10.22)

- urethral injury: RR 0.23 (95% CI 0.08 to 0.62)

- voiding difficulties: RR 2.83 (95% CI 2.05 to 3.89).

The findings should be viewed with caution because most of the data used in the pooling are derived from indirect comparisons of the interventions.

Other slings made of polypropylene (self-fashioned, Prolene® or Marlex®)
A polypropylene sling was compared with rectus fascial sling in a quasi-RCT, and with TVT in a cohort study. At median follow-up of about 2 years, cure and satisfaction rates were similar between fascial and polypropylene slings, but operating time and hospital stay were significantly shorter in the polypropylene group. Delayed voiding occurred in more women in the fascial sling group. There were no other significant differences between groups in complications reported (haematoma, dysuria, *de novo* urgency or urge UI) ($n = 50$).[848] [EL = 1−] The cohort study also found no difference in continence outcomes between groups at 20–23 months ($n = 80$).[729] [EL = 2−]

Eight case series describing the use of polypropylene mesh (not TVT) were identified that used a self-fashioned sling or a proprietary product (total $n = 900$; range 21–301).[849–856] Two of these described the use of a prosthesis that allows sling adjustment postoperatively ($n = 50$).[855,856] In six studies, between 10% and 62% had mixed UI.[849,850,852,853,855,856] Women in six studies had had prior continence surgery (11–62%),[849,851–855] and varying numbers of women across seven studies underwent concomitant surgery (8–100%).[849,850,852–856]

Duration of follow-up varied widely (1 month to 8 years), with six studies reporting mean/median follow-up of between 1 and 2 years. The outcomes reported were:

- subjective cure rates: 69–99% (median 77%)[849,850,852,854,856]

- objective cure rates: 62–96% (median 92%)[851,854,855]

- combined subjective and objective cure (no symptoms and negative stress test) rate: 87%[853]

- satisfaction rates: 77% and 91%.[852,855]

Five year follow-up of 23% of women from one case series has been published, at which 72% were cured. There were no cases of sling removal and 7% had *de novo* urgency.[857] [EL = 3]

Intra-operative complications were:

- haemorrhage requiring blood transfusion in 1%, 3% and 31%[849,851,856]

- haematoma: median 5% (range 0.7–10%)[849,852,853,856]

- bladder perforation/injury: median 0.4% (range 0–1%)[849,851,853,856]

- urethral perforation: median 0.3% (range 0–0.5%).[851,853,856]

No intra-operative complications were seen in one study.[855]

Postoperative complications were:

- UTI: median 6% (range 3–20%)[849,851,853,856]

- *de novo* DO: median 9% (range 5–16%)[849,851,853–855]

- urgency: median 19% (range 14–46%)[851,852,856]

- urinary retention was described in all studies, although the method of reporting varied; ISC was required for up to 3–6 months (four studies);[849,850,852,854] 3% from one study were using ISC at 1 year;[849] a further two studies reported that sling release (4%)[851] or postoperative immediate adjustment (using the attached prosthesis, 48%) was required for retention[855]

- prolapse developed in 0.3–12% (median 3%)[849,850,852,854]

- mesh exposure or vaginal erosion requiring removal of the tape: median 3% (range 0.3–8%)[849,852–854]

- no cases of mesh rejection in one study,[853] and no cases of urethral erosion in another.[854]

Complications relating to the surgical incision (all common) were:

- persistent abdominal or vaginal wall sinus[849,850]

- non-healing of vaginal wall (requiring sling excision)[850]

- wound infection[850,851,853]

- suprapubic pain or vaginal pain.[852,854]

Seroma was reported in 14% of women in one study.[856]

Uncommon complications (0.1% or more and less than 1%) were deep vein thrombosis,[849] osteomyelitis (resolved),[849] osteitis pubis (suprapubic sutures cut and removed),[849] small bowel obstruction and urinary obstruction.[854]

Slings made of silicone

No controlled trials evaluating the used of a silicone sling were identified. Three case series reported outcomes relating to this sling (reinforced with polyethylene) in women with stress UI. Two included 30 and 54 women,[858,859] while the third described the complication of sinus formation in 18% of 40 women who underwent the procedure.[860]

The majority of women in one series had undergone prior continence surgery;[859] in another, the decision to use the sling was made intra-operatively when colposuspension was seen not to be technically feasible.[858] Both included a proportion of women with mixed UI (17% and 60%).

Subjective cure rates were 79% at mean follow-up of 15 months,[858] and both subjective and objective (pad test) cure rates were 83% in the series with complete follow-up at 3 months.[859] Intra-operative complications were haemorrhage requiring blood transfusion (6%),[858] and vaginal perforation, and bladder or urethral perforation (7% each; one case of urethrovaginal fistula needing sling removal).[859] *De novo* DO and voiding difficulty was very common (more than 10%) in both; voiding difficulty required sling release in four of seven cases in one study.[859] Pulmonary embolism, enterocele, and sinus formation (which required removal or trimming of the sling) occurred in 4% of women in one study.[858] The third report described sinus formation in 18% of cases treated, with sling removal in each case at 3–16 months, following the procedure.[860]

Slings made of polytetrafluoroethylene

Three controlled trials evaluated a PTFE sling, each of which was small with maximum follow-up of about 2 years. Compared with open colposuspension in women with stress UI, and urethral hypermobility, cure rates with PTFE were not significantly different at 2.5 years (objective 85% versus 100%; subjective 93% versus 84%). At baseline, the proportion of women with DO was significantly lower in the PTFE group (41% versus 95%). *De novo* DO was reported in 24% versus 5%. Complications over the longer term in the sling group were erosion (12%) and urethrolysis for retention (6%) ($n = 36$).[668,669] [EL = 1+]

One RCT compared PTFE and rectus fascial slings in women with stress UI ($n = 48$; 92% of whom had had prior continence surgery). Combined objective and subjective cure rates were 88% and 81%, respectively, at 6 months. Urethral erosion, recurrent UTI and *de novo* DO were very common with PTFE, whereas no complications were reported in the fascial sling group.[861] [EL = 1−]

A quasi-RCT compared PTFE with a vaginal wall sling in women with stress or mixed (~60%) UI. Cure and satisfaction rates were high across both groups at mean follow-up of 22 months (75–100%), but no statistical analysis was reported. Complications reported were wound infection, UTI, bleeding, vaginitis and transient *de novo* urge UI ($n = 40$).[862] [EL = 1−]

Seven case series evaluated slings or a soft tissue patch made of PTFE in women with stress UI (total $n = 453$; range 24–115).[863–871] Some women in three studies had mixed UI (36–90%).[863–865,871] Between 26% and 100% of women across five studies (median 56%) had had prior continence surgery.[863–866,868,869,871] Concomitant surgery was undertaken in 26% and 78% of women in two studies.[868,869,871]

Duration of follow-up ranged from about 1 to 5 years. All except one study considered continence,[870] all considered complications and two reported satisfaction.[864,865,867] The median subjective cure rate was 83% (range 72–89%). The objective cure rates, reported in two studies, were 61% and 89%. Satisfaction was reported by 81–82% of women.[864,865,867]

Complications were:

- sling removal (all studies): median 8% (range 3–31%) for varying reasons (rejection, reactions to sling [sinus formation, granulation tissue, abdominal wound abscess, erosions of vaginal mucosa], urethral obstruction, urethral erosion, non-healing of vaginal incision, urinary retention, persistent pain, sling infections)

- wound complications or infections (three studies): median 15% (range 6–40%)[863–865,868,869]

- *de novo* urge UI or DO (four studies): median 9% (range 0–12%)[863–866,871]

- voiding difficulties (two studies): 22% and 37%[867–869]

- intermittent self-catheterisation (two studies): 3% and 8%[863,868,869]

- surgery for retention (two studies): 4% and 9%.[863–865]

Other complications noted were irritative symptoms and recurrent UTI (21%),[866] and pelvic pain (16%).[867] No cases of sling intolerance[863] or of bladder or urethral erosion were seen in two studies.[864,865]

Slings made of polyester

No controlled trials were identified for slings made of polyester. Four case series evaluated the use of a polyester graft mesh (Mersilene®), two with very limited baseline data for the women treated.[872–875] Each study included women with stress UI, and one stated that 69% of those followed up to 1 year had urgency or urge UI. Patient numbers ranged from 24 to 200 (median 102). Three studies noted that 25–54% of women had had prior continence surgery.[872,873,875] Concomitant surgery was undertaken in 55% of women in one.[873]

Duration of follow-up ranged from a mean of 2 years to 5 years. Subjective cure rates across the studies ranged from 50% to 96% (median 84%). The objective cure rate in 26% of women with follow-up of 5 years was 94%; compared with 95% at 1 year (one study).[873]

Complications reported were:

- intra-operative: haemorrhage 2%;[874] no cases of urethral or bladder injury[872]

- *de novo* urge UI or DO (two studies): 4% and 15%[872,874]

- retention or voiding difficulties (two studies): 1.5% and 15%;[873,874] surgical release for retention required in 1.5%.[873]

Other complications noted across the studies were: vaginal or inguinal sling erosion (4%; sling removed in one case), recurrent UTI (2%), superficial groin seroma/abscess (2.5%), dyspareunia (2.5%);[873] wound haematoma/infection (11%), exposure of Prolene® sutures (2%);[874] vesico-vaginal fistula (2%; repaired), minor wound complications (7%), and partial dehiscence of incision with exposure of part of sling which was resolved by trimming (3%).[875] No cases of urethral necrosis, graft rejection or sinus formation were reported in one series.[872]

Biological slings

Other relevant guidance

NICE IP guidance on biological slings states that 'current evidence on the safety and efficacy of the insertion of biological slings for stress urinary incontinence in women is adequate to support the use of this procedure provided that normal arrangements are in place for consent and clinical governance. Data on the long-term efficacy of the insertion of biological slings for stress urinary incontinence in women are limited to autologous slings. Clinicians should therefore audit patients in the longer term.'[29]

A Cochrane systematic review considered traditional suburethral slings; the review included studies evaluating synthetic as well as biological materials.[876] Therefore, the relevant studies included in the review are considered individually within this section.

Controlled trials evaluating biological slings

Nearly all RCTs of biological slings compare the autologous rectus fascial sling procedure with a range of other surgical interventions. RCTs evaluating dura mater and porcine dermal slings were also identified. Non-randomised comparisons of autologous and allograft rectus fascial or fascia lata slings were also considered.

Rectus fascial sling versus periurethral silicone

One RCT compared autologous rectus fascial sling with periurethral silicone injection in women with stress UI secondary to ISD in whom conservative treatment had failed. At 6 months, no significant differences were seen between groups in subjective cure or satisfaction, QOL (UDI-6,

IIQ) or on a 1 hour pad test. Significantly more women undergoing sling surgery were objectively cured (urodynamic assessment), but duration of the procedure, catheterisation, inpatient stay, and time to return to normal activities were significantly longer. No significant differences in other adverse effects were noted (voiding dysfunction, *de novo* DO, UTI). A survey of two-thirds of the women at 5 years found no statistically significant differences between groups in urinary symptoms or in satisfaction with surgery (*n* = 45).[557] [EL = 1+]

Continence surgery versus periurethral collagen
Open continence surgery (a suspension procedure in 46% and fascial sling in 54%) was compared with periurethral collagen in women with stress or mixed UI in one RCT, which found no differences in satisfaction or QOL (SF-36, IIQ) between groups at 1 year. Using intention-to-treat analysis (where treatment was considered to have failed in women with missing data), there was no significant difference in continence rates at 1 year (52% collagen, 55% surgery). If only the 89% of women who underwent the randomised intervention were considered, the continence rate with surgery was significantly higher (72% versus 53%). The incidence of adverse effects was significantly higher in the surgery group: urinary retention 13% versus 2%, transient voiding difficulty 36% versus 17%, UTI 6% versus 0% (*n* = 133).[560] [EL = 1+]

Rectus fascial sling versus tension-free vaginal tape
Two small RCTs compared TVT with an autologous rectus fascial sling, one of which also had a colposuspension arm (total *n* = 145). In the study with three arms, cure rates (negative stress test and symptom-free) were 87%, 88% and 93%, with TVT, open colposuspension and rectus fascial sling, respectively, at 1 year (*n* = 92).[658] [EL = 1+] The second study reported cure rates (using the same criteria) of 92% in both groups at 6 months. Complications reported were *de novo* DO (0% with TVT versus 0% or 4% with rectus fascial sling), wound pain (7% versus 28%), or urinary retention (13% versus 7%).[658,717] [EL = 1+]

Rectus fascial sling versus self-fashioned polypropylene mesh sling
A quasi-RCT compared a rectus fascial sling with a self-fashioned polypropylene mesh sling. At median follow-up of about 2 years, cure and satisfaction rates were similar but operating time and hospital stay were significantly shorter in the synthetic sling group. Delayed voiding occurred in more women in the fascial sling group. No other significant differences were seen between groups in complications (haematoma, dysuria, *de novo* urgency or urge UI) (*n* = 50).[848] [EL = 1−]

Rectus fascial sling versus polytetrafluoroethylene
One RCT compared rectus fascial and PTFE slings in women with stress UI, 92% of whom had had prior continence surgery. Combined objective and subjective cure rates were 81% and 88%, respectively, at 6 months. No complications were reported in the fascial sling group, whereas urethral erosion, recurrent UTI and *de novo* DO were very common with PTFE (*n* = 48).[861] [EL = 1−]

Rectus fascial sling versus vaginal wall sling
Rectus fascial and vaginal wall slings were compared in one RCT and in two non-randomised retrospective studies involving women with stress UI.[877–879] All women in the non-randomised studies had had prior continence surgery. Each study was considered to be of poor quality. The RCT reported high subjective cure, and satisfaction rates (80–100%), with median follow-up of 7 months (*n* = 26). Transient urinary retention and *de novo* urge UI were very common.[877] [EL = 1−] The retrospective studies reported similar 'success' rates with both interventions, ranging from 80% to 97%, with follow-up of 21 months, and 70 months versus 45 months (*n* = 232, *n* = 79). Other than the proportions requiring ISC (2% fascial versus 0% vaginal wall), no other significant differences were reported in the complications listed (voiding dysfunction, wound infection, urgency, *de novo* DO, bladder or urethral perforation, pain, seroma formation, rectocele).[878,879] [EL = 2−]

Comparing two techniques of fascial sling
One RCT compared two techniques of fascial sling in women with urodynamic stress UI (with urge UI in 82%), 89% of whom had had prior continence surgery. Women underwent a standard

fascial sling procedure or a 'sling on a string' (a shorter sling mounted on each end with a nylon thread), with baseline UDI scores lower in the standard group, which reflected differences in urge UI prevalence in groups (80% versus 86%). At 1 year, subjective cure rates were 84% using both techniques. Satisfaction and changes in IIQ scores were similar in both groups, whereas improvements in UDI scores were greater with the standard approach (adjusted for differences in baseline UDI data). Urinary tract complications (UTI, bladder injury or trauma, voiding difficulty and haematoma) were reported in 1–3% in at least one treatment arm ($n = 168$).[880] [EL = 1+]

A retrospective cohort study compared a rectus fascial sling with one reinforced with polyglactin mesh in women with urodynamic stress UI, one-third of whom also had urge UI ($n = 51$). Follow-up differed between groups (mean 8 versus 5 months). Overall, no clear difference was seen between groups in success rates, although results depended on the definition of success used (patient-determined, urodynamics or based on weekly leakage episodes). No significant differences between groups were noted in complications (wound infection, incisional hernia, voiding dysfunction, de novo DO).[881] [EL = 2−]

Dura mater sling versus open colposuspension
One RCT compared dura mater sling with open colposuspension in women with recurrent stress UI after hysterectomy. The cure rates (combined objective/subjective) were 92% versus 86%, at about 3 years. Significantly more women in the sling group had voiding difficulty or retention postoperatively, both of which were common, and more women developed rectocele in the colposuspension group. Bladder perforation and de novo urgency were common in both groups. Time to spontaneous voiding was significantly longer in the sling group ($n = 72$).[657] [EL = 1+]

Porcine dermis sling versus Stamey needle suspension
One RCT compared a porcine dermis suburethral sling with the Stamey needle suspension procedure in women with stress UI who were considered unsuitable for colposuspension; overall 60% had had prior continence surgery. At 2 years, subjective cure rates were 90% versus 70%. Intra-operative blood loss and postoperative infection were significantly more common in the sling group. Other common complications in both groups were bladder injury and de novo DO ($n = 20$).[656] [EL = 1+]

Porcine dermal collagen sling versus tension-free vaginal tape
In an RCT of women who had failed conservative treatment, no significant differences were seen between porcine dermal collagen sling and TVT in subjective cure or improvement at 1 or 3 years, nor in satisfaction at 3 years (assessed by mailed questionnaire). Operating time and hospital stay were not significantly different, nor was the rate of complications. The complications seen were haemorrhage (4% versus 3%), infection (2% versus 0%), the need for sling release or urethral dilatation (10% versus 5%), ISC (3% versus 3%), de novo urgency or urge UI (18% versus 15%), and dyspareunia (0% versus 3%) ($n = 142$).[719,720] [EL = 1+]

Autologous versus allograft slings
Seven non-randomised studies compared the outcomes of autologous and allograft slings in women with stress UI (54–60% in two studies having mixed UI). One also compared both interventions with a xenograft material (porcine dermis). All were retrospective reviews of cases undertaken, each with differences in duration of follow-up for the interventions evaluated, with drop-out rates of 4–34% of those treated in four studies; all were therefore considered to be of poor quality.[180,882–889] [EL = 2−] Women in six studies had had prior continence surgery (19–57%). Across four studies, 16–82% underwent concomitant surgery. Between 45 and 167 women were followed up (total 786) with duration of follow-up of between 3 months and about 3 years.

Four studies compared autologous with allograft (cadaveric) fascia lata,[883,885–888] three of which reported similar results for all outcomes (subjective cure, satisfaction, and UDI-6, IIQ-7 and SEAPI scores). The fourth study reported significantly higher cure rates in the autologous group.[883] In three studies that compared autologous rectus fascia (or fascia lata in one) with allograft fascia lata, two found a significantly higher cure rate in the autologous group.[180,884,889] The other did not report significant differences between groups in cure rate, although satisfaction rates were higher in the autologous group after 2 years follow-up. Operating time and hospital stay were shorter in the allograft group.[882] In the study with a xenograft arm, cure rates were significantly higher with autograft material.[889]

In studies that reported complications, these were:

- cases of sling failure, haemorrhage, suprapubic abscess, lower extremity neuropathy, persistent suprapubic pain and suprapubic haematoma in the allograft group[886–888]

- persistent thigh pain, abdominal wound infection and prolapse in 11%, 6% and 1%, respectively, of the autologous group[882,887,888]

- retention (4–7% autologous versus 2–4% allograft)[882,887,888] and UTI (27% versus 6%)[882] in both groups

- between 2% and 5% of autologous, allograft and xenograft groups underwent urethrolysis for persistent voiding dysfunction.[889]

Case series of biological slings

Autologous slings

Ten case series reported outcomes of the autologous rectus fascial sling.[890–899] Patient numbers in the studies ranged from 32 to 251 (total 1280). In six studies, only 67–95% of those treated were followed up. Six studies included women with mixed UI (34–58%). Prior continence surgery was documented for between 26% and 70% of women in six studies. Concomitant surgery was undertaken in 15–65% of women across six studies.

Each study reported a mean or median duration of follow-up ranging from about 2 to 6 years; in three studies, maximum follow-up of 15–18 years was reported.[894,896,897] Subjective cure rates ranged from 26% to 97% (median 81%); objective cure rate (one study) 93%; and cure that included subjective and objective elements 73% and 95% (two studies). Satisfaction rates of 86% and 92% were reported in two studies.

Intra-operative complications reported were:

- haemorrhage requiring transfusion: 4%[894]

- pelvic haematoma: 0.8%[895]

- retropubic haematoma or wound infection: 2%[897]

- wound infection: 3%[894]

- bladder perforation/injury: 0–7% (median 1.3%)[894,896,897,899]

- urethral injury: no cases.[896,899]

Postoperative complications were:

- *de novo* urgency, urge UI or DO (seven studies): median 14% (range 2–23%)

- voiding difficulty or retention either requiring intervention (sling removal or release, urethrolysis, ISC) or described as prolonged (eight studies): median 2% (range 1–9%)

- transient retention (five studies): median 33% (range 1.3–94%)

- lower abdominal pain (five studies): median 2.5% (range 0–25%)

- UTI (three studies): median 13% (range 4–41%); recurrent UTI (two studies): 4% and 22%

- sling erosion into urethra (two studies): 0% and 3%

- pelvic organ prolapse (two studies): 3–4%

- incisional hernia (two studies): 0.8–4.5%

- abdominal wall hernia (one study): 2%.

Allograft fascia lata slings

Six case series evaluated the use of allograft fascia lata slings in women with stress UI (with 50–87% with mixed UI in three).[900–905] Patient numbers ranged from 18 to 102 (total 295). Mean or median follow-up ranged from 9 to 13 months in five studies, and was 35 months in one. Three studies had follow-up data for 65–88% of the women treated. Concomitant surgery was undertaken in 11–59% in five studies, and prior continence surgery in 6–65% of women in four studies.

Median subjective cure rate was 70% (range 48–94%) across the studies, with satisfaction rates of 69% and 90% at 1 year (two studies). The study with longest follow-up reported significant improvement in QOL (IIQ-7 and UDI-6) at 1 year, which was sustained at 4 years.[905] Intra-operative bleeding was reported in one study (1%).[901]

Postoperative complications were:

- sling division or urethrolysis for retention (1% and 4%);[900] ISC at 1 year in 3%[904]

- *de novo* urge UI (15%)[901] or urgency (8%)[902]

- surgery for new onset or recurrent POP (2%);[901] another noted no cases of recurrent cystocele[902]

- vaginal pain, pressure or protrusion, and bladder or kidney infection very common in one study.[905]

No cases of bleeding, wound infection, or erosion were reported in one study.[904]

Slings made of other biological materials

Case series reporting the outcomes of slings made from other materials were identified: porcine dermal sling procedures,[906–908] vaginal wall slings[909–913] lyophilised dura mater,[914] and cadaveric dermal grafts.[915,916] The use of cadaveric human dermal sling, and bovine pericardium were described in two studies, but these studies are not considered further as both procedures used bone-anchors.[917,918]

The studies evaluating the porcine dermal or small intestinal mucosa slings were small (between 25 and 50 women), and had relatively short duration of follow-up. All reported cure, improvement and failure rates, using varying definitions, and complications. The three studies that evaluated the porcine dermal sling in women with stress UI (14% mixed UI in one)[908] had follow-up of 6 months or a mean of about 21 months.[906–908] In one study, all women had had prior continence surgery, compared with 18–26% in the other two studies. In one, 43% underwent concomitant prolapse surgery.[907] The cure rates ranged from 68% to 78%, with 9–15% improved, and failure rates of 10–25%. Common complications (1% or more and less than 10%) across the studies were UTI, wound infection, transient retention, and persisting or *de novo* urge UI.[906,907] Cases of sling erosion into the urethral wall,[907] retention requiring sling removal,[907] deep vein thrombosis[907] and bladder injury[908] were also reported. In one study pelvic pain for up to 3 months was common.

The case series evaluating the porcine small intestinal mucosa sling (32% of whom had concomitant surgery) reported cure and improvement rates of 79% and 9%, respectively, at 2 years. There was one case of *de novo* urge UI and three of suprapubic inflammation; no women had prolonged retention (*n* = 34).[919] [EL = 3]

In women who had stress UI and POP who underwent a lyophilised dura mater sling procedure, objective success (pad test) was seen in 89% at 6 months. There was a case each of the sling passing through the bladder and of haemorrhage requiring surgery (*n* = 36).[914] [EL = 3]

Two case series reported 6 or 12 month outcomes of cadaveric dermal grafts, in a total of 50 women with stress UI (28% had mixed in one study). The cure rate in both studies was 68%. Complications included a case of bladder perforation, suprapubic or vaginal infection (12%), and *de novo* urgency (12%).[915,916] [EL = 3]

Across the vaginal wall sling case series, results for 648 women treated (range 45–336) were reviewed: all had stress UI, with 47–65% in two studies having mixed UI.[909–913] Duration of follow-up ranged from means of 17 to 40 months, with one reporting a minimum 5 years follow-up. Success or cure (variously defined) was reported in 31–93% (median 83%), and satisfaction in 62% and 93% of studies that considered this. Complications reported were bladder injury (2%), wound infection (2–5%), *de novo* DO or urge UI (6–10%), retention (4–12%), suture removal (1–2%), pelvic organ prolapse (2–7%), UTI (3%), dyspareunia (4%) and suprapubic pain (0.5–2%). [EL = 3]

5.2.3 The effect of hysterectomy on continence

No evidence was identified that addressed the question of whether hysterectomy is an effective treatment for UI. While the procedure is often undertaken at the same time as surgery for UI, it is not possible to evaluate the independent impact of hysterectomy on continence.

There is some evidence regarding the influence of hysterectomy for reasons other than treatment of UI on continence status, but the data are inconsistent. A systematic review of studies found no increase in UI within the first 2 years after hysterectomy; although there was an increase in the risk of UI in women over 60 years of age who had undergone the procedure many years earlier; this was not found in younger women.[920]

Evidence statements for procedures for stress urinary incontinence

There has been little consistency between trials of continence surgery in the types of patients recruited, the incidence of previous surgery or concomitant procedures, and the prevalence of pre-existing urge incontinence or voiding difficulty. [EL = 3]

Outcome measures have been inconsistent so comparisons between studies are difficult. Some procedures may be indistinguishable in anything other than name. There is no strong evidence of superior effectiveness for any one surgical procedure. [EL = 3]

Procedures to augment sphincter pressure
Controlled trials evaluating urethral bulking agents (collagen, silicone, carbon-coated zirconium beads, hyaluronic acid/dextran copolymer) for the treatment of women with stress UI are few, enrol relatively small numbers of patients and are of mixed quality. Bulking agents may be less effective than open surgery for UI, but they are associated with fewer postoperative complications. [EL = 1+] Autologous fat is no better than placebo in effecting cure or improvement of incontinence, and is significantly less effective than collagen. [EL = 2+] Otherwise, there is no evidence of greater efficacy of one injectable over another. Polytetrafluoroethylene has not been assessed in controlled trials.

Repeat injections are required in the majority of patients to achieve initial benefit. [EL = 3] There are no data on the outcome of subsequent courses of treatment.

Controlled trials show that urethral bulking agents have relatively poor efficacy. Case series show that any benefit observed declines with time, and that complications, though common or very common, are mainly transient, and include acute retention, dysuria, haematuria, frequency, and UTI. *De novo* DO with urge UI was the only long-term complication documented. Uncommon but serious complications have been reported with autologous fat. [EL = 3]

Data supporting the use of artificial urinary sphincter in women with idiopathic UI are limited to case series. Subjective cure rates are high although complications requiring removal or revision are common. [EL = 3]

Retropubic suspension procedures
Open colposuspension is an effective treatment for stress UI in women and has longevity. There is no consistent difference in effectiveness between laparoscopic and open colposuspension for any outcome measures. [EL = 1+] However, laparoscopic colposuspension consumes more resources, and skills take longer to acquire than with open colposuspension. [EL = 4]

In general, most suspension procedures are effective in the short term but the longer term outcomes for anterior colporrhaphy, abdominal paravaginal repair and needle suspension are poor when used for stress incontinence alone. [EL = 3]

Complications are common for all suspension procedures; these include voiding difficulty, urgency syndrome or development of vaginal vault and posterior wall prolapse. There is no evidence that the Marshall–Marchetti–Krantz (MMK) procedure offers any significant advantage over open colposuspension. [EL = 1+] The MMK procedure is no longer in routine clinical practice owing to the serious additional complication of ostcitis pubis. [EL = 4]

Synthetic slings
Most RCT data regarding synthetic slings for the treatment of stress UI relate to a macroporous (type 1) polypropylene mesh inserted through the retropubic space using a bottom-up approach (e.g. TVT). This has been shown to have comparable efficacy to colposuspension (open or laparoscopic) with follow-up to 3 years. Hospital resource use is less and recovery time is shorter when compared with colposuspension. [EL = 1+] Limited data are available on outcomes beyond 3 years. [EL = 3]

Results from an economic model conducted alongside a systematic review suggest that a synthetic sling using a macroporous (type 1) polypropylene mesh, inserted through the retropubic space using a bottom-up approach (e.g. TVT) for the treatment of stress UI is more cost effective than other surgical procedures, open colposuspension in particular. This result is based on limited follow-up data and assumes that the relative differences between treatments do not change over time. Case series suggest that cure rates for TVT are sustained. Higher prevalence of prolapse in open colposuspension would increase the relative cost effectiveness of TVT.

Numerous alternative synthetic sling materials and techniques have been described where the tape may be inserted by a retropubic route, bottom-up or top-down, or via the obturator foramina, outside-in or inside-out. Based on case series, these techniques appear to be effective, but there are only limited comparative data. [EL = 3] Slings using a retropubic top-down approach appear to be as effective as bottom-up retropubic techniques. [EL = 1+] Slings inserted through the obturator foramen appear to be effective in the short term but there is limited high-level evidence of their effectiveness compared with more established techniques. [EL = 1+] Long-term outcomes are unknown.

Slings using materials other than a wholly macroporous construction (e.g. type 2, 3 or 4 meshes [made of polyester, polytetrafluoroethylene, or silicone]), cannot be assumed to be of comparable efficacy and safety to those using a macroporous (type 1) polypropylene mesh inserted through the retropubic space using a bottom-up approach (e.g. TVT). [EL = 4]

Intra-operative complications are rare except for bladder perforation, which, although common, appears to have no long-term sequelae provided it is recognised and remedied at the time of surgery. Long-term complications with synthetic slings include voiding difficulties and development of urgency and urge UI. There is a lack of high-level evidence on the relative safety of sling materials or techniques. Slings employing materials other than the wholly macroporous (type 1) appear to have higher rates of erosion and infection. [EL = 3]

Patients who have undergone prior surgery are more likely to have intra-operative complications. [EL = 3]

Biological slings
Autologous rectus fascial sling is the most widely evaluated biological sling, which is an effective treatment for stress UI and has longevity. [EL = 1+] Short-length suspended autologous fascial sling achieves similar outcomes to full-length slings at 1 year. [EL = 1+]

Limited data show that pubovaginal sling using porcine dermis is effective. [EL = 1+] Data relating to other biological slings (autologous or allograft fascia lata, vaginal wall sling, dura mater, porcine small intestinal mucosa) are few, and generally of low evidence level and poor quality. Complications with all slings are common and include voiding difficulties and development of urgency and urge UI.

Recommendations for procedures for stress urinary incontinence

Retropubic mid-urethral tape procedures using a 'bottom-up' approach with macroporous (type 1) polypropylene meshes are recommended as treatment options for stress UI if conservative management has failed. Open colposuspension and autologous rectus fascial sling are the recommended alternatives when clinically appropriate. [A]

Synthetic slings using a retropubic 'top-down' or a transobturator foramen approach are recommended as alternative treatment options for stress UI if conservative management has failed, provided women are made aware of the lack of long-term outcome data. [D]

Synthetic slings using materials other than polypropylene that are not of a macroporous (type 1) construction are not recommended for the treatment of stress UI. [D]

Intramural bulking agents (glutaraldehyde cross-linked collagen, silicone, carbon-coated zirconium beads or hyaluronic acid/dextran copolymer) should be considered for the management of stress UI if conservative management has failed. Women should be made aware that:

- repeat injections may be required to achieve efficacy

- efficacy diminishes with time

- efficacy is inferior to that of retropubic suspension or sling. [D]

In view of the associated morbidity, the use of an artificial urinary sphincter should be considered for the management of stress UI in women only if previous surgery has failed. Life-long follow-up is recommended. [D]

Laparoscopic colposuspension is not recommended as a routine procedure for the treatment of stress UI in women. The procedure should be performed only by an experienced laparoscopic surgeon working in a multidisciplinary team with expertise in the assessment and treatment of UI. [D (GPP)]

Anterior colporrhaphy, needle suspensions, paravaginal defect repair and the Marshall–Marchetti–Krantz procedure are not recommended for the treatment of stress UI. [A]

Autologous fat and polytetrafluoroethylene used as intramural bulking agents are not recommended for the treatment of stress UI. [D]

Research recommendation for procedures for stress urinary incontinence

Newer mid-urethral procedures should be further investigated and compared with pelvic floor muscle training and accepted surgical interventions in the treatment of stress urinary incontinence.

6. Competence of surgeons performing operative procedures for urinary incontinence in women

6.1 Introduction

The aim of surgery is to achieve cure of incontinence with minimum morbidity. Surgical outcomes are dependent on numerous factors including careful patient selection, accurate diagnosis and the expertise of the operating team, including in particular the skills of the surgeon. Some procedures for incontinence are technically simple, yet potentially harmful if carried out incompetently or in inappropriate patients. Others are complex and likely to require higher levels of expertise for their effective execution. The GDG were tasked specifically with describing the competence that should be expected of surgeons who are carrying out operations for incontinence in women.

Studies considered for the competence question

Competence of surgeons performing surgical procedures to treat UI or OAB in women were considered within a framework based on existing models of quality assurance, that is, with consideration of inputs (how competence is achieved), process/service (how competence is maintained), and how it is measured (e.g. auditing competence based on quality standards).

Little evidence relevant to the question was identified. Publications from professional or working groups were reviewed for existing guidance relating to competence of surgeons within this therapeutic area. Some volume–outcome data were available from intervention studies, notably of TVT, and from surveys of consultants undertaking continence surgery in the UK. Volume–outcome data relating to any type of surgery was also considered alongside that for continence surgery.

6.2 Achieving competence

Surgeons who perform operations for UI in women should have been properly trained in the specialist area of continence surgery. The route by which surgeons reach this area of practice varies. Specialist training programmes are provided by the Royal College of Obstetricians and Gynaecologists and by the Royal College of Surgeons Specialist Advisory Committee in Urology. The requirements of these training schemes are similar and are summarised as follows.

A surgeon should be knowledgeable in the anatomy, physiology and pathophysiology of female lower urinary tract and UI before undertaking surgery in this area.

He/she should possess the following generic skills related to surgery. The knowledge and generic skills described are necessary to ensure that the patient is given sufficient information on the options available to make an informed choice.

Knowledge:

- specific indications for surgery
- required preparation for surgery including preoperative investigations

- outcomes and complications of proposed procedure
- anatomy relevant to procedure
- steps involved in procedure
- alternative management options
- likely postoperative progress.

Other generic skills:

- be able to explain procedures and possible outcomes to patients and family and to obtain informed consent
- possess the necessary hand–eye dexterity to complete the procedure safely and efficiently, with appropriate use of assistance
- be able to communicate with and manage the operative team effectively
- be able to prioritise interventions.

Attitude:

- be able to recognise when to ask for advice from others
- demonstrate commitment to multidisciplinary team working with other health professionals involved in the care of women with UI.

A surgeon is expected to be able to perform an operation without supervision and be able to deal with the complications of that operation before he/she can be considered competent to perform it. The procedure should form part of his/her routine practice.

Existing surgeons should be able to demonstrate that their training, experience and current practice equates to the standards laid out for newly trained surgeons. They should work within the context of an integrated continence service, as recommended in the Department of Health's *Good Practice in Continence Services* (2000).[34]

Some aspects of continence surgery are likely to require a higher level of training than other procedures, which applies particularly to secondary surgical procedures. These procedures should be carried out in centres that are able to maintain their expertise and achieve good outcome for their patients[34] e.g. artificial urinary sphincter, urinary diversion, sacral nerve stimulation, augmentation cystoplasty and complex stress incontinence surgery.

6.3 Maintaining and measuring expertise and standards for practice

Surgeons undertaking continence surgery should be aware of and follow best practice in the management of UI, as laid out in this guideline. Surgeons should conform to standards of good medical practice (General Medical Council) and good surgical practice (Royal College of Surgeons). They should also conform to the standards of good practice as laid out by the British Association of Urological Surgeons Section of Female and Reconstructive Urology (BAUS-SFRU) and the British Society of Urogynaecology (BSUG), namely:

- Surgeons should participate in local and national audit.
- If a surgeon undertakes any new class of procedure for which he/she does not have appropriate training then he/she should seek formal training through a process of mentoring. This includes appropriate training of the surgical team.
- Before undertaking new procedures surgeons must notify their trust's clinical governance committee.
- Before utilising new materials or devices in previously established procedures, the trust's clinical governance committee should be informed.

- Any intention to undertake an evaluation of a new procedure should be registered with a relevant clinical trials database.

- The development of new techniques or modifications of established techniques should receive appropriate local ethical and clinical governance approval. New techniques are defined by NICE (Department of Health *Health Services Circular* 2003/011, 13/11/03) as one where 'a doctor no longer in a training post is using it for the first time in his or her NHS clinical practice'.

- A surgeon who encounters a serious adverse event related to the use of a device or implant, in the treatment of incontinence, should notify the MHRA through its Serious Adverse Event (SAE) reporting process.

- New procedures/classes of procedure should be notified to the Interventional Procedures Programme at NICE through the NICE website.

Measuring competence

For established surgeons, the best way to measure continuing competence is through comparative audit. All surgeons should have access to information about their personal results for continence surgery. This should include data on perioperative complications and long-term outcomes. They should also be able to compare those outcomes with the experience of others through national audit.

Examples of this include the databases set up by BSUG and BAUS-SFRU. Both systems offer the facility for surgeons to record every operation they do for incontinence, and are freely available for members of those organisations, although neither is well utilised at present.

Volume–outcome research

The necessary surgical volume of any operation required to maintain competence is inadequately defined. The volume–outcome relationship has been considered in many clinical areas, such as cardiology, gastroenterology, orthopaedics, ophthalmology and breast cancer surgery, but little evaluation has been undertaken in relation to continence surgery. In systematic reviews of this research, many methodological concerns have been raised over what is considered to be a heterogeneous body of research, consisting of observational studies. Most studies retrospectively analyse routinely collected data and are not designed to analyse the complex volume–outcome relationship, which leads to many problems when interpreting the data, namely:[921–923]

- inadequate consideration of confounders such as the effects of differences in case-mix and appropriateness of case selection on outcomes

- volume can relate to hospital or surgeon

- narrow outcomes are used in most studies, usually adverse (e.g. inpatient or 30 day mortality)

- thresholds for, or definitions of, high and low volume across and within procedures differ

- causality – it is unclear whether high volume–improved outcome relationships result from greater experience or whether the highest referral rate tends to be to those surgeons or centres who have the best results.

Hospital volume and surgeon volume may both be important, and the relative importance may vary from one procedure to another. For some procedures, such as trauma-related reconstruction, it may be the total amount of relevant surgery that is most important rather than the specific number of particular procedures. Complexity of procedures and whether their use is commonplace also influences whether a difference in outcomes can be seen for a given volume.

Although the evidence tends to suggest that higher volume is associated with better outcomes, the consistency and size of the effect varies for different procedures. A systematic review of 135 studies found a significant association between higher volume (hospital or surgeon) and better outcomes in about 70% of studies; none of the studies found a significant association between higher volume of any type of surgery and poorer outcome.[922] In these studies, the definition of low or high volume varied according to the procedure, with median low volumes of up to 100–200 for coronary angioplasty or coronary artery bypass graft surgery; and median low volume values ranging from 1 to 73 for other procedures described (mainly in the region of 10–30).[922]

Secondary surgery is unusual and can be technically challenging, and a centralisation argument probably applies. The centralisation argument holds that 'practice makes perfect' so concentration of cases into one centre that can carry out larger numbers of procedures will result in higher standards, not just in surgical technique, but also postoperative care.

Evidence for the effects of volume or hospital status on outcome of continence surgery
A few studies have reported the outcomes of continence surgery according to the volume of surgery undertaken. With the methodological issues relating to such studies in mind, the findings are described below.

A UK cohort study attempted to identify risk factors predictive of successful outcome 1 year after surgery for stress UI (colposuspension, anterior colporrhaphy or needle suspension). The outcomes considered were complications, symptom severity index, symptom impact index and activities of daily living. The number of cases performed by surgeons per year (20–42 versus 1–19) was not found to be associated with risk of a better or worse outcome (*n* = 232).[125,126] [EL = 2+]

Some information on volume–outcomes is available for TVT. One case series considered the cure rates for each of the ten surgeons who undertook the TVT procedure, which ranged from 72% to 92% and were not significantly associated with the number of procedures performed (11–250 per surgeon).[812] From the Finnish national data on TVT, it was estimated that the incidence of complications was 40% in hospitals where 15 or fewer operations had been undertaken, and about 14% in centres performing more than 15 operations.[813] [EL = 3]

Subgroup analysis of some aspects of the UK TVT/colposuspension RCT[659,660] was undertaken, including volume–outcome and recruitment numbers, although the study was not powered to do so.[924] It is difficult to put the numbers into context because those cases represent only a proportion of the continence surgery undertaken in those centres. Objective cure rates were higher for centres recruiting most patients; the categories analysed being more than 30 patients, 21–30, or fewer than 20. While it must be conceded that the effect of drop-outs on an intention-to-treat analysis is greater on units recruiting small numbers of patients, it may nevertheless be the case that there is a minimum workload consistent with optimal surgical outcome.

Other studies reflected on the learning curve with the TVT procedure. Three studies observed that the complication rate,[744,772,804] or specifically bladder injury,[925] was relatively higher during the surgeon's learning curve, the threshold/definition for which differed across the studies, from the first 5, 10–20, 50 or 100 procedures.

A survey of consultants performing continence surgery in the UK in 2001 was carried out in order to establish the type and volume of surgery undertaken, the nature of postoperative complications, investigations, and follow-up (*n* = 578; 54% response rate). The profile of respondents was general gynaecologists (40%), gynaecologists with a special interest in urogynaecology (31%), urologists (25%), subspecialist urogynaecologists (3%), with 2% not classified. Half the respondents stated that fewer than 50 procedures per year were adequate for good surgical results, whereas the other half considered that more than 50 procedures a year were necessary. The majority specialty view was 10–20 procedures per year (61% general gynaecologists and 59% urologists), or 20–50 per procedures per year (68% urogynaecology subspecialists and 61% gynaecologists with a special interest).[926] [EL = 3]

The results for the TVT device (7336 procedures) were also reported separately by the same authors, the survey participants being identified by the manufacturers of the device. Overall, 44% performed between one and ten TVT operations in the year evaluated (2001), and 28% performed over 25 during that year. Performing 10–20 cases of TVT under supervision was considered by 46% of surgeons in this survey to constitute adequate training, and 43% suggested that 20–50 cases of TVT are required to gain competence.[817] [EL = 3]

Hospital status
There is some conflicting evidence that outcomes relate in part to the training status of the institution in which they are performed. In the USA, teaching centres have been shown to have higher

30-day morbidity (predominantly wound complications) across a range of specialties (general surgery, orthopaedics, urology, and vascular surgery) than non-teaching centres. Mortality was not significantly different between centres for any of the seven specialties evaluated.[927] [EL = 2+]

Two studies considered outcome of continence surgery by hospital status (teaching versus non-teaching); exactly what is meant by 'teaching' hospitals is not clear. The risk of having complications from continence surgery was not significantly associated with hospital status in a UK cohort study (on multivariate analysis).[125,126] [EL = 2+] A case series of TVT reported that the risk of postoperative complications with TVT was higher when undertaken in teaching hospitals than in non-teaching hospitals (24% versus 16%; OR 0.55, 95% CI 0.35 to 0.85) ($n = 809$).[804] [EL = 3] While the studies report these observations, they do not explain the possible causes of the results seen. This may relate to overall case load, case mix (i.e. number of complex or secondary cases) or the impact of training on outcomes.

Evidence statements for competence of surgeons

There are limited data regarding the number of procedures required to learn any particular operation used in the management of urinary incontinence. There is similarly little evidence on annual workload required to maintain skills, optimise outcome and minimise morbidity. [EL = 4] From a survey of consultants performing continence surgery in the UK, the majority specialty view was that either 10–20 or 20–50 procedures per year are adequate for good surgical results. [EL = 3]

From evidence to recommendations
The GDG drew on the requirements for training schemes in gynaecology and urology in the UK to develop recommendations for training standards. The BAUS-SFRU and BSUG are currently developing training schemes and structured assessment methods specific for those undertaking continence surgery.

Cystourethroscopy is considered an integral part of several procedures used in the treatment of UI. Training in this technique is therefore deemed crucial to surgical competence in this area.

In relation to maintaining competence, the GDG agreed by consensus that a workload of 20 cases per procedure per annum was an appropriate volume, which was also supported by the survey of UK consultants. A volume of cases per procedure was recommended because a workload in one procedure does not necessarily maintain skills for other procedures. The minimum volume recommended was also agreed by GDG consensus.

Audit is an integral part of clinical governance. Regular audit of outcomes of continence surgery is considered essential to maintaining standards of practice.

Recommendations for competence of surgeons

Surgery for UI should be undertaken only by surgeons who have received appropriate training in the management of UI and associated disorders or who work within a multidisciplinary team with this training, and who regularly carry out surgery for UI in women. [D (GPP)]

Training should be sufficient to develop the knowledge and generic skills documented below.

Knowledge should include the:

- specific indications for surgery
- required preparation for surgery including preoperative investigations
- outcomes and complications of proposed procedure
- anatomy relevant to procedure
- steps involved in procedure
- alternative management options
- likely postoperative progress.

Generic skills should include:

- the ability to explain procedures and possible outcomes to patients and family and to obtain informed consent

- the necessary hand–eye dexterity to complete the procedure safely and efficiently, with appropriate use of assistance

- the ability to communicate with and manage the operative team effectively

- the ability to prioritise interventions

- the ability to recognise when to ask for advice from others

- a commitment to multidisciplinary team working. [D (GPP)]

Training should include competence in cystourethroscopy. [D (GPP)]

Operative competence of surgeons undertaking surgical procedures to treat UI or OAB in women should be formally assessed by trainers through a structured process. [D (GPP)]

Surgeons who are already carrying out procedures for UI should be able to demonstrate that their training, experience and current practice equates to the standards laid out for newly trained surgeons. [D (GPP)]

Surgery for UI or OAB in women should be undertaken only by surgeons who carry out a sufficient case load to maintain their skills. An annual workload of at least 20 cases of each primary procedure for stress UI is recommended. Surgeons undertaking fewer than five cases of any procedure annually should do so only with the support of their clinical governance committee; otherwise referral pathways should be in place within clinical networks. [D (GPP)]

There should be a nominated clinical lead within each surgical unit with responsibility for continence and prolapse surgery. The clinical lead should work within the context of an integrated continence service. [D (GPP)]

A national audit of continence surgery should be undertaken. [D (GPP)]

Surgeons undertaking continence surgery should maintain careful audit data and submit their outcomes to national registries such as those held by the British Society of Urogynaecology (BSUG) and British Association of Urological Surgeons Section of Female and Reconstructive Urology (BAUS-SFRU). [D (GPP)]

Appendix A

Declarations of interest

| GDG member | Description (industry/organisation) | | | | |
| | Personal | | Non-personal | | Non-current interests |
	Specific	Non-specific	Specific	Non-specific	
Elisabeth Adams	Occasional lecturing at meetings organised by pharmaceutical companies. Training for Gynecare. Attendance at international meetings (IUGA) through sponsorship (Gynecare, Yamanouchi, Boehringer Ingelheim, Pfizer, Galen).	None	Organise annual regional meeting for integration of continence services, sponsored in 2005 by Pfizer, SCA Hygiene, Boehringer Ingelheim, Yamanouchi, Janssen-Cilag. Hospital department involved in clinical trials (recently Boehringer Ingelheim, Pfizer, SCA Hygiene, Gynecare, Galen).	None	None
Alison Bardsley	Part of focus group/working party that looks at educational initiatives and training packs for professionals, information for patients and carers, and product development. Paid consultancy fee for meetings and speaking at training events (Coloplast, Schwarz Pharma, Eli Lilly, Boehringer Ingelheim). Advisory board, training and speaking (UCB Pharma).	None	Part of working group alongside other continence groups and organisations, as representative of RCN continence care forum; monies to RCN (Eli Lilly, Boehringer Ingelheim). Attendance at international meetings through part sponsorship (Galen, Coloplast).	None	None

(continued)

| GDG member | Description (industry/organisation) | | | | Non-current interests |
| | Personal | | Non-personal | | |
	Specific	Non-specific	Specific	Non-specific	
Linda Crumlin	Sponsored to attend ICS meeting (Pfizer).	None	None	None	Training for Boehringer Ingelheim.
Ian Currie	Training for Gynecare.	None	None	None	None
Lynda Evans	None	None	None	Tutor for chronically sick NHS patients, attending local and national meetings and NHS updates. Discussions of symptoms, responses and mediation arise as part of the programme delivery (expert patient programme – NHS).	Disability equality trainer and adviser (Disability Rights Commission).
Jeanette Haslam	Organisation, chair, presenter at study days; conference sponsorship (Johnson & Johnson, Gynecare). Chair of patient organisations' meetings, presentations to audiences of health professionals; conference sponsorship (Eli Lilly, Boehringer Ingelheim, Astellas). Course leader, presenter, tutor, 3rd level continence course (University of East London). Training for Gynecare.	None	None	None	None

Paul Hilton	None	None	None	None	Research funding from Gynecare (monies paid into research account). Previous research funding for nurse salary costs – paid directly to nurse from company (Gyne Ideas).
Margaret Jones	None	None	None	None	None
Malcolm Lucas	Sponsorship to attend international and national meetings. Advisory boards (Boston Scientific, Allergan, Galen, UCB Pharma, Yamanouchi).	Honoraria for speaking at meetings sponsored by companies (most pharmaceutical and some device companies involved in incontinence).	Hospital trust research department partial funding from Bard Ltd.	None	Advisory boards (UCB Pharma, Yamanouchi, Eli Lilly, Boehringer Ingelheim).
Julian Spinks	Speakers fees and honoraria in 2004 for meetings and authorship (Red Door Communications acting on behalf of Eli Lilly).	Consultant adviser to health department of a public relations company working with the pharmaceutical industry, various disease areas (Cohn and Wolfe acting on behalf of various pharmaceutical companies). Honoraria and speakers fees for focus groups and meetings on restless legs syndrome plus sponsorship of attendance at third European conference on Parkinson's disease and restless legs syndrome (Boehringer Ingelheim).	None	None	Honoraria for meetings and activities relating to smoking cessation in general and bupropion in particular (GlaxoSmithKline).

(continued)

GDG member	Description (industry/organisation)				Non-current interests
	Personal		Non-personal		
	Specific	Non-specific	Specific	Non-specific	
Joanne Townsend	Sponsorship to attend national/international continence meetings.	Teaching (Novo Nordisk, Eli Lilly, Astellas, Galen).	Sponsorship for training course for urogynaecology nurse specialists (Novo Nordisk, Eli Lilly, NEEN, Yamanouchi, RCN, Astellas).	Monies into trust urogynaecology fund for courses/presentations (Yamanouchi, Astellas, Mobilis, NEEN Healthcare) or to sponsor attendance at national/international meetings ICS and IUGA (Coloplast, Astratec, Gynecare).	None
Adrian Wagg	Principal investigator, prospective observational trial in UI (Eli Lilly, Boehringer Ingelheim). Sponsorship to ICI and/or ICS conferences/meetings (Pharmacia, Pfizer, Astellas). Lecture series for SCA Hygiene on continence May 2005.	None	Advisory board member (UK) – tolterodine (Pfizer), oxybutynin transdermal (UCB Pharma). European advisory board member – solifenacin (Yamanouchi). Royal College of Physicians (1 session/week) – continence programme CEEU. Research grants: Pfizer, Galen, Yamanouchi, UCB Pharma, Healthcare Commission. Studies: tolterodine in perception of bladder control (Pfizer); investigator solifenacin sunrise study (Yamanouchi).	Chairman of trustees for Continence Foundation	Occasional writing fees for pharmaceutical industry (Eli Lilly, Boehringer Ingelheim, UCB Pharma).
Paul Abrams (peer reviewer)	None	Advisory board member (Pfizer, Novartis); also lecturer for Novartis. Consultancy (Plethora).	Department in receipt of funds for projects; ice water test in bladder overactivity (Pfizer); nocturia (Ferring); RCT of two types of surgery for stress incontinence (AMS); drug trial OAB (Schwarz-Pharma).	Department in receipt of funds: developing non-invasive method for diagnosis of prostatic obstruction (Diagnostic Ultrasound).	None

Name					
Linda Cardozo (peer reviewer)	None	Global advisory board, European Faculty, Research PI and speaker at symposia (Astellas). European advisory board, research funding (UCB Pharma). Multicentre clinical trial (Cook). Clinical trial (Plethora).	None	None	Global advisory board, UK advisory board (chairman), clinical trials, lectures at symposia (Eli Lilly [for duloxetine in incontinence]). UK advisory board, clinical trial (multicentre) (Pfizer [tolterodine]). Adviser and lecturer (Gynecare, Johnson & Johnson).
June Cody (peer reviewer)	None	None	None	Coordinator of Cochrane Incontinence Group. The Health Services Research Unit has in the past and is currently receiving research funding from the NHS R&D Programme (University of Aberdeen Cochrane Collaboration).	None
Carol Coupland (peer reviewer)	None	None	None	None	None

Note: GDG members declared interests of all monetary values (not only those above the threshold stipulated by the NICE process). Some GDG members are involved in private practice; they consider that their private practice reflects their NHS clinical practice.

Appendix B

Guideline questions

Assessment and investigation

For each 'test', or form of investigation or assessment for UI, up to five questions were addressed, as indicated by ticks in the following matrix.

'Test'	Question				
	Test used to indicate alternative pathway?	Diagnostic accuracy (sensitivity, specificity, positive and negative predictive values)	Test used to direct treatment or predict outcome? Does it affect outcome?	Test used to direct treatment or predict outcome? Does it predict outcome?	Test used to measure severity? Test–retest reliability
Urinary history	✓	✓	✓	✗	✓
Bowel history	✓	✗	✗	✗	✗
Medical history	✓	✗	✗	✗	✗
Surgical history	✗	✗	✓	✗	✗
Obstetric history	✗	✗	✗	✗	✗
Drug history	✗	✗	✗	✗	✗
Social circumstances	✗	✗	✗	✗	✗
Expectations and motivation	✗	✗	✗	✗	✗
Cognitive function	✓	✗	✗	✗	✗
Physical examination	✓	✗	✗	✗	✗
Neurophysiology	✓	✓	✗	✗	✗
Pelvic floor muscle assessment	✗	✗	✓	✗	✓
Assessment of prolapse	✗	✓	✗	✗	✗
Urine testing	✓	✓	✓	✗	✗
Assessment of residual urine	✓	✓	✓	✗	✓
Symptom scoring and quality of life	✗	✗	✗	✗	✓
Bladder diary	✗	✗	✗	✗	✓
Pad testing	✗	✗	✓	✗	✓
Urodynamics	✓	✓	✓	✓	✓
Other tests of urethral competence (Q-tip, Fluid-Bridge, Bonney, Marshall)	✗	✓	✗	✓	✗
Cystoscopy	✓	✓	✗	✗	✗
Imaging	✓	✓	✓	✗	✗

✓ indicates the question was addressed; ✗ indicates that the question was not considered to be relevant to the 'test' and therefore the question was not addressed.

General

What is the impact of providing information to a woman with UI or OAB in terms of their satisfaction with the outcomes of treatment?

Conservative techniques

Conservative techniques for the treatment of UI
What is the effectiveness of conservative techniques for the treatment of UI or OAB in women?

Where the conservative techniques considered are:

- lifestyle changes (bowel habit, dietary factors, caffeine, fluid intake, smoking, weight, physical exercise)

- other behavioural therapies (toileting regimens)

- physical therapies (pelvic floor muscle training [PFMT], vaginal cones, biofeedback, electrical stimulation, transcutaneous electrical nerve stimulation [TENS], posterior tibial nerve stimulation, magnetic stimulation)

- drug treatment (antimuscarinic drugs, desmopressin, diuretics, duloxetine, oestrogens)

- complementary therapies (acupuncture, herbal medicines, hypnosis, aromatherapy, massage, reflexology, osteopathy).

(Effectiveness encompasses benefits, unwanted effects, cost effectiveness, and use of the interventions as monotherapy or in combination with other therapies, at any point in the care pathway.)

Sub-questions for conservative techniques
What is the comparative cost effectiveness of different conservative techniques?

Is one method of PFMT better than another?

Conservative techniques for the prevention of UI
What is the effectiveness of lifestyle changes, behavioural and physical therapies for the prevention of UI or OAB in women?

Non-therapeutic interventions (containment)
In what circumstances should containment be used as the only intervention for women with UI or OAB?

In what circumstances should containment be used prior to more definitive treatment for women with UI or OAB?

Does containment have an impact on quality of life, maintenance of independent living and rates of institutionalism, or return to work in women with UI or OAB?

Surgical procedures

What is the effectiveness of procedures to suspend the vaginal wall for the treatment of UI or OAB in women?

Where the procedures are:

- suprapubic: open colposuspension, laparoscopic colposuspension (Marshall–Marchetti–Krantz [MMK] or Burch colposuspension, vagino-obturator shelf procedure)

- bladder neck needle suspension (Pereyra, Stamey, Raz, Gittes)

- vaginal (anterior colporrhaphy).

What is the effectiveness of suburethral retropubic space slings using autologous/biological or synthetic material for the treatment of UI or OAB in women?

Where the suburethral retropubic space slings are:

- biological: autologous (fascia, dermis, tendon); allograft (fascia, dermis, dura); xenograft (porcine dermis, bovine pericardium, dura, small intestine submucosa)

- synthetic (e.g. tension-free vaginal tape, suprapubic arc sling).

What is the effectiveness of suburethral obturator foramen procedures using biological or synthetic tapes for the treatment of UI or OAB in women?

Where the suburethral obturator foramen procedures are:

- biological tapes
- synthetic tapes (e.g. transobturator tape, transobturator suburethral tape).

What is the effectiveness of implantable devices that have been designed to augment urethral sphincter pressures for the treatment of UI or OAB in women?

Where the devices are:

- intramural urethral injectables (bulking agents)/devices (e.g. collagen, hydroxyapatite, silicone [ACT Balloon], polytetrafluoroethylene)
- artificial urinary sphincters (AUS): extraurethral circumferential variable resistance devices (e.g. the AMS artificial urinary sphincter).

What is the effectiveness of augmentation cystoplasty for the treatment of UI or OAB in women?

What is the effectiveness of sacral nerve stimulation for the treatment of UI or OAB in women?

What is the effectiveness of detrusor myectomy for the treatment of OAB in women?

What is the effectiveness of urinary diversion for the treatment of UI or OAB in women?

What is the effectiveness of botulinum toxin for OAB in women?

What is the effectiveness of vanilloid receptor agonists for OAB in women?

What is the effectiveness of removal of concurrent pelvic pathology (hysterectomy) as a treatment for UI in women?

Optimal sequence questions

What is the optimal sequence of interventions and timescales for women with stress UI?

What is the optimal sequence of interventions and timescales for women with mixed UI?

What is the optimal sequence of interventions and timescales for women with overactive bladder (wet or dry)?

Competence

What are the core competencies required by a surgeon performing surgical procedures to treat UI or OAB in women?

Appendix C

Findings of urinary history taking compared with urodynamics

We found no studies in which clinical outcomes in women with UI diagnosed by clinical history alone were compared with those in women with UI diagnosed using urodynamics. However, several studies have evaluated the accuracy of the symptom of stress or urge UI relative to findings on urodynamic (UD) investigations in women undergoing assessment of their urinary symptoms. Most of these studies have been considered in two reviews and a health technology assessment of diagnostic methods for UI.[46–48] Two of the publications included studies of women with symptoms of stress, mixed or urge UI[46,48] and one included only studies evaluating women with stress UI.[47] The reviews that included women with stress, mixed or urge UI calculated and combined sensitivity and specificity data for the symptom of stress (be it with or without mixed symptoms) and for the symptom of urge UI (be it with or without mixed symptoms). The GDG considered that the mixed 'symptom' should be considered separately (because in practice women are categorised into those with stress, mixed or urge UI) and that the important question in relation to the comparison of urinary history with urodynamic findings is whether urodynamics gives additional information to that obtained from the history alone. In considering this question, the GDG took the approach that a clinical history would be taken for every woman, and that a positive history for a particular type of UI would always be followed by treatment appropriate to that type of UI.

Overall, 25 relevant studies that compared the diagnosis based on history with urodynamic findings were considered by the GDG. These studies used cystometry as the reference standard for diagnosis of UI, and therefore assumed that history taking had a lower diagnostic value in comparison. Fourteen studies included women with stress, mixed or urge UI, and eleven presented raw data in a way that allowed sensitivity, specificity, positive predictive value (PPV) and negative predictive value (NPV) to be calculated.[49–62] Two of these studies only reported accuracy data for stress and mixed UI.[61,62] Five studies only investigated how a history of urge UI or OAB compared with urodynamic findings of DO.[63–67] Six studies only investigated how a history of stress UI compared with the finding of urodynamic stress incontinence,[68–73] four of which provided some but not all accuracy data.

Multichannel cystometry (with or without uroflowmetry, urethral pressure profilometry, or cysto-urethrography) was the urodynamic method used in 24 studies. The remaining study used single-channel cystometry for women with urge UI (and suspected DO) and multichannel cystometry for women with stress UI.[50] All except four studies[62–64,70] stated that terminology used for urodynamic findings conformed to ICS standards.

With the exception of one study,[49] which involved primary and secondary care, all studies were conducted in secondary or tertiary care.

The GDG focused on the 11 studies that provided diagnostic accuracy data for stress, mixed and urge UI. Confidence intervals were calculated for each value, as this was considered to be more appropriate than pooling data from individual studies. Pooling the available data (by meta-analysis) or generating receiver operating characteristic curves was not considered to be appropriate because:

- the population in each study varied in terms of the relative proportions of stress, mixed or urge UI. The percentage of study participants with urodynamic stress incontinence varied from 34% to 63% (median 52%); the proportion with urodynamic stress incontinence plus DO ranged from 10% to 28% (median 19%), and for DO the range was 7–32% (median 17%)

Table C.1   '2 × 2' table for calculation of diagnostic accuracy parameters

	Reference standard (UD) positive	Reference standard (UD) negative	Total
Test (history) positive	a	b	a + b
Test (history) negative	c	d	c + d
Total	a + c	b + d	(a + b + c + d = total N in study)

Sensitivity = a/(a + c); specificity = d/(b + d); PPV = a/(a + b); NPV = d/(c + d)

- the methods used to obtain a history varied; a structured questionnaire or standardised form was used in seven of the 11 studies,[49–53,57,58] and the remainder only specified that a history had been taken[54–56,59]

- the studies were generally considered to be of poor quality; none stated whether urodynamic testing was undertaken blind to findings of history taking.

For the 11 studies that included women with stress, mixed or urge UI, and reported raw accuracy data for the three types of UI separately, the results are described below and also shown with 95% confidence intervals in Figures C.1 to C.12 (see evidence tables for full details of individual studies).[49–59]

The sensitivity, specificity, PPV and NPV values were calculated as shown in Table C.1. We consider that the NPV is of particular interest in terms of assessing whether urodynamics provides additional information compared with clinical history, because this quantity summarises the extent to which a negative history is associated with a negative finding on urodynamics (i.e. whether carrying out urodynamics would alter the diagnosis and, more importantly, management, for women who do not report a particular UI symptom).

In diagnostic accuracy studies 'prevalence' usually refers to the proportion within a study who have positive findings using the reference standard (and is given by (a + c)/(a + b + c + d)). The term 'prevalence' is used from here on for simplicity, to reflect the proportion of women in these studies who have a particular urodynamic finding. Sensitivity is normally unaffected by prevalence because it depends on the number of 'true positives' but not on the number of 'true negatives'. Similarly, specificity is normally unaffected by prevalence because it depends on the number of true negatives but not on the number of true positives. However, PPV and NPV both vary with prevalence because they both depend on the numbers of true positives and true negatives. PPV normally increases with increasing prevalence, whereas NPV normally decreases with increasing prevalence (provided sensitivity and specificity are both held fixed). PPV also increases with increasing sensitivity, provided specificity and prevalence are both held fixed. Similarly, NPV normally increases with increasing specificity, provided sensitivity and prevalence are both held fixed.

Stress urinary incontinence

Figures C.1 to C.4 show sensitivity, specificity, PPVs and NPVs of history of pure stress UI compared with urodynamic findings of stress UI (urodynamics being the reference standard), with 95% confidence intervals. The median values and ranges of results are shown in Table C.2.

Figures C.1 to C.4 show that there is considerable variation across the studies in sensitivities, specificities, PPVs and NPVs of a history of pure stress UI compared with positive findings of pure stress UI on multichannel cystometry. In general, there is a low level of agreement between the two methods. The median values show that:

- 66% of women who have urodynamic stress incontinence also have a history of pure stress UI

- 83% of women who do not have urodynamic stress incontinence also do not have a history of pure stress UI

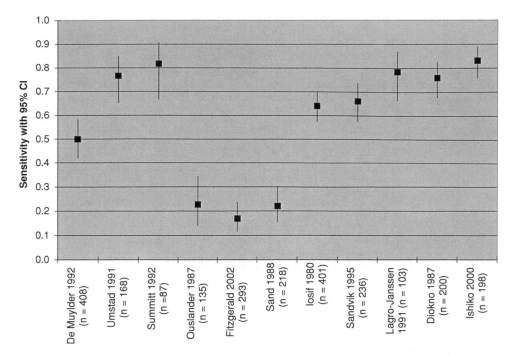

Figure C.1 Sensitivity of a history versus UD findings of stress UI; studies arranged in ascending order of USI prevalence (%): 34, 40, 44, 46, 51, 52, 53, 54, 58, 61, 63

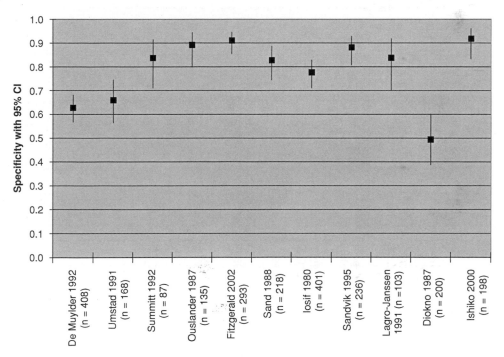

Figure C.2 Specificity of a history versus UD findings of stress UI; studies arranged in ascending order of USI prevalence (%): 34, 40, 44, 46, 51, 52, 53, 54, 58, 61, 63

Table C.2 Diagnostic accuracy data for urinary history of pure stress UI compared with urodynamic findings of stress UI

UI symptom	Sensitivity median (range)	Specificity median (range)	PPV median (range)	NPV median (range)
Stress UI	66% (17–83%)	83% (49–92%)	70% (41–95%)	69% (49–85%)

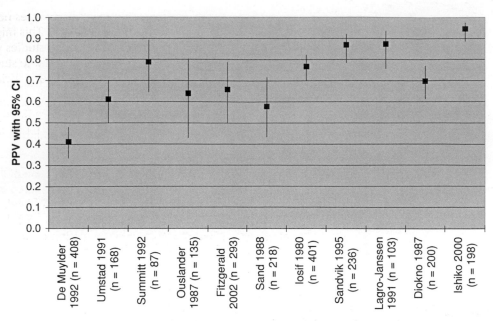

Figure C.3 PPV of a history versus UD findings of stress UI; studies arranged in ascending order of USI prevalence (%): 34, 40, 44, 46, 51, 52, 53, 54, 58, 61, 63

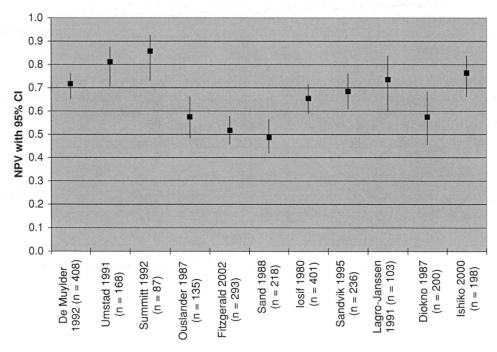

Figure C.4 NPV of a history versus UD findings of stress UI; studies arranged in ascending order of USI prevalence (%): 34, 40, 44, 46, 51, 52, 53, 54, 58, 61, 63

- 70% of women who have a history of pure stress UI also have urodynamic stress incontinence

- 69% of women who do not have a history of pure stress UI also do not have urodynamic stress incontinence.

We considered whether differences in prevalence of urodynamic stress incontinence might explain the variation in the results of individual studies. The studies in Figures C.1 to C.4 are arranged in ascending order of prevalence (from 34 to 63%, left to right). Figure C.3 shows that, as expected, the PPV increases with increasing USI prevalence (i.e. as the proportion of women with urodynamic stress UI in the study increases, the proportion of women who have positive findings from urodynamic studies as well as from history increases). However, NPV does not appear to follow the expected pattern of decreasing values with increasing prevalence. This might be because the sensitivities and specificities of the studies vary greatly, or because the studies vary in other ways. Three studies have a much lower sensitivity than the other eight. The three studies do not appear to be different to the others in any systematic way that would explain this variation.

It is possible that the method used to obtain a history might explain some of the variation between studies. However, the studies provided insufficient detail of the method of obtaining a history to allow this possible association to be explored in a meaningful way, and therefore it is not known how much this may influence the results seen.

The variation between studies might also reflect a lack of blind comparison of the results of history taking and urodynamic testing (again, the studies provide insufficient detail to explore this further), or the fact that urodynamics cannot be regarded as a gold standard. Indeed, there is some suggestion in Figures C.1 and C.2 that sensitivity and specificity vary with prevalence, which should not occur using a gold standard that provides a perfect classification of the presence/absence of stress UI.

Mixed urinary incontinence

Figures C.5 to C.8 show sensitivity, specificity, PPVs and NPVs of history compared with urodynamic findings of mixed UI (i.e. USI plus DO), with 95% confidence intervals. The median values and ranges of results are shown in Table C.3.

Figures C.5, C.6 and C.7 show that there is considerable variation across the studies in sensitivities, specificities and PPVs of a history of mixed UI compared with positive findings of USI plus DO on multichannel cystometry. The median values show that:

- 68% of women who have USI plus DO also have a history of mixed UI

- 77% of women who do not have urodynamic stress UI or DO also do not have a history of mixed UI

- 35% of women who have a history of mixed UI also have both USI plus DO.

Figure C.8 shows that the NPV is more consistent across studies than are the other quantities, i.e. at least 80% (median 90%) of women who do not have a history of mixed UI also do not have USI and DO on multichannel cystometry. Less variation is expected when the agreement between two forms of assessment is close to 100% (or 0%).

As expected, the PPV appears to increase with increasing prevalence of mixed findings of USI plus DO on multichannel cystometry.

The relationship between NPV and specificity is not strong in these studies; this could be because the prevalence of mixed UI varies widely between studies (from 10% to 28%).

Urge urinary incontinence

Figures C.9 to C.12 show sensitivity, specificity, PPVs and NPVs of the symptom of pure urge UI compared with urodynamic findings of detrusor overactivity, with 95% confidence intervals. The median values and ranges of results are shown in Table C.4.

Table C.3 Diagnostic accuracy data for urinary history of mixed UI compared with urodynamic findings of USI plus DO

UI symptom	Sensitivity median (range)	Specificity median (range)	PPV median (range)	NPV median (range)
Mixed UI	68% (42–85%)	77% (34–89%)	35% (18–70%)	90% (80–97%)

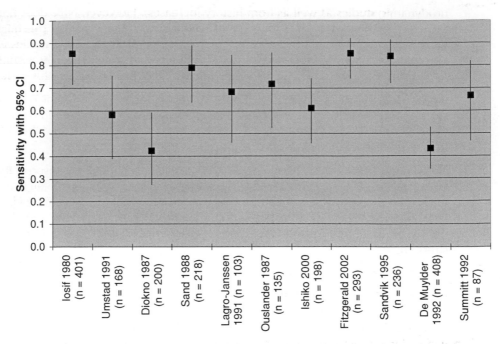

Figure C.5 Sensitivity of a history of mixed UI versus UD findings of USI plus DO; studies arranged in ascending order of USI plus DO prevalence (%): 10, 14, 17, 17, 18, 19, 21, 21, 24, 25, 28

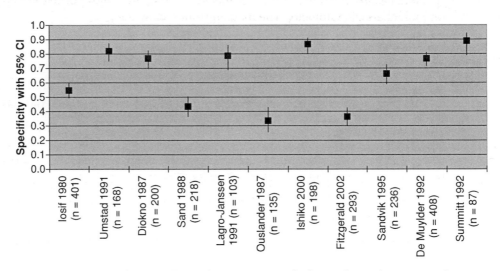

Figure C.6 Specificity of a history of mixed UI versus UD findings of USI plus DO; studies arranged in ascending order of USI plus DO prevalence (%): 10, 14, 17, 17, 18, 19, 21, 21, 24, 25, 28

Table C.4 Diagnostic accuracy data for urinary history of pure urge UI compared with urodynamic findings of detrusor overactivity

UI symptom	Sensitivity median (range)	Specificity median (range)	PPV median (range)	NPV median (range)
Urge UI	45% (14–86%)	96% (81–98%)	73% (25–81%)	91% (79–98%)

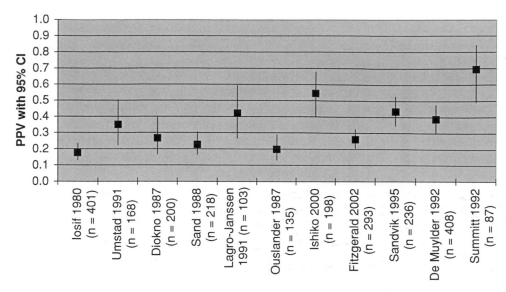

Figure C.7 PPV of a history of mixed UI versus UD findings of USI plus DO; studies arranged in ascending order of USI plus DO prevalence (%): 10, 14, 17, 17, 18, 19, 21, 21, 24, 25, 28

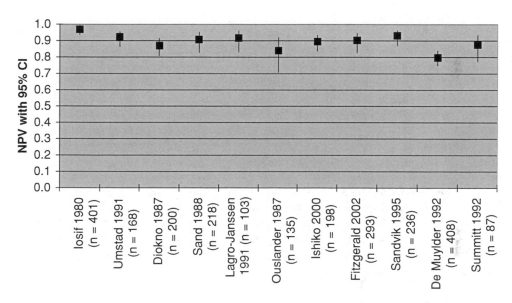

Figure C.8 NPV of a history of mixed UI versus UD findings of USI plus DO; studies arranged in ascending order of USI plus DO prevalence (%): 10, 14, 17, 17, 18, 19, 21, 21, 24, 25, 28

Figures C.9 and C.11 show that there is wide variation in the sensitivities and PPVs of urge UI across the studies. The median values show that:

- 45% of women who have DO also have a history of pure urge UI

- 73% of women who have a history of pure urge UI also have DO.

It is also noted that the relationship between PPV and sensitivity is not strong across these studies and this could be because the prevalence of DO varies from 7% to 32% (median 17%).

Conversely, specificity and NPVs for urge UI are both quite consistent, as shown in Figures C.10 and C.12. At least 81% of women (median 96%) who do not have DO also do not have a history of pure urge UI; and at least 79% (median 91%) of women who do not have a history of pure urge UI also do not have DO on multichannel cystometry. In other words, if there is no history of urge UI, the probability of finding DO on urodynamic testing is small. Again, the results of the individual

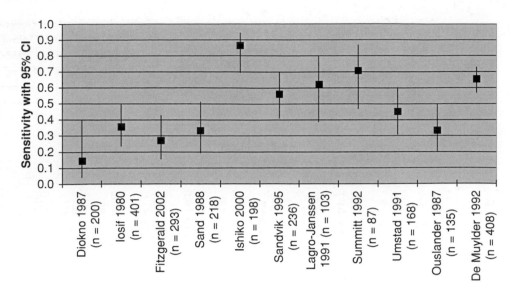

Figure C.9 Sensitivity of a history of urge UI versus UD findings of DO; studies arranged in ascending order of DO prevalence (%): 7, 12, 13, 14, 15, 17, 18, 20, 24, 27, 32

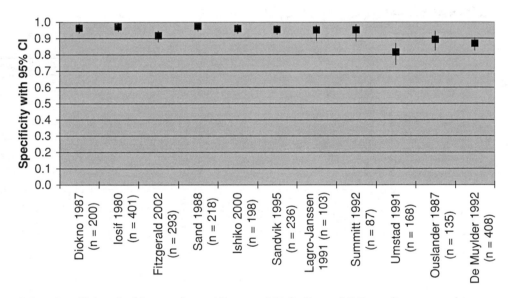

Figure C.10 Specificity of a history of urge UI versus UD findings of DO; studies arranged in ascending order of DO prevalence (%): 7, 12, 13, 14, 15, 17, 18, 20, 24, 27, 32

studies are quite consistent as is to be expected when the percentage agreement between two forms of assessment is close to 100%. There is a strong relationship between specificity and NPV in these studies, despite the variability in the prevalence of DO. This might be because the variations in prevalence are compensated by variations in sensitivity.

Other studies

The remaining studies that compared history and urodynamic findings did so in relation to only one or two types of UI. These also showed variability in their results. In two studies that only reported accuracy data for stress and mixed UI, the results were:[61,62]

- sensitivity: 33% and 39% stress UI; 49% and 68% mixed UI

- specificity: 83% and 86% stress UI; 48% and 57% mixed UI

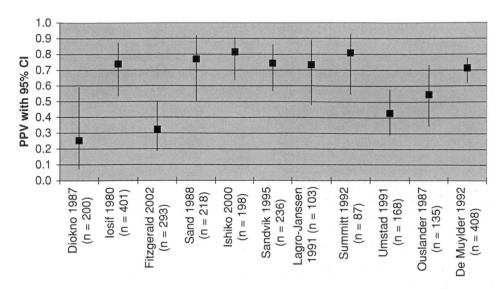

Figure C.11 PPV of a history of urge UI versus UD findings of DO; studies arranged in ascending order of DO prevalence (%): 7, 12, 13, 14, 15, 17, 18, 20, 24, 27, 32

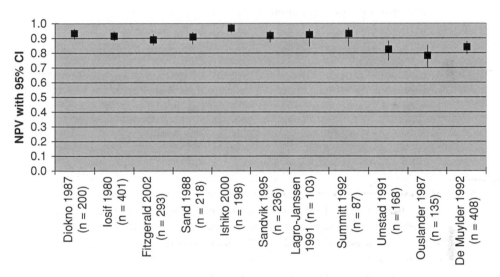

Figure C.12 NPV of a history of urge UI versus UD findings of DO; studies arranged in ascending order of DO prevalence (%): 7, 12, 13, 14, 15, 17, 18, 20, 24, 27, 32

- PPV: 56% and 74% stress UI; 33% and 53% mixed UI
- NPV: 58% and 66% stress UI; 53% and 80% mixed UI.

In one study that included women with any type of UI but for which only data for stress UI were reported, the sensitivity of history compared with urodynamics was 52%, specificity and PPV were both 85% and NPV was 53%.[70]

In the five studies that investigated how a history of urge UI and/or OAB compared with the urodynamic finding of DO, the results were:[63–67]

- sensitivity: median 40% (range 24–91%)
- specificity: median 86% (range 45–92%)
- PPV: median 54% (range 44–91%)
- NPV: median 68% (range 26–91%).

In five of six studies that investigated how a history of stress UI compared with a urodynamic finding of stress UI, sensitivities of 47–82% and PPVs of 52–100% were reported.[68–72] The remaining study reported sensitivity, specificity, PPV and NPV results using four different urodynamic methods in the assessment of women with urodynamic stress UI (including mixed UI). The ranges of results across the different methods were: sensitivity 49–91%, specificity 98–100%, PPV 82–100% and NPV 44–88%, the highest level of agreement being noted for observed urine loss with cough during multichannel cystometry.[73]

Conclusions

The available studies comparing history of stress, mixed or urge UI with findings of stress UI and/or DO on multichannel cystometry have poor internal and external validity. In addressing the question of whether urodynamic testing gives additional information to that obtained from history alone, with the limitations of the studies in mind, the following conclusions can be drawn:

- If a woman does not report mixed UI (i.e. if she reports pure stress UI or pure urge UI), the probability of finding USI plus DO on cystometry is small (around 10%), therefore urodynamic testing might be said to offer little additional diagnostic value. It is acknowledged that urodynamic investigation is not simply used to distinguish USI and DO, and that further information may be obtained about other elements of lower urinary tract function, for example the voiding pattern.

- If a woman does not report pure urge UI, the probability of finding DO on cystometry is small (again around 10%), therefore urodynamic testing offers little added diagnostic value.

The situation for pure stress UI is less clear-cut. Here 15–51% (median 31%) of women who do not report pure stress UI may nevertheless be found to have USI on cystometry. However, the lack of consistency between the NPVs in the available studies together with the lack of detailed information about the method of obtaining a history and the poor quality of the studies limit the extent to which the evidence would support urodynamic testing for women who do not report stress UI. Furthermore, a limitation of dealing with stress, mixed and urge UI as three separate entities is that the analysis ignores the interdependence between the different diagnoses.

History taking is regarded as the cornerstone of assessment of UI. Current practice is that women with UI are categorised according to their symptoms into those with stress, mixed or urge UI; women with mixed UI are treated according to the symptom they report to be the most troublesome. In the absence of evidence that urodynamic testing improves the outcome of women treated conservatively, and without robust evidence that urodynamic testing provides additional valuable information to the history alone in the initial assessment of women with UI, the GDG concluded that urodynamic testing is not required before initiating conservative treatment.

Appendix D

Economic evidence for urodynamics

The literature review identified two economic evaluations addressing the use of urodynamics in diagnosing stress UI. One study sought to compare the cost effectiveness of the cough stress test with simple cystometry against multichannel cystometry in a US setting.[928] Sensitivities and specificities for both methods were estimated from the literature, with baseline values derived from the mean of all reported values. The authors chose to use sensitivity as their measure of effectiveness on the grounds that the specificities for both diagnostic tests were close to 100%. With baseline values, the incremental cost effectiveness ratio (ICER) of multichannel urodynamics was calculated as $16,550 per correct diagnosis. Under the most favourable sensitivity analysis for multichannel cystometry, the ICER of multichannel cystometry is given as $1,679. Under some sensitivity analysis scenarios, cough stress test with simple cystometry dominates. The authors conclude that cough stress test with simple cystometrogram is more cost effective than multichannel cystometry. However, this conclusion is not warranted from their results because the value of a correct diagnosis is not considered, i.e. what cost per correct diagnosis would society consider to be good value for money?

The other paper used a decision analytic approach to compare the cost effectiveness of pre-operative testing with urodynamics versus no further testing, following a basic office assessment (BOA) diagnosis of pure stress UI within a US setting.[929] Clinical and population parameters for the model were estimated using a literature review together with additional articles referenced in recovered articles. The authors report that costs were considered from a societal perspective, although there is limited detail of the cost analysis and all the costs reported appear to be those that would be incurred by the healthcare provider or payer. With baseline values, the authors find that urodynamics is the most expensive and most effective strategy with an incremental cost per cure of $3,847 when compared with BOA and no further testing. Sensitivity analysis showed that the cost effectiveness result was particularly sensitive to changes in the proportion of the patient population having pure stress incontinence. If 85% or more of the population had pure stress incontinence then no further testing dominated, but the urodynamics strategy dominated when this fell to 79% or below. This makes it difficult to draw conclusions about the cost effectiveness of preoperative urodynamics in a population of women who are likely to have pure stress UI. Furthermore, the authors' conclusion that urodynamics before surgery is not cost effective is not supported, even under baseline assumptions, because the value of a cure or willingness to pay for a cure is not considered.

Using UK cost data, the decision analytic model developed by Weber et al. was used for this guideline to assess the preoperative cost effectiveness of urodynamics in a UK setting.[929] The decision tree was created in Microsoft Excel® but also, for validation purposes, in TreeAge Pro 2006®.

The model focuses on a hypothetical population of incontinent women who have failed conservative treatment and have a presumed diagnosis of pure stress UI. For baseline calculations, it is assumed that 80% of the cohort has pure stress UI, 18% have mixed UI and 2% have DO. It must be remembered that these are not intended as estimates of the prevalence of symptoms or urodynamic abnormalities in the whole population, but estimate the posterior probability after a basic office evaluation which includes detailed history and physical examination, urinalysis, a provocative stress test and measurement of residual urine.[929]

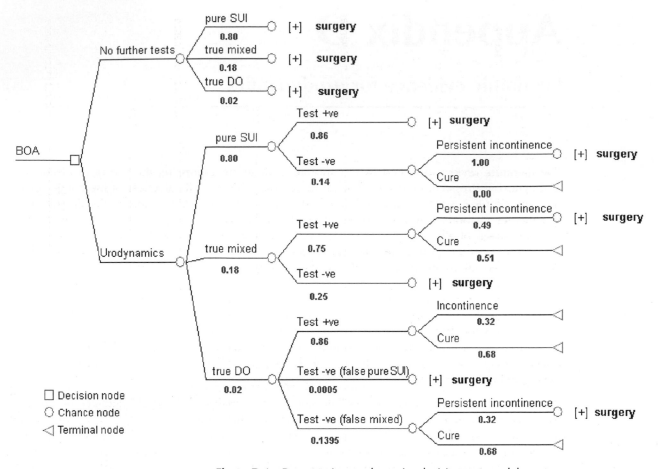

Figure D.1   Preoperative urodynamics decision tree model

The comparators in the model are no further testing prior to surgery or preoperative urodynamics in order to confirm a diagnosis of pure stress UI, mixed UI or DO.

The decision tree (Figure D.1) depicts the treatment pathway of the hypothetical cohort of patients. The pathway starts with the decision whether to undertake urodynamics testing or not, and patient flow from this decision proceeds from left to right with the branches indicating all feasible pathways. The pathway of any particular patient is also determined by chance events and these are represented in the model by chance nodes. Branches that emanate from chance nodes indicate all the possibilities that exist at such a point in the pathway. The outcome of each terminal node (or endpoint) in the tree is either 'cure' of incontinence or failure (persistent incontinence or retention).

In the no further testing arm, all patients are presumed to have pure stress UI and have surgery on that basis. The patient pathways following surgery are shown in the surgery sub-tree (Figure D.2). The top branch of the surgery sub-tree shows that cure rates with primary surgery for patients who have pure stress UI, mixed UI or DO are 86%, 78% or 31%, respectively.[929] For those patients who are not cured, the tree shows that urodynamic testing is used to establish whether there is retention or incontinence. For those with retention, urethrolysis* is performed, which is assumed to cure 72% of patients with retention.

In patients who have failed initial surgery but who are not diagnosed with retention, then the urodynamics is used to determine whether the underlying problem is recurrent hypermobility,

---

*   This model was developed in a US context. In the UK urethrolysis is rarely undertaken for retention. However, as this only affects a small proportion of the model cohort and the proportion is similar across treatment alternatives this feature of the model has minimal impact on model output.

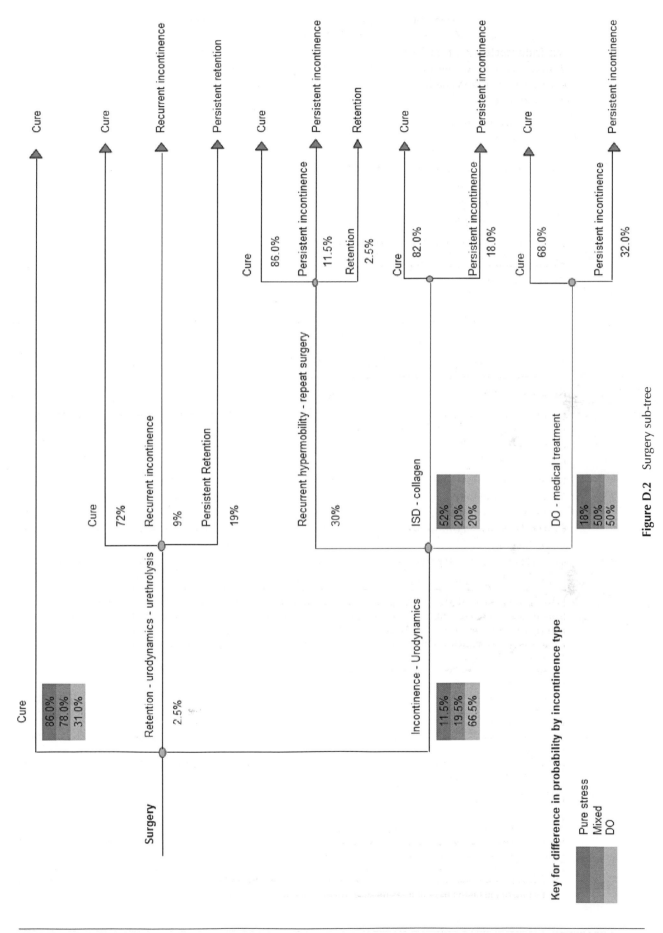

Figure D.2 Surgery sub-tree

Key for difference in probability by incontinence type

Pure stress
Mixed
DO

ISD or DO. For patients with recurrent hypermobility, repeat surgery is undertaken, which is assumed to cure 86% of patients, with the remainder having treatment failure and continuing incontinence (11.5%) or retention (2.5%). Patients with ISD receive a collagen injection, which has a cure rate of 82%, with 'failures' having persistent incontinence. Finally, patients with DO are given medical treatment, which cures 68%, with the remainder having persistent incontinence.

For patients in the urodynamics arm, the patient pathways are as described above for the surgery sub-tree if the diagnosis of pure stress UI is made. However, this will still include some false positives, as urodynamics does not have a specificity of 100%, which will affect the cure rate from initial surgery, collagen and medical treatment. For patients with a urodynamic finding of mixed UI or DO, medical treatment will be initiated. If medical treatment fails to cure patients, and the diagnosis was mixed UI, then surgery will be performed with the pathways as described above for the surgery sub-tree.

The cost parameters used in the model are shown in Table D.1.

The baseline values for clinical and population parameters are taken from Weber et al.[929] and are shown in Table D.2.

Table D.1 Cost parameters and source of data

Resource item	Costs	Source of UK data
Urodynamic testing	£140	2003 NHS Reference Cost – TOP HRG (M07op)
Initial TVT	£1,014	TVT HTA
Repeat TVT	£1,014	TVT HTA
Urethrolysis	£2,865	2004 NHS Reference Cost
Collagen injection	£1,305	TVT HTA (excluding theatre costs)
Medical treatment for DO	£36	BNF 50
Care related to incontinence for 1 year	£150	hcna.radcliffe-oxford.com/continen.htm
Care related to urinary retention for 1 year	£150	hcna.radcliffe-oxford.com/continen.htm

Urodynamic testing – The baseline estimate is the mean unit cost taken from the 2003 NHS Reference Cost for urodynamic investigation (HRG code M07op). The interquartile range for the unit costs was £94 to £163. A cost for urodynamic investigation was not included in the 2004 NHS Reference Costs.
Initial TVT – The baseline estimate is taken from an HTA of the clinical and cost effectiveness of TVT for the treatment of stress UI.[716]
Repeat TVT – The baseline estimate is the same as for the initial surgery. In Weber's model, repeat surgery was given a unit cost 3.4% greater than for initial surgery.
Urethrolysis – On the advice of the GDG, the baseline estimate was taken from the 2004 NHS Reference Cost mean unit cost for urethra major open procedures (HRG code L33). The interquartile range of unit costs given for this category of procedures is £1,205 to £2,757.
Collagen injection – The default value was taken from the HTA on TVT.[716] The authors note that this is likely to be an underestimate because it does not include theatre costs.
Medical treatment for detrusor overactivity – The baseline unit cost is based on a year's treatment with oxybutynin hydrochloride (non-proprietary) 5 mg twice daily (84-tab pack = £4.14).
Care related to incontinence for 1 year – The baseline estimates are much lower than those cited in the Weber paper but NICE requires that costs only be measured from the perspective of the NHS and personal social services. The source of the data was a continence healthcare needs assessment chapter available on the internet (hcna.radcliffe-oxford.com/continen.htm). This chapter refers to a study that reported the NHS- and patient-borne costs for a 3 month period, which was £37 (£37 × 4 = £148) in 1995 prices.[930] The simplifying assumption made is that removing patient-borne costs from this estimate, but adjusting for inflation, would more or less cancel each other out.
Care related to retention for 1 year – For baseline it was assumed that these would be the same as for incontinence. In Weber's paper, the costs were of a similar magnitude if slightly lower for retention.

Table D.2 Baseline values for clinical and population parameters

Parameter	Value
Pure stress UI in women with stress symptoms and positive cough stress test	80.00%
Pure mixed UI in women with stress symptoms and positive cough stress test	18.00%
Urodynamically confirmed DO in women with stress symptoms and positive cough stress test	2.00%
Urodynamic test positive for USI when USI is true condition (sensitivity or true +ve for USI)	86.00%
Urodynamic test positive for mixed incontinence when USI is true condition (false +ve for DO)	14.00%
Urodynamic test positive for mixed incontinence when mixed incontinence is true condition (true +ve for mixed)	75.00%
Urodynamic test positive for USI when mixed incontinence is true condition (false −ve for DO)	25.00%
Urodynamic test positive for DO when DO is true condition (sensitivity or true +ve for DO)	86.00%
Urodynamic test positive for USI when DO is true condition (false +ve for USI)	0.05%
Urodynamic test positive for mixed incontinence when DO is true condition (false +ve for mixed)	13.95%
Cure rate after initial retropubic bladder suspension for USI	86.00%
Cure rate after repeat retropubic bladder suspension for urethral hypermobility and USI	86.00%
Cure rate after initial retropubic bladder suspension for DO	31.00%
Cure rate after initial retropubic bladder suspension for mixed incontinence	78.00%
Cure rate after collagen injection for ISD	82.00%
Cure rate after urethrolysis for retention	72.00%
Cure rate for medical treatment for DO	68.00%
Cure rate for medical treatment for mixed incontinence	51.00%
Cure rate for medical treatment for USI	0.00%
Rate of retention after initial or repeat retropubic bladder suspension	2.50%
Rate of recurrent incontinence after urethrolysis	9.00%
Rate of persistent retention after urethrolysis	19.00%
Recurrent urethral hypermobility as cause of recurrent incontinence after retropubic bladder suspension for USI, DO or mixed incontinence	30.00%
ISD as aetiology of recurrent incontinence after retropubic bladder suspension for USI	52.00%
DO as aetiology of recurrent incontinence after retropubic bladder suspension for USI	18.00%
ISD as aetiology of recurrent incontinence after retropubic bladder suspension for DO or mixed incontinence	20.00%
DO as aetiology of recurrent incontinence after retropubic bladder suspension for DO or mixed incontinence	50.00%

Results

The results with the baseline parameter values are shown in Table D.3.

This means that for every 10 000 patients there would be approximately an additional 13 'cures' using urodynamics, compared with no further testing, and that these would be achieved at an approximate additional cost of £350,000, or £26,125 per additional cure.

However, without knowing how much a 'cure' is valued, it is not possible to say whether the additional urodynamic testing represents a cost effective use of resources. If we assume a willingness to pay threshold of £20,000 per QALY[36] then each cure would have to generate 1.3 QALYs in order for urodynamics to be considered cost effective with baseline values.

Table D.3 Results with baseline parameter values

Testing strategy	Cost	Cure rate	Incremental cost	Incremental cure	ICER
No further testing	£1,233	96.4%	–	–	–
Urodynamics	£1,268	96.5%	£35	0.13%	£26,125

Sensitivity analysis

A number of one-way sensitivity analyses were undertaken to assess how the model's results were affected by parameter uncertainty, and those having the greatest impact on the model output are shown below.

Cost parameters

Cost parameters do not affect the relative cure rates of the two alternatives. As the cure rate is fractionally higher for urodynamics with baseline values, this result will be unaffected with one-way sensitivity analysis on cost parameters. Therefore, urodynamics is always the more effective strategy for this subset of the sensitivity analysis.

Urodynamics	ICER (cost per cure)	Comment
£100	Urodynamics dominates	
£104	Urodynamics dominates	Threshold for dominance
£125	£15,162	Urodynamics more effective
£150	£33,434	Urodynamics more effective
£175	£51,706	Urodynamics more effective

TVT cost (initial and repeat)	ICER (cost per cure)	Comment
£800	£41,543	Urodynamics more effective
£1,000	£27,134	Urodynamics more effective
£1,200	£12,724	Urodynamics more effective
£1,377	Urodynamics dominates	Threshold for dominance
£1,400	Urodynamics dominates	

Population parameters

While this is referred to as one-way sensitivity analysis, it should be noted that the total population must add up to 100% and that this is not possible by varying just one of the population parameters. Therefore, one of the other population parameters is simultaneously adjusted to maintain the overall population at 100%.

Urodynamic stress UI proportion (varying mixed UI)	ICER (cost per cure)	Comment
72%	Urodynamics dominates	
74%	£2,988	Urodynamics more effective
76%	£7,764	Urodynamics more effective
78%	£14,787	Urodynamics more effective
80%	£26,125	Urodynamics more effective
82%	£47,525	Urodynamics more effective
84%	£103,061	Urodynamics more effective
86%	£596,173	Urodynamics more effective
87%	No further testing dominates	

DO proportion (varying urodynamic stress UI)	ICER (cost per cure)	Comment
0%	£17,335	Urodynamics more effective
1%	£19,669	Urodynamics more effective
2%	£26,125	Urodynamics more effective
3%	£130,016	Urodynamics more effective
4%	No further testing dominates	
5%	£4,007	No further testing more effective
10%	£10,086	No further testing more effective
20%	£11,432	No further testing more effective

DO proportion (varying mixed UI)	ICER (cost per cure)	Comment
0%	£13,391	Urodynamics more effective
1%	£16,517	Urodynamics more effective
2%	£26,125	Urodynamics more effective
3%	No further testing dominates	
4%	No further testing dominates	
5%	No further testing dominates	
6%	£1,249	No further testing more effective
7%	£2,736	No further testing more effective
10%	£4,660	No further testing more effective

Clinical parameters

Cure rate after TVT for urodynamic stress UI (varying retention)	ICER (cost per cure)	Comment
60%	Urodynamics dominates	
68%	Urodynamics dominates	Threshold for dominance
70%	£1,320	Urodynamics more effective
80%	£14,608	Urodynamics more effective

Cure rate after repeat TVT for urodynamic stress UI (varying retention)	ICER (cost per cure)	Comment
60%	Urodynamics dominates	
68%	Urodynamics dominates	Threshold for dominance
70%	£980	Urodynamics more effective
80%	£11,733	Urodynamics more effective

Cure rate after TVT for mixed (varying incontinence)	ICER (cost per cure)	Comment
40%	£1,969	Urodynamics more effective
60%	£5,919	Urodynamics more effective
80%	£35,715	Urodynamics more effective
87%	No further testing dominates	Threshold for dominance
90%	No further testing dominates	

Cure rate for medical treatment of DO	ICER (cost per cure)	Comment
40%	No further testing dominates	Threshold for dominance
50%	£75,577	Urodynamics more effective
60%	£36,770	Urodynamics more effective
70%	£24,370	Urodynamics more effective
80%	£18,270	Urodynamics more effective
90%	£14,643	Urodynamics more effective

Cure rate for medical treatment for mixed UI	ICER (cost per cure)	Comment
30%	No further testing dominates	
32%	No further testing dominates	Threshold for dominance
40%	£99,042	Urodynamics more effective
50%	£28,953	Urodynamics more effective
60%	£9,952	Urodynamics more effective
70%	£1,102	Urodynamics more effective
72%	Urodynamics dominates	Threshold for dominance
80%	Urodynamics dominates	

Discussion

In this model, the use of urodynamics can save unnecessary surgery in a population that would all have surgery in its absence. This can produce cost savings, which to a greater or lesser extent offset the additional costs of testing. Also, the way treatment pathways are defined in the model, most patients will ultimately get surgery if they fail on medical treatment.

The results with the baseline values suggest that the costs and effectiveness of both of the testing strategies is very similar. This result is unpicked in order to gain a better understanding of the model and its workings.

Patients with pure stress incontinence

The cure rate (effectiveness) is the same irrespective of the testing regimen (no further testing versus urodynamics) as all patients ultimately get surgery. This is automatically true with no further testing, where all patients receive surgery. However, with urodynamics, even those patients with a false negative ultimately get surgery as it is assumed that the cure rate for medical treatment in such patients is 0%. Not surprisingly, the urodynamic testing arm is more costly for such patients – no surgery costs are saved and there are additional costs of urodynamic testing and medical treatment for false negative patients.

Conclusions: effectiveness same, costs lower under no further testing.

Patients with true mixed urinary incontinence

The cure rate is higher with urodynamic testing. Patients who have a positive diagnosis for mixed UI are treated with medical treatment, which has a cure rate of 51%. Patients with false negative results for mixed UI on urodynamics or those who fail medical treatment all proceed to surgery. The failure rate with surgery is the same as in the no further testing arm. However, because this represents just a subset of the total (the rest being cured by medical treatment), the overall failure rate is reduced. The urodynamics arm is also cheaper for these patients because the additional testing costs are more than offset by reduced surgery arising from the cures achieved by medical treatment.

Conclusions: urodynamics more effective, costs higher under no further testing

Patients with true detrusor overactivity

For these patients, the cure rate is higher with no further testing. This perhaps rather counter-intuitive result arises because surgery/repeat surgery produces a higher cure rate than medical treatment (83% versus 68%). Of course, the subset of patients who have a false diagnosis of mixed UI will go on to surgery but the 83% cure rate in these patients applies to only about 4% of all true DO patients. However, the costs in the no further testing group are higher because urodynamics saves a lot of unnecessary surgery.

Conclusions: no further testing more effective, cost higher under no further testing.

The above shows that the effectiveness of each strategy varies according to the patient's true UI status. Similarly, neither testing strategy is cheaper for all incontinence types. Therefore, the population characteristics are likely to be important in determining the relative cost effectiveness of the strategies given the other underlying assumptions in the model. This is borne out in the sensitivity analysis which shows that urodynamics dominates when the proportion with true USI is 72% or less, but that no further testing dominates when the proportion with USI is 87% or more.

The baseline results show that the ICER is £26,125 per cure. This begs the question as to what would be considered a cost effective cost per cure for the NHS.

In order to estimate an approximate figure for this, the following assumptions were made:

1 year of cure represents a QALY gain = 0.05[931]
Cure lasts 15 years with no relapse
Discount rate = 3.5%*

$$\text{QALY gain per cured patient} = \sum_{i=1}^{15} 0.05/1.035^{i-1} = 0.60$$

Therefore, for a cost effectiveness threshold of £20,000 per QALY we would be willing to pay in the order of £12,000 per cure. For the baseline values this would suggest that urodynamics is not cost effective, with a cost per cure of £26,125. However, this may be an overestimate of the cost per cure for the model's default parameters, as it does not take into account 'downstream' savings from reduced continence care in cure savings. If we assume that there is a cost saving of £150 per year of cure, then the net present value of these 'downstream' savings for each cured patient is as follows:

$$\text{Net present value of savings for cured patient}^{\dagger} = \sum_{i=1}^{14} £150/1.035^{i} = £1,638$$

So for 10,000 patients:

Incremental cure = 13

$\rightarrow 13 \times 0.6 = 7.8$ QALYs

Incremental cost = £350,000 − (13 × £1,638) = £328,000

ICER = £25,000 per cure *or* £42,000 per QALY

Using the default values, the model suggests that preoperative urodynamic testing would not be considered cost effective. Sensitivity analysis shows that cost effectiveness results are extremely sensitive to various model parameters, particularly the proportion of patients with USI. For a cost effectiveness threshold of £20,000 per QALY we would be willing to pay in the order of £12,000 per cure. For the baseline values this would suggest that urodynamics is not cost effective with a cost per cure of £26,125, but that it would be if the proportion with true stress UI was 77.3%.

---

* This is the discount rate recommended in the NICE technical manual for costs and benefits.[36] 'Discounting' is a technique which is used to convert cost or effects that occur in the future into a net present value, so that interventions with differential timings of costs and consequences can be compared on an equivalent basis. This is necessary because society exhibits 'time preference', preferring to receive goods and services sooner rather than later and to defer costs to future generations. The concept of 'time preference' could be considered to be embodied in the proverb that 'a bird in the hand is worth two in the bush'.

† The first year saving is captured in the model.

Appendix E

Costing first-line conservative treatments for urinary incontinence

In costing potential first-line conservative treatments, it is necessary to focus solely on the resources associated with those treatments considered by the GDG. This is not to say that assessment and treatment should not be offered during the same session but that those resources devoted to determining treatment option or the need for a referral should not be considered as part of the cost of providing treatment.

Considerable heterogeneity exists within many of the conservative treatments for UI. As far as possible, the cost estimates presented here are based on 'standard' or 'typical' treatment (as informed by expert opinion on the GDG) but in practice such a standard may not exist. Therefore, the actual costs of particular conservative treatments will vary according to the actual practice followed.

Labour costs

Labour costs can be considered a *variable cost* of producing a given treatment. This means that for each additional patient treated, there is a demand on staff time and therefore labour costs vary with the quantity of treatment supplied.

For the purposes of this costing, labour costs are based on *Unit Costs of Health and Social Care 2004*.[932] This provides a unit cost (cost per hour, cost per consultation, etc.) for a range of professional staff working in a health- or social care setting. As far as possible, the unit costs are based on the *long run opportunity costs* of employing an additional member of staff. Therefore, in addition to wages/salary the unit costs also include salary oncosts, qualifications and continuing training. The calculations also make an allowance for the impact that holidays, sickness and training days have on the actual hours worked.

Importantly for the costings undertaken here, they also incorporate the *direct overheads* associated with delivering health care through professional and *capital costs*. Direct overheads, includes those activities such as clerical support and administration which relate directly to the provision of a particular service or treatment. Capital costs relate to the costs of building and land but for hospital-based staff, at least, exclude equipment.

Consumable costs

These are also *variable costs* and relate to resources that are used up in the provision of a service or treatment. It cannot be reused. Again, these costs vary with the quantity of treatment actually provided.

Equipment (capital) costs

In an economic evaluation, *capital costs* (which include equipment, buildings and land) should not be ignored. After all, buying medical equipment carries an *opportunity cost*. That said, these costs differ from operating costs such as labour and consumables in certain respects. The purchase of equipment requires an upfront payment (or investment) before treatment can begin. This payment is a *fixed cost* and does not vary with the quantity of treatment provided. This capital can then often be used over a number of years before it needs to be replaced.

Capital costs have two facets:

- Opportunity cost – the money spent on the equipment could have been invested in some other venture yielding positive benefits. This is calculated by applying an interest rate to the sum invested in the equipment.

- Depreciation cost – the equipment has a certain lifespan and depreciates over time. Eventually, the equipment has to be replaced.

In economic evaluation, the usual practice is to annuitise the initial capital outlay over the expected life of the equipment. This gives an 'equivalent annual cost', which can then be divided by the number of patients treated annually to assign a unit cost of using that equipment. Calculating the equivalent annual cost means making an allowance for the differential timing of costs, which involves *discounting*.

The formula for calculating the equivalent annual cost is given below:

$$E = (K - [S \div \{1 + r\}^n]) \div A(n, r)$$

where:

E = equivalent annual cost
K = purchase price of equipment
S = resale value
r = discount (interest rate)
n = equipment lifespan
A(n, r) = annuity factor* (n years at interest rate r)

Pelvic floor muscle training

Description of treatment and assumptions

It is difficult to define a 'standard' or 'typical' PFMT session and therefore costs will vary according to the actual practices employed.

- Costings are based on treatment being undertaken by a senior 1 grade women's health physiotherapist[†] in a hospital physiotherapy department.

- There are a total of six sessions with the therapist.[‡]

- The initial session lasts 1 hour; subsequent sessions last half an hour.

- Consumables at the initial session include gloves, single-use KY Jelly, wipes (×2), paper towels (×4).

- Consumables at subsequent sessions include gloves, wipes (×2), paper towels (×4).

- Additional consumables may include exercise diaries and advice leaflets (often provided free by companies) but these are negligible and not included.

---

[*]   Converts a present value into an annuity, a series of equal annual payments.

[†]   Remuneration for a continence nurse specialist grade f–g/band 6–7 is similar.

[‡]   Estimates from GDG members that four to eight sessions are typically offered.

Labour costs

Contact time with patient: $(1 \times 1) + (5 \times 0.5) = 3.5$ hours
Unit cost: £37 per hour
Labour cost: £37 $\times$ 3.5 = £129.50

Consumables

Item	Quantity	Unit cost	Cost
Gloves	6	£0.02	£0.11
KY Jelly	1	£0.80	£0.80
Couch roll	6	£0.04	£0.22
Paper towels	24	Less than £0.01	£0.07
Wipes	12	£0.03	£0.30
Total			**£1.50**

Total cost for PFMT: £131 (£94 to £168)*

PFMT + biofeedback

Description of treatment and assumptions

Not only is it difficult to define a 'standard' for PFMT but biofeedback can also take many different forms. Costs will therefore vary according to actual practice and biofeedback equipment used:

- Number of sessions and duration is typically the same as for 'ordinary' PFMT. Therefore, costs of PFMT + Biofeedback have been estimated by adding the costs associated with biofeedback to PFMT alone (see above).

- Biofeedback is undertaken using a Verity NeuroTrac™ Simplex (hand-held single-channel EMG unit), a Neen Educator® and a Neen Periform vaginal probe.

- It is assumed that the NeuroTrac device is loaned to patients for home use for 3 months and that it has a lifespan of 5 years (i.e. the cost of equipment is spread over 20 patients).

- Educators and probes are for single-patient use and are treated as consumable costs.

PFMT costs: £131

Additional biofeedback costs

Consumables

Item	Quantity	Unit cost	Cost
Neen Educator	1	£19.50	£19.50
Neen Periform	1	£10.25	£10.25
Total			**£29.75**

---

*   Range based on four to eight sessions.

Equipment

Item	Cost	Equivalent annual cost	Cost/patient
Verity NeuroTrac Simplex	£99	£19.84	£4.96

Total cost for PFMT + biofeedback: £166

Cones

Description of treatment and assumptions

Treatment is often not provided by the NHS, and women will often buy cones over the counter after GP advice and self-treat. An estimate is provided here of the cost to the NHS of providing this as a first-line treatment, including the cost of cones.

- It is assumed that the labour costs are one-third of those for PFMT*

- Consumables are cones and KY Jelly.

Labour costs

$1/3 \times £129.50 = £43$[933]

Consumables

Item	Quantity	Unit cost	Cost
KY Jelly	1	£1.29	£1.29
Cones	1	£24.95	£24.95
Total			**£26.24**

Total cost for cones: £69

Electrical stimulation

Description of treatment and assumptions

- Initial 1 hour appointment with senior 1 grade women's health physiotherapist in a hospital physiotherapy department to determine appropriate programme.

- Patient is loaned a neuromuscular stimulator for 3 months (Neen 'Peri-calm').

- Patient has two follow-up appointments[†], lasting 30 minutes.

- It is assumed that the Neen Pericalm device is loaned to patients for home use for 3 months and that it has a lifespan of 5 years (i.e. the cost of equipment is spread over 20 patients).

- A Neen Periform vaginal electrode is used (×1).

- Other consumables include gloves (×3), KY Jelly (×3), couch roll (×3), wipes (×6) and paper towels (×12).

---

*   Teaching time is one-third of that for PFMT; see Link.[933]

†   Again, actual practice on follow-up may vary.

Labour costs

Contact time with patient: $(1 \times 1) + (2 \times 0.5) = 2$ hours
Unit cost: £37 per hour
Labour cost: £37 $\times$ 2 = £74.00

Consumables

Item	Quantity	Unit cost	Cost
Gloves	3	£0.02	£0.06
KY Jelly	3	£0.80	£2.40
Couch roll	3	£0.04	£0.11
Paper towels	12	Less than £0.01	£0.04
Wipes	6	£0.03	£0.15
Neen Periform	1	£10.25	£10.25
Total			**£13.01**

Equipment

Item	Cost	Equivalent annual cost	Cost/patient
Neen Pericalm	£83.89	£19.84	£4.20

Total cost for electrical stimulation: £91

Electrical stimulation (clinic based)

Description of treatment and assumptions

- Initial 1 hour appointment with senior 1 grade women's health physiotherapist in a hospital physiotherapy department to determine appropriate programme.

- Patient has twelve follow-up appointments*, lasting 30 minutes.

- A Neen Periform vaginal electrode is used ($\times$1).

- Other consumables include gloves ($\times$13), KY Jelly ($\times$13), couch roll ($\times$13), wipes ($\times$26) and paper towels ($\times$52).

- In addition it was assumed that the following clinic equipment was used: Genesis Medical Unomax Data Reader.

- It was assumed that these equipment items would each have a lifespan of 5 years and be used on 200 patients per year.

Labour costs

Contact time with patient: $(1 \times 1) + (12 \times 0.5) = 7$ hours
Unit cost: £37 per hour
Labour cost: £37 $\times$ 7 = £259

---

* Again actual practice on follow-up may vary.

Consumables

Item	Quantity	Unit cost	Cost
KY Jelly	13	£0.80	£10.38
Gloves	13	£0.02	£0.24
Couch roll	13	£0.04	£0.47
Paper towels	52	£0.00	£0.16
Wipes	26	£0.03	£0.65
Neen Periform	1	£10.25	£10.25
Total			**£22.15**

Equipment

Item	Cost	Equivalent annual cost	Cost/patient
Genesis Medical Nomax 2	£220	£41.29	£0.21
Data Reader	£285	£53.49	£0.27

Total cost for clinic-based electrical stimulation: £282

Bladder training

Description of treatment and assumptions

- Costings are based on treatment being undertaken by a senior 1 grade women's health physiotherapist* in a hospital physiotherapy department.

- Patients are seen five times over a 4 month period.

- Initial appointment is 1 hour, follow-up sessions last 15–30 minutes.

- Bladder/baseline charts are normally provided free by pharmaceutical companies.

- Other consumables include gloves ($\times$5), KY Jelly ($\times$1), couch roll ($\times$5), assessment forms ($\times$1), wipes ($\times$10) and paper towels ($\times$20).

Labour costs

Contact time with patient:	$(1 \times 1) + (4 \times 0.375) = 2.5$ hours
Unit cost:	£37 per hour
Labour cost:	£37 $\times$ 2.5 = £92.50

Consumables

Item	Quantity	Unit cost	Cost
Gloves	5	£0.02	£0.09
KY Jelly	1	£0.80	£0.80
Couch roll	5	£0.04	£0.18
Paper towels	20	Less than £0.01	£0.06
Wipes	10	£0.03	£0.25
Assessment forms	1	£0.41	£0.41
Total			**£1.50**

Total cost for bladder training: £94

---

* Treatment is also undertaken by continence nurse specialists (grade e–h) in clinics; costs are similar.

Drugs

Description of treatment and assumptions

- Assumes one review consultation with GP.

- The duration of GP consultations is 9.36 minutes (GMP workload survey).

- Drug costs are for 52 weeks.

Labour costs

Contact time with patient: 0.156 hours
Unit cost: £135 per hour
Labour cost: £135 × 0.156 = £21

Drug costs (taken from BNF 50, September 2005)

Drug	Dose	Daily frequency	Cost per pack (£)	Pack size	Cost per day (£)	Cost for 12 weeks (£)	Cost for 1 year (£)	Cost for 1 year incl. GP review (£)
Duloxetine	40 mg	2	30.80	56	1.10	92	402	423
Flavoxate	200 mg	3	11.87	90	0.40	33	144	165
Oxybutynin	5 mg	2	4.14	84	0.10	8	36	57
ER oxybutynin	10 mg	1	24.68	30	0.82	69	300	321
Oxybutynin patches	3.9 mg	0.29	27.20	8	0.97	82	355	376
Propiverine	15 mg	3	24.45	56	1.31	110	478	499
Solifenacin	5 mg	1	27.62	30	0.92	77	336	357
Solifenacin	10 mg	1	35.91	30	1.20	101	437	458
Tolterodine	2 mg	2	30.56	56	1.09	92	398	419
ER tolterodine	4 mg	1	29.03	28	1.04	87	378	399
Trospium	20 mg	2	26.00	60	0.87	73	316	337

At the time of publication, costs for darifenacin were not yet available.

Various conservative treatments combined

PFMT + duloxetine

Description of treatment and assumptions

- As for PFMT and drug therapy alone, except it is assumed that drug review can be part of a PFMT session with no time implication. The cost of this multicomponent treatment is therefore less than the sum of its parts.

Costs

PFMT cost: £131
Duloxetine cost: £423
Less GP review of medication: −£21

Total cost: £533

Lifestyle and physical therapy

Description of treatment and assumptions

- It is assumed that the lifestyle advice is given by the therapist (senior 1 grade women's health physiotherapist or continence nurse specialist).

- Physical therapy is as described previously but with behavioural advice (fluid intake, BMI, constipation, smoking, etc.) incorporated into the first session and subsequent $1/2$ hour sessions when necessary – this is assumed to add 15 minutes to contact time between patient and therapist.

The additional cost of adding lifestyle advice to physical therapy is the labour cost of that advice.

Labour costs

Contact time with patient: $(1 \times 0.25) = 0.25$ hours
Unit cost: £37 per hour
Labour cost: $£37 \times 0.25 = £9.25$

Combining behavioural advice with physical therapy adds approximately **£9** to the cost of conservative treatment.

Bladder training + drugs

Description of treatment and assumptions

- As for bladder training and drug therapy alone, except it is assumed that drug review can be part of a bladder training session with no time implication. The cost of this multicomponent treatment is therefore less than the sum of its parts.

Costs

Bladder training cost: £94
Oxybutynin cost: £57 (1 year's treatment)
ER tolterodine: £399
Less GP review of medication: −£21

Total cost (bladder training + oxybutynin):   £130

Total cost (bladder training + ER tolterodine):   £472

Appendix F

Cost effectiveness analysis for duloxetine

First-line treatment: PFMT versus duloxetine

A decision tree model was developed in Microsoft Excel to compare the cost effectiveness of PFMT and duloxetine as a first-line treatment for women with moderate to severe stress UI, which is assumed to be 14 or more leakage episodes per week. Treatment effects and costs were based on a 52 week time frame. The structure of the model is shown below in Figure F.1. Patients are given either PFMT or duloxetine as a first-line treatment for their stress UI.

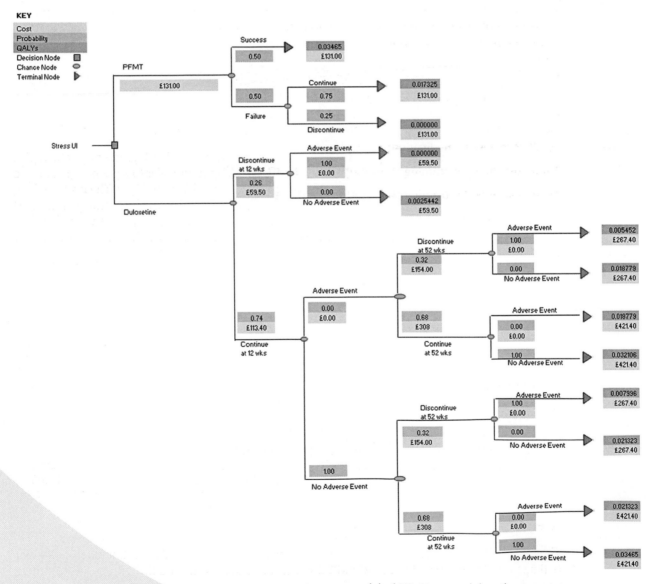

Figure F.1 Decision tree model of PFMT versus duloxetine

Patients in the PFMT arm can either 'succeed' or 'fail'. If patients 'fail' on PFMT, they either continued treatment, on the basis that they derive some treatment effect, or discontinued treatment. It is assumed that there are no adverse effects from PFMT.

Patients who take duloxetine as their first-line treatment have either continued or discontinued by 12 weeks, the period for which there is most trial data.

The structure of the model allows patients on duloxetine to have an adverse event whether they continued or discontinued. However, under baseline assumptions, it is assumed that adverse events are the reason for discontinuation and that patients who continued do not experience any adverse events. Patients who continued beyond 12 weeks can, by 52 weeks, either continue on treatment or have discontinued. Again, they may have continued/discontinued with or without adverse events.

Cost parameters

Item	Cost
PFMT	£131
Duloxetine cost per day	£1.10
GP consultation	£21.00
Review consultations	1
Additional duloxetine-attributable consultations, weeks 12–52	0
Drug adverse effects	£0

The cost of PFMT in the model is based on six sessions with a senior 1 grade physiotherapist. The first session is 1 hour and subsequent sessions last half an hour (refer to Appendix E for more details on cost derivation). The daily cost of duloxetine is derived from BNF 50. The cost of taking duloxetine also includes one review GP consultation, of 9.36 minutes duration, with the cost taken from *Unit Costs of Health and Social Care 2004*.[932] It is additionally assumed at baseline that adverse effects of duloxetine do not impose any costs on the NHS and that there are no further review GP consultations after week 12.

Probability parameters

Event	Probability
PFMT successful	50%
Continued PFMT if fail	75%
Continued duloxetine at 12 weeks	74%
Continued duloxetine at 52 weeks (if continued at 12 weeks)	68%
Adverse event if continued duloxetine at 12 weeks (weeks 0–12)	0%
Adverse event if continued duloxetine at 52 weeks (weeks 12–52)	0%
Adverse event if discontinued duloxetine by 12 weeks (weeks 0-12)	100%
Adverse event if discontinued duloxetine by 52 weeks (weeks 12–52)	100%

The probabilities that PFMT is successful, that patients continue PFMT if treatment fails, and that patients continue duloxetine at 12 and 52 weeks are taken from a published cost effectiveness analysis.[426]

Incontinence outcome parameters

Incontinence outcome	Value
Reduction in leakage episodes (PFMT success)	55%
Reduction in leakage episodes (PFMT fail/continued)	27.5%
Reduction in leakage episodes (PFMT fail/discontinued)	0%
Reduction in leakage episodes (duloxetine continued)	55%
Reduction in leakage episodes (duloxetine discontinued)	0%
Reduction in leakage episodes (duloxetine discontinued by 12 weeks)	42%
Reduction in leakage episodes (duloxetine discontinued by 52 weeks)	55%
Days on duloxetine if discontinued by 12 weeks	35 days
Weeks on duloxetine for those who discontinued by 52 weeks	32 weeks

The data above relate to the percentage reduction in leakage episodes and are taken from a published cost effectiveness analysis.[426] Similarly, the days on duloxetine if discontinued by 12 weeks is also taken from this source. For those women who continued at 12 weeks but discontinued by 52 weeks, it is assumed that they stop taking duloxetine halfway through this 40 week period.

QALY parameters

Outcome	QALYs
QALY gain – pretreatment to continent	0.063
PFMT success	0.035
PFMT fail – continued	0.017
PFMT fail – discontinued	0.0
Duloxetine continued at 12 weeks	0.008
Duloxetine continued at 12–52 weeks	0.027
Duloxetine discontinued by 12 weeks	0.003
Duloxetine discontinued at 52 weeks	0.013
Duloxetine adverse effects by 12 weeks	−0.003
Duloxetine adverse effects by 52 weeks	−0.013

The QALY gain of treatment was derived from a published cost effectiveness analysis[426] and from information submitted to guideline developers within the stakeholder process. In a cost–utility analysis of TVT versus colposuspension, QALYs were derived from women who completed an EQ-5D questionnaire at baseline and 6 months after hospital discharge.[931] For TVT, the baseline estimate of QOL was 0.778 (0.785 for colposuspension) and at 6 months this had risen to 0.806. The cure rate for TVT patients was 66% and this can be used to estimate the QOL of a cure, as not all patients are dry at 6 months:

$$0.806 = (QOL_{cure} \times 0.66) + (0.34 \times 0.778)$$

$$QOL_{cure} = (0.806 - [0.34 \times 0.778]) \div 0.66 = 0.82$$

A published HTA report reviewing evidence on the clinical and cost effectiveness of TVT reports this QOL data, including the fact that a cure is associated with a QOL of 0.82. However, in its own cost effectiveness model, it uses QALY values of 0.85 and 0.80 for continent and incontinent women respectively.[716]

The published cost effectiveness analysis of duloxetine includes surgery as a follow-up treatment for patients in whom conservative management is unsuccessful.[426] The authors assume that in such patients there is a pre-surgery disutility of 0.05. However, these pre-surgery patients have had conservative management, which it is assumed has led to some reduction in leakage episodes, with a concomitant utility gain. The overall utility gain is calculated thus:

$$\text{Pre-PFMT disutility} \times 0.79 = \text{Post-PFMT disutility} = 0.05$$

$$\text{Pre-PFMT disutility} = 0.063$$

A brief explanation of this formula is as follows:

- post-PFMT disutility is one and the same as pre-surgery disutility (0.05)

- pre-surgery patients:

    □ 75% continued with PFMT and had a 27.5% reduction in leakage episodes
    □ 25% did not continue with PFMT and had a 0% reduction in leakage episodes
    □ weighted reduction in leakage episodes $= (0.75 \times 0.275) + (0.25 \times 0) = 0.21$

- therefore the post-PFMT disutility is only 79% (i.e., $1 - 0.21 = 0.79$) of the pre-PFMT disutility and therefore the disutility of moderate to severe UI prior to any reduction in leakage episodes is 0.063.

The other QALY parameters are derived in a linear fashion from the percentage reduction in leakage episodes associated with the particular outcome (each terminal node on the tree) and the maximum QALY gain attainable from pretreatment to continent. In other words, if the QALY gain in achieving continence is 0.063 then a 55% reduction in leakage episodes is assumed to produce a 0.035 (i.e., 0.063×0.55) gain in QALYs. On the assumption that adverse effects are the main cause of discontinuation, it seems a reasonable approximation to say that the disutility from adverse event must be at least as great as any utility gain from reduced UI symptoms.

Results

Treatment	Cost for 52 weeks	QALY	Incremental cost	Incremental QALY	ICER
PFMT	£131	0.024		0.004	Dominates
Duloxetine	£291	0.019	£160		

Using baseline assumptions, PFMT 'dominates' duloxetine. This means that it is both more effective and less costly.

Sensitivity analysis

Sensitivity analysis is used in economic evaluation to assess how sensitive the results of the model are to the assumptions made about the model parameters, particularly those parameters where considerable uncertainty exists as to their actual value.

One-way sensitivity analysis involves altering the value of a single parameter, holding all the others constant, to determine how sensitive the cost effectiveness conclusion is to the assumptions made about that particular parameter. Multi-way sensitivity analysis means that several default parameters are changed simultaneously, although one of the difficulties with this technique is the huge number of possible permutations that exist.

The results of some sensitivity analyses for this model are shown below. As the default shows PFMT to be dominant (produces more benefit for less cost), parameter values have been varied in favour of duloxetine. The rationale for this is that confidence in the robustness of the default conclusion – that PFMT is more cost effective – will be strengthened if the conclusion holds under less favourable scenarios for PFMT.

Cost differential between PFMT and duloxetine

Duloxetine cost – PFMT cost	ICER (cost/QALY)	Comment
£160	PFMT dominates	PFMT more cost effective
£140	PFMT dominates	PFMT more cost effective
£120	PFMT dominates	PFMT more cost effective
£100	PFMT dominates	PFMT more cost effective
£80	PFMT dominates	PFMT more cost effective
£60	PFMT dominates	PFMT more cost effective
£40	PFMT dominates	PFMT more cost effective
£20	PFMT dominates	PFMT more cost effective
£0	PFMT dominates	PFMT more cost effective
−£10	£2,097	PFMT more cost effective[a]
−£20	£4,282	PFMT more cost effective[a]
−£30	£6,466	PFMT more cost effective[a]
−£40	£8,923	PFMT more cost effective[a]
−£50	£11,107	PFMT more cost effective[a]
−£60	£13,291	PFMT more cost effective[a]
−£70	£15,476	PFMT more cost effective[a]
−£80	£17,660	PFMT more cost effective[a]
−£90	£19,900	Borderline – NICE ICER threshold

[a] Based on NICE threshold.

PFMT is always the more effective treatment. The ICER is for PFMT relative to duloxetine.

Keeping all the other model parameter values constant, the annual cost of duloxetine would have to fall to £41 a year (i.e., drug costs would have to fall to £0.08 per day from their current level of £1.10) for the relative cost effectiveness of PFMT to be called into question.

Continued duloxetine at 12 weeks

Continued duloxetine at 12 weeks	ICER (cost/QALY)	Comment
75%	PFMT dominates	PFMT more cost effective
80%	PFMT dominates	PFMT more cost effective
85%	PFMT dominates	PFMT more cost effective
90%	PFMT dominates	PFMT more cost effective
95%	£227,000	PFMT more cost effective[a]
100%	£105,000	PFMT more cost effective[a]

[a] Based on NICE threshold.

Holding all other parameter values constant, it is necessary for 92% of patients on duloxetine to continue at 12 weeks in order for duloxetine to generate more QALYs than PFMT. However, even for a zero discontinuation rate at 12 weeks, the additional benefit falls a long way short of being cost effective because of the large cost differential between the two strategies.

Continued duloxetine at 52 weeks

Continued duloxetine at 52 weeks	ICER (cost/QALY)	Comment
70%	PFMT dominates	PFMT more cost effective
75%	PFMT dominates	PFMT more cost effective
80%	PFMT dominates	PFMT more cost effective
85%	PFMT dominates	PFMT more cost effective
90%	PFMT dominates	PFMT more cost effective
95%	£229,000	PFMT more cost effective[a]
100%	£108,000	PFMT more cost effective[a]

[a] Based on NICE threshold.

Similarly, 91% of patients who continued at 12 weeks must still be on duloxetine at 52 weeks ($0.74 \times 0.91 = 67\%$ of all patients) for duloxetine to generate more QALYs than PFMT. However, even if there is no discontinuation after 12 weeks, the small gain in QALYs (0.002) is considered poor value at an incremental cost of £200 per patient.

Continued PFMT if fail

Continued PFMT if fail	ICER (cost/QALY)	Comment
70%	PFMT dominates	PFMT more cost effective
60%	PFMT dominates	PFMT more cost effective
50%	PFMT dominates	PFMT more cost effective
40%	PFMT dominates	PFMT more cost effective
30%	PFMT dominates	PFMT more cost effective
20%	£588,000	PFMT more cost effective[a]
10%	£140,000	PFMT more cost effective[a]
0%	£80,000	PFMT more cost effective[a]

[a] Based on NICE threshold.

Duloxetine is more effective than PFMT for low values of this parameter. Therefore, the ICER is calculated for duloxetine relative to PFMT.

The conclusion that PFMT is cost effective is not sensitive to the assumption made about those who fail with PFMT but continue with their pelvic floor exercises, if all other parameter values are held constant.

Reduction in leakage episodes if continue with PFMT after 'failure'

Reduction in leakage episodes if PFMT fail/continued	ICER (cost/QALY)	Comment
25%	PFMT dominates	PFMT more cost effective
20%	PFMT dominates	PFMT more cost effective
15%	PFMT dominates	PFMT more cost effective
10%	PFMT dominates	PFMT more cost effective
5%	£194,000	PFMT more cost effective[a]
0%	£80,000	PFMT more cost effective[a]

[a] Based on NICE threshold.

The conclusion that PFMT is cost effective is not sensitive to the assumption made about the reduction in leakage episodes for those who continue pelvic floor exercises after PFMT has failed, if all other parameter values are held constant.

Multi-way sensitivity analysis
In the following example all of the following have been changed:

Parameter	Default	New value
Duloxetine cost per day	£1.10	£0.90
Review consultations	1	0
PFMT successful	50%	40%
Continue PFMT if fail	75%	50%
Continued duloxetine at 12 weeks	74%	80%
Continued duloxetine at 80 weeks	68%	80%

Under this scenario, the ICER for duloxetine is £27,000 per QALY. According to the NICE threshold, this would suggest that duloxetine was borderline cost effective. However, this figure has only been achieved by biasing all the changes to parameter values in favour of duloxetine.

Clearly, it is possible to set parameter values in the model so that duloxetine is cost effective. However, the plausibility of such values is contingent on duloxetine being considerably more efficacious than PFMT, and this is not supported by the best available evidence at this time.

Second-line treatment: surgery versus duloxetine

Given the finding that PFMT dominated duloxetine as a first-line treatment, a further decision tree model was developed, using TreeAge Pro 2006, to compare the cost effectiveness of surgery versus duloxetine for women with moderate to severe stress UI in whom first-line treatment with PFMT has been unsuccessful. A 2 year time frame was used for this model to reflect the fact that surgery has long-lasting effects that are not contingent on recurrent treatment costs. The decision tree for this model is shown in Figure F.2.

Patients in the surgery arm have primary surgery that can either 'succeed' or 'fail'. A proportion of patients in whom primary surgery fails will choose to have a second operation or even a third if the second also fails. The model does not include complications arising from surgery, most of which would be minor. Although they are extremely rare (less than 1 in 10 000 cases), severe complications (for example transfusion, ITU admission, death) may occur.

The duloxetine 'sub-tree' is the same as in the first-line treatment model, with the addition of continue/discontinued branches at 2 years for those still taking the drug at 52 weeks.

As with the first-line model, the decision tree structure for duloxetine includes patient pathways that allow for continuation on therapy with adverse events and for discontinuation in the absence of adverse events. However, the simplifying default assumptions for model parameters is that adverse events cause discontinuation and that patients who continued with duloxetine did not experience any adverse events.

Cost parameters

Resource item	Value
Surgery (TVT)	£1,014
Gynaecology outpatient consultation	£124
Urodynamics	£140
Urodynamics prior to primary surgery	1
Urodynamics prior to secondary surgery	1
Duloxetine cost per day	£1.10
GP consultation	£21.00
Review consultations for duloxetine	1
Drug adverse effects	£0

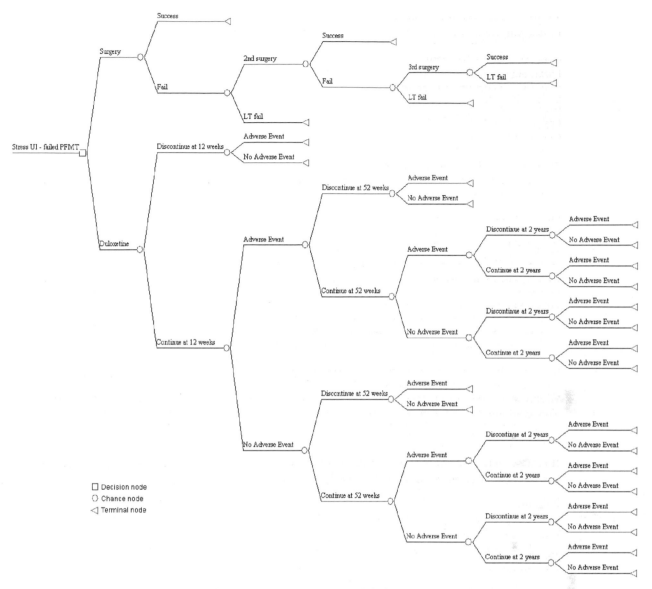

Figure F.2 Decision tree model of surgery versus duloxetine

The cost of surgery is based on a published economic evaluation of TVT.[716] It is assumed that a patient will have a gynaecology outpatient consultation prior to primary surgery and following a 'failed' operation. The cost of a gynaecology outpatient consultation is based on the mean value reported in the 2004 NHS Reference Costs for a first attendance for an outpatient gynaecology consultation. It is additionally assumed that urodynamics will be undertaken prior to primary or secondary surgery, reflecting current practice. The cost of urodynamics is taken from the mean unit cost for urodynamics reported in the 2003 NHS Reference Costs. The daily cost of duloxetine is derived from BNF 50. The cost of taking duloxetine also includes one review GP consultation, of 9.36 minutes duration, with the cost taken from *Unit Costs of Health and Social Care* 2004.[932] It is additionally assumed at baseline that adverse effects of duloxetine do not impose any costs on the NHS and that there are no further review GP consultations after week 12. In accordance with NICE methodology, costs occurring in the second year are discounted at 3.5%.

Probability parameters

The adverse event probabilities are a simplifying assumption of this model. The other probabilities are taken from a published cost effectiveness study.[426] The surgery success rate parameter is taken from an RCT of open colposuspension versus TVT.[659,660]

Event	Probability
Surgery (TVT) successful	66%
Have second surgery if primary surgery fails	75%
Have third surgery if second surgery fails	30%
Adverse event if continued duloxetine	0%
Adverse event if discontinued duloxetine	100%
Continued duloxetine at 12 weeks	74%
Continued duloxetine at 52 weeks	68%[a]
Continued duloxetine at 2 years	90%[a]

[a] Expressed as a proportion of those continuing from the previous period.

Incontinence outcome parameters

Incontinence outcome	Value
Reduction in leakage episodes (surgery success)	100%
Reduction in leakage episodes (surgery fail)	50%
Reduction in leakage episodes (duloxetine continued)	55%
Reduction in leakage episodes (duloxetine discontinued)	0%
Reduction in leakage episodes (duloxetine discontinued by 12 weeks)	42%
Reduction in leakage episodes (duloxetine discontinued after 12 weeks)	55%
Days on duloxetine if discontinued by 12 weeks	35 days
Weeks on duloxetine for those who discontinue by 52 weeks	32 weeks
Weeks on duloxetine for those who discontinue by 2 years	78 weeks

It is assumed that women who stop taking duloxetine between 12 and 52 weeks, and between the first and second year, do so at the midpoint of these time intervals.

QALY parameters

Outcome	QALYs
QALY gain – pretreatment to continent	0.063
Duloxetine continued at 12 weeks	0.008
Duloxetine continued at 12–52 weeks	0.026
Duloxetine continued at 2 years[a]	0.069
Duloxetine discontinued by 12 weeks	0.003
Duloxetine discontinued by 52 weeks	0.013
Duloxetine discontinued by 2 years[a]	0.052
Duloxetine adverse effects at 12 weeks	−0.003
Duloxetine adverse effects at 52 weeks	−0.013
Duloxetine adverse effects at 2 years[a]	−0.017
Surgery success[a]	0.126
Surgery long-term fail[a]	0.063

[a] Not discounted.

Again, it is assumed that adverse effects are the main cause of discontinuation and that the disutility from adverse event must be at least as great as any utility gain from reduced UI symptoms. The other QALY values are derived by assuming a linear relationship between QALY gain and the reduction in leakage episodes.

QALYs occurring in the second year of the model are discounted at 3.5% in accordance with NICE guidance.

Results

Treatment	Cost	QALY	Incremental cost	Incremental QALY	ICER
Duloxetine	£477	0.0345			
Surgery	£1,655	0.1143	£1,178	0.0798	£14,765

Using baseline assumptions, surgery would be considered as the more cost effective treatment with an ICER well within the £20,000 per QALY threshold for cost effectiveness suggested by NICE.

Sensitivity analysis

A series of one-way sensitivity analyses was undertaken to establish the parameter thresholds to achieve a £20,000 cost per QALY. Given the baseline result, this means varying parameter values in favour of duloxetine.

Parameter	Value at which surgery cost per QALY = £20,000
Cost of surgery (TVT)	£1,450
Cost of duloxetine per day	£0.09
Surgery 'success'	48%
Reduction in leakage episodes for surgery 'success'	80%
Reduction in leakage episodes for duloxetine 'success'	100%
QALY gain from cure	0.0465

For all other parameter values, the ICER remains below £20,000 per QALY.

Discussion

This model suggests that surgery is more cost effective than duloxetine as a second-line treatment for stress UI in women who have failed PFMT. Sensitivity analysis suggested that this result was not greatly affected by the assumptions used to inform parameter values.

The model was restricted to a 2 year follow-up because of a lack of long-term effectiveness data, particularly for duloxetine. Although, the effectiveness of surgery may decline over time, the limited time frame of the model still represents a considerable bias against surgery, as it does not allow for long-lasting effects and the continuing costs that would be required for medical therapy. However, this bias is offset to some extent by the decision not to include complications arising from surgery, to simplify the model.

The surgery success rate parameter is taken from an RCT of open colposuspension versus TVT,[659,660] but this is a lower value than published case series; our assumptions may therefore underestimate the success of primary surgery. While it is probably inaccurate to say that the success of surgery does not decline with subsequent procedures, the assumption that this is the case simplifies the model.

However, the model also shows duloxetine to be a much cheaper strategy than surgery and therefore it could be considered as a second-line treatment for women who would choose it in preference to surgery, as lower cost care does not impose opportunity costs on the NHS.

Appendix G

A partial cost–consequence analysis for surgical treatment options for OAB

Most women can be treated successfully for OAB with conservative measures but a small proportion with more severe symptoms may require surgery. Sacral nerve stimulation (SNS) is a relatively new but effective treatment option for patients in this category but is expensive and currently only available in a limited number of centres in the UK. However, alternatives to SNS often involve major surgery, such as augmentation cystoplasty or urinary diversion, and are also expensive. The associated long-term morbidity, and risk of further surgical intervention, appears to be higher for cystoplasty and urinary diversion than it is for SNS, therefore a cost–consequence analysis was undertaken.*

Literature review

A literature review did not identify any studies that carried out a full economic evaluation of SNS for patients with UI, although, a cost analysis was undertaken for a report by the Australian Medicare Services Advisory Committee (MSAC).[934] A full economic analysis was not considered by MSAC because of uncertainty about treatment costs, particularly in relation to patients for whom the implant is unsuitable or fails. The authors also justified their costing approach because of uncertainty surrounding treatment on health outcomes.

The MSAC report estimated that the 6 month treatment costs of SNS for patients with urge incontinence or urinary retention were AUD11,000 per patient initiated to treatment with percutaneous sacral nerve evaluation (PNE). PNE equipment and implant cost accounted for AUD6,567 and surgery and re-surgery costs for AUD4,464. It was further estimated that SNS could produce savings of between AUD245 and AUD574 per patient in laundry costs and incontinence products over the 6 month period. The report noted that such savings would increase if the device continued to be effective but they also noted that not all revision surgery may be captured in the first 6 months. Using data from the literature,[515] they estimated that approximately 30% of urge incontinence patients tested with PNE would be dry at 6 months with a cost effectiveness ratio of AUD35,000 (95% CI AUD28,000 to AUD 46,000) per additional person free of incontinence when compared with no treatment.

Cost analysis

The costings are based on a successfully treated patient over 10 years. However, there are clearly patients with all treatments who do not have successful outcomes. Such patients will then go down a different treatment pathway that also has resource implications, which could be considerable. A full costing analysis would account for this but it was not possible to do this fully within the constraints of the guideline. However, where data are available, some indication of alternative

---

* Cost–consequence analysis is a limited form of economic evaluation that considers costs alongside consequences (or outcomes) without calculating an ICER. It was not possible within the constraints of this guideline to undertake a more sophisticated economic evaluation, especially as these treatment options are likely to be low volume.

pathways will be given in the event of treatment failure. Costs that are known to occur in the future are discounted at a rate of 3.5% per annum:

Sacral nerve stimulation

Item	Unit cost	Source of cost data
Percutaneous nerve evaluation	£687	Procedure – 2004 NHS Reference Costs (HRG code R19, day case)
	£1,200	Tined lead
Permanent implant	£687	Procedure – 2004 NHS Reference Costs (HRG code R19, day case)
	£6,870	Implant device

Total initial treatment cost = £9,444

Approximately 50% of patients get sufficient improvement in symptoms from PNE to proceed to the permanent implant. Other treatment options would have to be considered for the patients who are deemed not suitable for SNS after PNE.

Of those who have the permanent implant, approximately 65–70% have a satisfactory outcome. In those where the outcome is unsatisfactory, augmentation cystoplasty or urinary diversion may be considered.

A battery change is required after 7 years and costs £4,400. This would again require a day case procedure (HRG code R19). A proportion of patients with satisfactory SNS outcomes will also require revision surgery, which is usually undertaken as a day case procedure. Estimates of the requirement for further surgery are indicated below.[512]

- surgical revision rate: 33%

- replacement or relocation of implanted pulse generator: 15%

- permanent device removal: 9%

Augmentation cystoplasty

Item	Unit cost	Source of cost data
Procedure	£3,440	2004 NHS Reference Costs (HRG code L14)

Total initial treatment cost = £3,440

It has been estimated that:[536]

- 80% of patients treated would need to self-catheterise.

- 6% will need a re-operation for bleeding or for bowel obstruction. This would be a major abdominal procedure with a 2004 NHS Reference Cost of between £1,600 and £3,000 depending on age (HRG code F41/F42).

- 25% of patients will have symptomatic infections and need long-term antibiotics (low-dose trimethoprim or cefalexin and receive six full-week courses of oral ciprofloxacin per annum).

- There is a 60% cumulative risk of stones over 10 years, and this will usually require intermediate bladder endoscopy to resolve (code L18), which has a NHS 2004 Reference Cost of between £500 and £1,000 depending on whether it is done as a day case or elective inpatient procedure.

- Long-term complications mean that about 6% of patients need repeat abdominal surgery within 10 years. This repeat surgery would cost £3,440 or more if a conversion to urinary diversion was considered.

Urinary diversion

Item	Unit cost	Source of cost data
Procedure	£5,536	2004 NHS Reference Costs (HRG code L14)

Total initial treatment cost = £5,536

Furthermore, it has been estimated that:[935]

- All patients would need to use stoma products for the rest of their lives.

- There is a 60% cumulative risk of stones over 10 years which usually require intermediate bladder endoscopy to resolve (HRG code L18).

- 25% of patients will have symptomatic infections and need long-term antibiotics (low-dose trimethoprim or cefalexin and receive six full-week courses of oral ciprofloxacin per annum).

- The risk of stoma complications is approximately 80% over 10 years and, of these, approximately 50% would require revision surgery , which would cost between £1,600 and £3,000 depending on age

Botulinum toxin A

Item	Unit cost	Source of cost data
Botulinum A (200 units)	£258	BNF 51
Procedure	£458	2004 NHS Reference Costs (HRG code L19, day case)

A patient successfully treated would require repeat injections every 8 months. Future treatment costs were discounted using a 3.5% annual discount rate to give the 10 year cost of treatment.

10 year treatment cost = £9,296

Additionally, it has been estimated that 20% of patients would fail to respond with botulinum toxin A and these patients would be considered for alternative treatment after their initial injections. Of the patients who continue, 20% would need to self-catheterise half the time.

Cost–consequence comparison

Treatment	Cost (10 year)	Consequences
Sacral nerve stimulation	£8,437 + replacement battery + surgical revisions	Up to two-thirds of patients achieve continence or substantial improvement in symptoms after SNS; the available data show that beneficial effects appear to persist for up to 3–5 years after implantation. Around one-third of patients may require re-operation, most often owing to pain at the implant site, infection, or the need for adjustment and modification of the lead system. Permanent removal of the electrodes may be required in one in ten patients. Developments in the devices and leads have resulted in reduced rates of complications since introduction of the technique.
Augmentation cystoplasty	£3,440 + complication costs + self-catheterisation costs	Data on augmentation cystoplasty in women with UI or OAB are limited to case series. Cure or improvement has been reported in at least half of patients with idiopathic DO. Postoperative complications such as bowel disturbance, metabolic acidosis, mucus production and/or retention in the bladder, UTI and urinary retention are common or very common. There is a high incidence of recurrent UTI postoperatively, and many patients will need to self-catheterise. Malignant transformation in the bowel segment or urothelium has been reported in a small number of cases.
Urinary diversion	£5,536 + complication costs	There are limited data on the outcomes of urinary diversion in women with UI or OAB. Where the procedure has been used in men and women with benign conditions, vesical infection, stoma-related problems and the need for surgical revisions occur very commonly.
Botulinum toxin A	£9,296 + self-catheterisation costs	Data on the use of botulinum toxin A in the management of idiopathic detrusor overactivity are limited. The available data show cure or improvement in about half of patients, with duration of benefit between 3 and 12 months.

Discussion

This guideline has made a recommendation that SNS be used in the treatment of UI due to DO in women who have not responded to conservative treatments and we expect it to be a low-volume intervention. SNS has high initial treatment costs and requires a battery replacement after approximately 7 years. However, as this cost–consequence analysis shows, the alternative treatment options for this group of women with refractory incontinence are all expensive, and the incremental costs of SNS when compared with the alternatives are much less (and possibly even negative) than when looking at the costs of SNS in isolation.

A cost–consequence analysis does not demonstrate cost effectiveness and it is difficult to compare effectiveness in a quantitative way. However not only does major surgery such as augmentation cystoplasty or urinary diversion carry a high cost over time but the morbidity is also high and only around 50% of patients are satisfied with the outcome. Although botulinum toxin A injection appears to offer promising results the current evidence is limited; it is assumed that repeated injections will be required. The incremental costs over time are therefore likely to be very high. We believe that this cost–consequence analysis provides an economic justification for the recommendation made.

References

1. Abrams P, Cardozo L, Fall M, *et al.* The standardisation of terminology of lower urinary tract function: report from the Standardisation Sub-committee of the International Continence Society. *Neurourology and Urodynamics* 2002;21(2):167–78.

2. Thomas TM, Plymat KR, Blannin J, *et al.* Prevalence of urinary incontinence. *British Medical Journal* 1980;281(6250):1243–5.

3. Perry S, Shaw C, Assassa P, *et al.* An epidemiological study to establish the prevalence of urinary symptoms and felt need in the community: the Leicestershire MRC Incontinence Study. Leicestershire MRC Incontinence Study Team. *Journal of Public Health Medicine* 2000;22(3):427–34.

4. Dugan E, Roberts CP, Cohen SJ, *et al.* Why older community-dwelling adults do not discuss urinary incontinence with their primary care physicians. *Journal of the American Geriatrics Society* 2001;49(4):462–5.

5. Papanicolaou S, Pons M, Hampel C, *et al.* Medical resource utilisation and cost of care for women seeking treatment for urinary incontinence in an outpatiend setting. Examples from three countries participating in the PURE study. *Maturitas* 2005;52 Supplement 2:S35–S47.

6. Shaw C, Tansey R, Jackson C, *et al.* Barriers to help seeking in people with urinary symptoms. *Family Practice* 2001;18(1):48–52.

7. Hunskaar S, Burgio K, Clark A, Lapitan M, Nelson R, Sillen U. Epidemiology of urinary (UI) and feacal (FI) incontinence and pelvic organprolapse (POP). In: Abrams P, Khoury S, Cardozo L, Wein A, eds. *WHO-ICS International Consultation on Incontinence.* 3rd ed. Paris: Health Publications Ltd; 2005. p. 255–312.

8. McGrother CW, Donaldson MM, Shaw C, *et al.* Storage symptoms of the bladder: prevalence, incidence and need for services in the UK. *BJU International* 2004;93(6):763–9.

9. Hannestad YS, Rortveit G, Sandvik H, *et al.* A community-based epidemiological survey of female urinary incontinence: the Norwegian EPINCONT study. Epidemiology of Incontinence in the County of Nord-Trondelag. *Journal of Clinical Epidemiology* 2000;53(11):1150–7.

10. Sandvik H, Hunskaar S, Seim A, *et al.* Validation of a severity index in female urinary incontinence and its implementation in an epidemiological survey. *Journal of Epidemiology and Community Health* 1993;47(6):497–9.

11. Minassian VA, Drutz HP, Al-Badr A. Urinary incontinence as a worldwide problem. *International Journal of Gynaecology and Obstetrics* 2003;82(3):327–38.

12. Stewart WF, Van Rooyen JB, Cundiff GW, *et al.* Prevalence and burden of overactive bladder in the United States. *World Journal of Urology* 2003;20(6):327–36.

13. Milsom I, Abrams P, Cardozo L, *et al.* How widespread are the symptoms of an overactive bladder and how are they managed? A population-based prevalence study. [erratum appears in *BJU International* 2001;88(7):807]. *BJU International* 2001;87(9):760–6.

14. McGrother CW, Donaldson MM, Hayward T, *et al.* Urinary storage symptoms and comorbidities: a prospective population cohort study in middle-aged and older women. *Age and Ageing* 2006;35(1):16–24.

15. Norton PA, MacDonald LD, Sedgwick PM, *et al.* Distress and delay associated with urinary incontinence, frequency, and urgency in women. *British Medical Journal* 1988;297(6657):1187–9.

16. Macaulay AJ, Stern RS, Holmes DM, *et al.* Micturition and the mind: psychological factors in the aetiology and treatment of urinary symptoms in women. *British Medical Journal Clinical Research Ed.* 1987;294(6571):540–3.

17. Thom DH, Haan MN, Van den Eeden SK. Medically recognized urinary incontinence and risks of hospitalization, nursing home admission and mortality. *Age and Ageing* 1997;26(5):367–74.

18. Wilson L, Brown JS, Shin GP, *et al.* Annual direct cost of urinary incontinence. *Obstetrics and Gynecology* 2001;98(3):398–406.

19. Milsom I. The prevalence of urinary incontinence. *Acta Obstetricia et Gynecologica Scandinavica* 2000;79(12):1056–9.

20. Turner DA, Shaw C, McGrother CW, *et al.* The cost of clinically significant urinary storage symptoms for community dwelling adults in the UK. *BJU International* 2004;93(9):1246–52.

21. Hu TW and Wagner TH. Health-related consequences of overactive bladder: an economic perspective. *BJU International* 2005;96 Supplement 1:43–5.

22. National Institute for Clinical Excellence. *Infection Control: Prevention of Healthcare-Associated Infection in Primary and Community Care.* London: National Institute for Clinical Excellence; 2003.

23. National Institute for Health and Clinical Excellence. *Referral Guidelines for Suspected Cancer.* London: National Institute for Health and Clinical Excellence; 2005.

24. National Collaborating Centre for Primary Care. *Routine Postnatal Care of Women and Their Babies.* London: National Institute for Health and Clinical Excellence; 2006.

25. National Institute for Clinical Excellence. *Improving Outcomes in Urological Cancer: the Manual.* London: National Institute for Clinical Excellence; 2002.

26. National Institute for Clinical Excellence. *Sacral Nerve Stimulation for Urge Incontinence and Urgency-Frequency.* London: National Institute for Clinical Excellence; 2004.

27. National Institute for Clinical Excellence. *Intramural Urethral Bulking Procedures for Stress Urinary Incontinence in Women.* London: National Institute for Health and Clinical Excellence; 2005.

28. National Institute for Health and Clinical Excellence. *Insertion of Extraurethral (Non-Circumferential) Retropubic Adjustable Compression Devices for Stress Urinary Incontinence in Women.* London: National Institute for Health and Clinical Excellence; 2005.

29. National Institute for Health and Clinical Excellence. *Insertion of Biological Slings for Stress Urinary Incontinence in Women.* London: National Institute for Health and Clinical Excellence; 2006.

30. National Institute for Clinical Excellence. *Bone-Anchored Cystourethropexy.* London: National Institute for Clinical Excellence; 2003.

31. Abrams P, Cardozo LD, Khoury S, Wein A. *Incontinence. Volume 1. Basics and Evaluation.* Paris: Health Publication Ltd; 2005.

32. Abrams P, Cardozo L, Khoury S, Wein A. *Incontinence. Volume 2. Management.* Paris: Health Publication Ltd; 2005.

33. Royal College of Physicians of London. *Incontinence: Causes, Management and Provision of Services.* London: Royal College of Physicians of London; 1995.

34. Department of Health. *Good Practice in Continence Services.* London: Department of Health; 2000.

35. Department of Health. *National Service Framework for Older People.* London: Department of Health; 2001.

36. National Institute for Clinical Excellence. *Guideline Development Methods: Information for National Collaborating Centres and Guideline Developers.* London: National Institute for Clinical Evidence; 2005.

37. Oxman AD, Sackett DL, Guyatt GH. Users' guides to the medical literature. I. How to get started. The Evidence-Based Medicine Working Group. *JAMA: the journal of the American Medical Association* 1993;270(17):2093–5.

38. Guyatt GH, Sackett DL, Cook DJ. Users' guides to the medical literature. II. How to use an article about therapy or prevention. A. Are the results of the study valid? Evidence-Based Medicine Working Group. *JAMA: the journal of the American Medical Association* 1993;270(21):2598–601.

39. Guyatt GH, Sackett DL, Cook DJ. Users' guides to the medical literature. II. How to use an article about therapy or prevention. B. What were the results and will they help me in caring for my patients? Evidence-Based Medicine Working Group. *JAMA: the journal of the American Medical Association* 1994;271(1):59–63.

40. Jaeschke R, Guyatt G, Sackett DL. Users' guides to the medical literature. III. How to use an article about a diagnostic test. A. Are the results of the study valid? Evidence-Based Medicine Working Group. *JAMA: the journal of the American Medical Association* 1994;271(5):389–91.

41. Jaeschke R, Guyatt GH, Sackett DL. Users' guides to the medical literature. III. How to use an article about a diagnostic test. B. What are the results and will they help me in caring for my patients? The Evidence-Based Medicine Working Group. *JAMA: the journal of the American Medical Association* 1994;271(9):703–7.

42. Sackett DL, Straus SE, Richardson WS, Rosenberg W, Haynes RB. *Evidence-Based Medicine. How to Practice and Teach EBM.* 2nd ed. Edinburgh: Churchill Livingstone; 2000.

43. Scottish Intercollegiate Guidelines Network. *Sign 50: a Guideline Developers' Handbook.* No. 50. Edinburgh: Scottish Intercollegiate Guideline Network; 2001.

44. Drummond MF, O'Brien B, Stoddart GL, Torrance GW. *Methods for the Economic Evaluation of Health Care Programmes.* Oxford University Press; 1997.

45. Newcombe RG and Altman DG. Proportions and their differences. In: Altman DG, Machin D, Bryant TN, Gardner MJ, eds. *Statistics with Confidence.* 2nd ed. BMJ Books; 2000. p. 45–56.

46. Jensen JK, Nielsen FR, Ostergard DR. The role of patient history in the diagnosis of urinary incontinence. *Obstetrics and Gynecology* 1994;83(5 Part 2):904–10.

47. Harvey MA and Versi E. Predictive value of clinical evaluation of stress urinary incontinence: a summary of the published literature. *International Urogynecology Journal* 2001;12(1):31–7.

48. Martin JL, Williams KS, Abrahams KR, *et al.* Systematic review and evaluation of methods of assessing urinary incontinence. *Health Technology Assessment* 2006;10:(6).

49. Lagro-Janssen AL, Debruyne FM, and van Weel C. Value of the patient's case history in diagnosing urinary incontinence in general practice. *British Journal of Urology* 1991;67(6):569–72.

50. Summitt RL Jr, Stovall TG, Bent AE, *et al.* Urinary incontinence: correlation of history and brief office evaluation with multichannel urodynamic testing. *American Journal of Obstetrics and Gynecology* 1992;166(6 Part 1):1835–40.

51. Sand PK, Hill RC, Ostergard DR. Incontinence history as a predictor of detrusor stability. *Obstetrics and Gynecology* 1988;71(2):257–60.

52. Ouslander J, Staskin D, Raz S, *et al.* Clinical versus urodynamic diagnosis in an incontinent geriatric female population. *Journal of Urology* 1987;137(1):68–71.

53. de Muylder X, Claes H, Neven P, *et al.* Usefulness of urodynamic investigations in female incontinence. *European Journal of Obstetrics, Gynecology, and Reproductive Biology* 1992;44(3):205–8.

54. Diokno AC, Wells TJ, Brink CA. Urinary incontinence in elderly women: urodynamic evaluation. *Journal of the American Geriatrics Society* 1987;35(10):940–6.

55. Iosif S, Henriksson L, Ulmsten U. Urethrocystometry as a routine method for the objective evaluation of women with urinary incontinence. *Archives of Gynecology* 1980;230(1):41–7.

56. Umstad MP and Glenning PP. Urodynamic investigation in the management of incontinent women. *Asia-Oceania Journal of Obstetrics and Gynaecology* 1991;17(4):307–13.

57. Ishiko O, Hirai K, Sumi T, *et al.* The urinary incontinence score in the diagnosis of female urinary incontinence. *International Journal of Gynaecology and Obstetrics* 2000;68(2):131–7.

58. Sandvik H, Hunskaar S, Vanvik A, *et al.* Diagnostic classification of female urinary incontinence: an epidemiological survey corrected for validity. *Journal of Clinical Epidemiology* 1995;48(3):339–43.

59. FitzGerald MP and Brubaker L. Urinary incontinence symptom scores and urodynamic diagnoses. *Neurourology and Urodynamics* 2002;21(1):30–5.

60. Sunshine TJ and Glowacki GA. Clinical correlation of urodynamic testing in patients with urinary incontinence. *Journal of Gynecologic Surgery* 1989;5(1):93–8.

61. Weidner AC, Myers ER, Visco AG, et al. Which women with stress incontinence require urodynamic evaluation? *American Journal of Obstetrics and Gynecology* 2001;184(2):20–7.

62. Carey MP, Dwyer PL, Glenning PP. The sign of stress incontinence–should we believe what we see? *Australian and New Zealand Journal of Obstetrics and Gynaecology* 1997;37(4):436–9.

63. Cantor TJ and Bates CP. A comparative study of symptoms and objective urodynamic findings in 214 incontinent women. *British Journal of Obstetrics and Gynaecology* 1980;87(10):889–92.

64. Awad SA and McGinnis RH. Factors that influence the incidence of detrusor instability in women. *Journal of Urology* 1983;130(1):114–15.

65. Walter S and Olesen KP. Urinary incontinence and genital prolapse in the female: Clinical, urodynamic and radiological examinations. *British Journal of Obstetrics and Gynaecology* 1982;89(5):393–401.

66. Petros PP and Ulmsten U. Urge incontinence history is an accurate predictor of urge incontinence. *Acta Obstetricia et Gynecologica Scandinavica* 1992;71(7):537–9.

67. Digesu GA, Khullar V, Cardozo L, et al. Overactive bladder symptoms: do we need urodynamics? *Neurourology and Urodynamics* 2003;22(2):105–8.

68. Glezerman M, Glasner M, Rikover M. Evaluation of reliability of history in women complaining of urinary stress incontinence. *European Journal of Obstetrics, Gynecology, and Reproductive Biology* 1986;21(3):159–64.

69. Versi E, Cardozo L, Anand D, et al. Symptoms analysis for the diagnosis of genuine stress incontinence. *British Journal of Obstetrics and Gynaecology* 1991;98(8):815–19.

70. Fischer-Rasmussen W, Iversen HR, Stage P. Predictive values of diagnostic tests in the evaluation of female urinary stress incontinence. *Acta Obstetricia et Gynecologica Scandinavica* 1986;65(4):291–4.

71. Hastie KJ and Moisey CU. Are urodynamics necessary in female patients presenting with stress incontinence? *British Journal of Urology* 1989;63(2):155–6.

72. Videla FL and Wall LL. Stress incontinence diagnosed without multichannel urodynamic studies. *Obstetrics and Gynecology* 1998;91(6):965–8.

73. Swift SE and Ostergard DR. Evaluation of current urodynamic testing methods in the diagnosis of genuine stress incontinence. *Obstetrics and Gynecology* 1995;86(1):85–91.

74. Hilton P and Stanton SL. Algorithmic method for assessing urinary incontinence in elderly women. *British Medical Journal Clinical Research Ed.* 1981;282(6268):940–2.

75. Romanzi LJ, Polaneczky M, Glazer HI. Simple test of pelvic muscle contraction during pelvic examination: correlation to surface electromyography. *Neurourology and Urodynamics* 1999;18(6):603–12.

76. Laycock J and Jerwood D. Pelvic floor muscle assessment: The PERFECT scheme. *Physiotherapy* 2001;87(12):631–42.

77. Bo K and Finckenhagen HB. Vaginal palpation of pelvic floor muscle strength: inter-test reproducibility and comparison between palpation and vaginal squeeze pressure. *Acta Obstetricia et Gynecologica Scandinavica* 2001;80(10):883–7.

78. Jeyaseelan SM, Haslam J, Winstanley J, et al. Digital vaginal assessment: An inter-tester reliability study. *Physiotherapy* 2001;87(5):243–50.

79. Swift SE, Tate SB, Nicholas J. Correlation of symptoms with degree of pelvic organ support in a general population of women: what is pelvic organ prolapse? *American Journal of Obstetrics and Gynecology* 2003;189(2):372–7.

80. Samuelsson EC, Victor A, Tibblin G, et al. Signs of genital prolapse in a Swedish population of women 20 to 59 years of age and possible related factors. *American Journal of Obstetrics and Gynecology* 1999;180(2 Part 1):299–305.

81. Bradley CS and Nygaard IE. Vaginal wall descensus and pelvic floor symptoms in older women. *Obstetrics and Gynecology* 2005;106(4):759–66.

82. Buchsbaum GM, Albushies DT, Guzick DS. Utility of urine reagent strip in screening women with incontinence for urinary tract infection. *International Urogynecology Journal* 2004;15(6):391–3.

83. Ouslander JG, Schapira M, Schnelle JF, et al. Does eradicating bacteriuria affect the severity of chronic urinary incontinence in nursing home residents? *Annals of Internal Medicine* 1995;122(10):749–54.

84. Ding YY, Sahadevan S, Pang WS, et al. Clinical utility of a portable ultrasound scanner in the measurement of residual urine volume. *Singapore Medical Journal* 1996;37(4):365–8.

85. Goode PS, Locher JL, Bryant RL, et al. Measurement of postvoid residual urine with portable transabdominal bladder ultrasound scanner and urethral catheterization. *International Urogynecology Journal* 2000;11(5):296–300.

86. Ouslander JG, Simmons S, Tuico E, et al. Use of a portable ultrasound device to measure post-void residual volume among incontinent nursing home residents. *Journal of the American Geriatrics Society* 1994;42(11):1189–92.

87. Nygaard IE. Postvoid residual volume cannot be accurately estimated by bimanual examination. *International Urogynecology Journal* 1996;7(2):74–6.

88. Amarenco G, Arnould B, Carita P, et al. European psychometric validation of the CONTILIFE: a Quality of Life questionnaire for urinary incontinence. *European Urology* 2003;43(4):391–404.

89. Uebersax JS, Wyman JF, Shumaker SA, et al. Short forms to assess life quality and symptom distress for urinary incontinence in women: the Incontinence Impact Questionnaire and the Urogenital Distress Inventory. Continence Program for Women Research Group. *Neurourology and Urodynamics.* 1995;14(2):131–9.

90. Avery K, Donovan J, Peters TJ, *et al*. ICIQ: A brief and robust measure for evaluating the symptoms and impact of urinary incontinence. *Neurourology and Urodynamics* 2004;23(4):322–30.

91. Jackson S, Donovan J, Brookes S, *et al*. The bristol female lower urinary tract symptoms questionnaire: Development and psychometric testing. *British Journal of Urology* 1996;77(6):805–12.

92. Kulseng-Hanssen S and Borstad E. The development of a questionnaire to measure the severity of symptoms and the quality of life before and after surgery for stress incontinence. *BJOG: an International Journal of Obstetrics and Gynaecology* 2003;110(11):983–8.

93. Patrick DL, Martin ML, Bushnell DM, *et al*. Quality of life of women with urinary incontinence: further development of the incontinence quality of life instrument (I-QOL). *Urology* 1999;53(1):71–6.

94. Wagner TH, Patrick DL, Bavendam TG, *et al*. Quality of life of persons with urinary incontinence: development of a new measure. *Urology* 1996;47(1):67–71.

95. Bushnell DM, Martin ML, Summers KH, *et al*. Quality of life of women with urinary incontinence: cross-cultural performance of 15 language versions of the I-QOL. *Quality of Life Research* 2005;14(8):1901–13.

96. Stothers L. Reliability, validity, and gender differences in the quality of life index of the SEAPI-QMM incontinence classification system. *Neurourology and Urodynamics* 2004;23(3):223–8.

97. Kelleher CJ, Cardozo LD, Khullar V, *et al*. A new questionnaire to assess the quality of life of urinary incontinent women. *British Journal of Obstetrics and Gynaecology* 1997;104(12):1374–9.

98. Hagen S, Hanley J, Capewell A. Test–retest reliability, validity, and sensitivity to change of the urogenital distress inventory and the incontinence impact questionnaire. *Neurourology and Urodynamics* 2002;21(6):534–9.

99. Wyman JF, Harkins SW, Choi SC, *et al*. Psychosocial impact of urinary incontinence in women. *Obstetrics and Gynecology*. 1987; 70(3 Part 1):378–81.

100. Stach-Lempinen B, Kujansuu E, Laippala P, *et al*. Visual analogue scale, urinary incontinence severity score and 15 D - Psychometric testing of three different health-related quality-of-life instruments for urinary incontinent women. *Scandinavian Journal of Urology and Nephrology* 2001;35(6):476–83.

101. Matza LS, Thompson CL, Krasnow J, *et al*. Test–retest reliability of four questionnaires for patients with overactive bladder: The overactive bladder questionnaire (OAB-q), patient perception of bladder condition (PPBC), urgency questionnaire (UQ), and the primary OAB symptom questionnaire (POSQ). *Neurourology and Urodynamics* 2005;24(3):215–25.

102. Hanley J, Capewell A, Hagen S. Validity study of the severity index, a simple measure of urinary incontinence in women. *British Medical Journal* 2001;322(7294):1096–7.

103. Larsson G and Victor A. The frequency/volume chart in genuine stress incontinent women. *Neurourology and Urodynamics* 1992;11(1):23–31.

104. Groutz A, Blaivas JG, Chaikin DC, *et al*. Noninvasive outcome measures of urinary incontinence and lower urinary tract symptoms: a multicenter study of micturition diary and pad tests. *Journal of Urology* 2000;164(3 Part 1):698–701.

105. Nygaard I and Holcomb R. Reproducibility of the seven-day voiding diary in women with stress urinary incontinence. *International Urogynecology Journal* 2000;11(1):15–17.

106. Wyman JF, Choi SC, Harkins SW, *et al*. The urinary diary in evaluation of incontinent women: a test–retest analysis. *Obstetrics and Gynecology* 1988;71:(6 Part 1)812–17.

107. Locher JL, Goode PS, Roth DL, *et al*. Reliability assessment of the bladder diary for urinary incontinence in older women. *Journals of Gerontology Series A-Biological Sciences and Medical Sciences* 2001;56(1):M32–M35.

108. Kinn AC and Larsson B. Pad test with fixed bladder volume in urinary stress incontinence. *Acta Obstetricia et Gynecologica Scandinavica* 1987;66(4):369–71.

109. Simons AM, Yoong WC, Buckland S, *et al*. Inadequate repeatability of the one-hour pad test: The need for a new incontinence outcome measure. *British Journal of Obstetrics and Gynaecology* 2001;108(3):315–19.

110. Lose G, Gammelgaard J, Jorgensen TJ. The one-hour pad-weighing test: Reproducibility and the correlation between the test result, the start volume in the bladder, and the diuresis. *Neurourology and Urodynamics* 1986;5(1):17–21.

111. Jorgensen L, Lose G, Andersen JT. One-hour pad-weighing test for objective assessment of female urinary incontinence. *Obstetrics and Gynecology* 1987;69(1):39–42.

112. Klarskov P and Hald T. Reproducibility and reliability of urinary incontinence assessment with a 60 min test. *Scandinavian Journal of Urology and Nephrology* 1984;18(4):293–8.

113. Christensen SJ, Colstrup H, Hertz JB. Inter- and intra-departmental variations of the perineal pad weighing test. *Neurourology and Urodynamics* 1986;5(1):23–8.

114. Fantl JA, Harkins SW, Wyman JF, *et al*. Fluid loss quantiation test in women with urinary incontinence: A test–retest analysis. *Obstetrics and Gynecology* 1987;70(5):739–43.

115. Devreese AM, De Weerdt WJ, Feys HM, *et al*. Functional assessment of urinary incontinence: the perineal pad test. *Clinical Rehabilitation* 1996;10(3):210–15.

116. Lose G, Rosenkilde P, Gammelgaard J, *et al*. Pad-weighing test performed with standardized bladder volume. *Urology* 1988;32(1):78–80.

117. Rasmussen A, Mouritsen L, Dalgaard A, *et al*. Twenty-four hour pad weighing test: reproducibility and dependency of activity level and fluid intake. *Neurourology and Urodynamics* 1994;13(3):261–5.

118. Lose G, Jorgensen L, Thunedborg P. 24-hour home pad weighing test versus 1-hour ward test in the assessment of mild stress incontinence. *Acta Obstetricia et Gynecologica Scandinavica* 1989;68(3):211–15.

119. Karantanis E, Allen W, Stevermuer TL, *et al*. The repeatability of the 24-hour pad test. *International Urogynecology Journal* 2005;16(1):63–8.

120. Victor A, Larsson G, Asbrink AS. A simple patient-administered test for objective quantitation of the symptom of urinary incontinence. *Scandinavian Journal of Urology and Nephrology* 1987;21(4):277–9.

121. Versi E, Orrego G, Hardy E, *et al*. Evaluation of the home pad test in the investigation of female urinary incontinence. *British Journal of Obstetrics and Gynaecology* 1996;103(2):162–7.

122. Glazener CM and Lapitan MC. Urodynamic investigations for management of urinary incontinence in adults. (Cochrane Review). In: *Cochrane Database of Systematic Reviews*, Issue 3, 2002. Oxford: Update Software.

123. Ramsay IN, Ali HM, Hunter M, *et al*. A randomized controlled trial of urodynamic investigations prior to conservative treatment of urinary incontinence in the female. *International Urogynecology Journal* 1995;6(5):277–81.

124. Thompson PK, Duff DS, Thayer PS. Stress incontinence in women under 50: does urodynamics improve surgical outcome? *International Urogynecology Journal* 2000;11(5):285–9.

125. Black N, Griffiths J, Pope C, *et al*. Impact of surgery for stress incontinence on morbidity: Cohort study. *British Medical Journal* 1997;315(7121):1493–8.

126. Hutchings A, Griffiths J, Black NA. Surgery for stress incontinence: factors associated with a successful outcome. *British Journal of Urology* 1998;82(5):634–41.

127. Francis LN, Sand PK, Hamrang K, *et al*. A urodynamic appraisal of success and failure after retropubic urethropexy. *Journal of Reproductive Medicine for the Obstetrician and Gynecologist* 1987;32(9):693–6.

128. Kujansuu E. Urodynamic analysis of successful and failed incontinence surgery. *International Journal of Gynecology and Obstetrics* 1983;21(5):353–60.

129. Digesu GA, Khullar V, Cardozo L, *et al*. Preoperative pressure-flow studies: useful variables to predict the outcome of continence surgery. *BJU International* 2004;94(9):1296–9.

130. Rodriguez LV, de Almeida F, Dorey F, *et al*. Does Valsalva leak point pressure predict outcome after the distal urethral polypropylene sling? Role of urodynamics in the sling era. *Journal of Urology* 2004;172(1):210–14.

131. Kilicarslan H, Gokce G, Ayan S, *et al*. Predictors of outcome after *in situ* anterior vaginal wall sling surgery. *International Urogynecology Journal* 2003;14(5):339–41.

132. Sand PK, Bowen LW, Panganiban R, *et al*. The low pressure urethra as a factor in failed retropubic urethropexy. *Obstetrics and Gynecology* 1987;69(3 Part 1):399–402.

133. Meschia M, Bruschi F, Barbacini P, *et al*. Recurrent incontinence after retropubic surgery. *Journal of Gynecologic Surgery* 1993;9(1):25–8.

134. Weil A, Reyes H, Bischoff P. Modifications of the urethral rest and stress profiles after different types of surgery for urinary stress incontinence. *British Journal of Obstetrics and Gynaecology* 1984;91(1):46–55.

135. Herschorn S and Glazer AA. Early experience with small volume periurethral polytetrafluoroethylene for female stress urinary incontinence. *Journal of Urology* 2000;163(6):1838–42.

136. Paick JS, Ku JH, Shin JW, *et al*. Complications associated with the tension-free vaginal tape procedure: The Korean experience. *International Urogynecology Journal* 2005;16(3):215–19.

137. Paick JS, Ku JH, Kim SW, *et al*. Tension-free vaginal tape procedure for the treatment of mixed urinary incontinence: significance of maximal urethral closure pressure. *Journal of Urology* 2004;172(3):1001–5.

138. Paick JS, Ku JH, Shin JW, *et al*. Tension-free vaginal tape procedure for urinary incontinence with low Valsalva leak point pressure. *Journal of Urology* 2004;172(4 Part 1):1370–3.

139. Monga AK and Stanton SL. Urodynamics: Prediction, outcome and analysis of mechanisms for cure of stress incontinence by periurethral collagen. *British Journal of Obstetrics and Gynaecology* 1997;104(2):158–62.

140. McLennan MT, Melick CF, Bent AE. Leak-point pressure: clinical application of values at two different volumes. *International Urogynecology Journal* 2000;11(3):136–41.

141. Bergman A and Bhatia NN. Uroflowmetry for predicting postoperative voiding difficulties in women with stress urinary incontinence. *British Journal of Obstetrics and Gynaecology* 1985;92(8):835–8.

142. Hong B, Park S, Kim HS, *et al*. Factors predictive of urinary retention after a tension-free vaginal tape procedure for female stress urinary incontinence. *Journal of Urology* 2003;170(3):852–6.

143. Minassian VA, Al-Badr A, Drutz HP, *et al*. Tension-free vaginal tape, Burch, and slings: Are there predictors for early postoperative voiding dysfunction? *International Urogynecology Journal* 2004;15(3):183–7.

144. Bombieri L, Freeman RM, Perkins EP, *et al*. Why do women have voiding dysfunction and de novo detrusor instability after colposuspension? *BJOG: an International Journal of Obstetrics and Gynaecology* 2002;109(4):402–12.

145. Ouslander J, Leach G, Abelson S, *et al*. Simple versus multichannel cystometry in the evaluation of bladder function in an incontinent geriatric population. *Journal of Urology* 1988;140(6):1482–6.

146. Fonda D, Brimage PJ, D'Astoli M. Simple screening for urinary incontinence in the elderly: comparison of simple and multichannel cystometry. *Urology* 1993;42(5):536–40.

147. Sutherst JR and Brown MC. Comparison of single and multichannel cystometry in diagnosing bladder instability. *British Medical Journal Clinical Research Ed.* 1984;288(6432):1720–2.

148. Sand PK, Hill RC, Ostergard DR. Supine urethroscopic and standing cystometry as screening methods for the detection of detrusor instability. *Obstetrics and Gynecology* 1987;70(1):57–60.

149. Scotti RJ and Myers DL. A comparison of the cough stress test and single-channel cystometry with multichannel urodynamic evaluation in genuine stress incontinence. *Obstetrics and Gynecology* 1993;81(3):430–3.

150. Hsu TH, Rackley RR, Appell RA. The supine stress test: a simple method to detect intrinsic urethral sphincter dysfunction. *Journal of Urology* 1999;162(2):460–3.

151. Lobel RW and Sand PK. The empty supine stress test as a predictor of intrinsic urethral sphincter dysfunction. *Obstetrics and Gynecology* 1996;88(1):128–32.

152. Hanzal E, Berger E, Koelbl H. Reliability of the urethral closure pressure profile during stress in the diagnosis of genuine stress incontinence. *British Journal of Urology* 1991;68(4):369–71.

153. Swithinbank LV, James M, Shepherd A, *et al*. Role of ambulatory urodynamic monitoring in clinical urological practice. *Neurourology and Urodynamics* 1999;18(3):215–22.

154. Radley SC, Rosario DJ, Chapple CR, *et al*. Conventional and ambulatory urodynamic findings in women with symptoms suggestive of bladder overactivity. *Journal of Urology* 2001;166(6):2253–8.

155. Davis G, McClure G, Sherman R, *et al*. Ambulatory urodynamics of female soldiers. *Military Medicine* 1998;163(12):808–12.

156. Webb RJ, Ramsden PD, Neal DE. Ambulatory monitoring and electronic measurement of urinary leakage in the diagnosis of detrusor instability and incontinence. *British Journal of Urology* 1991;68(2):148–52.

157. McInerney PD, Vanner TF, Harris SA, *et al*. Ambulatory urodynamics. *British Journal of Urology* 1991;67(3):272–4.

158. Davila GW. Ambulatory urodynamics in urge incontinence evaluation. *International Urogynecology Journal* 1994;5(1):25–30.

159. Pelsang RE and Bonney WW. Voiding cystourethrography in female stress incontinence. *American Journal of Roentgenology* 1996;166(3):561–5.

160. Kadar N. The value of bladder filling in the clinical detection of urine loss and selection of patients for urodynamic testing. *British Journal of Obstetrics and Gynaecology* 1988;95(7):698–704.

161. Digesu GA, Hutchings A, Salvatore S, *et al*. Reproducibility and reliability of pressure flow parameters in women. *BJOG: an International Journal of Obstetrics and Gynaecology* 2003;110(8):774–6.

162. Homma Y, Kondo Y, Takahashi S, *et al*. Reproducibility of cystometry in overactive detrusor. *European Urology* 2000;38(6):681–5.

163. Caputo RM and Benson JT. The Q-tip test and urethrovesical junction mobility. *Obstetrics and Gynecology* 1993;82(6):892–6.

164. Montella JM, Ewing S, Cater J. Visual assessment of urethrovesical junction mobility. *International Urogynecology Journal* 1997;8(1):13–17.

165. Cogan SL, Weber AM, Hammel JP. Is urethral mobility really being assessed by the pelvic organ prolapse quantification (POP-Q) system? *Obstetrics and Gynecology* 2002;99(3):473–6.

166. Noblett K, Lane FL, Driskill CS. Does pelvic organ prolapse quantification exam predict urethral mobility in stages 0 and I prolapse? *International Urogynecology Journal* 2005;16(4):268–71.

167. Migliorini GD and Glenning PP. Bonney's test - Fact or fiction? *British Journal of Obstetrics and Gynaecology* 1987;94(2):157–9.

168. Bhatia NN and Bergman A. Urodynamic appraisal of the Bonney test in women with stress urinary incontinence. *Obstetrics and Gynecology* 1983;62(6):696–9.

169. Miyazaki FS and Grody MHT. The Bonney test: A reassessment. *American Journal of Obstetrics and Gynecology* 1997;177(6):1322–9.

170. Bergman A and Bhatia NN. Urodynamic appraisal of the Marshall-Marchetti test in women with stress urinary incontinence. *Urology* 1987;29(4):458–62.

171. Sutherst JR and Brown MC. Detection of urethral incompetence in women using the fluid-bridge test. *British Journal of Urology* 1980;52(2):138–42.

172. Sutherst JR and Brown M. Detection of urethral incompetence. Erect studies using the fluid-bridge test. *British Journal of Urology* 1981;53(4):360–3.

173. Niecestro RM, Wheeler Jr JS, Nanninga J, *et al*. Use of Stresscath for diagnosing stress incontinence. *Urology* 1992;39(3):266–9.

174. Bergman A, Koonings PP, Ballard CA. Negative Q-tip test as a risk factor for failed incontinence surgery in women. *Journal of Reproductive Medicine* 1989;34(3):193–7.

175. Cundiff GW and Bent AE. The contribution of urethrocystoscopy to evaluation of lower urinary tract dysfunction in women. *International Urogynecology Journal* 1996;7(6):307–11.

176. Scotti RJ, Ostergard DR, Guillaume AA, *et al*. Predictive value of urethroscopy as compared to urodynamics in the diagnosis of genuine stress incontinence. *Journal of Reproductive Medicine* 1990;35(8):772–6.

177. Bergman A, Ballard CA, Platt LD. Ultrasonic evaluation of urethrovesical junction in women with stress urinary incontinence. *Journal of Clinical Ultrasound* 1988;16(5):295–300.

178. Khullar V, Cardozo LD, Salvatore S, *et al*. Ultrasound: a noninvasive screening test for detrusor instability. *British Journal of Obstetrics and Gynaecology* 1996;103(9):904–8.

179. Robinson D, Anders K, Cardozo L, *et al*. Can ultrasound replace ambulatory urodynamics when investigating women with irritative urinary symptoms? *BJOG: an International Journal of Obstetrics and Gynaecology* 2002;109(2):145–8.

180. Heit M. Intraurethral ultrasonography: correlation of urethral anatomy with functional urodynamic parameters in stress incontinent women. *International Urogynecology Journal* 2000;11(4):204–11.

181. Grischke EM, Anton H, Stolz W, *et al*. Urodynamic assessment and lateral urethrocystography. A comparison of two diagnostic procedures for female urinary incontinence. *Acta Obstetricia et Gynecologica Scandinavica* 1991;70(3):225–9.

182. Bergman A, McKenzie C, Ballard CA, *et al*. Role of cystourethrography in the preoperative evaluation of stress urinary incontinence in women. *Journal of Reproductive Medicine* 1988;33(4):372–6.

183. Bergman A, McKenzie CJ, Richmond J, *et al*. Transrectal ultrasound versus cystography in the evaluation of anatomical stress urinary incontinence. *British Journal of Urology* 1988;62(3):228–34.

184. Department of Health. *The NHS Plan: a Plan for Investment, a Plan for Reform*. No. Cm 4818-I. London: The Stationery Office Limited; 2000.

185. The Bristol Royal Infirmary Inquiry. *Learning from Bristol: the Report of the Public Inquiry Into Children's Heart Surgery at the Bristol Royal Infirmary 1984–1995*. Command Paper: CM 5207. London: The Bristol Royal Infirmary Inquiry/COI Communications; 2001.

186. Waitzkin H. Doctor–patient communication. Clinical implications of social scientific research. *Journal of the American Medical Association* 1984;252(17):2441–6.

187. Spence-Jones C, Kamm MA, Henry MM, *et al*. Bowel dysfunction: A pathogenic factor in uterovaginal prolapse and urinary stress incontinence. *British Journal of Obstetrics and Gynaecology* 1994;101(2):147–52.

188. Alling ML, Lose G, Jorgensen T. Risk factors for lower urinary tract symptoms in women 40 to 60 years of age. *Obstetrics and Gynecology* 2000;96(3):446–51.

189. Song YF, Zhang WJ, Song J, *et al*. Prevalence and risk factors of urinary incontinence in Fuzhou Chinese women. *Chinese Medical Journal* 2005;118(11):887–92.

190. Dallosso HM, McGrother CW, Matthews RJ, *et al*. The association of diet and other lifestyle factors with overactive bladder and stress incontinence: A longitudinal study in women. *BJU International* 2003;92(1):69–77.

191. Dallosso HM, McGrother CW, Matthews RJ, *et al*. Nutrient composition of the diet and the development of overactive bladder: A longitudinal study in women. *Neurourology and Urodynamics* 2004;23(3):204–10.

192. Dallosso H, Matthews R, McGrother C, *et al*. Diet as a risk factor for the development of stress urinary incontinence: A longitudinal study in women. *European Journal of Clinical Nutrition* 2004;58(6):920–6.

193. Nuotio M, Jylha M, Koivisto A-M, *et al*. Association of smoking with urgency in older people. *European Urology* 2001;40(2):206–12.

194. Bryant CM, Dowell CJ, Fairbrother G. Caffeine reduction education to improve urinary symptoms. *British Journal of Nursing* 2002;11(8):560–5.

195. Arya LA, Myers DL, Jackson ND. Dietary caffeine intake and the risk for detrusor instability: a case-control study. *Obstetrics and Gynecology* 2000;96(1):85–9.

196. Creighton SM and Stanton SL. Caffeine: Does it affect your bladder? *British Journal of Urology* 1990;66(6):613–14.

197. Tomlinson BU, Dougherty MC, Pendergast JF, *et al*. Dietary caffeine, fluid intake and urinary incontinence in older rural women. *International Urogynecology Journal* 1999;10(1):22–8.

198. James JE, Sawczuk D, Merrett S. The effect of chronic caffeine consumption on urinary incontinence in psychogeriatric inpatients. *Psychology and Health* 1989;3(4):297–305.

199. Dougherty MC, Dwyer JW, Pendergast JF, *et al*. A randomized trial of behavioral management for continence with older rural women. *Research in Nursing and Health* 2002;25(1):3–13.

200. Hannestad YS, Rortveit G, Daltveit AK, *et al*. Are smoking and other lifestyle factors associated with female urinary incontinence? The Norwegian EPINCONT Study. *BJOG: an International Journal of Obstetrics and Gynaecology* 2003;110(3):247–54.

201. Asplund R and Aberg HE. Nocturia in relation to body mass index, smoking and some other life-style factors in women. *Climacteric* 2004;7(3):267–73.

202. Bradley CS, Kennedy CM, Nygaard IE. Pelvic floor symptoms and lifestyle factors in older women. *Journal of Women's Health* 2005;14(2):128–36.

203. Dowd TT, Campbell JM, Jones JA. Fluid intake and urinary incontinence in older community-dwelling women. *Journal of Community Health Nursing* 1996;13(3):179–86.

204. Swithinbank L, Hashim H, Abrams P. The effect of fluid intake on urinary symptoms in women. *Journal of Urology* 2005;174 (1):187–9.

205. Fantl JA, Wyman JF, McClish DK, *et al*. Efficacy of bladder training in older women with urinary incontinence. *JAMA: the journal of the American Medical Association* 1991;265(5):609–13.

206. Wyman JF, Elswick RK, Wilson MS, *et al*. Relationship of fluid intake to voluntary micturitions and urinary incontinence in women. *Neurourology and Urodynamics* 1991;10(5):463–73.

207. Tampakoudis P, Tantanassis T, Grimbizis G, *et al*. Cigarette smoking and urinary incontinence in women - A new calculative method of estimating the exposure to smoke. *European Journal of Obstetrics, Gynecology, and Reproductive Biology* 1995;63(1):27–30.

208. Burgio KL, Matthews KA, Engel BT. Prevalence, incidence and correlates of urinary incontinence in healthy, middle-aged women. *Journal of Urology* 1991;146(5):1255–9.

209. Roe B and Doll H. Lifestyle factors and continence status: comparison of self-report data from a postal survey in England. *Journal of Wound, Ostomy, and Continence Nursing* 1999; 26(6):312–13,315–19.

210. Subak LL, Whitcomb E, Shen H, *et al*. Weight loss: a novel and effective treatment for urinary incontinence. *Journal of Urology* 2005;174(1):190–5.

211. Bump RC, Sugerman HJ, Fantl JA, *et al*. Obesity and lower urinary tract function in women: Effect of surgically induced weight loss. *American Journal of Obstetrics and Gynecology* 1992;167(2):392–9.

212. Deitel M, Stone E, Kassam HA, *et al*. Gynecologic-obstetric changes after loss of massive excess weight following bariatric surgery. *Journal of the American College of Nutrition* 1988;7(2):147–53.

213. Ahroni JH, Montgomery KF, Watkins BM. Laparoscopic adjustable gastric banding: weight loss, co-morbidities, medication usage and quality of life at one year. *Obesity Surgery* 2005;15(5):641–7.

214. Subak LL, Johnson C, Whitcomb E, *et al*. Does weight loss improve incontinence in moderately obese women? *International Urogynecology Journal* 2002;13(1):40–3.

215. Nygaard IE. Does prolonged high-impact activity contribute to later urinary incontinence? A retrospective cohort study of female olympians. *Obstetrics and Gynecology* 1997;90(5):718–22.

216. Eliasson K, Nordlander I, Larson B, *et al*. Influence of physical activity on urinary leakage in primiparous women. *Scandinavian Journal of Medicine and Science in Sports* 2005;15(2):87–94.

217. Nygaard I, DeLancey JOL, Arnsdorf L, *et al.* Exercise and incontinence. *Obstetrics and Gynecology* 1990;75(5):848–51.

218. Bo K and Borgen JS. Prevalence of stress and urge urinary incontinence in elite athletes and controls. *Medicine and Science in Sports and Exercise* 2001;33(11):1797–802.

219. Bo K, Maehlum S, Oseid S, *et al.* Prevalence of stress urinary incontinence among physically active and sedentary female students. *Scandinavian Journal of Sports Sciences* 1989;11(3):113–16.

220. Bo K. Pelvic floor muscle training is effective in treatment of female stress urinary incontinence, but how does it work?. *International Urogynecology Journal* 2004;15(2):76–84.

221. Abrams P, Cardozo L, Fall M, *et al.* The standardisation of terminology in lower urinary tract function: report from the standardisation sub-committee of the International Continence Society. *Urology* 2003;61(1):37–49.

222. Thakar R and Stanton S. Regular review: management of urinary incontinence in women. *British Medical Journal* 2000;321(7272):1326–31.

223. Berghmans LC, Hendriks HJ, Bo K, *et al.* Conservative treatment of stress urinary incontinence in women: a systematic review of randomized clinical trials. *British Journal of Urology* 1998;82(2):181–91.

224. Hay-Smith EJC and Dumoulin C. Pelvic floor muscle training versus no treatment, or inactive control treatments, for urinary incontinence in women. (Cochrane Review). In: *Cochrane Database of Systematic Reviews*, Issue 1, 2006. Oxford: Update Software.

225. Herbison P, Plevnik S, Mantle J. Weighted vaginal cones for urinary incontinence. (Cochrane Review). In: *Cochrane Database of Systematic Reviews*, Issue 1, 2002. Oxford: Update Software.

226. Bo K, Talseth T, Holme I. Single blind, randomised controlled trial of pelvic floor exercises, electrical stimulation, vaginal cones, and no treatment in management of genuine stress incontinence in women. *British Medical Journal* 1999;318(7182):487–93.

227. Miller JM, Ashton-Miller JA, DeLancey JO. A pelvic muscle precontraction can reduce cough-related urine loss in selected women with mild SUI. *Journal of the American Geriatrics Society* 1998;46(7):870–4.

228. Henalla SM, Hutchins CJ, Robinson P, *et al.* Non-operative methods in the treatment of female genuine stress incontinence of urine. *Journal of Obstetrics and Gynaecology* 1989;9(3):222–5.

229. Ghoniem GM, Van Leeuwen JS, Elser DM, *et al.* A randomized controlled trial of duloxetine alone, pelvic floor muscle training alone, combined treatment and no active treatment in women with stress urinary incontinence. *Journal of Urology* 2005;173(5): 1647–53.

230. Burns PA, Pranikoff K, Nochajski TH, *et al.* A comparison of effectiveness of biofeedback and pelvic muscle exercise treatment of stress incontinence in older community-dwelling women. *Journal of Gerontology* 1993;48(4):M167–M174.

231. Lagro-Janssen AL, Debruyne FM, Smits AJ, *et al.* The effects of treatment of urinary incontinence in general practice. *Family Practice* 1992;9(3):284–9.

232. Lagro-Janssen TL, Debruyne FM, Smits AJ, *et al.* Controlled trial of pelvic floor exercises in the treatment of urinary stress incontinence in general practice. *British Journal of General Practice* 1991;41(352):445–9.

233. Lagro-Janssen T and Van WC. Long-term effect of treatment of female incontinence in general practice. *British Journal of General Practice* 1998;48(436):1735–8.

234. Bo K, Hagen RH, Kvarstein B, *et al.* Pelvic floor muscle exercise for the treatment of female stress urinary incontinence: III. Effects of two different degrees of pelvic floor muscle exercises. *Neurourology and Urodynamics* 1990;9(5):489–502.

235. Bo K, Hagen R, Kvarstein B, *et al.* Female stress urinary incontinence and participation in different sports and social activities. *Scandinavian Journal of Sports Sciences* 1989;11(3):117–21.

236. Glazener CM, Herbison GP, Wilson PD, *et al.* Conservative management of persistent postnatal urinary and faecal incontinence: randomised controlled trial. *British Medical Journal* 2001;323(7313):593–6.

237. Glazener C, Herbison GP, MacArthur C, *et al.* Randomised controlled trial of conservative management of postnatal urinary and faecal incontinence: six year follow up. *British Medical Journal* 2005;330(7487):337–40.

238. Wilson PD and Herbison GP. A randomized controlled trial of pelvic floor muscle exercises to treat postnatal urinary incontinence. *International Urogynecology Journal* 1998;9(5):257–64.

239. Ewings P, Spencer S, Marsh H, *et al.* Obstetric risk factors for urinary incontinence and preventative pelvic floor exercises: cohort study and nested randomized controlled trial. [erratum appears in J Obstet Gynaecol. 2005 Nov;25(8):834-5]. *Journal of Obstetrics and Gynaecology* 2005;25(6):558–64.

240. Bo K and Talseth T. Long-term effect of pelvic floor muscle exercise 5 years after cessation of organized training. *Obstetrics and Gynecology* 1996;87(2):261–5.

241. Bo K, Kvarstein B, Nygaard I. Lower urinary tract symptoms and pelvic floor muscle exercise adherence after 15 years. *Obstetrics and Gynaecology* 2005;105(5 Part 1):999–1005.

242. Janssen CC, Lagro-Janssen AL, Felling AJ. The effects of physiotherapy for female urinary incontinence: individual compared with group treatment. *BJU International* 2001;87(3):201–6.

243. Demain S, Smith JF, Hiller L, *et al.* Comparison of group and individual physiotherapy for female urinary incontinence in primary care. *Physiotherapy* 2001;87(5):235–42.

244. Ishiko O, Hirai K, Sumi T, *et al.* Hormone replacement therapy plus pelvic floor muscle exercise for postmenopausal stress incontinence: A randomized, controlled trial. *Journal of Reproductive Medicine for the Obstetrician and Gynecologist* 2001;46(3): 213–20.

245. Millard RJ. Clinical Efficacy of Tolterodine with or Without a Simplified Pelvic Floor Exercise Regimen. *Neurourology and Urodynamics* 2004;23(1):48–53.

246. Arvonen T, Fianu-Jonasson A, Tyni-Lenne R. Effectiveness of two conservative modes of physical therapy in women with urinary stress incontinence. *Neurourology and Urodynamics* 2001;20(5):591–9.

247. Cammu H and Van Nylen M. Pelvic floor exercises versus vaginal weight cones in genuine stress incontinence. *European Journal of Obstetrics, Gynecology, and Reproductive Biology* 1998;77(1):89–93.

248. Laycock J and Jerwood D. Does pre-modulated interferential therapy cure genuine stress incontinence? *Physiotherapy* 1993;79(8):553–60.

249. Laycock J, Brown J, Cusack C, *et al.* Pelvic floor reeducation for stress incontinence: comparing three methods. *British Journal of Community Nursing* 2001;6(5):230–7.

250. Olah KS, Bridges N, Denning J, *et al.* The conservative management of patients with symptoms of stress incontinence: A randomized, prospective study comparing weighted vaginal cones and interferential therapy. *American Journal of Obstetrics and Gynecology* 1990;162(1):87–92.

251. Seo JT, Yoon H, Kim YH. A randomized prospective study comparing new vaginal cone and FES-Biofeedback. *Yonsei Medical Journal* 2004;45(5):879–84.

252. Pieber D, Zivkovic F, Tamussino K, *et al.* Pelvic floor exercise alone or with vaginal cones for the treatment of mild to moderate stress urinary incontinence in premenopausal women. *International Urogynecology Journal* 1995;6(1):14–17.

253. Delneri C and Di Benedetto P. Pelvic floor rehabilitation. A comparison of two methods of treatment: Vaginal cones versus functional electrical stimulation. *Europa Medicophysica* 2000;36(1):45–8.

254. Berghmans LC, Frederiks CM, de Bie RA, *et al.* Efficacy of biofeedback, when included with pelvic floor muscle exercise treatment, for genuine stress incontinence. *Neurourology and Urodynamics* 1996;15(1):37–52.

255. Castleden CM, Duffin HM, Mitchell EP. The effect of physiotherapy on stress incontinence. *Age and Ageing* 1984;13(4): 235–7.

256. Glavind K, Nohr SB, Walter S. Biofeedback and physiotherapy versus physiotherapy alone in the treatment of genuine stress urinary incontinence. *International Urogynecology Journal* 1996;7(6):339–43.

257. Sherman RA. Behavioral treatment of exercise-induced urinary incontinence among female soldiers. *Military Medicine* 1997;162(10):690–4.

258. Shepherd AM, Montgomery E, Anderson RS. Treatment of genuine stress incontinence with a new perineometer. *Physiotherapy* 1983;69(4):113.

259. Aukee P, Immonen P, Penttinen J, *et al.* Increase in pelvic floor muscle activity after 12 weeks' training: A randomized prospective pilot study. *Urology* 2002;60(6):1020–3.

260. Aukee P, Immonen P, Laaksonen DE, *et al.* The effect of home biofeedback training on stress incontinence. *Acta Obstetricia et Gynecologica Scandinavica* 2004;83(10):973–7.

261. Pages IH, Jahr S, Schaufele MK, *et al.* Comparative analysis of biofeedback and physical therapy for treatment of urinary stress incontinence in women. *American Journal of Physical Medicine and Rehabilitation* 2001;80(7):494–502.

262. Sung MS, Choi YH, Back SH, *et al.* The effect of pelvic floor muscle exercises on genuine stress incontinence among Korean women–focusing on its effects on the quality of life. *Yonsei Medical Journal* 2000;41(2):237–51.

263. Sung MS, Hong JY, Choi YH, *et al.* FES-biofeedback versus intensive pelvic floor muscle exercise for the prevention and treatment of genuine stress incontinence. *Journal of Korean Medical Science* 2000;15(3):303–8.

264. Morkved S, Bo K, Fjortoft T. Effect of adding biofeedback to pelvic floor muscle training to treat urodynamic stress incontinence. *Obstetrics and Gynecology* 2002;100(4):730–9.

265. Wang AC, Wang Y-Y, Chen M-C. Single-blind, randomized trial of pelvic floor muscle training, biofeedback-assisted pelvic floor muscle training, and electrical stimulation in the management of overactive bladder. *Urology* 2004;63(1):61–6.

266. Aksac B, Aki S, Karan A, *et al.* Biofeedback and pelvic floor exercises for the rehabilitation of urinary stress incontinence. *Gynecologic and Obstetric Investigation* 2003;56(1):23–7.

267. Wong KS, Fung KY, Fung SM, *et al.* Biofeedback of pelvic floor muscles in the management of genuine stress incontinence in Chinese women: randomised controlled trial. *Physiotherapy* 2001;87(12):644–8.

268. Sand PK, Richardson DA, Staskin DR, *et al.* Pelvic floor electrical stimulation in the treatment of genuine stress incontinence: A multicenter, placebo-controlled trial. *American Journal of Obstetrics and Gynecology* 1995;173(1):72–9.

269. Yamanishi T, Yasuda K, Sakakibara R, *et al.* Randomized, double-blind study of electrical stimulation for urinary incontinence due to detrusor overactivity. *Urology* 2000;55(3):353–7.

270. Luber KM and Wolde-Tsadik G. Efficacy of functional electrical stimulation in treating genuine stress incontinence: A randomized clinical trial. *Neurourology and Urodynamics* 1997;16(6):543–51.

271. Jeyaseelan SM, Haslam EJ, Winstanley J, *et al.* An evaluation of a new pattern of electrical stimulation as a treatment for urinary stress incontinence: a randomized, double-blind, controlled trial. *Clinical Rehabilitation* 2000;14(6):631–40.

272. Brubaker L, Benson JT, Bent A, *et al.* Transvaginal electrical stimulation for female urinary incontinence. *American Journal of Obstetrics and Gynecology* 1997;177(3):536–40.

273. Barroso JC, Ramos JG, Martins-Costa S, *et al.* Transvaginal electrical stimulation in the treatment of urinary incontinence. *BJU International* 2004;93(3):319–23.

274. Amaro JL, Gameiro MO, Padovani CR. Effect of intravaginal electrical stimulation on pelvic floor muscle strength. *International Urogynecology Journal* 2005;16(5):355–8.

275. Berghmans B, Van Waalwijk vD, Nieman F, *et al.* Efficacy of physical therapeutic modalities in women with proven bladder overactivity. *European Urology* 2002;41(6):581–7.

276. Hahn I, Sommar S, Fall M. A comparative study of pelvic floor training and electrical stimulation for the treatment of genuine female stress urinary incontinence. *Neurourology and Urodynamics* 1991;10(6):545–54.

277. Smith JJ, III. Intravaginal stimulation randomized trial. *Journal of Urology* 1996;155(1):127–30.

278. Hofbauer J, Preisinger F, Nurnberger N. The value of physical therapy in genuine female stress incontinence. [German]. *Zeitschrift fur Urologie und Nephrologie* 1990;83(5):249–54.

279. Spruijt J, Vierhout M, Verstraeten R, *et al.* Vaginal electrical stimulation of the pelvic floor: A randomized feasibility study in urinary incontinent elderly women. *Acta Obstetricia et Gynecologica Scandinavica* 2003;82(11):1043–8.

280. Knight S, Laycock J, Naylor D. Evaluation of neuromuscular electrical stimulation in the treatment of genuine stress incontinence. *Physiotherapy* 1998;84(2):61–71.

281. Lo SK, Naidu J, Cao Y. Additive effect of interferential therapy over pelvic floor exercise alone in the treatment of female urinary stress and urge incontinence: a randomized controlled trial. *Hong Kong Physiotherapy Journal* 2003;21:37–42.

282. Blowman C, Pickles C, Emery S, *et al.* Prospective double blind controlled trial of intensive physiotherapy with and without stimulation of the pelvic floor in treatment of genuine stress incontinence. *Physiotherapy* 1991;77(10):661–4.

283. Soomro NA, Khadra MH, Robson W, *et al.* A crossover randomized trial of transcutaneous electrical nerve stimulation and oxybutynin in patients with detrusor instability. *Journal of Urology* 2001;166(1):146–9.

284. Walsh IK, Johnston RS, Keane PF. Transcutaneous sacral neurostimulation for irritative voiding dysfunction. *European Urology* 1999;35(3):192–6.

285. Hasan ST, Robson WA, Pridie AK, *et al.* Transcutaneous electrical nerve stimulation and temporary S3 neuromodulation in idiopathic detrusor instability. *Journal of Urology* 1996;155(6):2005–11.

286. Karademir K, Baykal K, Sen B, *et al.* A peripheric neuromodulation technique for curing detrusor overactivity: Stoller afferent neurostimulation. *Scandinavian Journal of Urology and Nephrology* 2005;39(3):230–3.

287. Vandoninck V, van Balken MR, Agro EF, *et al.* Percutaneous tibial nerve stimulation in the treatment of overactive bladder: Urodynamic data. *Neurourology and Urodynamics* 2003;22(3):227–32.

288. van Balken MR, Vandoninck V, Gisolf KW, *et al.* Posterior tibial nerve stimulation as neuromodulative treatment of lower urinary tract dysfunction. *Journal of Urology* 2001;166(3):914–18.

289. Vandoninck V, van Balken MR, Finazzi AE, *et al.* Posterior tibial nerve stimulation in the treatment of urge incontinence. *Neurourology and Urodynamics* 2003;22(1):17–23.

290. Klingler HC, Pycha A, Schmidbauer J, *et al.* Use of peripheral neuromodulation of the S3 region for treatment of detrusor overactivity: a urodynamic-based study. *Urology* 2000;56(5):766–71.

291. Govier FE, Litwiller S, Nitti V, *et al.* Percutaneous afferent neuromodulation for the refractory overactive bladder: results of a multicenter study. *Journal of Urology* 2001;165(4):1193–8.

292. Congregado Ruiz B, Pena Outeirino X, Campoy Martinez P, *et al.* Peripheral afferent nerve stimulation for treatment of lower urinary tract irritative symptoms. *European Urology* 2004;45(1):65–9.

293. van der Pal F, van Balken MR, Heesakkers JP, *et al.* Correlation between quality of life and voiding variables in patients treated with percutaneous tibial nerve stimulation. *BJU International* 2006;97(1):113–16.

294. Van der Pal F., van Balken MR, Heesakkers JP, *et al.* Percutaneous tibial nerve stimulation in the treatment of refractory overactive bladder syndrome: is maintenance treatment necessary? *BJU International* 2006;97(3):547–50.

295. But I. Conservative treatment of female urinary incontinence with functional magnetic stimulation. *Urology* 2003;61(3):558–61.

296. But I, Faganelj M, Sostaric A. Functional magnetic stimulation for mixed urinary incontinence. *Journal of Urology* 2005;173(5):1644–6.

297. Galloway NT, El Galley RE, Sand PK, *et al.* Extracorporeal magnetic innervation therapy for stress urinary incontinence. *Urology* 1999;53(6):1108–11.

298. Chandi DD, Groenendijk PM, Venema PL. Functional extracorporeal magnetic stimulation as a treatment for female urinary incontinence: 'The chair'. *BJU International – Supplement* 2004;93(4):539–42.

299. Wallace SA, Roe B, Williams K, Palmer M. Bladder training for urinary incontinence in adults. (Cochrane Review). In: *Cochrane Database of Systematic Reviews*, Issue 1, 2004. Oxford: Update Software.

300. Hadley EC. Bladder training and related therapies for urinary incontinence in older people. *Journal of the American Medical Association* 1986;256(3):372–9.

301. Ostaszkiewicz J, Johnston L, Roe B. Habit retraining for the management of urinary incontinence in adults. (Cochrane Review). In: *Cochrane Database of Systematic Reviews*, Issue 2, 2004. Oxford: Update Software.

302. Ostaszkiewicz J, Johnston L, Roe B. Timed voiding for the management of urinary incontinence in adults. (Cochrane Review). In: *Cochrane Database of Systematic Reviews*, Issue 1, 2004. Oxford: Update Software.

303. Eustice S, Roe B, Paterson J. Prompted voiding for the management of urinary incontinence in adults. (Cochrane Review). In: *Cochrane Database of Systematic Reviews*, Issue 2, 2000. Oxford: Update Software.

304. Ostaszkiewicz J, Roe B, Johnston L. Effects of timed voiding for the management of urinary incontinence in adults: systematic review. *Journal of Advanced Nursing* 2005;52(4):420–31.

305. Jarvis GJ and Millar DR. Controlled trial of bladder drill for detrusor instability. *British Medical Journal* 1980;281(6251):1322–3.

306. Colombo M, Zanetta G, Scalambrino S, *et al.* Oxybutynin and bladder training in the management of female urinary urge incontinence: A randomized study. *International Urogynecology Journal and Pelvic Floor Dysfunction* 1995;6(2):63–7.

307. Jarvis GJ. A controlled trial of bladder drill and drug therapy in the management of detrusor instability. *British Journal of Urology* 1981;53(6):565–6.

308. Szonyi G, Collas DM, Ding YY, *et al.* Oxybutynin with bladder retraining for detrusor instability in elderly people: a randomized controlled trial. *Age and Ageing* 1995;24(4):287–91.

309. Wiseman PA, Malone-Lee J, Rai GS. Terodiline with bladder retraining for treating detrusor instability in elderly people. *British Medical Journal* 1991;302(6783):994–6.

310. Castleden CM, Duffin HM, Gulati RS. Double-blind study of imipramine and placebo for incontinence due to bladder instability. *Age and Ageing* 1986;15(5):299–303.

311. Mattiasson A, Blaakaer J, Hoye K, *et al.* Simplified bladder training augments the effectiveness of tolterodine in patients with an overactive bladder. *BJU International* 2003;91(1):54–60.

312. Yoon HS, Song HH, Ro YJ. A comparison of effectiveness of bladder training and pelvic muscle exercise on female urinary incontinence. *International Journal of Nursing Studies* 2003;40(1):45–50.

313. Wyman JF, Fantl JA, McClish DK, *et al.* Comparative efficacy of behavioral interventions in the management of female urinary incontinence. Continence Program for Women Research Group. *American Journal of Obstetrics and Gynecology* 1998;179(4):999–1007.

314. Burgio KL, Locher JL, Goode PS, *et al.* Behavioral vs drug treatment for urge urinary incontinence in older women: a randomized controlled trial. [see comments]. *JAMA: the journal of the American Medical Association* 1998;280(23):1995–2000.

315. Goode PS. Behavioral and drug therapy for urinary incontinence. *Urology* 2004;63(3 Supplement 1):58–64.

316. Johnson TM, Burgio KL, Redden DT, *et al.* Effects of behavioral and drug therapy on nocturia in older incontinent women. *Journal of the American Geriatrics Society* 2005;53(5):846–50.

317. Goode PS, Burgio KL, Locher JL, *et al.* Urodynamic changes associated with behavioral and drug treatment of urge incontinence in older women. *Journal of the American Geriatrics Society* 2002;50(5):808–16.

318. Burgio KL. Behavioral training with and without biofeedback in the treatment of urge incontinence in older women: A randomized controlled trial. *JAMA: the journal of the American Medical Association* 2002;288(18):2293–9.

319. Goode PS, Burgio KL, Locher JL, *et al.* Effect of behavioral training with or without pelvic floor electrical stimulation on stress incontinence in women: a randomized controlled trial. *JAMA: the journal of the American Medical Association* 2003;290(3):345–52.

320. Subak LL, Quesenberry CP Jr, Posner SF, *et al.* The effect of behavioral therapy on urinary incontinence: a randomized controlled trial. *Obstetrics and Gynecology* 2002;100(1):72–8.

321. McFall SL, Yerkes AM, Cowan LD. Outcomes of a small group educational intervention for urinary incontinence: Health-related quality of life. *Journal of Aging and Health* 2000;12(3):301–17.

322. McFall SL, Yerkes AM, Cowan LD. Outcomes of a small group educational intervention for urinary incontinence: episodes of incontinence and other urinary symptoms. *Journal of Aging and Health* 2000;12(2):250–67.

323. McDowell BJ, Engberg S, Sereika S, *et al.* Effectiveness of behavioral therapy to treat incontinence in homebound older adults. *Journal of the American Geriatrics Society* 1999;47(3):309–18.

324. Engberg S, Sereika SM, McDowell BJ, *et al.* Effectiveness of prompted voiding in treating urinary incontinence in cognitively impaired homebound older adults. *Journal of Wound, Ostomy, and Continence Nursing* 2002;29(5):252–65.

325. Burgio KL, Locher JL, Goode PS. Combined behavioral and drug therapy for urge incontinence in older women. *Journal of the American Geriatrics Society* 2000;48(4):370–4.

326. Schnelle JF. Treatment of urinary incontinence in nursing home patients by prompted voiding. *Journal of the American Geriatrics Society* 1990;38(3):356–60.

327. Hu TW, Igou JF, Kaltreider DL, *et al.* A clinical trial of a behavioral therapy to reduce urinary incontinence in nursing homes. Outcome and implications. *JAMA: the journal of the American Medical Association* 1989;261(18):2656–62.

328. Schnelle JF, Traughber B, Morgan DB, *et al.* Management of geriatric incontinence in nursing homes. *Journal of Applied Behavior Analysis* 1983;16(2):235–41.

329. Schnelle JF, Traughber B, Sowell VA, *et al.* Prompted voiding treatment of urinary incontinence in nursing home patients. A behavior management approach for nursing home staff. *Journal of the American Geriatrics Society* 1989;37(11):1051–7.

330. Schnelle JF, Alessi CA, Simmons SF, *et al.* Translating clinical research into practice: a randomized controlled trial of exercise and incontinence care with nursing home residents. *Journal of the American Geriatrics Society* 2002;50(9):1476–83.

331. Ouslander JG, Schnelle JF, Uman G, *et al.* Does oxybutynin add to the effectiveness of prompted voiding for urinary incontinence among nursing home residents? A placebo-controlled trial. *Journal of the American Geriatrics Society* 1995;43(6):610–17.

332. Colling J, Ouslander J, Hadley BJ, *et al.* The effects of patterned urge-response toileting (PURT) on urinary incontinence among nursing home residents. *Journal of the American Geriatrics Society* 1992;40(2):135–41.

333. Tobin GW and Brocklehurst JC. The management of urinary incontinence in local authority residential homes for the elderly. *Age and Ageing* 1986;15(5):292–8.

334. Jirovec MM and Templin T. Predicting success using individualized scheduled toileting for memory-impaired elders at home. *Research in Nursing and Health* 2001;24(1):1–8.

335. Haeusler G, Leitich H, van Trotsenburg M, *et al.* Drug therapy of urinary urge incontinence: a systematic review. *Obstetrics and Gynecology* 2002;100(5 Part 1):1003–16.

336. Herbison P, Hay-Smith J, Ellis G, *et al.* Effectiveness of anticholinergic drugs compared with placebo in the treatment of overactive bladder: systematic review. *British Medical Journal* 2003;326(7394):841–4.

337. Hay-Smith J, Herbison P, Ellis G, Moore K. Anticholinergic drugs versus placebo for overactive bladder syndrome in adults. (Cochrane Review). In: *Cochrane Database of Systematic Reviews*, Issue 3, 2002. Oxford: Update Software.

338. Harvey MA, Baker K, Wells GA. Tolterodine versus oxybutynin in the treatment of urge urinary incontinence: a meta-analysis. *American Journal of Obstetrics and Gynecology* 2001;185(1):56–61.

339. Hay-Smith J, Herbison P, Ellis G, Morris A. Which anticholinergic drug for overactive bladder symptoms in adults. (Cochrane Review). In: *Cochrane Database of Systematic Reviews*, Issue 3, 2005. Oxford: Update Software.

340. Chapple C, Khullar V, Gabriel Z, *et al.* The effects of antimuscarinic treatments in overactive bladder: A systematic review and meta-analysis. *European Urology* 2005;48(1):5–26.

341. Haab F, Stewart L, Dwyer P. Darifenacin, an M3 selective receptor antagonist, is an effective and well-tolerated once-daily treatment for overactive bladder. *European Urology* 2004;45(4):420–9.

342. Steers W, Corcos J, Foote J, *et al.* An investigation of dose titration with darifenacin, an M3-selective receptor antagonist. *BJU International* 2005;95(4):580–6.

343. Cardozo L and Dixon A. Increased warning time with darifenacin: a new concept in the management of urinary urgency. *Journal of Urology* 2005;173(4):1214–18.

344. Zinner N, Susset J, Gittelman M, *et al.* Efficacy, tolerability and safety of darifenacin, an M(3) selective receptor antagonist: an investigation of warning time in patients with OAB. *International Journal of Clinical Practice* 2006;60(1):119–26.

345. Chapple CR, Parkhouse H, Gardener C, *et al.* Double-blind, placebo-controlled, cross-over study of flavoxate in the treatment of idiopathic detrusor instability. *British Journal of Urology* 1990;66(5):491–4.

346. Meyhoff HH, Gerstenberg TC, Nordling J. Placebo–the drug of choice in female motor urge incontinence? *British Journal of Urology* 1983;55(1):34–7.

347. Milani R, Scalambrino S, Carrera S, *et al.* Comparison of flavoxate hydrochloride in daily dosages of 600 versus 1200 mg for the treatment of urgency and urge incontinence. *Journal of International Medical Research* 1988;16(3):244–8.

348. Lose G, Jorgensen L, Thunedborg P. Doxepin in the treatment of female detrusor overactivity: a randomized double-blind crossover study. *Journal of Urology* 1989;142(4):1024–6.

349. Abrams P, Freeman R, Anderstrom C, *et al.* Tolterodine, a new antimuscarinic agent: as effective but better tolerated than oxybutynin in patients with an overactive bladder. *British Journal of Urology* 1998;81(6):801–10.

350. Drutz HP, Appell RA, Gleason D, *et al.* Clinical efficacy and safety of tolterodine compared to oxybutynin and placebo in patients with overactive bladder. *International Urogynecology Journal* 1999;10(5):283–9.

351. Dmochowski RR, Sand PK, Zinner NR, *et al.* Comparative efficacy and safety of transdermal oxybutynin and oral tolterodine versus placebo in previously treated patients with urge and mixed urinary incontinence. *Urology* 2003;62(2):237–42.

352. Homma Y, Paick JS, Lee JG, *et al.* Clinical efficacy and tolerability of extended-release tolterodine and immediate-release oxybutynin in Japanese and Korean patients with an overactive bladder: a randomized, placebo-controlled trial. *BJU International* 2003;92(7):741–7.

353. Dmochowski RR, Davila GW, Zinner NR, *et al.* Efficacy and safety of transdermal oxybutynin in patients with urge and mixed urinary incontinence. *Journal of Urology* 2002;168(2):580–6.

354. Enzelsberger H, Helmer H, Kurz C. Intravesical instillation of oxybutynin in women with idiopathic detrusor instability: a randomised trial. *British Journal of Obstetrics and Gynaecology* 1995;102(11):929–30.

355. Dorschner W, Stolzenburg JU, Griebenow R, *et al.* Efficacy and cardiac safety of propiverine in elderly patients – a double-blind, placebo-controlled clinical study. *European Urology* 2000;37(6):702–8.

356. Mazur D, Wehnert J, Dorschner W, *et al.* Clinical and urodynamic effects of propiverine in patients suffering from urgency and urge incontinence. A multicentre dose-optimizing study. *Scandinavian Journal of Urology and Nephrology* 1995;29(3):289–94.

357. Chapple CR, Arano P, Bosch JL, *et al.* Solifenacin appears effective and well tolerated in patients with symptomatic idiopathic detrusor overactivity in a placebo- and tolterodine-controlled phase 2 dose-finding study. [erratum appears in BJU Int. 2004 May;93(7):1135]. *BJU International* 2004;93(1):71–7.

358. Cardozo L, Lisec M, Millard R, *et al.* Randomized, double-blind placebo controlled trial of the once daily antimuscarinic agent solifenacin succinate in patients with overactive bladder. *Journal of Urology* 2004;172(5 Part 1):1919–24.

359. Chapple CR, Rechberger T, Al Shukri S, *et al.* Randomized, double-blind placebo- and tolterodine-controlled trial of the once-daily antimuscarinic agent solifenacin in patients with symptomatic overactive bladder. *BJU International* 2004;93(3):303–10.

360. Haab F, Cardozo L, Chapple C, *et al.* Long-term open-label solifenacin treatment associated with persistence with therapy in patients with overactive bladder syndrome. *European Urology* 2005;47(3):376–84.

361. Kelleher CJ, Cardozo L, Chapple CR, *et al.* Improved quality of life in patients with overactive bladder symptoms treated with solifenacin. *BJU International* 2005;95(1):81–5.

362. Malone-Lee JG, Walsh JB, Maugourd MF. Tolterodine: a safe and effective treatment for older patients with overactive bladder. *Journal of the American Geriatrics Society* 2001;49(6):700–5.

363. Jonas U, Hofner K, Madersbacher H, *et al.* Efficacy and safety of two doses of tolterodine versus placebo in patients with detrusor overactivity and symptoms of frequency, urge incontinence, and urgency: urodynamic evaluation. The International Study Group. [erratum appears in World J Urol 1997;15(3):210]. *World Journal of Urology* 1997;15(2):144–51.

364. Jacquetin B and Wyndaele J. Tolterodine reduces the number of urge incontinence episodes in patients with an overactive bladder. *European Journal of Obstetrics, Gynecology, and Reproductive Biology* 2001;98(1):97–102.

365. Abrams P, Malone-Lee J, Jacquetin B, *et al.* Twelve-month treatment of overactive bladder: efficacy and tolerability of tolterodine. *Drugs and Aging* 2001;18(7):551–60.

366. Millard R, Tuttle J, Moore K, *et al.* Clinical efficacy and safety of tolterodine compared to placebo in detrusor overactivity. *Journal of Urology* 1999;161(5):1551–5.

367. Van Kerrebroeck P, Kreder K, Jonas U, *et al.* Tolterodine once-daily: superior efficacy and tolerability in the treatment of the overactive bladder. *Urology* 2001;57(3):414–21.

368. Swift S, Garely A, Dimpfl T, *et al.* A new once-daily formulation of tolterodine provides superior efficacy and is well tolerated in women with overactive bladder. *International Urogynecology Journal* 2003;14(1):50–4.

369. Zinner NR, Mattiasson A, Stanton SL. Efficacy, safety, and tolerability of extended-release once-daily tolterodine treatment for overactive bladder in older versus younger patients. *Journal of the American Geriatrics Society* 2002;50(5):799–807.

370. Chancellor M, Freedman S, Mitcheson HD, *et al.* Tolterodine, an effective and well tolerated treatment for urge incontinence and other overactive bladder symptoms. *Clinical Drug Investigation* 2000;19(2):83–91.

371. Landis JR, Kaplan S, Swift S, et al. Efficacy of antimuscarinic therapy for overactive bladder with varying degrees of incontinence severity. Journal of Urology 2004;171(2 Part 1):752–6.

372. Pleil AM, Reese PR, Kelleher CJ, et al. Health-related quality of life of patients with overactive bladder receiving immediate-release tolterodine. Hepac: Health Economics in Prevention and Care 2001;2(2):69–75.

373. Kelleher CJ, Kreder KJ, Pleil AM, et al. Long-term health-related quality of life of patients receiving extended-release tolterodine for overactive bladder. American Journal of Managed Care 2002;8(19):S608–S615.

374. Kreder K, Mayne C, Jonas U. Long-term safety, tolerability and efficacy of extended-release tolterodine in the treatment of overactive bladder. European Urology 2002;41(6):588–95.

375. Khullar V, Hill S, Laval KU, et al. Treatment of urge-predominant mixed urinary incontinence with tolterodine extended release: a randomized, placebo-controlled trial. Urology 2004;64(2):269–74.

376. Cardozo L, Chapple CR, Toozs-Hobson P, et al. Efficacy of trospium chloride in patients with detrusor instability: a placebo-controlled, randomized, double-blind, multicentre clinical trial. BJU International 2000;85(6):659–64.

377. Alloussi S, Laval K-U, Eckert R, et al. Trospium chloride (Spasmo-lyt(TM)) in patients with motor urge syndrome (detrusor instability): A double-blind, randomised, multicentre, placebo-controlled study. Journal of Clinical Research 1998;1:439–51.

378. Frohlich G, Bulitta M, Strosser W. Trospium chloride in patients with detrusor overactivity: meta-analysis of placebo-controlled, randomized, double-blind, multi-center clinical trials on the efficacy and safety of 20 mg trospium chloride twice daily. International Journal of Clinical Pharmacology and Therapeutics 2002;40(7):295–303.

379. Ulshofer B, Bihr A-M, Bodeker R-H, et al. Randomised, double-blind, placebo-controlled study on the efficacy and tolerance of trospium chloride in patients with motor urge incontinence. Clinical Drug Investigation 2001;21(8):563–9.

380. Zinner N, Gittelman M, Harris R, et al. Trospium chloride improves overactive bladder symptoms: a multicenter phase III trial. Journal of Urology 2004;171(6 Part 1):2311–15.

381. Rudy D, Cline K, Harris R, et al. Multicenter phase III trial studying trospium chloride in patients with overactive bladder. Urology 2006;67(2):275–80.

382. Milani R, Scalambrino S, Milia R, et al. Double-blind crossover comparison of flavoxate and oxybutynin in women affected by urinary urge syndrome. International Urogynecology Journal 1993;4(1):3–8.

383. Holmes DM, Montz FJ, Stanton SL. Oxybutinin versus propantheline in the management of detrusor instability. A patient-regulated variable dose trial. British Journal of Obstetrics and Gynaecology 1989;96(5):607–12.

384. Madersbacher H, Halaska M, Voigt R, et al. A placebo-controlled, multicentre study comparing the tolerability and efficacy of propiverine and oxybutynin in patients with urgency and urge incontinence. BJU International 1999;84(6):646–51.

385. Jeong GL, Jae YH, Myung-Soo C, et al. Tolterodine: As effective but better tolerated than oxybutynin in Asian patients with symptoms of overactive bladder. International Journal of Urology 2002;9(5):247–52.

386. Malone-Lee J, Shaffu B, Anand C, et al. Tolterodine: superior tolerability than and comparable efficacy to oxybutynin in individuals 50 years old or older with overactive bladder: a randomized controlled trial. Journal of Urology 2001;165(5):1452–6.

387. Giannitsas K, Perimenis P, Athanasopoulos A, et al. Comparison of the efficacy of tolterodine and oxybutynin in different urodynamic severity grades of idiopathic detrusor overactivity. European Urology 2004;46(6):776–82.

388. Leung HY, Yip SK, Cheon C, et al. A randomized controlled trial of tolterodine and oxybutynin on tolerability and clinical efficacy for treating Chinese women with an overactive bladder. BJU International 2002;90(4):375–80.

389. Appell RA, Sand P, Dmochowski R, et al. Prospective randomized controlled trial of extended-release oxybutynin chloride and tolterodine tartrate in the treatment of overactive bladder: results of the OBJECT Study. Mayo Clinic Proceedings 2001;76(4):358–63.

390. Sand PK, Miklos J, Ritter H, et al. A comparison of extended-release oxybutynin and tolterodine for treatment of overactive bladder in women. International Urogynecology Journal 2004;15(4):243–8.

391. Diokno AC, Appell RA, Sand PK, et al. Prospective, randomized, double-blind study of the efficacy and tolerability of the extended-release formulations of oxybutynin and tolterodine for overactive bladder: results of the OPERA trial. Mayo Clinic Proceedings 2003;78(6):687–95.

392. Armstrong RB, Luber KM, Peters KM. Comparison of dry mouth in women treated with extended-release formulations of oxybutynin or tolterodine for overactive bladder. International Urology and Nephrology 2005;37(2):247–52.

393. Chu FM, Dmochowski RR, Lama DJ, et al. Extended-release formulations of oxybutynin and tolterodine exhibit similar central nervous system tolerability profiles: a subanalysis of data from the OPERA trial. American Journal of Obstetrics and Gynecology 2005;192(6):1849–54.

394. Appell RA, Abrams P, Drutz HP, et al. Treatment of overactive bladder: long-term tolerability and efficacy of tolterodine. World Journal of Urology 2001;19(2):141–7.

395. Takei M, Homma Y, Akino H, et al. Long-term safety, tolerability and efficacy of extended-release tolterodine in the treatment of overactive bladder in Japanese patients. International Journal of Urology 2005;12(5):456–64.

396. Halaska M, Ralph G, Wiedemann A, et al. Controlled, double-blind, multicentre clinical trial to investigate long-term tolerability and efficacy of trospium chloride in patients with detrusor instability. World Journal of Urology 2003;20(6):392–9.

397. Chapple CR, Martinez-Garcia R, Selvaggi L, et al. A comparison of the efficacy and tolerability of solifenacin succinate and extended release tolterodine at treating overactive bladder syndrome: Results of the STAR trial. European Urology 2005;48(3):464–70.

398. Davila GW, Daugherty CA, Sanders SW, et al. A short-term, multicenter, randomized double-blind dose titration study of the efficacy and anticholinergic side effects of transdermal compared to immediate release oral oxybutynin treatment of patients with urge urinary incontinence. Journal of Urology 2001;166(1):140–5.

399. Barkin J, Corcos J, Radomski S, et al. A randomized, double-blind, parallel-group comparison of controlled- and immediate-release oxybutynin chloride in urge urinary incontinence. Clinical Therapeutics 2004;26(7):1026–36.

400. Anderson RU, Mobley D, Blank B, *et al.* Once daily controlled versus immediate release oxybutynin chloride for urge urinary incontinence. OROS Oxybutynin Study Group. *Journal of Urology* 1999;161(6):1809–12.

401. Birns J, Lukkari E, Malone-Lee JG. A randomized controlled trial comparing the efficacy of controlled-release oxybutynin tablets (10 mg once daily) with conventional oxybutynin tablets (5 mg twice daily) in patients whose symptoms were stabilized on 5 mg twice daily of oxybutynin. *BJU International* 2000;85(7):793–8.

402. Versi E, Appell R, Mobley D, *et al.* Dry mouth with conventional and controlled-release oxybutynin in urinary incontinence. The Ditropan XL Study Group. *Obstetrics and Gynecology* 2000;95(5):718–21.

403. Diokno A, Sand P, Labasky R, *et al.* Long-term safety of extended-release oxybutynin chloride in a community-dwelling population of participants with overactive bladder: a one-year study. *International Urology and Nephrology* 2002;34(1):43–9.

404. Getsios D, Caro JJ, Ishak KJ, *et al.* Oxybutynin Extended Release and Tolterodine Immediate Release: A Health Economic Comparison. *Clinical Drug Investigation* 2004;24(2):81–8.

405. Hughes DA and Dubois D. Cost-effectiveness analysis of extended-release formulations of oxybutynin and tolterodine for the management of urge incontinence. *Pharmacoeconomics* 2004;22(16):1047–59.

406. Guest JF, Abegunde D, Ruiz FJ. Cost effectiveness of controlled-release oxybutynin compared with immediate-release oxybutynin and tolterodine in the treatment of overactive bladder in the UK, France and Austria. *Clinical Drug Investigation* 2004;24(6): 305–21.

407. Getsios D, Caro JJ, Ishak KJ, *et al.* Canadian economic comparison of extended-release oxybutynin and immediate-release tolterodine in the treatment of overactive bladder. *Clinical Therapeutics* 2004;26(3):431–8.

408. Arikian SR, Casciano J, Doyle JJ, *et al.* A pharmacoeconomic evaluation of two new products for the treatment of overactive bladder. *Managed Care Interface* 2000;13(2):88–94.

409. O'Brien BJ, Goeree R, Bernard L, *et al.* Cost-Effectiveness of tolterodine for patients with urge incontinence who discontinue initial therapy with oxybutynin: a Canadian perspective. *Clinical Therapeutics* 2001;23(12):2038–49.

410. Kobelt G, Jonsson L, Mattiasson A. Cost-effectiveness of new treatments for overactive bladder: the example of tolterodine, a new muscarinic agent: a Markov model. *Neurourology and Urodynamics* 1998;17(6):599–611.

412. Shaya FT, Blume S, Gu A, *et al.* Persistence with overactive bladder pharmacotherapy in a Medicaid population. *American Journal of Managed Care* 2005;11:(Supplement 4)S121-S129.

413. Lose G, Lalos O, Freeman RM, *et al.* Efficacy of desmopressin (Minirin) in the treatment of nocturia: a double-blind placebo-controlled study in women. *American Journal of Obstetrics and Gynecology* 2003;189(4):1106–13.

414. Lose G, Mattiasson A, Walter S, *et al.* Clinical experiences with desmopressin for long-term treatment of nocturia. *Journal of Urology* 2004;172(3):1021–5.

415. Asplund R, Sundberg B, Bengtsson P. Oral desmopressin for nocturnal polyuria in elderly subjects: a double-blind, placebo-controlled randomized exploratory study. *BJU International* 1999;83(6):591–5.

416. Hilton P and Stanton SL. The use of desmopressin (DDAVP) in nocturnal urinary frequency in the female. *British Journal of Urology* 1982;54(3):252–5.

417. Robinson D, Cardozo L, Akeson M, *et al.* Antidiuresis: a new concept in managing female daytime urinary incontinence. *BJU International* 2004;93(7):996–1000.

418. Pedersen PA and Johansen PB. Prophylactic treatment of adult nocturia with bumetanide. *British Journal of Urology* 1988;62(2): 145–7.

419. Mariappan P, Ballantyne Z, N'Dow JMO, Alhasso AA. Serotonin and noradrenaline reuptake inhibitors (SNRI) for stress urinary incontinence in adults. (Cochrane Review). In: *Cochrane Database of Systematic Reviews*, Issue 1, 2006. Oxford: Update Software.

420. Norton PA, Zinner NR, Yalcin I, *et al.* Duloxetine versus placebo in the treatment of stress urinary incontinence. *American Journal of Obstetrics and Gynecology* 2002;187(1):40–8.

421. Millard RJ, Moore K, Rencken R, *et al.* Duloxetine vs placebo in the treatment of stress urinary incontinence: a four-continent randomized clinical trial. *BJU International* 2004;93(3):311–18.

422. Dmochowski RR, Miklos JR, Norton PA, *et al.* Duloxetine versus placebo for the treatment of North American women with stress urinary incontinence. *Journal of Urology* 2003;170(4 Part 1):1259–63.

423. Van Kerrebroeck P, Abrams P, Lange R, *et al.* Duloxetine versus placebo in the treatment of European and Canadian women with stress urinary incontinence. *BJOG: an International Journal of Obstetrics and Gynaecology* 2004;111(3):249–57.

424. Kinchen KS, Obenchain R, Swindle R. Impact of duloxetine on quality of life for women with symptoms of urinary incontinence. *International Urogynecology Journal* 2005;16(5):337–44.

425. Cardozo L, Drutz HP, Baygani SK, *et al.* Pharmacological treatment of women awaiting surgery for stress urinary incontinence. *Obstetrics and Gynecology* 2004;104(3):511–19.

426. Das Gupta R, Caiado M, Bamber L. An evaluation of the cost-effectiveness of duloxetine as a treatment for women with moderate-to-severe stress urinary incontinence. *Journal of Medical Economics* 2006;9:1–25.

427. Moehrer B, Hextall A, Jackson S. Oestrogens for urinary incontinence in women. (Cochrane Review). In: *Cochrane Database of Systematic Reviews*, Issue 2, 2003. Oxford: Update Software.

428. Cardozo L, Lose G, McClish D, *et al.* A systematic review of the effects of estrogens for symptoms suggestive of overactive bladder. *Acta Obstetricia et Gynecologica Scandinavica* 2004;83(10):892–7.

429. Fantl JA, Cardozo L, McClish DK. Estrogen therapy in the management of urinary incontinence in postmenopausal women: a meta-analysis. First report of the Hormones and Urogenital Therapy Committee. *Obstetrics and Gynecology* 1994;83(1):12–18.

430. Al Badr A, Ross S, Soroka D, *et al.* What is the available evidence for hormone replacement therapy in women with stress urinary incontinence? *Journal of Obstetrics and Gynaecology Canada: JOGC* 2003;25(7):567–74.

431. Dessole S, Rubattu G, Ambrosini G, *et al.* Efficacy of low-dose intravaginal estriol on urogenital aging in postmenopausal women. *Menopause* 2004;11(1):49–56.

432. Fantl JA, Bump RC, Robinson D, *et al.* Efficacy of estrogen supplementation in the treatment of urinary incontinence. The Continence Program for Women Research Group. *Obstetrics and Gynecology* 1996;88(5):745–9.

433. Jackson S, Shepherd A, Brookes S, *et al.* The effect of oestrogen supplementation on post-menopausal urinary stress incontinence: a double-blind placebo-controlled trial. *British Journal of Obstetrics and Gynaecology* 1999;106(7):711–18.

434. Wilson PD, Faragher B, Butler B, *et al.* Treatment with oral piperazine oestrone sulphate for genuine stress incontinence in post-menopausal women. *British Journal of Obstetrics and Gynaecology* 1987;94(6):568–74.

435. Cardozo L, Rekers H, Tapp A, *et al.* Oestriol in the treatment of postmenopausal urgency: a multicentre study. *Maturitas* 1993;18(1): 47–53.

436. Lose G and Englev E. Oestradiol-releasing vaginal ring versus oestriol vaginal pessaries in the treatment of bothersome lower urinary tract symptoms. *BJOG: an International Journal of Obstetrics and Gynaecology* 2000;107(8):1029–34.

437. Ouslander JG, Greendale GA, Uman G, *et al.* Effects of oral estrogen and progestin on the lower urinary tract among female nursing home residents. *Journal of the American Geriatrics Society* 2001;49(6):803–7.

438. Rufford J, Hextall A, Cardozo L, *et al.* A double-blind placebo-controlled trial on the effects of 25 mg estradiol implants on the urge syndrome in postmenopausal women. *International Urogynecology Journal* 2003;14(2):78–83.

439. Simunic V, Banovic I, Ciglar S, *et al.* Local estrogen treatment in patients with urogenital symptoms. *International Journal of Gynecology and Obstetrics* 2003;82(2):187–97.

440. Walter S, Wolf H, Barlebo H, *et al.* Urinary incontinence in postmenopausal women treated with oestrogens. *Urologia Internationalis* 1978;33:135–43.

441. Samsioe G, Jansson I, Mellstrom D, *et al.* Occurrence, nature and treatment of urinary incontinence in a 70-year-old female population. *Maturitas* 1985;7(4):335–42.

442. Molander U, Milsom I, Ekelund P, *et al.* Effect of oral oestriol on vaginal flora and cytology and urogenital symptoms in the post-menopause. *Maturitas* 1990;12(2):113–20.

443. Eriksen PS and Rasmussen H. Low-dose 17 beta-estradiol vaginal tablets in the treatment of atrophic vaginitis: a double-blind placebo controlled study. *European Journal of Obstetrics, Gynecology, and Reproductive Biology* 1992;44(2): 137–44.

444. Grady D, Brown JS, Vittinghoff E, *et al.* Postmenopausal hormones and incontinence: the Heart and Estrogen/Progestin Replacement Study. *Obstetrics and Gynecology* 2001;97(1):116–20.

445. Hulley S, Grady D, Bush T, *et al.* Randomized trial of estrogen plus progestin for secondary prevention of coronary heart disease in postmenopausal women. Heart and Estrogen/progestin Replacement Study (HERS) Research Group. *JAMA: the journal of the American Medical Association* 1998;280(7):605–13.

446. Hendrix SL, Cochrane BB, Nygaard IE, *et al.* Effects of estrogen with and without progestin on urinary incontinence. *JAMA: the journal of the American Medical Association* 2005;293(8):935–48.

447. Rossouw JE, Anderson GL, Prentice RL, *et al.* Risks and benefits of estrogen plus progestin in healthy postmenopausal women: principal results From the Women's Health Initiative randomized controlled trial. *JAMA: the journal of the American Medical Association* 2002;288(3):321–33.

448. Anderson GL, Limacher M, Assaf AR, *et al.* Effects of conjugated equine estrogen in postmenopausal women with hysterectomy: the Women's Health Initiative randomized controlled trial. *JAMA: the journal of the American Medical Association* 2004;291(14):1701–12.

449. Goldstein SR, Johnson S, Watts NB, *et al.* Incidence of urinary incontinence in postmenopausal women treated with raloxifene or estrogen. *Menopause* 2005;12(2):160–4.

450. Steinauer JE, Waetjen LE, Vittinghoff E, *et al.* Postmenopausal hormone therapy: does it cause incontinence? *Obstetrics and Gynecology* 2005;106(5 Part 1):940–5.

451. Wagg A and Malone-Lee J. The management of urinary incontinence in the elderly. *British Journal of Urology* 1998;82 Supplement 1:11–17.

452. Lekan-Rutledge D, Doughty D, Moore KN, *et al.* Promoting social continence: products and devices in the management of urinary incontinence. *Urologic Nursing* 2003;23(6):416–29.

453. Tannenbaum C and DuBeau CE. Urinary incontinence in the nursing home: practical approach to evaluation and management. *Clinics in Geriatric Medicine* 2004;20(3):437–52.

454. Holtedahl K, Verelst M, Schiefloe A. A population based, randomized, controlled trial of conservative treatment for urinary incontinence in women. *Acta Obstetricia et Gynecologica Scandinavica* 1998;77(6):671–7.

455. Shekelle PG, Morton SC, Clark KA, *et al.* Systematic review of risk factors for urinary tract infection in adults with spinal cord dysfunction. *Journal of Spinal Cord Medicine* 1999;22(4):258–72.

456. Thyssen H and Lose G. New disposable vaginal device (continence guard) in the treatment of female stress incontinence. Design, efficacy and short term safety. *Acta Obstetricia et Gynecologica Scandinavica* 1996;75(2):170–3.

457. Thyssen H and Lose G. Long-term efficacy and safety of a disposable vaginal device (Continence Guard) in the treatment of female stress incontinence. *International Urogynecology Journal* 1997;8(3):130–3.

458. Thyssen H, Sander P, Lose G. A vaginal device (Continence guard) in the management of urge incontinence in women. *International Urogynecology Journal* 1999;10(4):219–22.

459. Nilsson CG. Effectiveness of the conveen continence guard (a disposable vaginal device) in the treatment of complicated female stress incontinence. *Acta Obstetricia et Gynecologica Scandinavica* 2000;79(12):1052–5.

460. Thyssen H, Bidmead J, Lose G, *et al.* Two disposable intravaginal devices were similarly effective for treatment of stress urinary incontinence. *Evidence-based Obstetrics and Gynecology* 2002;4(3):144–5.

461. Mouritsen L. Effect of vaginal devices on bladder neck mobility in stress incontinent women. *Acta Obstetricia et Gynecologica Scandinavica* 2001;80(5):428–31.

462. Thyssen H, Bidmead J, Lose G, *et al.* A new intravaginal device for stress incontinence in women. *BJU International* 2001;88:889–92.

463. Morris AR and Moore KH. The Contiform incontinence device – efficacy and patient acceptability. *International Urogynecology Journal* 2003;14(6):412–17.

464. Bernier F and Harris L. Treating stress incontinence with the bladder neck support prosthesis. *Urologic Nursing* 1995;15(1):5–9.

465. Versi E, Griffiths DJ, Harvey M-A. A new external urethral occlusive device for female urinary incontinence. *Obstetrics and Gynecology* 1998;92(2):286–91.

466. Tincello DG, Adams EJ, Bolderson J, *et al.* A urinary control device for management of female stress incontinence. *Obstetrics and Gynecology* 2000;95(3):417–20.

467. Bellin P, Smith J, Poll W, *et al.* Results of a multicenter trial of the CapSure (Re/Stor) continence shield on women with stress urinary incontinence. *Urology* 1998;51(5):697–706.

468. Eckford SD, Jackson SR, Lewis PA, *et al.* The continence control pad – A new external urethral occlusion device in the management of stress incontinence. *British Journal of Urology* 1996;77(4):538–40.

469. North BB. A disposable adhesive patch for stress urinary incontinence. *Family Medicine* 1998;30(4):258–64.

470. Brubaker L, Harris T, Gleason D, *et al.* The external urethral barrier for stress incontinence: a multicenter trial of safety and efficacy. Miniguard Investigators Group. *Obstetrics and Gynecology* 1999;93(6):932–7.

471. Bachmann G and Wiita B. External occlusive devices for management of female urinary incontinence. *Journal of Women's Health* 2002;11(9):793–800.

472. Nielsen KK, Kromann-Andersen B, Jacobsen H, *et al.* The urethral plug: A new treatment modality for genuine urinary stress incontinence in women. *Journal of Urology* 1990;144(5):1199–202.

473. Nielsen KK, Walter S, Maegaard E, *et al.* The urethral plug II: An alternative treatment in women with genuine urinary stress incontinence. *British Journal of Urology* 1993;72(4):428–32.

474. Choe JM and Staskin DR. Clinical usefulness of urinary control urethral insert devices. *International Urogynaecology Journal* 1997;8:307–13.

475. Dunn M, Brandt D, Nygaard I. Treatment of exercise incontinence with a urethral insert: a pilot study in women. *Physician and Sportsmedicine* 2002;30(1):45–8.

476. Sand PK, Staskin D, Miller J, *et al.* Effect of a urinary control insert on quality of life in incontinent women. *International Urogynecology Journal* 1999;10(2):100–5.

477. Miller JL and Bavendam T. Treatment with the reliance(TM) urinary control insert: One-year experience. *Journal of Endourology* 1996;10(3):287–92.

478. Robinson H, Schulz J, Flood C, *et al.* A randomized controlled trial of the NEAT expandable tip continence device. *International Urogynecology Journal* 2003;14(3):199–203.

479. Elliott DS and Boone TB. Urethral devices for managing stress urinary incontinence. *Journal of Endourology* 2000;14(1):79–83.

480. Sirls LT, Foote JE, Kaufman JM, *et al.* Long-term results of the FemSoft urethral insert for the management of female stress urinary incontinence. *International Urogynecology Journal* 2002;13(2):88–95.

481. Robert M and Mainprize TC. Long-term assessment of the incontinence ring pessary for the treatment of stress incontinence. *International Urogynecology Journal* 2002;13(5):326–9.

482. Kelly J. Urinary incontinence: alternative therapies that are standard treatment. *Alternative and Complementary Therapies* 1997;3(4):261–8.

483. Ellis N. The effect of acupuncture on nocturnal urinary frequency and incontinence in the elderly. *Complementary Medical Research* 1990;4(1):16–17.

484. Ellis N. A pilot study to evaluate the effect of acupuncture on nocturia in the elderly. *Complementary Therapies in Medicine* 1993;1(3):164–7.

485. Zheng H, Sun Y, Xu Z, *et al.* Flow dynamics of urine in female patients with stress urinary incontinence treated by acupuncture and moxibustion. *International Journal of Clinical Acupuncture* 1992;3(3):243–7.

486. Emmons SL and Otto L. Acupuncture for overactive bladder: a randomized controlled trial. *Obstetrics and Gynecology* 2005;106(1):138–43.

487. Chang PL. Urodynamic studies in acupuncture for women with frequency, urgency and dysuria. *Journal of Urology* 1988;140(3):563–6.

488. Chang PL, Wu CJ, Huang MH. Long-term outcome of acupuncture in women with frequency, urgency and dysuria. *American Journal of Chinese Medicine* 1993;21(3–4):231–6.

489. Philp T, Shah PJR, Worth PHL. Acupuncture in the treatment of bladder instability. *British Journal of Urology* 1988;61(6):490–3.

490. Kubista E, Altmann P, Kucera H, *et al.* Electro-acupuncture's influence on the closure mechanism of the female urethra in incontinence. *American Journal of Chinese Medicine* 1976;4(2):177–81.

491. Bergstrom K, Carlsson CPO, Lindholm C, *et al.* Improvement of urge- and mixed-type incontinence after acupuncture treatment among elderly women – A pilot study. *Journal of the Autonomic Nervous System* 2000;79(2–3):173–80.

492. Freeman RM and Baxby K. Hypnotherapy for incontinence caused by the unstable detrusor. *British Medical Journal* 1982;284(6332):1831–4.

493. Freeman RM. A psychological approach to detrusor instability incontinence in women. *Stress Medicine* 1987;3(1):9–14.

494. Smith N, D'Hooghe V, Duffin S, *et al*. Hypnotherapy for the unstable bladder: four case reports. *Contemporary Hypnosis* 1999;16(2):87–94.

495. Diment AD. Hypnosis in the treatment of urinary incontinence. *Australian Journal of Clinical and Experimental Hypnosis* 1980;8(1):13–20.

496. Steels E, Ryan J, Seipel T, *et al*. Crataeva and equisetum reduce urinary incontinence symptoms. *Australian Continence Journal* 2002;8(3):46–8.

497. Harvey MA. Pelvic floor exercises during and after pregnancy: a systematic review of their role in preventing pelvic floor dysfunction. *Journal of Obstetrics and Gynaecology Canada: JOGC* 2003;25(6):487–98.

498. Hay-Smith J, Herbison P, Morkved S. Physical therapies for prevention of urinary and faecal incontinence in adults. (Cochrane Review). In: *Cochrane Database of Systematic Reviews*, Issue 2, 2002. Oxford: Update Software.

499. Diokno AC, Sampselle CM, Herzog AR, *et al*. Prevention of urinary incontinence by behavioral modification program: a randomized, controlled trial among older women in the community. *Journal of Urology* 2004;171(3):1165–71.

500. Sampselle CM, Messer KL, Seng JS, *et al*. Learning outcomes of a group behavioral modification program to prevent urinary incontinence. *International Urogynecology Journal* 2005;16(6):441–6.

501. Reilly ET, Freeman RM, Waterfield MR, *et al*. Prevention of postpartum stress incontinence in primigravidae with increased bladder neck mobility: a randomised controlled trial of antenatal pelvic floor exercises. *BJOG: an International Journal of Obstetrics and Gynaecology* 2002;109(1):68–76.

502. Sampselle CM, Miller JM, Mims BL, *et al*. Effect of pelvic muscle exercise on transient incontinence during pregnancy and after birth. *Obstetrics and Gynecology* 1998;91(3):406–12.

503. Morkved S, Bo K, Schei B, *et al*. Pelvic floor muscle training during pregnancy to prevent urinary incontinence: A single-blind randomized controlled trial. *Obstetrics and Gynecology* 2003;101(2):313–19.

504. Hughes P and Jackson S. *Influence of Pregnancy and Childbirth on LUT and Colorectal Symptoms and the Effect of Pelvic Floor Exercises*. Thesis. University of Bristol; 2005.

505. King JK and Freeman RM. Is antenatal bladder neck mobility a risk factor for postpartum stress incontinence? *British Journal of Obstetrics and Gynaecology* 1998;105(12):1300–7.

506. Chiarelli P and Cockburn J. Promoting urinary continence in women after delivery: randomised controlled trial. *British Medical Journal* 2002;324(7348):1241–4.

507. Sleep J and Grant A. Pelvic floor exercises in postnatal care. *Midwifery* 1987;3(4):158–64.

508. Morkved S and Bo K. The effect of postpartum pelvic floor muscle exercise in the prevention and treatment of urinary incontinence. *International Urogynecology Journal* 1997;8(4):217–22.

509. Meyer S, Hohlfeld P, Achtari C, *et al*. Pelvic floor education after vaginal delivery. *Obstetrics and Gynecology* 2001;97 (5 Part 1):673–7.

510. Chiarelli P, Murphy B, Cockburn J. Promoting urinary continence in postpartum women: 12-month follow-up data from a randomised controlled trial. *International Urogynecology Journal* 2004;15(2):99–105.

511. Morkved S and Bo K. Effect of postpartum pelvic floor muscle training in prevention and treatment of urinary incontinence: A one-year follow up. *British Journal of Obstetrics and Gynaecology* 2000;107(8):1022–8.

512. Brazzelli M, Murray A, Fraser C. Efficacy and safety of sacral nerve stimulation for urinary urge incontinence: A systematic review. *Journal of Urology* 2006;175(3):835–41.

513. Latini JM, Alipour M, Kreder KJ. Efficacy of sacral neuromodulation for symptomatic treatment of refractory urinary urge incontinence. *Urology* 2006;67(3):550–3.

514. Weil EH, Ruiz-Cerda JL, Eerdmans PH, *et al*. Sacral root neuromodulation in the treatment of refractory urinary urge incontinence: a prospective randomized clinical trial. *European Urology* 2000;37(2):161–71.

515. Schmidt RA, Jonas U, Oleson KA, *et al*. Sacral nerve stimulation for treatment of refractory urinary urge incontinence. Sacral Nerve Stimulation Study Group. *Journal of Urology* 1999;162(2):352–7.

516. Hassouna MM, Siegel SW, Nyeholt AABL, *et al*. Sacral neuromodulation in the treatment of urgency-frequency symptoms: A multicenter study on efficacy and safety. *Journal of Urology* 2000;163(6):1849–54.

517. Siegel SW, Catanzaro F, Dijkema HE, *et al*. Long-term results of a multicenter study on sacral nerve stimulation for treatment of urinary urge incontinence, urgency-frequency, and retention. *Urology*. 2000;56(6 Supplement 1):87–91.

518. Spinelli M, Bertapelle P, Cappellano F, *et al*. Chronic sacral neuromodulation in patients with lower urinary tract symptoms: results from a national register. *Journal of Urology* 2001;166(2):541–5.

519. Everaert K, De RD, Baert L, *et al*. Patient satisfaction and complications following sacral nerve stimulation for urinary retention, urge incontinence and perineal pain: A multicenter evaluation. *International Urogynecology Journal* 2000;11(4):231–6.

520. Grunewald V, Hofner K, Thon WF, *et al*. Sacral electrical neuromodulation as an alternative treatment option for lower urinary tract dysfunction. *Restorative Neurology and Neuroscience* 1999;14(2–3):189–93.

521. Aboseif S, Tamaddon K, Chalfin S, *et al*. Sacral neuromodulation as an effective treatment for refractory pelvic floor dysfunction. *Urology* 2002;60(1):52–6.

522. Bosch JL and Groen J. Sacral nerve neuromodulation in the treatment of patients with refractory motor urge incontinence: long-term results of a prospective longitudinal study. *Journal of Urology* 2000;163(4):1219–22.

523. Cappellano F, Bertapelle P, Spinelli M, *et al*. Quality of life assessment in patients who undergo sacral neuromodulation implantation for urge incontinence: an additional tool for evaluating outcome. *Journal of Urology* 2001;166(6):2277–80.

524. Janknegt RA, Hassouna MM, Siegel SW, *et al*. Long-term effectiveness of sacral nerve stimulation for refractory urge incontinence. *European Urology* 2001;39(1):101–6.

525. Scheepens WA, Van Koeveringe GA, de Bie RA, *et al.* Long-term efficacy and safety results of the two-stage implantation technique in sacral neuromodulation. *BJU International* 2002;90(9):840–5.

526. Shaker HS and Hassouna M. Sacral nerve root neuromodulation: an effective treatment for refractory urge incontinence. *Journal of Urology* 1998;159(5):1516–19.

527. Amundsen CL and Webster GD. Sacral neuromodulation in an older, urge-incontinent population. *American Journal of Obstetrics and Gynecology* 2002;187(6):1462–5.

528. Hedlund H, Schultz A, Talseth T, *et al.* Sacral neuromodulation in Norway: clinical experience of the first three years. *Scandinavian Journal of Urology and Nephrology Supplementum.* 2002;210:87–95.

529. Weil EH, Ruiz-Cerda JL, Eerdmans PH, *et al.* Clinical results of sacral neuromodulation for chronic voiding dysfunction using unilateral sacral foramen electrodes. *World Journal of Urology.* 1998;16(5):313–21.

530. Awad SA, Al-Zahrani HM, Gajewski JB, *et al.* Long-term results and complications of augmentation ileocystoplasty for idiopathic urge incontinence in women. *British Journal of Urology* 1998;81(4):569–73.

531. Hasan ST, Marshall C, Robson WA, *et al.* Clinical outcome and quality of life following enterocystoplasty for idiopathic detrusor instability and neurogenic bladder dysfunction. *British Journal of Urology* 1995;76(5):551–7.

532. Mundy AR and Stephenson TP. 'Clam' ileocystoplasty for the treatment of refractory urge incontinence. *British Journal of Urology* 1985;57(6):641–6.

533. Kockelbergh RC, Tan JBL, Bates CP, *et al.* Clam enterocystoplasty in general urological practice. *British Journal of Urology* 1991;68(1):38–41.

534. Leng WW, Blalock HJ, Fredriksson WH, *et al.* Enterocystoplasty or detrusor myectomy? Comparison of indications and outcomes for bladder augmentation. *Journal of Urology* 1999;161(3):758–63.

535. Edlund C, Peeker R, Fall M. Clam ileocystoplasty: Successful treatment of severe bladder overactivity. *Scandinavian Journal of Urology and Nephrology* 2001;35(3):190–5.

536. Greenwell TJ, Venn SN, Mundy AR. Augmentation cystoplasty. *BJU International* 2001;88(6):511–25.

537. Singh G, Wilkinson JM, Thomas DG. Supravesical diversion for incontinence: a long-term follow-up. *British Journal of Urology.* 1997;79(3):348–53.

538. Cox R and Worth PHL. Ileal loop diversion in women with incurable stress incontinence. *British Journal of Urology* 1987;59(5):420–2.

539. Swami KS, Feneley RCL, Hammonds JC, *et al.* Detrusor myectomy for detrusor overactivity: A minimum 1-year follow-up. *British Journal of Urology* 1998;81(1):68–72.

540. Kumar SP and Abrams PH. Detrusor myectomy: long-term results with a minimum follow-up of 2 years. *BJU International* 2005;96(3):341–4.

541. Rapp DE, Lucioni A, Katz EE, *et al.* Use of botulinum-A toxin for the treatment of refractory overactive bladder symptoms: An initial experience. *Urology* 2004;63(6):1071–5.

542. Kuo H-C. Clinical effects of suburothelial injection of botulinum A toxin on patients with nonneurogenic detrusor overactivity refractory to anticholinergics. *Urology* 2005;66(1):94–8.

543. Schulte-Baukloh H, Weiss C, Stolze T, *et al.* Botulinum-A toxin detrusor and sphincter injection in treatment of overactive bladder syndrome: objective outcome and patient satisfaction. *European Urology* 2005;48(6):984–90.

544. Schulte-Baukloh H, Weiss C, Stolze T, *et al.* Botulinum-A toxin for treatment of overactive bladder without detrusor overactivity: Urodynamic outcome and patient satisfaction. *Urology* 2005;66(1):82–7.

545. Flynn MK, Webster GD, Amundsen CL. The effect of botulinum-A toxin on patients with severe urge urinary incontinence. *Journal of Urology* 2004;172(6 Part 1):2316–20.

546. Werner M, Schmid DM, Schussler B. Efficacy of botulinum-A toxin in the treatment of detrusor overactivity incontinence: a prospective nonrandomized study. *American Journal of Obstetrics and Gynecology* 2005;192(5):1735–40.

547. Rajkumar GN, Small DR, Mustafa AW, *et al.* A prospective study to evaluate the safety, tolerability, efficacy and durability of response of intravesical injection of botulinum toxin type A into detrusor muscle in patients with refractory idiopathic detrusor overactivity. *BJU International* 2005;96(6):848–52.

548. Ghei M, Maraj BH, Miller R, *et al.* Effects of botulinum toxin B on refractory detrusor overactivity: a randomized, double-blind, placebo controlled, crossover trial. *Journal of Urology* 2005;174(5):1873–7.

549. Dykstra D, Enriquez A, Valley M. Treatment of overactive bladder with botulinum toxin type B: A pilot study. *International Urogynecology Journal* 2003;14(6):424–6.

550. Palma PC, Thiel M, Riccetto CL, *et al.* Resiniferatoxin for detrusor instability refractory to anticholinergics. *International Braz J Urol* 2004;30(1):53–8.

551. Kuo HC. Effectiveness of intravesical resiniferatoxin for anticholinergic treatment refractory detrusor overactivity due to nonspinal cord lesions. *Journal of Urology* 2003;170(3):835–9.

552. Abrams P, Hilton P, Lucas M, *et al.* A proposal for a new classification for operative procedures for stress urinary incontinence. *BJU International* 2005;96(3):232–3.

553. Department of Health. Hospital Episode Statistics [www.hesonline.nhs.uk].

554. Pickard R, Reaper J, Wyness L, Cody DJ, McClinton S, N'Dow J. Periurethral injection therapy for urinary incontinence in women. (Cochrane Review). In: *Cochrane Database of Systematic Reviews*, Issue 2, 2003. Oxford: Update Software.

555. ter Meulen PH, Berghmans LC, and van Kerrebroeck PE. Systematic review: efficacy of silicone microimplants (Macroplastique) therapy for stress urinary incontinence in adult women. *European Urology* 2003;44(5):573–82.

556. Bano F, Barrington JW, Dyer R. Comparison between porcine dermal implant (Permacol) and silicone injection (Macroplastique) for urodynamic stress incontinence. *International Urogynecology Journal* 2005;16(2):147–50.

557. Maher CF, O'Reilly BA, Dwyer PL, et al. Pubovaginal sling versus transurethral Macroplastique for stress urinary incontinence and intrinsic sphincter deficiency: A prospective randomised controlled trial. *BJOG: an International Journal of Obstetrics and Gynaecology* 2005;112(6):797–801.

558. Andersen RC. Long-term follow-up comparison of Durasphere and Contigen in the treatment of stress urinary incontinence. *Journal of Lower Genital Tract Disease* 2002;6(4):239–43.

559. Lightner D, Calvosa C, Andersen R, et al. A new injectable bulking agent for treatment of stress urinary incontinence: Results of a multicenter, randomized, controlled, double-blind study of Durasphere. *Urology* 2001;58(1):12–15.

560. Corcos J, Collet JP, Shapiro S, et al. Multicenter randomized clinical trial comparing surgery and collagen injections for treatment of female stress urinary incontinence. *Urology* 2005;65(5):898–904.

561. Lee PE, Kung RC, Drutz HP. Periurethral autologous fat injection as treatment for female stress urinary incontinence: a randomized double-blind controlled trial. *Journal of Urology* 2001;165(1):153–8.

562. Chrouser KL, Fick F, Goel A, et al. Carbon coated zirconium beads in beta-glucan gel and bovine glutaraldehyde cross-linked collagen injections for intrinsic sphincter deficiency: Continence and satisfaction after extended followup. *Journal of Urology* 2004;171(3):1152–5.

563. Haab F, Zimmern PE, Leach GE. Urinary stress incontinence due to intrinsic sphincteric deficiency: experience with fat and collagen periurethral injections.[erratum appears in J Urol 1997 Jul;158(1):188]. *Journal of Urology* 1997;157(4):1283–6.

564. Faerber GJ, Belville WD, Ohl DA, et al. Comparison of transurethral versus periurethral collagen injection in women with intrinsic sphincter deficiency. *Techniques in Urology* 1998;4(3):124–7.

565. Schulz JA, Nager CW, Stanton SL, et al. Bulking agents for stress urinary incontinence: Short-term results and complications in a randomized comparison of periurethral and transurethral injections. *International Urogynecology Journal* 2004;15(4):261–5.

566. Henalla SM, Hall V, Duckett JR, et al. A multicentre evaluation of a new surgical technique for urethral bulking in the treatment of genuine stress incontinence. *BJOG: an International Journal of Obstetrics and Gynaecology* 2000;107(8):1035–9.

567. Usman F and Henalla S. A single transurethral Macroplastique(TM) injection as primary treatment for stress incontinence in women. *Journal of Obstetrics and Gynaecology* 1998;18(1):56–60.

568. Gurdal M, Tekin A, Erdogan K, et al. Endoscopic silicone injection for female stress urinary incontinence due to intrinsic sphincter deficiency: Impact of coexisting urethral mobility on treatment outcome. *Urology* 2002;60(6):1016–19.

569. Sheriff MK, Foley S, McFarlane J, et al. Endoscopic correction of intractable stress incontinence with silicone micro-implants. *European Urology* 1997;32(3):284–8.

570. Radley SC, Chapple CR, Mitsogiannis IC, et al. Transurethral implantation of Macroplastique for the treatment of female stress urinary incontinence secondary to urethral sphincter deficiency. *European Urology* 2001;39(4):383–9.

571. Tamanini JT, D'Ancona CA, Tadini V, et al. Macroplastique implantation system for the treatment of female stress urinary incontinence. *Journal of Urology* 2003;169(6):2229–33.

572. Tamanini JT, D'Ancona CA, Netto NR Jr. Treatment of intrinsic sphincter deficiency using the Macroplastique Implantation System: two-year follow-up. *Journal of Endourology* 2004;18(9):906–11.

573. Barranger E, Fritel X, Kadoch O, et al. Results of transurethral injection of silicone micro-implants for females with intrinsic sphincter deficiency. *Journal of Urology* 2000;164(5):1619–22.

574. Koelbl H, Saz V, Doerfler D, et al. Transurethral injection of silicone microimplants for intrinsic urethral sphincter deficiency. *Obstetrics and Gynecology* 1998;92(3):332–6.

575. Harriss DR, Iacovou JW, Lemberger RJ, et al. Peri-urethral silicone microimplants (Macroplastique(TM)) for the treatment of genuine stress incontinence. *British Journal of Urology* 1996;78(5):722–8.

576. Richardson TD, Kennelly MJ, Faerber GJ. Endoscopic injection of glutaraldehyde cross-linked collagen for the treatment of intrinsic sphincter deficiency in women. *Urology* 1995;46(3):378–81.

577. Cross CA, English SF, Cespedes RD, et al. A followup on transurethral collagen injection therapy for urinary incontinence. *Journal of Urology* 1998;159(1):106–8.

578. Khullar V, Cardozo LD, Abbott D, et al. GAX collagen in the treatment of urinary incontinence in elderly women: A two year follow up. *British Journal of Obstetrics and Gynaecology* 1997;104(1):96–9.

579. Bent AE, Foote J, Siegel S, et al. Collagen implant for treating stress urinary incontinence in women with urethral hypermobility. *Journal of Urology* 2001;166(4):1354–7.

580. Monga AK, Robinson D, Stanton SL. Periurethral collagen injections for genuine stress incontinence: A 2-year follow-up. *British Journal of Urology* 1995;76(2):156–60.

581. Stanton SL and Monga AK. Incontinence in elderly women: Is periurethral collagen an advance? *British Journal of Obstetrics and Gynaecology* 1997;104(2):154–7.

582. Gorton E, Stanton S, Monga A, et al. Periurethral collagen injection: A long-term follow-up study. *BJU International* 1999;84(9):966–71.

583. Corcos J and Fournier C. Periurethral collagen injection for the treatment of female stress urinary incontinence: 4-year follow-up results. *Urology* 1999;54(5):815–18.

584. Herschorn S, Steele DJ, Radomski SB. Followup of intraurethral collagen for female stress urinary incontinence. *Journal of Urology* 1996;156(4):1305–9.

585. Herschorn S and Radomski SB. Collagen injections for genuine stress urinary incontinence: Patient selection and durability. *International Urogynecology Journal* 1997;8(1):18–24.

586. Winters JC, Chiverton A, Scarpero HM, et al. Collagen injection therapy in elderly women: Long-term results and patient satisfaction. *Urology* 2000;55(6):856–60.

587. Stricker P and Haylen B. Injectable collagen for type 3 female stress incontinence: The first 50 Australian patients. *Medical Journal of Australia* 1993;158(2):89–91.

588. Homma Y, Kawabe K, Kageyama S, *et al.* Injection of glutaraldehyde cross-linked collagen for urinary incontinence: two-year efficacy by self-assessment. *International Journal of Urology* 1996;3(2):124–7.

589. Elsergany R, Elgamasy A-N, Ghoniem GM. Transurethral collagen injection for female stress incontinence. *International Urogynecology Journal* 1998;9(1):13–18.

590. Tschopp PJ, Wesley-James T, Spekkens A, *et al.* Collagen injections for urinary stress incontinence in a small urban urology practice: Time to failure analysis of 99 cases. *Journal of Urology* 1999;162(3 Part 1):779–83.

591. Swami S, Batista JE, Abrams P. Collagen for female genuine stress incontinence after a minimum 2-year follow-up. *British Journal of Urology* 1997;80(5):757–61.

592. Stothers L, Goldenberg SL, Leone EF. Complications of periurethral collagen injection for stress urinary incontinence. *Journal of Urology* 1998;159(3):806–7.

593. Smith DN, Appell RA, Winters JC, *et al.* Collagen injection therapy for female intrinsic sphincteric deficiency. *Journal of Urology* 1997;157(4):1275–8.

594. Ang LP, Tay KP, Lim PH, *et al.* Endoscopic injection of collagen for the treatment of female urinary stress incontinence. *International Journal of Urology* 1997;4(3):254–8.

595. Stenberg A, Larsson G, Johnson P, *et al.* DiHA Dextran Copolymer, a new biocompatible material for endoscopic treatment of stress incontinent women. Short term results. *Acta Obstetricia et Gynecologica Scandinavica* 1999;78(5):436–42.

596. Stenberg AM, Larsson G, Johnson P. Urethral injection for stress urinary incontinence: Long-term results with dextranomer/hyaluronic acid copolymer. *International Urogynecology Journal* 2003;14(5):335–8.

597. Van Kerrebroeck P., Ter MF, Larsson G, *et al.* Treatment of stress urinary incontinence using a copolymer system: Impact on quality of life. *BJU International* 2004;94(7):1040–3.

598. Van Kerrebroeck P., Ter MF, Larsson G, *et al.* Efficacy and safety of a novel system (NASHA/Dx copolymer using the Implacer device) for treatment of stress urinary incontinence. *Urology* 2004;64(2):276–81.

599. Chapple CR, Haab F, Cervigni M, *et al.* An open, multicentre study of NASHA/Dx Gel (Zuidex) for the treatment of stress urinary incontinence. *European Urology* 2005;48(3):488–94.

600. Pannek J, Brands FH, Senge T. Particle migration after transurethral injection of carbon coated beads for stress urinary incontinence. *Journal of Urology* 2001;166(4):1350–3.

601. Madjar S, Covington-Nichols C, Secrest CL. New periurethral bulking agent for stress urinary incontinence: Modified technique and early results. *Journal of Urology* 2003;170(6 Part 1):2327–9.

602. Schulman CC, Simon J, Wespes E, *et al.* Endoscopic injection of teflon for female urinary incontinence. *European Urology* 1983;9(4):246–7.

603. Beckingham IJ, Wemyss-Holden G, Lawrence WT. Long-term follow-up of women treated with perurethral Teflon injections for stress incontinence. *British Journal of Urology* 1992;69(6):580–3.

604. Deane AM, English P, Hehir M. Teflon injection in stress incontinence. *British Journal of Urology* 1985;57(1):78–80.

605. Vesey SG, Rivett A, O'Boyle PJ. Teflon injection in female stress incontinence. Effect on urethral pressure profile and flow rate. *British Journal of Urology* 1988;62(1):39–41.

606. Harrison SC, Brown C, O'Boyle PJ. Periurethral Teflon for stress urinary incontinence: medium-term results. *British Journal of Urology* 1993;71(1):25–7.

607. Kiilholma P and Makinen J. Disappointing effect of endoscopic teflon injection for female stress incontinence. *European Urology* 1991;20(3):197–9.

608. Mayer R, Lightfoot M, Jung I. Preliminary evaluation of calcium hydroxylapatite as a transurethral bulking agent for stress urinary incontinence. *Urology* 2001;57(3):434–8.

609. Costa P, Mottet N, Rabut B, *et al.* The use of an artificial urinary sphincter in women with type III incontinence and a negative Marshall test. *Journal of Urology* 2001;165(4):1172–6.

610. Diokno AC, Hollander JB, Alderson TP. Artificial urinary sphincter for recurrent female urinary incontinence: Indications and results. *Journal of Urology* 1987;138(4):778–80.

611. Webster GD, Perez LM, Khoury JM, *et al.* Management of type III stress urinary incontinence using artificial urinary sphincter. *Urology* 1992;39(6):499–503.

612. Appell RA. Techniques and results in the implantation of the artificial urinary sphincter in women with type III stress urinary incontinence by a vaginal approach. *Neurourology and Urodynamics.* 1988;7(6):613–19.

613. Light JK and Scott FB. Management of urinary incontinence in women with the artificial urinary sphincter. *Journal of Urology* 1985;134(3):476–8.

614. Petero VG Jr and Diokno AC. Comparison of the long-term outcomes between incontinent men and women treated with artificial urinary sphincter. *Journal of Urology* 2006;175(2):605–9.

615. Amid PK. Classification of biomaterials and their related complications in abdominal wall surgery. *Hernia* 1997;1(1):15–21.

616. Lapitan MC, Cody DJ, Grant AM. Open retropubic colposuspension for urinary incontinence in women. (Cochrane Review). In: *Cochrane Database of Systematic Reviews*, Issue 3, 2005. Oxford: Update Software.

617. Moehrer B, Ellis G, Carey M, Wilson PD. Laparoscopic colposuspension for urinary incontinence in women. (Cochrane Review). In: *Cochrane Database of Systematic Reviews*, Issue 1, 2002. Oxford: Update Software.

618. Moehrer B, Carey M, Wilson D. Laparoscopic colposuspension: a systematic review. *BJOG: an International Journal of Obstetrics and Gynaecology* 2003;110(3):230–5.

619. Glazener CM and Cooper K. Bladder neck needle suspension for urinary incontinence in women. (Cochrane Review). In: *Cochrane Database of Systematic Reviews*, Issue 2, 2004. Oxford: Update Software.

620. Glazener CM and Cooper K. Anterior vaginal repair for urinary incontinence in women. (Cochrane Review). In: *Cochrane Database of Systematic Reviews*, Issue 1, 2001. Oxford: Update Software.

621. Black NA, Downs SH, Hilton P. The effectiveness of surgery for stress incontinence in women: A systematic review. *British Journal of Urology* 1996;78(4):497–510.

622. Leach GE, Dmochowski RR, Appell RA, *et al.* Female Stress Urinary Incontinence Clinical Guidelines Panel summary report on surgical management of female stress urinary incontinence. The American Urological Association. *Journal of Urology* 1997;158 (3 Part 1):875–80.

623. Jarvis GJ. Surgery for genuine stress incontinence. *British Journal of Obstetrics and Gynaecology* 1994;101(5):371–4.

624. Ankardal M, Milsom I, Stjerndahl J-H, *et al.* A three-armed randomized trial comparing open Burch colposuspension using sutures with laparoscopic colposuspension using sutures and laparoscopic colposuspension using mesh and staples in women with stress urinary incontinence. *Acta Obstetricia et Gynecologica Scandinavica* 2005;84(8):773–9.

625. Fatthy H, El HM, Samaha I, *et al.* Modified Burch colposuspension: Laparoscopy versus laparotomy. *Journal of the American Association of Gynecologic Laparoscopists* 2001;8(1):99–106.

626. Cheon WC, Mak JHL, Liu JYS. Prospective randomised controlled trial comparing laparoscopic and open colposuspension. *Hong Kong Medical Journal* 2003;9(1):10–14.

627. Ustun Y, Engin-Ustun Y, Gungor M, *et al.* Randomized comparison of Burch urethropexy procedures concomitant with gynecologic operations. *Gynecologic and Obstetric Investigation* 2005;59(1):19–23.

628. Su TH, Wang KG, Hsu CY, *et al.* Prospective comparison of laparoscopic and traditional colposuspensions in the treatment of genuine stress incontinence. *Acta Obstetricia et Gynecologica Scandinavica* 1997;76(6):576–82.

629. Kitchener HC, Dunn G, Lawton V, *et al.* Laparoscopic versus open colposuspension – results of a prospective randomised controlled trial. *BJOG* 2006;113:1007–13.

630. Persson J and Wolner-Hanssen P. Laparoscopic Burch colposuspension for stress urinary incontinence: A randomized comparison of one or two sutures on each side of the urethra. *Obstetrics and Gynecology* 2000;95(1):151–5.

631. Ross J. Two techniques of laparoscopic Burch repair for stress incontinence: a prospective, randomized study. *Journal of the American Association of Gynecologic Laparoscopists* 1996;3(3):351–7.

632. Piccione F, Zullo F, Palomba S, *et al.* Different techniques of laparoscopic Burch colposuspension. *Italian Journal of Gynaecology and Obstetrics* 2001;13(1):10–13.

633. Zullo F, Palomba S, Piccione F, *et al.* Laparoscopic burch colposuspension: A randomized controlled trial comparing two transperitoneal surgical techniques. *Obstetrics and Gynecology* 2001;98(5):783–8.

634. Zullo F, Morelli M, Russo T, *et al.* Two techniques of laparoscopic retropubic urethropexy. *Journal of the American Association of Gynecologic Laparoscopists* 2002;9(2):178–81.

635. Zullo F, Palomba S, Russo T, *et al.* Laparoscopic colposuspension using sutures or prolene meshes: a 3-year follow-up. *European Journal of Obstetrics, Gynecology, and Reproductive Biology* 2004;117(2):201–3.

636. McCrery RJ and Thompson PK. Outcomes of urethropexy added to paravaginal defect repair: A randomized trial of Burch versus Marshall-Marchetti-Krantz. *Journal of Pelvic Medicine and Surgery* 2005;11(3):137–43.

637. Colombo M, Scalambrino S, Maggioni A, *et al.* Burch colposuspension versus modified Marshall-Marchetti-Krantz urethropexy for primary genuine stress urinary incontinence: A prospective, randomized clinical trial. *American Journal of Obstetrics and Gynecology* 1994;171(6):1573–9.

638. Quadri G, Magatti F, Belloni C, *et al.* Marshall-Marchetti-Krantz urethropexy and Burch colposuspension for stress urinary incontinence in women with low pressure and hypermobility of the urethra: Early results of a prospective randomized clinical trial. *American Journal of Obstetrics and Gynecology* 1999;181(1):12–18.

639. Liapis AE, Asimiadis V, Loghis CD, *et al.* A randomized prospective study of three operative methods for genuine stress incontinence. *Journal of Gynecologic Surgery* 1996;12(1):7–14.

640. Colombo M, Vitobello D, Proietti F, *et al.* Randomised comparison of Burch colposuspension versus anterior colporrhaphy in women with stress urinary incontinence and anterior vaginal wall prolapse. *BJOG: an International Journal of Obstetrics and Gynaecology* 2000;107(4):544–51.

641. Kammerer-Doak DN, Dorin MH, Rogers RG, *et al.* A randomized trial of burch retropubic urethropexy and anterior colporrhaphy for stress urinary incontinence. *Obstetrics and Gynecology* 1999;93(1):75–8.

642. Bergman A, Koonings PP, Ballard CA. Primary stress urinary incontinence and pelvic relaxation: Prospective randomized comparison of three differnt operations. *American Journal of Obstetrics and Gynecology* 1989;161(1):97–101.

643. Klutke JJ, Klutke CG, Bergman J, *et al.* Urodynamics changes in voiding after anti-incontinence surgery: an insight into the mechanism of cure. *Urology* 1999;54(6):1003–7.

644. Bergman A, Ballard CA, Koonings PP. Comparison of three different surgical procedures for genuine stress incontinence: Prospective randomized study. *American Journal of Obstetrics and Gynecology* 1989;160(5 Part 1):1102–6.

645. Bergman A and Elia G. Three surgical procedures for genuine stress incontinence: Five-year follow-up of a prospective randomized study. *American Journal of Obstetrics and Gynecology* 1995;173(1):66–71.

646. Athanassopoulos A and Barbalias G. Burch colposuspension versus Stamey endoscopic bladder neck suspension: A urodynamic appraisal. *Urologia Internationalis* 1996;56(1):23–7.

647. Mundy AR. A trial comparing the stamey bladder neck suspension procedure with colposuspension for the treatment of stress incontinence. *British Journal of Urology* 1983;55(6):687–90.

648. Gilja I, Puskar D, Mazuran B, *et al.* Comparative analysis of bladder neck suspension using Raz, Burch and transvaginal Burch procedures. A 3-year randomized prospective study. *European Urology* 1998;33(3):298–302.

649. German KA, Kynaston H, Weight S, *et al.* A prospective randomized trial comparing a modified needle suspension procedure with the vagina/obturator shelf procedure for genuine stress incontinence. *British Journal of Urology* 1994;74(2):188–90.

650. Palma PC, Soffiatti SA, Almeida SC, *et al.* Stress urinary incontinence: a comparative study of surgical treatment by the Marshall-Marchetti-Krantz technique with endoscopic suspension of the bladder neck. Second report. *Asia-Oceania Journal of Obstetrics and Gynaecology* 1988;14(1):31–6.

651. Colombo M, Milani R, Vitobello D, *et al.* A randomized comparison of Burch colposuspension and abdominal paravaginal defect repair for female stress urinary incontinence. *American Journal of Obstetrics and Gynecology* 1996;175(1):78–84.

652. Berglund AL and Lalos O. The pre- and postsurgical nursing of women with stress incontinence. *Journal of Advanced Nursing* 1996;23(3):502–11.

653. Berglund AL, Eisemann M, Lalos A, *et al.* Predictive factors of the outcome of primary surgical treatment of stress incontinence in women. *Scandinavian Journal of Urology and Nephrology* 1997;31(1):49–55.

654. Lalos O, Berglund A-L, Bjerle P. The long-term outcome of retropubic urethrocystopexy (sutures and fibrin sealant) and pubococcygeal repair. *Acta Obstetricia et Gynecologica Scandinavica* 2000;79(2):135–9.

655. Di Palumbo V. Four-corner bladder and urethral retropubic suspension versus anterior colporrhaphy in the correction of stress urinary incontinence with urethrocystocele 3-4. Randomized clinical trial. *Urogynaecologia International Journal* 2003;17(2): 57–68.

656. Hilton P. A clinical and urodynamic study comparison the Stamey bladder neck suspension and suburethral sling procedures in the treatment of genuine stress incontinence. *British Journal of Obstetrics and Gynaecology* 1989;96(2):213–20.

657. Enzelsberger H, Helmer H, Schatten C. Comparison of Burch and Lyodura sling procedures for repair of unsuccessful incontinence surgery. *Obstetrics and Gynecology* 1996;88(2):251–6.

658. Bai SW, Sohn WH, Chung DJ, *et al.* Comparison of the efficacy of Burch colposuspension, pubovaginal sling, and tension-free vaginal tape for stress urinary incontinence. *International Journal of Gynaecology and Obstetrics* 2005;91(3):246–51.

659. Ward K, Hilton P, United Kingdom and Ireland Tension-free Vaginal Tape Trial Group. Prospective multicentre randomised trial of tension-free vaginal tape and colposuspension as primary treatment for stress incontinence. *British Medical Journal* 2002;325(7355):67–73.

660. Ward KL and Hilton P. A prospective multicenter randomized trial of tension-free vaginal tape and colposuspension for primary urodynamic stress incontinence: Two-year follow-up. *American Journal of Obstetrics and Gynecology* 2004;190(2):324–31.

661. Liapis A, Bakas P, Creatsas G. Burch colposuspension and tension-free vaginal tape in the management of stress urinary incontinence in women. *European Urology* 2002;41(4):469–73.

662. Wang AC and Chen M-C. Comparison of tension-free vaginal taping versus modified Burch colposuspension on urethral obstruction: A randomized controlled trial. *Neurourology and Urodynamics* 2003;22(3):185–90.

663. El-Barky E, El-Shazly A, El-Wahab OA, *et al.* Tension free vaginal tape versus Burch colposuspension for treatment of female stress urinary incontinence. *International Urology and Nephrology* 2005;37(2):277–81.

664. Valpas A, Kivela A, Penttinen J, *et al.* Tension-free vaginal tape and laparoscopic mesh colposuspension for stress urinary incontinence. *Obstetrics and Gynecology* 2004;104(1):42–9.

665. Valpas A, Kivela A, Penttinen J, *et al.* Tension-free vaginal tape and laparoscopic mesh colposuspension in the treatment of stress urinary incontinence: immediate outcome and complications–a randomized clinical trial. *Acta Obstetricia et Gynecologica Scandinavica* 2003;82(7):665–71.

666. Paraiso MF, Walters MD, Karram MM, *et al.* Laparoscopic Burch colposuspension versus tension-free vaginal tape: a randomized trial. *Obstetrics and Gynecology* 2004;104(6):1249–58.

667. Ustun Y, Engin-Ustun Y, Gungor M, *et al.* Tension-free vaginal tape compared with laparoscopic Burch urethropexy. *Journal of the American Association of Gynecologic Laparoscopists* 2003;10(3):386–9.

668. Sand PK, Winkler H, Blackhurst DW, *et al.* A prospective randomized study comparing modified Burch retropubic urethropexy and suburethral sling for treatment of genuine stress incontinence with low-pressure urethra. *American Journal of Obstetrics and Gynecology* 2000;182(1 Part 1):30–4.

669. Culligan PJ, Goldberg RP, Sand PK. A randomized controlled trial comparing a modified Burch procedure and a suburethral sling: Long-term follow-up. *International Urogynecology Journal* 2003;14(4):229–33.

670. Tamussino KF, Zivkovic F, Pieber D, *et al.* Five-year results after anti-incontinence operations. *American Journal of Obstetrics and Gynecology* 1999;181(6):1347–52.

671. Cosiski Marana HR, Moreira de AJ, Matheus de SM, *et al.* Evaluation of long-term results of surgical correction of stress urinary incontinence. *Gynecologic and Obstetric Investigation* 1996;41(3):214–19.

672. van Geelen JM, Theeuwes AGM, Eskes TKAB, *et al.* The clinical and urodynamic effects of anterior vaginal repair and Burch colposuspension. *American Journal of Obstetrics and Gynecology* 1988;159(1):137–44.

673. Demirci F, Yildirim U, Demirci E, *et al.* Ten-year results of Marshall Marchetti Krantz and anterior colporraphy procedures. *Australian and New Zealand Journal of Obstetrics and Gynaecology* 2002;42(5):513–14.

674. Park GS and Miller Jr EJ. Surgical treatment of stress urinary incontinence: A comparison of the Kelly plication, Marshall-Marchetti-Krantz, and Pereyra procedures. *Obstetrics and Gynecology* 1988;71(4):575–9.

675. Luna MT, Hirakawa T, Kamura T, *et al.* Comparison of the anterior colporrhaphy procedure and the Marshall-Marchetti-Krantz operation in the treatment of stress urinary incontinence among women. *Journal of Obstetrics and Gynaecology Research* 1999;25(4): 255–60.

676. Giberti C, Pacella M, Banchero R, *et al.* Needle suprapubic urethropexy (Npu) versus retropubic urethropexy (Rpu) for the treatment of female stress urinary incontinence. *Acta Urologica Italica* 1995;9(2):81–4.

677. Christensen H, Laybourn C, Eickhoff JH, *et al.* Long-term results of the stamey bladder-neck suspension procedure and of the burch colposuspension. *Scandinavian Journal of Urology and Nephrology* 1997;31(4):349–53.

678. Wang AC. Burch colposuspension vs. Stamey bladder neck suspension. A comparison of complications with special emphasis on detrusor instability and voiding dysfunction. *Journal of Reproductive Medicine* 1996;41(7):529–33.

679. Riggs JA. Retropubic cystourethropexy: A review of two operative procedures with long-term follow-up. *Obstetrics and Gynecology* 1986;68(1):98–105.

680. Spencer JR, O'Conor J, V, Schaeffer AJ. A comparison of endoscopic suspension of the vesical neck with suprapubic vesicourethropexy for treatment of stress urinary incontinence. *Journal of Urology* 1987;137(3):411–15.

681. Clemens JQ, Stern JA, Bushman WA, *et al.* Long-term results of the Stamey bladder neck suspension: Direct comparison with the Marshall-Marchetti-Krantz procedure. *Journal of Urology* 1998;160(2):372–6.

682. Alcalay M, Monga A, Stanton SL. Burch colposuspension: a 10-20 year follow up. *British Journal of Obstetrics and Gynaecology* 1995;102(9):740–5.

683. Herbertsson G and Iosif CS. Surgical results and urodynamic studies 10 years after retropubic colpourethrocystopexy. *Acta Obstetricia et Gynecologica Scandinavica* 1993;72(4):298–301.

684. Ladwig D, Miljkovic-Petkovic L, Hewson AD. Simplified colposuspension: A 15-year follow-up. *Australian and New Zealand Journal of Obstetrics and Gynaecology* 2004;44(1):39–45.

685. Eriksen BC, Hagen B, Eik-Nes SH, *et al.* Long-term effectiveness of the Burch colposuspension in female urinary stress incontinence. *Acta Obstetricia et Gynecologica Scandinavica* 1990;69(1):45–50.

686. Kiilholma P, Makinen J, Chancellor MB, *et al.* Modified Burch colposuspension for stress urinary incontinence in females. *Surgery, Gynecology and Obstetrics* 1993;176(2):111–15.

687. Akpinar H, Cetinel B, Demirkesen O, *et al.* Long-term results of Burch colposuspension. *International Journal of Urology* 2000;7(4):119–25.

688. Feyereisl J, Dreher E, Haenggi W, *et al.* Long-term results after Burch colposuspension. *American Journal of Obstetrics and Gynecology* 1994;171(3):647–52.

689. Kjolhede P. Long-term efficacy of Burch colposuspension: A 14-year follow-up study. *Acta Obstetricia et Gynecologica Scandinavica* 2005;84(8):767–72.

690. Kjolhede P, Wahlstrom J, Wingren G. Pelvic floor dysfunction after Burch colposuspension – A comprehensive study. Part II. *Acta Obstetricia et Gynecologica Scandinavica* 2005;84(9):902–8.

691. Kjolhede P, Wahlstrom J, Wingren G. Pelvic floor dysfunction after Burch colposuspension – A comprehensive study. Part I. *Acta Obstetricia et Gynecologica Scandinavica* 2005;84(9):894–901.

692. Langer R, Lipshitz Y, Halperin R, *et al.* Long-Term (10–15 years) follow-up after Burch colposuspension for urinary stress incontinence. *International Urogynecology Journal* 2001;12(5):323–6.

693. Burch JC. Cooper's ligament urethrovesical suspension for stress incontinence. Nine years' experience–results, complications, technique. *American Journal of Obstetrics and Gynecology* 1968;100(6):764–74.

694. Galloway NT, Davies N, Stephenson TP. The complications of colposuspension. *British Journal of Urology* 1987;60(2):122–4.

695. Lim PH, Brown AD, Chisholm GD. The Burch Colposuspension operation for stress urinary incontinence. *Singapore Medical Journal* 1990;31(3):242–6.

696. Kinn AC. Burch colposuspension for stress urinary incontinence. 5-year results in 153 women. *Scandinavian Journal of Urology and Nephrology* 1995;29(4):449–55.

697. Ou CS and Rowbotham R. Five-year follow-up of laparoscopic bladder neck suspension using synthetic mesh and surgical staples. *Journal of Laparoendoscopic and Advanced Surgical Techniques-Part A* 1999;9(3):249–52.

698. Ou CS, Presthus J, Beadle E. Laparoscopic bladder neck suspension using hernia mesh and surgical staples. *Journal of Laparoendoscopic Surgery* 1993;3(6):563–6.

699. Ross JW. Multichannel urodynamic evaluation of laparoscopic Burch colposuspension for genuine stress incontinence. *Obstetrics and Gynecology* 1998;91(1):55–9.

700. Briel RC. Follow-up of a new modification of the Marshall-Marchetti-Krantz (MMK) procedure. *Archives of Gynecology* 1986;239(1):1–9.

701. Zorzos I and Paterson PJ. Quality of life after a Marshall-Marchetti-Krantz procedure for stress urinary incontinence. *Journal of Urology* 1996;155(1):259–62.

702. Czaplicki M, Dobronski P, Torz C, *et al.* Long-term subjective results of Marshall-Marchetti-Krantz procedure. *European Urology* 1998;34(2):118–23.

703. Raz S, Sussman EM, Erickson DB, *et al.* The Raz bladder neck suspension: Results in 206 patients. *Journal of Urology* 1992;148(3 Part 1):845–50.

704. Korman HJ, Sirls LT, Kirkemo AK. Success rate of modified Pereyra bladder neck suspension determined by outcomes analysis. *Journal of Urology* 1994;152(5 Part 1):1453–7.

705. Sirls LT, Keoleian CM, Korman HJ, *et al.* The effect of study methodology on reported success rates of the modified Pereyra bladder neck suspension. *Journal of Urology* 1995;154(5):1732–5.

706. Gilja I. Tansvaginal needle suspension operation: the way we do it. Clinical and urodynamic study: long-term results. *European Urology* 2000;37(3):325–30.

707. Kelly MJ, Knielsen K, Bruskewitz R, *et al.* Symptom analysis of patients undergoing modified Pereyra bladder neck suspension for stress urinary incontinence. Pre- and postoperative findings. *Urology* 1991;37(3):213–19.

708. Elkabir JJ and Mee AD. Long-term evaluation of the Gittes procedure for urinary stress incontinence. *Journal of Urology* 1998;159(4):1203–5.

709. Takahashi S, Miyao N, Hisataki T, *et al.* Complications of Stamey needle suspension for female stress urinary incontinence. *Urologia Internationalis* 2002;68(3):148–51.

710. Gofrit ON, Landau EH, Shapiro A, *et al.* The Stamey procedure for stress incontinence: Long-term results. *European Urology* 1998;34(4):339–43.

711. Huland H and Bucher H. Endoscopic bladder neck suspension (Stamey-Pereyra) in female urinary stress incontinence. Long-term follow-up of 66 patients. *European Urology* 1984;10(4):238–41.

712. Hilton P and Mayne CJ. The Stamey endoscopic bladder neck suspension: A clinical and urodynamic investigation, including actuarial follow-up over four years. *British Journal of Obstetrics and Gynaecology* 1991;98(11):1141–9.

713. Ashken MH, Abrams PH, Lawrence WT. Stamey endoscopic bladder neck suspension for stress incontinence. *British Journal of Urology* 1984;56(6):629–34.

714. Kuczyk MA, Klein S, Grunewald V, *et al.* A questionnaire-based outcome analysis of the Stamey bladder neck suspension procedure for the treatment of urinary stress incontinence: The Hannover experience. *British Journal of Urology* 1998;82(2):174–80.

715. O'Sullivan DC, Chilton CP, Munson KW. Should Stamey colposuspension be our primary surgery for stress incontinence? *British Journal of Urology* 1995;75(4):457–60.

716. Cody J, Wyness L, Wallace S, *et al.* Systematic review of the clinical effectiveness and cost-effectiveness of tension-free vaginal tape for treatment of urinary stress incontinence. *Health Technology Assessment* 2003;7(21):1–189.

717. Wadie BS, Edwan A, Nabeeh AM. Autologous fascial sling vs polypropylene tape at short-term followup: a prospective randomized study. *Journal of Urology* 2005;174(3):990–3.

718. Lo TS, Horng SG, Liang CC, *et al.* Ultrasound and urodynamic comparison between caudocranial and craniocaudal tension-free vaginal tape for stress urinary incontinence. *Urology* 2005;66(4):754–8.

719. Arunkalaivanan AS and Barrington JW. Randomized trial of porcine dermal sling (Pelvicol implant) vs. tension-free vaginal tape (TVT) in the surgical treatment of stress incontinence: a questionnaire-based study. *International Urogynecology Journal* 2003;14(1):17–23.

720. Abdel-Fattah M, Barrington JW, Arunkalaivanan AS. Pelvicol pubovaginal sling versus tension-free vaginal tape for treatment of urodynamic stress incontinence: A prospective randomized three-year follow-up study. *European Urology* 2004;46(5):629–35.

721. Liapis A, Bakas P, Giner M, *et al.* Tension-Free Vaginal Tape versus Tension-Free Vaginal Obturator in Women with Stress Urinary Incontinence. *Gynecologic and Obstetric Investigation* 2006;62(3):160–4.

722. Mellier G, Benayed B, Bretones S, *et al.* Suburethral tape via the obturator route: Is the TOT a simplification of the TVT? *International Urogynecology Journal* 2004;15(4):227–32.

723. Fischer A, Fink T, Zachmann S, *et al.* Comparison of retropubic and outside-in transoburator sling systems for the cure of female genuine stress urinary incontinence. *European Urology* 2005;48(5):799–804.

724. Rechberger T, Rzeczniczuk K, Skorupski P, *et al.* A randomized comparison between monofilament and multifilament tapes for stress incontinence surgery. *International Urogynecology Journal and Pelvic Floor Dysfunction* 2003;14(6):432–6.

725. Lim YN, Muller R, Corstiaans A, *et al.* Suburethral slingplasty evaluation study in North Queensland Australia: The SUSPEND trial. *Australian and New Zealand Journal of Obstetrics and Gynaecology* 2005;45(1):52–9.

726. Andonian S, Chen T, St-Denis B, *et al.* Randomized clinical trial comparing suprapubic arch sling (SPARC) and tension-free vaginal tape (TVT): One-year results. *European Urology* 2005;47(4):537–41.

727. Tseng L-H, Wang AC, Lin Y-H, *et al.* Randomized comparison of the suprapubic arc sling procedure vs tension-free vaginal taping for stress incontinent women. *International Urogynecology Journal* 2005;16(3):230–5.

728. Hammad FT, Kennedy-Smith A, Robinson RG. Erosions and urinary retention following polypropylene synthetic sling: Australasian survey. Editorial comment. *European Urology* 2005;47(5):641–7.

729. Hung MJ, Liu FS, Shen PS, *et al.* Analysis of two sling procedures using polypropylene mesh for treatment of stress urinary incontinence. *International Journal of Gynaecology and Obstetrics* 2004;84(2):133–41.

730. Lo TS, Horng SG, Chang CL, *et al.* Tension-free vaginal tape procedure after previous failure in incontinence surgery. *Urology* 2002;60(1):57–61.

731. Azam U, Frazer MI, Kozman EL, *et al.* The tension-free vaginal tape procedure in women with previous failed stress incontinence surgery. *Journal of Urology* 2001;166(2):554–6.

732. Tomoe H, Kondo A, Takei MM, *et al.* Quality of life assessments in women operated on by tension-free vaginal tape (TVT). *International Urogynecology Journal* 2005;16(2):114–18.

733. Moran PA, Ward KL, Johnson D, *et al.* Tension-free vaginal tape for primary genuine stress incontinence: A two-centre follow-up study. *BJU International* 2000;86(1):39–42.

734. Ulmsten U, Johnson P, Rezapour M. A three-year follow up of tension free vaginal tape for surgical treatment of female stress urinary incontinence. *British Journal of Obstetrics and Gynaecology* 1999;106(4):345–50.

735. Ulmsten U, Falconer C, Johnson P, *et al.* A multicenter study of tension-free vaginal tape (TVT) for surgical treatment of stress urinary incontinence. *International Urogynecology Journal* 1998;9(4):210–13.

736. Huang KH, Kung FT, Liang HM, *et al.* Concomitant surgery with tension-free vaginal tape. *Acta Obstetricia et Gynecologica Scandinavica* 2003;82(10):948–53.

737. De Matteis G., Colagrande S, Maglioni Q, *et al*. A new procedure for the treatment of SUI. Our experience. *Int J Urogynecol* 2000;14(2):71–7.

738. Pang MW, Chan LW, Yip SK. One-year urodynamic outcome and quality of life in patients with concomitant tension-free vaginal tape during pelvic floor reconstruction surgery for genitourinary prolapse and urodynamic stress incontinence. *International Urogynecology Journal* 2003;14(4):256–60.

739. Mazouni C, Karsenty G, Bretelle F, *et al*. Urinary complications and sexual function after the tension-free vaginal tape procedure. *Acta Obstetricia et Gynecologica Scandinavica* 2004;83(10):955–61.

740. Mutone N, Brizendine E, Hale D. Clinical Outcome of Tension-Free Vaginal Tape Procedure for Stress Urinary Incontinence Without Preoperative Urethral Hypermobility. *Journal of Pelvic Medicine and Surgery* 2003;9(2):75–81.

741. Sokol AI, Jelovsek JE, Walters MD, *et al*. Incidence and predictors of prolonged urinary retention after TVT with and without concurrent prolapse surgery. *American Journal of Obstetrics and Gynecology* 2005;192(5):1537–43.

742. Dietz HP, Ellis G, Wilson PD, *et al*. Voiding function after tension-free vaginal tape: A longitudinal study. *Australian and New Zealand Journal of Obstetrics and Gynaecology* 2004;44(2):152–5.

743. Flock F, Reich A, Muche R, *et al*. Hemorrhagic complications associated with tension-free vaginal tape procedure. *Obstetrics and Gynecology* 2004;104(5 Part 1):989–94.

744. Neuman M. Tension-free vaginal tape bladder penetration and long-lasting transvesical prolene material. *Journal of Pelvic Medicine and Surgery* 2004;10(6):307–9.

745. Glavind K and Tetsche MS. Sexual function in women before and after suburethral sling operation for stress urinary incontinence: A retrospective questionnaire study. *Acta Obstetricia et Gynecologica Scandinavica* 2004;83(10):965–8.

746. Ghezzi F, Serati M, Cromi A, *et al*. Impact of tension-free vaginal tape on sexual function: Results of a prospective study. *International Urogynecology Journal* 2006;17(1):54–9.

747. Rezapour M and Ulmsten U. Tension-free vaginal tape (TVT) in women with recurrent stress urinary incontinence – A long-term follow up. *International Urogynecology Journal* 2001;12(Supplement 2):S9–S11.

748. Rezapour M, Falconer C, Ulmsten U. Tension-free vaginal tape (TVT) in stress incontinent women with intrinsic sphincter deficiency (ISD) – A long-term follow-up. *International Urogynecology Journal* 2001;12(Supplement 2):S12–S14.

749. Rezapour M and Ulmsten U. Tension-free vaginal tape (TVT) in women with mixed urinary incontinence – A long-term follow-up. *International Urogynecology Journal* 2001;12(Supplement 2):S15–S18.

750. Zhu L, Lang J-H, Li Y, *et al*. Postoperative evaluation of tension-free vaginal tape procedure. *Chinese Medical Sciences Journal* 2005;20(2):116–18.

751. Rardin CR, Kohli N, Rosenblatt PL, *et al*. Tension-free vaginal tape: outcomes among women with primary versus recurrent stress urinary incontinence. *Obstetrics and Gynecology* 2002;100(5 Part 1):893–7.

752. Mukherjee K and Constantine G. Urinary stress incontinence in obese women: Tension-free vaginal tape is the answer. *BJU International* 2001;88(9):881–3.

753. Abouassaly R, Steinberg JR, Lemieux M, *et al*. Complications of tension-free vaginal tape surgery: A multi-institutional review. *BJU International* 2004;94(1):110–13.

754. Bodelsson G, Henriksson L, Osser S, *et al*. Short term complications of the tension free vaginal tape operation for stress urinary incontinence in women. *BJOG: an International Journal of Obstetrics and Gynaecology* 2002;109(5):566–9.

755. Niemczyk P, Klutke JJ, Carlin BI, *et al*. United States experience with tension-free vaginal tape procedure for urinary stress incontinence: Assessment of safety and tolerability. *Techniques in Urology* 2001;7(4):261–5.

756. Deans CL, Morris AR, O'Sullivan R, *et al*. Voiding difficulty and other adverse events after tension free vaginal tape. *Australian and New Zealand Continence Journal* 2004;10(2):34–6.

757. Virtanen HS and Kiilholma P. Urogynecologic ultrasound is a useful aid in the assessment of female stress urinary incontinence – A prospective study with TVT procedure. *International Urogynecology Journal* 2002;13(4):218–23.

758. Wang KH, Wang KH, Neimark M, *et al*. Voiding dysfunction following TVT procedure. *International Urogynecology Journal* 2002;13(6):353–7.

759. Abdel-Hady e and Constantine G. Outcome of the use of tension-free vaginal tape in women with mixed urinary incontinence, previous failed surgery, or low valsalva pressure. *Journal of Obstetrics and Gynaecology Research* 2005;31(1):38–42.

760. Karram MM, Segal JL, Vassallo BJ, *et al*. Complications and untoward effects of the tension-free vaginal tape procedure. *Obstetrics and Gynecology* 2003;101(5 Part 1):929–32.

761. Moss E, Toozs-Hobson P, Cardozo L, *et al*. A multicentre review of the tension-free vaginal tape procedure in clinical practice. *Journal of Obstetrics and Gynaecology* 2002;22(5):519–22.

762. Segal JL, Vassallo B, Kleeman S, *et al*. Prevalence of persistent and de novo overactive bladder symptoms after the tension-free vaginal tape. *Obstetrics and Gynecology* 2004;104(6):1263–9.

763. Qureshi A, Nicolaou J, Lynch CB, *et al*. Outcome of tension-free vaginal tape (TVT) procedure in women with stress urinary incontinence – Patients' perspective. *Journal of Obstetrics and Gynaecology* 2003;23(3):297–300.

764. Walsh K, Generao SE, White MJ, *et al*. The influence of age on quality of life outcome in women following a tension-free vaginal tape procedure. *Journal of Urology* 2004;171(3):1185–8.

765. Manikandan R, Kujawa M, Pearson E, *et al*. Results of the tension-free vaginal tape procedure for stress incontinence: Patient's perspective. *International Journal of Urology* 2004;11(4):206–12.

766. Carta G, Cerrone L, Iovenitti P. Tension-free vaginal tape procedure for treatment of USI: Subjective and objective efficacy evaluation. *Clinical and Experimental Obstetrics and Gynecology* 2002;29(4):247–50.

767. Sander P, Moller LMA, Rudnicki PM, et al. Does the tension-free vaginal tape procedure affect the voiding phase? Pressure-flow studies before and 1 year after surgery. BJU International 2002;89(7):694–8.

768. Soulie M, Cuvillier X, Benaissa A, et al. The tension-free transvaginal tape procedure in the treatment of female urinary stress incontinence: A French prospective multicentre study. European Urology 2001;39(6):709–15.

769. Laurikainen E and Kiilholma P. The tension-free vaginal tape procedure for female urinary incontinence without preoperative urodynamic evaluation. Journal of the American College of Surgeons 2003;196(4):579–83.

770. Levin I, Groutz A, Gold R, et al. Surgical Complications and Medium-Term Outcome Results of Tension-Free Vaginal Tape: A Prospective Study of 313 Consecutive Patients. Neurourology and Urodynamics 2004;23(1):7–9.

771. Nilsson CG and Kuuva N. The tension-free vaginal tape procedure is successful in the majority of women with indications for surgical treatment of urinary stress incontinence. BJOG: an International Journal of Obstetrics and Gynaecology 2001;108(4): 414–19.

772. Lebret T, Lugagne P-M, Herve J-M, et al. Evaluation of tension-free vaginal tape procedure: Its safety nd efficacy in the treatment of female stress urinary incontinence during the learning phase. European Urology 2001;40(5):543–7.

773. Lo TS, Chang TC, Chao AS, et al. Tension-free vaginal tape procedure on genuine stress incontinent women with coexisting genital prolapse. Acta Obstetricia et Gynecologica Scandinavica 2003;82(11):1049–53.

774. Davis TL, Lukacz ES, Luber KM, et al. Determinants of patient satisfaction after the tension-free vaginal tape procedure. American Journal of Obstetrics and Gynecology 2004;191(1):176–81.

775. Wang AC and Lo TS. Tension-free vaginal tape. A minimally invasive solution to stress urinary incontinence in women. Journal of Reproductive Medicine 1998;43(5):429–34.

776. Haab F, Sananes S, Amarenco G, et al. Results of the tension-free vaginal tape procedure for the treatment of type II stress urinary incontinence at a minimum followup of 1 year. Journal of Urology 2001;165(1):159–62.

777. Meschia M, Pifarotti P, Bernasconi F, et al. Tension-free vaginal tape: Analysis of outcomes and complications in 404 stress incontinent women. International Urogynecology Journal 2001;12(Supplement 2):S24–S27.

778. Richter HE, Norman AM, Burgio KL, et al. Tension-free vaginal tape: A prospective subjective and objective outcome analysis. International Urogynecology Journal 2005;16(2):109–13.

779. Lo TS, Huang HJ, Chang CL, et al. Use of intravenous anesthesia for tension-free vaginal tape therapy in elderly women with genuine stress incontinence. Urology 2002;59(3):349–53.

780. Wang AC. An assessment of the early surgical outcome and urodynamic effects of the tension-free vaginal tape (TVT). International Urogynecology Journal 2000;11(5):282–4.

781. Palma PCR, Riccetto CLZ, Dambros M, et al. Tension-free vaginal tape (TVT): Minimally invasive technique for stress urinary incotinence (SUI). International Braz J Urol 2002;28(5):458–63.

782. Ulmsten U, Henriksson L, Johnson P, et al. An ambulatory surgical procedure under local anesthesia for treatment of female urinary incontinence. International Urogynecology Journal 1996;7(2):81–6.

783. Gateau T, Faramarzi-Roques R, Le NL, et al. Clinical and urodynamic repercussions after TVT procedure and how to diminish patient complaints. European Urology 2003;44(3):372–6.

784. Vassallo BJ, Kleeman SD, Segal JL, et al. Tension-free vaginal tape: A quality-of-life assessment. Obstetrics and Gynecology 2002;100(3):518–24.

785. Cetinel B, Demirkesen O, Onal B, et al. Are there any factors predicting the cure and complication rates of tension-free vaginal tape? International Urogynecology Journal 2004;15(3):188–93.

786. Fiori M, Gunelli R, Mercuriali M, et al. Tension-free vaginal tape and female stress incontinence: Further evidence of effectiveness. Urologia Internationalis 2004;72(4):325–8.

787. Allahdin S, McKinley CA, Mahmood TA. Tension free vaginal tape: A procedure for all ages. Acta Obstetricia et Gynecologica Scandinavica 2004;83(10):937–40.

788. Allahdin S, McKinley CA, Mahmood TA, et al. Tension-free vaginal tape: 162 Cases in a district general hospital. Journal of Obstetrics and Gynaecology 2004;24(5):539–41.

789. Price N and Jackson SR. Clinical audit of the use of tension-free vaginal tape as a surgical treatment for urinary stress incontinence, set against NICE guidelines. Journal of Obstetrics and Gynaecology 2004;24(5):534–8.

790. Schiotz HA. Tension-free vaginal tape (TVT) – A new surgical procedure for female stress incontinence. Journal of Obstetrics and Gynaecology 2000;20(2):158–61.

791. Munir N, Bunce C, Gelister J, et al. Outcome following TVT sling procedure: A comparison of outcome recorded by surgeons to that reported by their patients at a London District General Hospital. European Urology 2005;47(5):635–40.

792. Yalcin O, Isikoglu M, Beji NK. Results of TVT operations alone and combined with other vaginal surgical procedures. Archives of Gynecology and Obstetrics 2004;269(2):96–8.

793. Lo TS, Wang AC, Horng SG, et al. Ultrasonographic and urodynamic evaluation after tension free vagina tape procedure (TVT). Acta Obstetricia et Gynecologica Scandinavica 2001;80(1):65–70.

794. Al-Badr A, Ross S, Soroka D, et al. Voiding patterns and urodynamics after a tension-free vaginal tape procedure. Journal of Obstetrics and Gynaecology Canada: JOGC 2003;25(9):725–30.

795. Magatti F, Sirtori PL, Rumi C, et al. TVT procedure for the treatment of SUI: Our experience. Urogynaecologia International Journal 2002;16(1):17–27.

796. Neuman M. Low incidence of post-TVT genital prolapse. International Urogynecology Journal 2003;14(3):191–2.

797. Sevestre S, Ciofu C, Deval B, et al. Results of the tension-free vaginal tape technique in the elderly. European Urology 2003;44(1):128–31.

798. Deval B, Jeffry L, Al NF, *et al.* Determinants of patient dissatisfaction after a tension-free vaginal tape procedure for urinary incontinence. *Journal of Urology* 2002;167(5):2093–7.

799. Kinn AC. Tension-free vaginal tape evaluated using patient self-reports and urodynamic testing – a two-year follow-up. *Scandinavian Journal of Urology and Nephrology* 2001;35(6):484–90.

800. Jeffry L, Deval B, Birsan A, *et al.* Objective and subjective cure rates after tension-free vaginal tape for treatment of urinary incontinence. *Urology* 2001;58(5):702–6.

801. Liapis A, Bakas P, Creatsas G. Management of stress urinary incontinence in women with the use of tension-free vaginal tape. *European Urology* 2001;40(5):548–51.

802. Paick JS, Kim SW, Ku JH, *et al.* Preoperative maximal flow rate may be a predictive factor for the outcome of tension-free vaginal tape procedure for stress urinary incontinence. *International Urogynecology Journal* 2004;15(6):413–17.

803. Kuuva N and Nilsson CG. Tension-free vaginal tape procedure: An effective minimally invasive operation for the treatment of recurrent stress urinary incontinence? *Gynecologic and Obstetric Investigation* 2003;56(2):93–8.

804. Schraffordt Koops SE, Bisseling TM, Heintz APM, *et al.* Prospective analysis of complications of tension-free vaginal tape from The Netherlands tension-free vaginal tape study. *American Journal of Obstetrics and Gynecology* 2005;193(1):45–52.

805. Schraffordt Koops SE, Bisseling TM, Heintz AP, *et al.* Quality of life before and after TVT, a prospective multicentre cohort study, results from the Netherlands TVT database. *BJOG: an International Journal of Obstetrics and Gynaecology* 2006;113(1):26–9.

806. Schraffordt Koops SE, Bisseling TM, Van Brummen HJ, *et al.* What determines a successful tension-free vaginal tape? A prospective multicenter cohort study: Results from the Netherlands TVT database. *American Journal of Obstetrics and Gynecology* 2006;194(1):65–74.

807. Debodinance P, Delporte P, Engrand JB, *et al.* Tension-free vaginal tape (TVT) in the treatment of urinary stress incontinence: 3 years experience involving 256 operations. *European Journal of Obstetrics, Gynecology, and Reproductive Biology* 2002;105(1):49–58.

808. Bunyavejchevin S, Santingamkun A, Wisawasukmongchol W. The three years results of tension free vaginal tape (TVT) for the treatment of stress urinary incontinence in Thai women. *Journal of the Medical Association of Thailand* 2005;88(1):5–8.

809. Tsivian A, Mogutin B, Kessler O, *et al.* Tension-free vaginal tape procedure for the treatment of female stress urinary incontinence: Long-term results. *Journal of Urology* 2004;172(3):998–1000.

810. Nilsson CG, Kuuva N, Falconer C, *et al.* Long-term results of the tension-free vaginal tape (TVT) procedure for surgical treatment of female stress urinary incontinence. *International Urogynecology Journal* 2001;12(Supplement 2):S5–S8.

811. Nilsson CG, Falconer C, Rezapour M. Seven-year follow-up of the tension-free vaginal tape procedure for treatment of urinary incontinence. *Obstetrics and Gynecology* 2004;104(6):1259–62.

812. Holmgren C, Nilsson S, Lanner L, *et al.* Long-term results with tension-free vaginal tape on mixed and stress urinary incontinence. *Obstetrics and Gynecology* 2005;106(1):38–43.

813. Kuuva N and Nilsson CG. A nationwide analysis of complications associated with the tension-free vaginal tape (TVT) procedure. *Acta Obstetricia et Gynecologica Scandinavica* 2002;81(1):72–7.

814. Tamussino KF, Hanzal E, Kolle D, *et al.* Tension-free vaginal tape operation: results of the Austrian registry. *Obstetrics and Gynecology* 2001;98(5 Part 1):732–6.

815. Tamussino K, Hanzal E, Kolle D, *et al.* The Austrian tension-free vaginal tape registry. *International Urogynecology Journal* 2001;12:(Supplement 2)S28–S29.

816. Kolle D, Tamussino K, Hanzal E, *et al.* Bleeding complications with the tension-free vaginal tape operation. *American Journal of Obstetrics and Gynecology* 2005;193(6):2045–9.

817. Duckett JR, Tamilselvi A, Moran PA, *et al.* Tension-free vaginal tape (TVT) in the United Kingdom. *Journal of Obstetrics and Gynaecology* 2004;24(7):794–7.

818. Pugsley H, Barbrook C, Mayne CJ, *et al.* Morbidity of incontinence surgery in women over 70 years old: A retrospective cohort study. *BJOG: an International Journal of Obstetrics and Gynaecology* 2005;112(6):786–90.

819. Karantanis E, Fynes MM, Stanton SL. The tension-free vaginal tape in older women. *BJOG: an International Journal of Obstetrics and Gynaecology* 2004;111(8):837–41.

820. Gordon D, Gold R, Pauzner D, *et al.* Tension-free vaginal tape in the elderly: Is it a safe procedure? *Urology* 2005;65(3):479–82.

821. Rafii A, Darai E, Haab F, *et al.* Body mass index and outcome of tension-free vaginal tape. *European Urology* 2003;43(3):288–92.

822. Lovatsis D, Gupta C, Dean E, *et al.* Tension-free vaginal tape procedure is an ideal treatment for obese patients. *American Journal of Obstetrics and Gynecology* 2003;189(6):1601–4.

823. Rafii A, Paoletti X, Haab F, *et al.* Tension-Free Vaginal Tape and Associated Procedures: A Case Control Study. *European Urology* 2004;45(3):356–61.

824. Meltomaa S, Backman T, Haarala M. Concomitant vaginal surgery did not affect outcome of the tension-free vaginal tape operation during a prospective 3-year followup study. *Journal of Urology* 2004;172(1):222–6.

825. Rardin CR, Kohli N, Miklos JR, *et al.* Outcomes of tension-free vaginal tape in women with intrinsic sphincter deficiency with or without urethral hypermobility. *Journal of Pelvic Medicine and Surgery* 2005;11(6):321–7.

826. Deval B, Levardon M, Samain E, *et al.* A French multicenter clinical trial of SPARC for stress urinary incontinence. *European Urology* 2003;44(2):254–8.

827. Kobashi KC and Govier FE. Perioperative complications: the first 140 polypropylene pubovaginal slings. *Journal of Urology* 2003;170(5):1918–21.

828. Hodroff MA, Sutherland SE, Kesha JB, *et al.* Treatment of stress incontinence with the SPARC sling: intraoperative and early complications of 445 patients. *Urology* 2005;66(4):760–2.

829. Bafghi A, Benizri EI, Trastour C, *et al.* Multifilament polypropylene mesh for urinary incontinence: 10 Cases of infections requiring removal of the sling. *BJOG: an International Journal of Obstetrics and Gynaecology* 2005;112(3):376–8.

830. Ijland MM, Fischer DC, Kieback DG, et al. Midline intravaginal slingplasty for treatment of urinary stress incontinence: results of an independent audit up to 2 years after surgery. *International Urogynecology Journal* 2005;16(6):447–54.

831. Baessler K, Hewson AD, Tunn R, et al. Severe mesh complications following intravaginal slingplasty. *Obstetrics and Gynecology* 2005;106(4):713–16.

832. Siegel AL, Kim M, Goldstein M, et al. High incidence of vaginal mesh extrusion using the intravaginal slingplasty sling. *Journal of Urology* 2005;174:(4 l)1308–11.

833. Palma PC, Dambros M, Riccetto CZ, et al. The Ibero-American experience with a re-adjustable minimally invasive sling. *BJU International* 2005;95(3):341–5.

834. Palma P, Riccetto C, Herrmann V, et al. Transobturator SAFYRE sling is as effective as the transvaginal procedure. *International Urogynecology Journal* 2005;16(6):487–91.

835. De Leval J. Novel Surgical Technique for the Treatment of Female Stress Urinary Incontinence: Transobturator Vaginal Tape Inside-Out. *European Urology* 2003;44(6):724–30.

836. Costa P, Grise P, Droupy S, et al. Surgical treatment of female stress urinary incontinence with a Trans-Obturator-Tape (T.O.T.) Uratape: Short term results of a prospective multicentric study. *European Urology* 2004;46(1):102–7.

837. Cindolo L, Salzano L, Rot G, et al. Tension-free transobturator approach for female stress urinary incontinence. *Minerva Urologica e Nefrologica* 2004;56(1):89–98.

838. Delorme E, Droupy S, De TR, et al. Transobturator Tape (Uratape): A New Minimally-Invasive Procedure to Treat Female Urinary Incontinence. *European Urology* 2004;45(2):203–7.

839. Krauth JS, Rasoamiaramanana H, Barletta H, et al. Sub-urethral tape treatment of female urinary incontinence - Morbidity assessment of the trans-obturator route and a new tape (I-STOP): A multi-centre experiment involving 604 cases. *European Urology* 2005;47(1):102–7.

840. Lukban JC. Suburethral sling using the transobturator approach: A quality-of-life analysis. *American Journal of Obstetrics and Gynecology* 2005;193(6):2138–43.

841. Naidu A, Lim YN, Barry C, et al. Transobturator tape for stress incontinence: the North Queensland experience. *Australian and New Zealand Journal of Obstetrics and Gynaecology* 2005;45(5):446–9.

842. Spinosa J-P and Dubuis P-Y. Suburethral sling inserted by the transobturator route in the treatment of female stress urinary incontinence: Preliminary results in 117 cases. *European Journal of Obstetrics, Gynecology, and Reproductive Biology* 2005;123(2):212–17.

843. Deval B, Ferchaux J, Berry R, et al. Objective and subjective cure rates after trans-obturator tape (OBTAPE) treatment of female urinary incontinence. *European Urology* 2006;49(2):373–7.

844. Roumeguere T, Quackels T, Bollens R, et al. Trans-obturator vaginal tape (TOT) for female stress incontinence: one year follow-up in 120 patients. *European Urology* 2005;48(5):805–9.

845. Domingo S, Alama P, Ruiz N, et al. Diagnosis, management and prognosis of vaginal erosion after transobturator suburethral tape procedure using a nonwoven thermally bonded polypropylene mesh. *Journal of Urology* 2005;173(5):1627–30.

846. Debodinance P. Trans-obturator urethral sling for the surgical correction of femal stress urinary incontinence: Outside-in (Monarc®) versus inside-out (TVT-O®). Are the two ways reassuring? *European Journal of Obstetrics and Gynecology and Reproductive Biology* 2006. In press.

847. David-Montefiore E, Frobert J-L, Grisard-Anaf M, et al. Peri-operative complications and pain after the suburethral sling procedure for urinary stress incontinence: A french prospective randomised multicentre study comparing the retropubic and transobturator routes. *European Urology* 2006;49(1):133–8.

848. Kuo HC. Comparison of video urodynamic results after the pubovaginal sling procedure using rectus fascia and polypropylene mesh for stress urinary incontinence. *Journal of Urology* 2001;165(1):163–8.

849. Spence-Jones C, DeMarco E, Lemieux M-C, et al. Modified urethral sling for the treatment of genuine stress incontinence and latent incontinence. *International Urogynecology Journal* 1994;5(2):69–75.

850. Bryans FE. Marlex gauze hammock sling operation with Cooper's ligament attachment in the management of recurrent urinary stress incontinence. *American Journal of Obstetrics and Gynecology* 1979;133(3):292–4.

851. Demirci F, Ozdemir I, Alhan A. The midurethral polypropylene sling for stress incontinence: 22-Month results of 81 patients. *Archives of Gynecology and Obstetrics* 2005;272(2):145–50.

852. Costantini E, Mearini L, Mearini E, et al. Assessing outcome after a modified vaginal wall sling for stress incontinence with intrinsic sphincter deficiency. *International Urogynecology Journal* 2005;16(2):138–46.

853. Laurikainen E, Rosti J, Pitkanen Y, et al. The Rosti sling: A new, minimally invasive, tension-free technique for the surgical treatment of female urinary incontinence – The first 217 patients. *Journal of Urology* 2004;171(4):1576–80.

854. Rodriguez LV and Raz S. Prospective analysis of patients treated with a distal urethral polypropylene sling for symptoms of stress urinary incontinence: surgical outcome and satisfaction determined by patient driven questionnaires. *Journal of Urology* 2003;170(3):857–63.

855. Iglesias X and Espun~a M. Surgical treatment of urinary stress incontinence using a method for postoperative adjustment of sling tension (Remeex System). *International Urogynecology Journal* 2003;14(5):326–30.

856. Martinez AM, Ramos NM, Requena JF, et al. Analysis of retropubic colpourethrosuspension results by suburethral sling with REMEEX prosthesis. *European Journal of Obstetrics, Gynecology, and Reproductive Biology* 2003;106(2):179–83.

857. Rutman M, Itano N, Deng D, et al. Long-term durability of the distal urethral polypropylene sling procedure for stress urinary incontinence: minimum 5-year followup of surgical outcome and satisfaction determined by patient reported questionnaires. *Journal of Urology* 2006;175(2):610–13.

858. Korda A, Peat B, Hunter P. Experience with silastic slings for female urinary incontinence. *Australian and New Zealand Journal of Obstetrics and Gynaecology* 1989;29(2):150–4.

859. Stanton SL, Brindley GS, Holmes DM. Silastic sling for urethral sphincter incompetence in women. *British Journal of Obstetrics and Gynaecology* 1985;92(7):747–50.

860. Duckett JR and Constantine G. Complications of silicone sling insertion for stress urinary incontinence. *Journal of Urology* 2000;163(6):1835–7.

861. Barbalias G, Liatsikos E, Barbalias D. Use of slings made of indigenous and allogenic material (Goretex) in type III urinary incontinence and comparison between them. *European Urology* 1997;31(4):394–400.

862. Choe JM, Ogan K, Battino BS. Antimicrobial mesh versus vaginal wall sling: a comparative outcomes analysis. *Journal of Urology* 2000;163(6):1829–34.

863. Errando C, Batista JE, Arano P. Polytetrafluoroethylene sling for failure in female stress incontinence surgery. *World Journal of Urology* 1996;14(Supplement 1):S48–S50.

864. Choe JM and Staskin DR. Gore-Tex patch sling: 7 years later. *Urology* 1999;54(4):641–6.

865. Staskin DR, Choe JM, Breslin DS. The Gore-tex sling procedure for female sphincteric incontinence: indications, technique, and results. *World Journal of Urology* 1997;15(5):295–9.

866. Barbalias GA, Liatsikos EN, Athanasopoulos A. Gore-Tex sling urethral suspension in type III female urinary incontinence: Clinical results and urodynamic changes. *International Urogynecology Journal* 1997;8(6):344–50.

867. Yamada T, Arai G, Masuda H, *et al.* The correction of type 2 stress incontinence with a polytetrafluoroethylene patch sling: 5-year mean follow up. *Journal of Urology* 1998;160:(3 I)746–9.

868. Weinberger MW and Ostergard DR. Postoperative catheterization, urinary retention, and permanent voiding dysfunction after polytetrafluoroethylene suburethral sling placement. *Obstetrics and Gynecology* 1996;87(1):50–4.

869. Weinberger MW and Ostergard DR. Long-term clinical and urodynamic evaluation of the polytetrafluoroethylene suburethral sling for treatment of genuine stress incontinence. *Obstetrics and Gynecology* 1995;86(1):92–6.

870. Bent AE, Ostergard DR, Zwick-Zaffuto M. Tissue reaction to expanded polytetrafluoroethylene suburethral sling for urinary incontinence: Clinical and histologic study. *American Journal of Obstetrics and Gynecology* 1993;169(5):1198–204.

871. Petros PP. The intravaginal slingplasty operation, a minimally invasive technique for cure of urinary incontinence in the female. *Australian and New Zealand Journal of Obstetrics and Gynaecology* 1996;36(4):453–61.

872. Guner H, Yildiz A, Erdem A, *et al.* Surgical treatment of urinary stress incontinence by a suburethral sling procedure using a Mersilene mesh graft. *Gynecologic and Obstetric Investigation* 1994;37(1):52–5.

873. Young SB, Howard AE, Baker SP. Mersilene mesh sling: Short- and long-term clinical and urodynamic outcomes. *American Journal of Obstetrics and Gynecology* 2001;185(1):32–40.

874. Kersey J, Martin MR, Mishra P. A further assessment of the gauze hammock sling operation in the treatment of stress incontinence. *British Journal of Obstetrics and Gynaecology* 1988;95(4):382–5.

875. Kersey J. The gauze hammock sling operation in the treatment of stress incontinence. *British Journal of Obstetrics and Gynaecology* 1983;90(10):945–9.

876. Bezerra CA, Bruschini H, Cody DJ. Traditional suburethral sling operations for urinary incontinence in women. (Cochrane Review). In: *Cochrane Database of Systematic Reviews*, Issue 3, 2005. Oxford: Update Software.

877. Viseshsindh W, Kochakarn W, Waikakul W, *et al.* A randomized controlled trial of pubovaginal sling versus vaginal wall sling for stress urinary incontinence. *Journal of the Medical Association of Thailand* 2003;86(4):308–15.

878. Kaplan SA, Santarosa RP, Te AE. Comparison of fascial and vaginal wall slings in the management of intrinsic sphincter deficiency. *Urology* 1996;47(6):885–9.

879. Rodrigues P, Hering F, Meler A, *et al.* Pubo-fascial versus vaginal sling operation for the treatment of stress urinary incontinence: A prospective study. *Neurourology and Urodynamics* 2004;23(7):627–31.

880. Lucas M, Emery S, Stephenson T. *A Randomised Study to Assess and Compare the Clinical Effectiveness of Two Surgical Techniques for the Treatment of Stress Urinary Incontinence in Women.* No. RC080. Cardiff: The Wales Office of Research and Development for Health and Social Care; 2000.

881. Maher C, Carey M, Dwyer P, *et al.* Pubovaginal or Vicryl mesh rectus fascia sling in intrinsic sphincter deficiency. *International Urogynecology Journal* 2001;12(2):111–16.

882. Flynn BJ and Yap WT. Pubovaginal sling using allograft fascia lata versus autograft fascia for all types of stress urinary incontinence: 2-year minimum followup. *Journal of Urology* 2002;167(2 Part 1):608–12.

883. Almeida SH, Gregorio E, Grando JP, *et al.* Pubovaginal sling using cadaveric allograft fascia for the treatment of female urinary incontinence. *Transplantation Proceedings* 2004;36(4):995–6.

884. Soergel TM, Shott S, Heit M. Poor surgical outcomes after fascia lata allograft slings. *International Urogynecology Journal* 2001;12(4):247–53.

885. McBride AW, Ellerkmann RM, Bent AE, *et al.* Comparison of long-term outcomes of autologous fascia lata slings with Suspend Tutoplast fascia lata allograft slings for stress incontinence. *American Journal of Obstetrics and Gynecology* 2005;192(5):1677–81.

886. Wright EJ, Iselin CE, Carr LK, *et al.* Pubovaginal sling using cadaveric allograft fascia for the treatment of intrinsic sphincter deficiency. *Journal of Urology* 1998;160(3 Part 1):759–62.

887. Brown SL, Govier FE, Morgan TO Jr, *et al.* Cadaveric versus autologous fascia lata for the pubovaginal sling: Surgical outcome and patient satisfaction. *Journal of Urology* 2000;164(5):1633–7.

888. O'Reilly KJ and Govier FE. Intermediate term failure of pubovaginal slings using cadaveric fascia lata: A case series. *Journal of Urology* 2002;167(3):1356–8.

889. Simsiman AJ, Powell CR, Stratford RR, *et al.* Suburethral sling materials: Best outcome with autologous tissue. *American Journal of Obstetrics and Gynecology* 2005;193(6):2112–16.

890. Chou EC, Flisser AJ, Panagopoulos G, *et al.* Effective treatment for mixed urinary incontinence with a pubovaginal sling. *Journal of Urology* 2003;170(2 Part 1):494–7.

891. Hassouna ME and Ghoniem GM. Long-term outcome and quality of life after modified pubovaginal sling for intrinsic sphincteric deficiency. *Urology* 1999;53(2):287–91.

892. Reichelt O, Weirich T, Wunderlich H, *et al.* Pubovaginal cutaneous fascial sling procedure for stress urinary incontinence: 10 Years' experience. *Urologia Internationalis* 2004;72(4):318–23.

893. Cross CA, Cespedes RD, McGuire EJ. Our experience with pubovaginal slings in patients with stress urinary incontinence. *Journal of Urology* 1998;159(4):1195–8.

894. Hawkins E, Taylor D, Hughes-Nurse J. Long term follow up of the cruciate fascial sling for women with genuine stress incontinence. *BJOG: an International Journal of Obstetrics and Gynaecology* 2002;109(3):327–38.

895. Morgan TO Jr, Westney OL, McGuire EJ. Pubovaginal sling: 4-year outcome analysis and quality of life assessment. *Journal of Urology* 2000;163(6):1845–8.

896. Chaikin DC, Rosenthal J, Blaivas JG. Pubovaginal fascial sling for all types of stress urinary incontinence: Long-term analysis. *Journal of Urology* 1998;160(4):1312–16.

897. Muller SC, Steinbach F, Maurer FM, *et al.* Long-term results of fascial sling procedure. *International Urogynecology Journal* 1993;4(4):199–203.

898. Borup K and Nielsen JB. Results in 32 women operated for genuine stress incontinence with the pubovaginal sling procedure ad modum Ed McGuire. *Scandinavian Journal of Urology and Nephrology* 2002;36(2):128–33.

899. Zaragoza MR. Expanded indications for the pubovaginal sling: treatment of type 2 or 3 stress incontinence. *Journal of Urology* 1996;156(5):1620–2.

900. FitzGerald MP, Edwards SR, Fenner D. Medium-term follow-up on use of freeze-dried, irradiated donor fascia for sacrocolpopexy and sling procedures. *International Urogynecology Journal* 2004;15(4):238–42.

901. Amundsen CL, Visco AG, Ruiz H, *et al.* Outcome in 104 pubovaginal slings using freeze-dried allograft fascia lata from a single tissue bank. *Urology* 2000;56(6 Supplement 1):2–8.

902. Elliott DS and Boone TB. Is fascia lata allograft material trustworthy for pubovaginal sling repair? *Urology* 2000;56(5):772–5.

903. Huang YH, Lin AT, Chen KK, *et al.* High failure rate using allograft fascia lata in pubovaginal sling surgery for female stress urinary incontinence. *Urology* 2001;58(6):943–6.

904. Walsh IK, Nambirajan T, Donellan SM, *et al.* Cadaveric fascia lata pubovaginal slings: Early results on safety, efficacy and patient satisfaction. *BJU International* 2002;90(4):415–19.

905. Richter HE, Burgio KL, Holley RL, *et al.* Cadaveric fascia lata sling for stress urinary incontinence: A prospective quality-of-life analysis. *American Journal of Obstetrics and Gynecology* 2003;189(6):1590–6.

906. Giri SK, Drumm J, Saunders JA, *et al.* Day-case sling surgery for stress urinary incontinence: feasibility and safety. *BJU International* 2005;95(6):827–32.

907. Kinn AC, Larson B, Hammarstrom M. Urethropexy with porcine dermal sling in complicated stress incontinence. *International Urogynecology Journal* 1994;5(1):31–4.

908. Jarvis GJ and Fowlie A. Clinical and urodynamic assessment of the porcine dermis bladder sling in the treatment of genuine stress incontinence. *British Journal of Obstetrics and Gynaecology* 1985;92(11):1189–91.

909. Raz S, Stothers L, Young GPH, *et al.* Vaginal wall sling for anatomical incontinence and intrinsic sphincter dysfunction: Efficacy and outcome analysis. *Journal of Urology* 1996;156(1):166–70.

910. Kaplan SA, Te AE, Young GPH, *et al.* Prospective analysis of 373 consecutive women with stress urinary incontinence treated with a vaginal wall sling: The Columbia-Cornell University experience. *Journal of Urology* 2000;164(5):1623–7.

911. Litwiller SE, Nelson RS, Fone PD, *et al.* Vaginal wall sling: Long-term outcome analysis of factors contributing to patient satisfaction and surgical success. *Journal of Urology* 1997;157(4):1279–82.

912. Palma PCR, Riccetto CLZ, as Filho AC, *et al.* Is the anterior vaginal wall sling a good alternative for intrinsic sphincteric insufficiency? *International Braz J Urol* 2002;28(4):349–55.

913. Mikhail MS, Rosa H, Packer P, *et al.* A modified vaginal wall patch sling technique as a first-line surgical approach for genuine stress incontinence with urethral hypermobility: Long-term follow up. *International Urogynecology Journal* 2004;15(2):132–7.

914. Rottenberg RD, Weil A, Brioschi P-A. Urodynamic and clinical assessment of the Lyodura sling operation for urinary stress incontinence. *British Journal of Obstetrics and Gynaecology* 1985;92(8):829–34.

915. Owens DC and Winters JC. Pubovaginal Sling Using Duraderm Graft: Intermediate Follow-Up and Patient Satisfaction. *Neurourology and Urodynamics* 2004;23(2):115–18.

916. Onur R and Singla A. Solvent-dehydrated cadaveric dermis: A new allograft for pubovaginal sling surgery. *International Journal of Urology* 2005;12(9):801–5.

917. Wang D, Bresette JF, Smith III JJ. Initial Experience with Acellular Human Dermal Allograft (Repliform) Pubovaginal Sling for Stress Urinary Incontinence. *Journal of Pelvic Medicine and Surgery* 2004;10(1):23–6.

918. Pelosi MA, Pelosi MA, III, Pelekanos M. The YAMA UroPatch sling for treatment of female stress urinary incontinence: a pilot study. *Journal of Laparoendoscopic and Advanced Surgical Techniques-Part A* 2002;12(1):27–33.

919. Jones JS, Rackley RR, Berglund R, *et al.* Porcine small intestinal submucosa as a percutaneous mid-urethral sling: 2-Year results. *BJU International* 2005;96(1):103–6.

920. Brown JS, Sawaya G, Thom DH, *et al.* Hysterectomy and urinary incontinence: a systematic review. *Lancet* 2000;356(9229):535–9.

921. Nuffield Institute for Health and NHS Centre for Reviews and Dissemination. Hospital volume and health care outcomes, costs and patient access. *Effective Health Care* 1996;2(8):1–16.

922. Halm EA, Lee C, Chassin MR. Is volume related to outcome in health care? A systematic review and methodologic critique of the literature. *Annals of Internal Medicine* 2002;137(6):511–20.

923. Khuri SF, Hussaini BE, Kumbhani DJ, *et al*. Does volume help predict outcome in surgical disease?. *Advances in Surgery* 2005;39:379–453.

924. Hilton P. Trials of surgery for stress incontinence–thoughts on the 'Humpty Dumpty principle'. *BJOG: an International Journal of Obstetrics and Gynaecology* 2002;109(10):1081–8.

925. McLennan MT and Melick DF. Bladder perforation during tension-free vaginal tape procedures: analysis of learning curve and risk factors. *Obstetrics and Gynecology* 2005;106(5 Part 1):1000–4.

926. Duckett JR, Jain S, Tamilselvi A, *et al*. National audit of incontinence surgery in the United Kingdom. *Journal of Obstetrics and Gynaecology* 2004;24(7):785–93.

927. Khuri SF, Najjar SF, Daley J, *et al*. Comparison of surgical outcomes between teaching and nonteaching hospitals in the Department of Veterans Affairs. *Annals of Surgery* 2001;234(3):370–83.

928. Holley RL, Richter HE, Goode PS, *et al*. Cost-effectiveness of the cough stress test with simple cystometrogram versus urodynamics in the diagnosis of genuine stress urinary incontinence. *Journal of Gynecologic Techniques* 1999;5(4):135–9.

929. Weber AM, Taylor RJ, Wei JT, *et al*. The cost-effectiveness of preoperative testing (basic office assessment vs urodynamics) for stress urinary incontinence in women. *BJU International* 2002;89(4):356–63.

930. Clayton J, Smith K, Qureshi H, *et al*. Collecting patients' views and perceptions of continence services: the development of research instruments. *Journal of Advanced Nursing* 1998;28(2):353–61.

931. Manca A, Sculpher MJ, Ward K, *et al*. A cost–utility analysis of tension-free vaginal tape versus colposuspension for primary urodynamic stress incontinence. *BJOG: an International Journal of Obstetrics and Gynaecology* 2003;110(3):255–62.

932. Curtis L and Netten A. *Unit Costs of Health and Social Care 2004*. Canterbury: University of Kent at Canterbury, Personal Social Services Research Unit; 2004.

933. Link C. Medical treatment of urinary incontinence in women. *CME Bulletin Gynaecology* 2001;2(3):80–3.

934. Medicare Services Advisory Committee. *Sacral Nerve Stimulation for Refractory Urinary Urge Incontinence Or Urinary Retention*. Canberra: AusInfo; 2001.

935. Madersbacher S, Schmidt J, Eberle JM, *et al*. Long-term outcome of ileal conduit diversion. *Journal of Urology* 2003;169(3):985–90.

936. Cundiff GW, Harris RL, Coates KW, *et al*. Clinical predictors of urinary incontinence in women. *American Journal of Obstetrics and Gynecology* 1997;177(2):262–6.

937. Radley SC, Jones GL, Tanguy EA, *et al*. Computer interviewing in urogynaecology: concept, development and psychometric testing of an electronic pelvic floor assessment questionnaire in primary and secondary care. *BJOG: an International Journal of Obstetrics and Gynaecology* 2006;113(2):231–8.

938. Weber AM and Walters MD. Cost-effectiveness of urodynamic testing before surgery for women with pelvic organ prolapse and stress urinary incontinence. *American Journal of Obstetrics and Gynecology* 2000;183(6):1338–46.

939. Bo K, Talseth T, Vinsnes A. Randomized controlled trial on the effect of pelvic floor muscle training on quality of life and sexual problems in genuine stress incontinent women. *Acta Obstetricia et Gynecologica Scandinavica* 2000;79(7):598–603.

940. Elser DM, Wyman JF, McClish DK, *et al*. The effect of bladder training, pelvic floor muscle training, or combination training on urodynamic parameters in women with urinary incontinence. Continence Program for Women Research Group. *Neurourology and Urodynamics* 1999;18(5):427–36.

941. Engberg S, McDowell BJ, Weber E, *et al*. Assessment and management of urinary incontinence among homebound older adults: a clinical trial protocol. *Advanced Practice Nursing Quarterly* 1997;3(2):48–56.

942. Homma Y and Kawabe K. Health-related quality of life of Japanese patients with overactive bladder treated with extended-release tolterodine or immediate-release oxybutynin: a randomized, placebo-controlled trial. *World Journal of Urology* 2004;22(4):251–6.

943. Freeman R, Hill S, Millard R, *et al*. Reduced perception of urgency in treatment of overactive bladder with extended-release tolterodine. *Obstetrics and Gynecology* 2003;102(3):605–11.

944. Asplund R, Sundberg B, Bengtsson P. Desmopressin for the treatment of nocturnal polyuria in the elderly: A dose titration study. *British Journal of Urology* 1998;82(5):642–6.

945. Grady D, Wenger NK, Herrington D, *et al*. Postmenopausal hormone therapy increases risk for venous thromboembolic disease. The Heart and Estrogen/progestin Replacement Study. *Annals of Internal Medicine* 2000;132(9):689–96.

946. Bosch JL and Groen J. Sacral (S3) segmental nerve stimulation as a treatment for urge incontinence in patients with detrusor instability: results of chronic electrical stimulation using an implantable neural prosthesis. *Journal of Urology* 1995;154(2 Part 1):504–7.

947. Ruud Bosch JLH and Groen J. Neuromodulation: Urodynamic effects of sacral (S3) spinal nerve stimulation in patients with detrusor instability or detrusor hyperflexia. *Behavioural Brain Research* 1998;92(2):141–50.

948. Ankardal M, Ekerydh A, Crafoord K, *et al*. A randomised trial comparing open Burch colposuspension using sutures with laparoscopic colposuspension using mesh and staples in women with stress urinary incontinence. *BJOG: an International Journal of Obstetrics and Gynaecology* 2004;111(9):974–81.

949. Colombo M, Vitobello D, Proietti F, *et al*. Results and complications of the modified Marshall-Marchetti-Krantz procedure. *Italian Journal of Gynaecology and Obstetrics* 1998;10(3):91–6.

950. Liapis A, Pyrgiotis E, Kontoravdis A, *et al*. Genuine stress incontinence: Prospective randomized comparizon of two operative methods. *European Journal of Obstetrics Gynecology and Reproductive Biology* 1996;64(1):69–72.

951. Meschia M, Buonaguidi A, Colombo M, *et al*. Tension-free vaginal tape: An Italian multi-center study. *Urogynaecologia International Journal* 1999;13(1):9–17.

952. Olsson I and Kroon U-B. A three-year postoperative evaluation of tension-free vaginal tape. *Gynecologic and Obstetric Investigation* 1999;48(4):267–9.

953. Kuo HC. Long-term surgical results of pubovaginal sling procedure using polypropylene mesh in the treatment of stress urinary incontinence. *Urologia Internationalis* 2005;74(2):147–52.

954. Kuo HC. Anatomical and functional results of pubovaginal sling procedure using polypropylene mesh for the treatment of stress urinary incontinence. *Journal of Urology* 2001;166(1):152–7.

955. Kuo HC. The surgical results of the pubovaginal sling procedure using polypropylene mesh for stress urinary incontinence. *BJU International* 2001;88(9):884–8.

956. Kuo HC. Sonographic evaluation of anatomic results after the pubovaginal sling procedure for stress urinary incontinence. *Journal of Ultrasound in Medicine* 2001;20(7):739–47.

957. De Almeida FG, Rodriguez LV, Raz S. Polypropylene distal urethral sling for treatment of female stress urinary incontinence. *Brazilian Journal of Urology* 2002;28(3):254–8.

958. Shah SM, Bukkapatnam R, Rodriguez LV. Impact of vaginal surgery for stress urinary incontinence on female sexual function: Is the use of polypropylene mesh detrimental? *Urology* 2005;65(2):270–4.

959. Yamada T, Kamata S, Nagahama K, *et al.* Polytetrafluoroethylene patch sling for type 2 or type 3 stress urinary incontinence. *International Journal of Urology* 2001;8(12):675–80.

960. FitzGerald MP, Mollenhauer J, Brubaker L. Failure of allograft suburethral slings. *BJU International* 1999;84(7):785–8.

Index